W9-CEK-221

A SADLY TROUBLED HISTORY

MCGILL-QUEEN'S/ASSOCIATED MEDICAL SERVICES STUDIES IN THE
HISTORY OF MEDICINE, HEALTH, AND SOCIETY

SERIES EDITORS: S.O. FREEDMAN AND J.T.H. CONNOR

Volumes in this series have financial support from Associated Medical
Services, Inc. (AMS). Associated Medical Services Inc. was established in 1936
by Dr Jason Hannah as a pioneer prepaid not-for-profit health-care
organization in Ontario. With the advent of medicare, AMS became a
charitable organization supporting innovations in academic medicine and
health services, specifically the history of medicine and health care, as well as
innovations in health professional education and bioethics.

A Sadly Troubled History

The Meanings of Suicide in the Modern Age

JOHN C. WEAVER

McGill-Queen's University Press
Montreal & Kingston • London • Ithaca

© McGill-Queen's University Press 2009

ISBN 978-0-7735-3513-8

Legal deposit second quarter 2009
Bibliothèque nationale du Québec

Printed in Canada on acid-free paper that is 100% ancient forest free
(100% post-consumer recycled), processed chlorine free

This book has been published with the help of a grant from the Canadian
Federation for the Humanities and Social Sciences, through the Aid to
Scholarly Publications Programme, using funds provided by the Social
Sciences and Humanities Research Council of Canada.

McGill-Queen's University Press acknowledges the support of the Canada
Council for the Arts for our publishing program. We also acknowledge
the financial support of the Government of Canada through the Book
Publishing Industry Development Program (BPIDP) for our publishing
activities.

Library and Archives Canada Cataloguing in Publication

Weaver, John C.
    A sadly troubled history : the meanings of suicide in the modern age /
John C. Weaver.

(McGill-Queen's/Associated Medical Services studies in the history of
medicine, health, and society ; 33)
Includes bibliographical references and index.
ISBN 978-0-7735-3513-8

1. Suicide – New Zealand – History. 2. Suicide – Queensland – History.
3. Suicide. I. Title. II. Series.

HV6545.W43   2009 362.280993   C2008-907494-7

Typeset by Jay Tee Graphics Ltd. in 10.5/13 Sabon

Contents

Tables and Graphs

TABLES

GRAPHS

Preface

My resolve to write a book on a disturbing and complex subject requires an explanation. I grew up in the closed world of small-town Ontario and knew people who had taken their own lives. I wondered then and now about their demise. Decades later, when completing research for *The Great Land Rush and the Making of the Modern World, 1650–1900*, I came across a finding aid for a series of records unlike any I had seen before. That encounter in the State Archives of Queensland led to the current book, but neither immediately nor directly. Prepared for genealogists, the finding aid listed all extant coroners' inquests for the entire state arranged by the name of the deceased. A preliminary excursion into the bundles of files disclosed an extraordinary collection of depositions with information on environmental hazards, chance occurrences, risky conduct, violence, and self-destruction. When used carefully, I felt at the time, these records would disclose plenty about "common" lives. A later trip to Wellington, New Zealand, turned up equally rich inquest files covering a much longer period. The records in both jurisdictions turned out to be among the best, if not *the* best, series of accessible inquests in the common-law world. The original proceedings had been open to the public, and access to material older than fifty years remains unrestricted. Doctors felt no obligation of confidentiality to deceased patients, and so they occasionally commented on physical and mental illnesses.

I searched for sets of comparable records in Canada and the United States and found chronologically fragmented collections or ones that covered only a city or county. Victor Bailey had discovered and used to good effect the coroner's inquest records for Hull, England, from 1837 to 1900. Often in common-law jurisdictions, officials charged with investigating sudden deaths were county-based coroners or local magistrates. Thus inquest records remained in local courthouses or were destroyed to save space; in Australia and New Zealand, however, judicial affairs were far more centralized and fit a larger pattern of surveillance. Magistrates had to send files to the attorney general's office for review. Here they remained until transferred to archives, where they comprise a truly immense body of contemporary reflections on life's troubles and sorrows. The scope, utility, and limitations of these records are discussed in chapter 3.

I made a preliminary exploration of the Queensland files in June and July 1999, accompanied by Sean Gouglas, then my doctoral student and later a faculty member at the University of Alberta. Homicide inquests and inquiries into industrial accidents held remarkable material. Sean and I elected to write about homicide and the criminal justice system.[1] As we leafed through bundle after bundle, suicide inquests surfaced with regularity, and because the witnesses' depositions covered aspects of everyday life, these cases recommended further research. With support from the Social Sciences and Humanities Research Council of Canada (SSHRCC), I secured the help of two wise and meticulous research assistants: Jonathan Richards in Queensland and Doug Munro in New Zealand. Their commitment to the project lasted after the end of our formal association. Jonathan continued to help while writing his own book, *The Secret War: A True History of the Queensland Native Police*.[2] Doug assisted even as he worked on his study of historians of the South Pacific.[3]

To write at length about suicide is a foolhardy undertaking, I now realize, because the topic has received plenty of attention for over a century and a half. I had to master this international literature without prior exposure. The data collection was onerous and claimed my summers for half a dozen years. My colleague and co-researcher David Wright encouraged me to collect information about mental illness from the files, and that led to our collaboration for an article about the treatment of "shell shock" in New Zealand after World War I.[4] More background literature had to be absorbed. David organized an international workshop on the history of suicide in August 2006; it advanced my planning for the current book. A small conferences grant from SSHRCC, aid from the Wilson Centre for Canadian History, and assistance from McMaster University supported that workshop, which brought together historians, anthropologists, and criminologists who worked on suicide in Europe, North and South America, southern Africa, and Japan. The congenial scholars whom David arranged to attend the workshop furthered my education.

I was encouraged by other colleagues, too, notably the chairs of the Department of History at McMaster University, Virginia Aksan and Ken Cruikshank; former dean of Humanities, Nasrin Rahimieh; former provost Ken Norrie; acting provost Robert McNutt; provost Ilene Busch-Vishniac; and vice-presidents of research Mamdouh Shoukri and Mohamed Elbestawi. My inaugural lectures as University Professor drew on the research; they prompted questions and suggestions from colleagues, including Ken Norrie, Viv Nelles, Wayne Thorpe, David Hitchcock, Inga Dolinina, Neil McLaughlin, and Peter Archibald. Parts of the manuscript were read by David Wright, Cyril Levitt, Viv Nelles, and Neil McLaughlin. David Rosenbloom kindly reviewed the entire manuscript. Reports from the anonymous reviewers led to a host of improvements. Over the course of many conversations, Richard Hill, director of the Treaty of Waitangi Research Unit, Stout Research Centre for New Zealand Studies, advanced my understanding of New Zealand history. Joan Weaver tolerated reports on tragedy and assisted with the preparation of the manuscript. Adam Weaver hosted my research trips to Wellington and kept me apprised of social science theory. At McGill-Queen's University Press, Roger Martin and Joan McGilvray steered the manuscript through the review and production stages with diligence. Elizabeth Hulse, as copy editor, improved the text and saved me from many errors. Ruth Pinko prepared a fine index. Canadian academic publishing achieves international recognition because a community of skilled and rigorous professionals works in concert with focused scholars. This book's failings, however, are entirely of my making.

I benefited from the assistance of staff at the Queensland State Archives, the Queensland State Library, the Fryer Library at the University of Queensland, the National Archives of New Zealand (now Archives New Zealand), the National Library of New Zealand, and the Turnbull Library in the National Library of New Zealand. Alison Ainsworth from the Department of Internal Affairs, Government of New Zealand, assisted by arranging searches through death certificates for missing ages.

Publication of this book was assisted with a grant from the Aid to Scholarly Publications Programme of the Canadian Federation for the Humanities and Social Sciences and a grant from Associated Medical Services, Hannah Publications Support Program.

This is not research for the faint of heart. I wonder how military historians handle emotionally the combat deaths of young men and the slaughter of civilians; they may be insulated, for they rarely encounter the words of these people close to the moment of destruction. Jonathan, Doug, and I could not avoid reacting viscerally to our investigations. Leaning across an archive table, one of us would remark from time to time, "I have come across a bad one." A few especially distressing cases had to be photocopied, because we found it painful to write notes. These upsetting instances usually involved young people or homicide-suicides. Once we had read these case files, we had to take a break and talk things over. If only we could have reached through time to pull someone back from a precipice! Additional painful incidents separated this research from other forms of historical inquiry. "What are you working on," people asked. Too often, after one of us replied, the questioner recounted a suicide tragedy. Because heart-rending interludes punctuated research, an analytical history of suicide was going to be insufficient for us; Jonathan and Doug often insisted on that point. Therefore I have attempted to resurrect strong feelings to further an understanding of a complex, often taboo subject, as well as to apply an emotional hue to social history. It may appear obvious to point out the costs of incivility, to catalogue the enduring burdens of war, and to dwell on people's need for fulfillment; it may appear commonplace to bring to light the trials of mental illness and alcoholism and to affirm the dignity of individuals. So be it. These are among my aims.

A SADLY TROUBLED HISTORY

Introduction

People everywhere are conscious of the passage of time, have memories, can imagine the future, and can reflect on life's purpose. Why am I here? Why have certain things happened to me? What will happen to me in the future? Will my fortunes rise or fall? Is my life meaningful? These and other closely related questions frame the human condition. How people actually broach such issues remains elusive and exceedingly difficult to document. Nevertheless, their centrality to life demands that we grapple with them if we are at all interested in how people have lived their lives, imagined their material or emotional state, and charted their future. We should be interested, not for mere curiosity, but in order to reaffirm the preciousness of life, discern all that threatens its enjoyment, and strive for personal conduct and social action that may ameliorate troubles for others and ourselves.

Biographers can offer reasoned speculation about the human condition in relation to a single individual. But social historians have been deterred from intimate explorations, partly because of an apparent lack of documentation. During the late 1960s and early 1970s, the computer revolution rendered manageable census manuscripts and other materials assembled by state bureaucracies and justice systems. Routinely generated information manipulated by computers still generates benchmarks for social history, and reconstructions of the past have gained appreciably. However, the statistically based findings that sit mute on the page are detached from people's reactions to their circumstances – circumstances and conditions that at best are feebly hinted at in tables and graphs. Computation opened discussions about wealth distribution, social mobility, fertility, morbidity, crime, and more, but the ever more sophisticated ventures have taken history a long distance away from the perceptions and emotions of contemporaries. Social historians interested in everyday life accordingly have long lamented the rarity of diaries or the lack of extensive collections of letters written by ordinary people; they have exulted when these items turned up, although on account of the scarcity of such material, they have not developed schema for structuring abundant narrative accounts into a meaningful whole. But more than a lack of sources and an absence of models stand in the way of comprehending the human condition.

SEEKING THE INACCESSIBLE

There can be no easily won insights into the human condition, even if there were abundant confessions or close observations of how people coped with setbacks or handled the stock-taking episodes in their lives, because the topic runs squarely into obstacles between us and the thoughts of others. Notwithstanding psychiatry's efforts, the mental life of others remains inaccessible because humans lack the god's eye. Putting that claim of supreme inaccessibility to the test, writers laboured ingeniously during two centuries to explain suicide. They were puzzled as to why some people saw no point in living, even as the great majority dedicated themselves to prolonging life and feared its inevitable end. With a paramount conundrum of the human condition at their centre, suicide studies present social historians with theories and data that nearly connect material circumstances to the most profoundly emotional experiences conceivable.[1] Attempts to understand suicide have coaxed into print an immense body of speculation, observation, and theory; the better studies cautiously suggested how people factored the human condition at various times and places, at various stages in the life course, and for men and women separately and jointly.

Seeking reasons for what seemed the perverse deed of self-destruction, secular commentators by the early nineteenth century enumerated crises in the human condition, leaving the impression that life's setbacks, hazardous excesses in personal conduct, or mental illnesses sufficed to explain suicide. On the face of it, nineteenth-century studies documented glimpses into inner torment. However, contemporary moral and political precepts shaped their descriptions of life's sorrows and troubles. A few who investigated suicide projected flashes of illumination, not necessarily when they tried to explain how lives could go awry but when they pushed deeper, identified enigmas, and wondered why some people had less resilience toward adversity than others; some conceded imperfections in their research methods, remarked on limits to evidence, and explained that theories did little justice to the assorted experiences of real people whose troubles were being condensed into hypotheses.

Despite biased assumptions, rigid theories, overreaching assertions, flaws in research designs, and the too-frequent erasure of the individual – matters considered in this book's first two chapters – suicide scholars during nearly two centuries of inquiry raised awareness about the diversity of life's sorrows. Many writers, however, did not visualize the deceased as persons tormented by existential crises but, rather, as exemplars of troubles susceptible to reformatory action or medical intervention. In the chapters that follow, the peculiar situation of suicidal conduct as rational to the individual but a widely accepted mark of mental illness will be a topic of discussion. Suicide scholars did not set out to assist social historians but of course pursued their own goals, including the establishment of new academic disciplines.

The pursuit of diagnostic precision and the quest for effective therapeutic or preventive measures have driven and continue to drive research. Some who engaged in these life-saving missions have recognized that it is insufficient to connect suicide only with life's bounty of troubles; rather, it is vital to try to comprehend how troubles and sorrows are managed in the self-reflexive thoughts of others. How people imagine their past, present, and future – core considerations in the human condition – must be at the centre of meaningful studies of suicide. Precisely this fact makes these studies significant for social historians and for the effort, attempted in this book, of combining society and psyche through historical inquiry.

Understandably, the ambition to probe people's lives through the exceptional act of suicide is fraught with epistemological difficulties. First, as noted already, political biases have intruded in many studies, often forcefully and obviously so. Second, a few scholars have homed in on individuals' variable capacity to weather adversity, but because of the elusive goal of knowing how people truly think about themselves, recondite writers have admitted a tension between, on the one hand, their research results and plausible assertions and, on the other, frank recognition of their limits to knowledge about other individuals. Positivist social scientists down to the present day do not proclaim this obstacle, but they have learned to step away from rigid pronouncements. They call for more research. On that score *A Sadly Troubled History* has plenty to offer, although the findings may provide uncomfortable reading since the book stresses the importance of the individual and draws attention to the gap between what can be known about a private life and what remains interior to that person. As well, it indicates how in the past government agencies failed to report all instances of suicide. It is possible that the types of errors and obfuscations found in the first half of the twentieth century, in jurisdictions that took inquests seriously, still occur today in countries that pay little attention to the cause of death once foul play is ruled out.

The scope of evidence for the current book is immense, its scale unusually intimate. Yet no amount of testimony can dispel skepticism about the motivations and memories of those giving evidence; as well, no investigation of the practices of judicial authorities and government agencies can fully dispel unease about the possible manipulation and compression of information in bureaucracies. The thousands of case files used in the research for this book expose these difficulties, but in the course of doing so, they also suggest a few remedies, especially with regard to the under-counting of suicides by the government officials responsible for determining the cause of death and reporting numbers. Tensions between empirical findings and reservations about what can be known about private lives set the mood for the central chapters of this book, which explore case histories. Rarely has so much highly personal information been assembled in a study of suicide or, likely, for a social history; rarely have so many witnesses' statements and suicide notes been cited in an effort to comprehend hardships. However, not even a paper avalanche of depositions and letters can break through the epistemological barrier that limits access to the minds of others. Despite a wealth of information and the cleverness of authors who have made the study of suicide their life's work and who have inspired ideas recalled in this book, there endure barriers to knowledge – barriers affirmed even by men and women who left testaments bearing on their self-destruction but who could not precisely explain their actions and who anticipated that no one else would understand either. "No one will ever quite understand why I did this," wrote Ella Krimmer, one of the thousands who appear in this study. "I can't go on as I am."[2] The benefit of looking into case histories arises from the humility and compassion they foster as much as from insights they offer about motives.

Even if we are barred from perfect understanding, we can gain insights into how many, many people were affected by and thought about the great disruptions of the first half of the twentieth century, as well as the routine challenges of work, romance, illness, and aging. Rich documentation exists for these crises in the life course. Historical incidents may help survivors deal with their questions, because many individuals whom we will encounter in this book not only described their torment but thought about the feelings of family and friends. Ella Krimmer did: "Don't think I haven't thought of everyone and the hurt this will bring."[3] Many suicide notes conveyed compassion and gave instructions. A plain recounting of a few tales could possibly achieve the purposes of sensitizing and consoling, but a collection of cases would require the application of selection criteria. In part, I chose to include cases based on their ties to themes taken from leading studies, although doubts raised by conflicting theories and from the core epistemological limitation mean that my analytical remarks are precarious, even if defensible. I also selected cases that exemplified the leading motives suggested by a statistical analysis of the more significant variables (age, gender, occupation, employment status, marital status, war experience, and health) found in thousands of files. Thus the hundreds of cases cited throughout the book were not chosen to illustrate a theory, to slight the bewildering diversity of troubles, or to show all suicidal individuals in a favourable light. In addition to encountering eloquent calm letters of solace, you will read words of vengeance, hatred, braggadocio, and mockery.

THE GUIDING QUESTIONS

Because of this book's interior-mental subject matter, which involves some conjecture, I take a pragmatic approach to truth and accept that its real determination, beyond what I think are strong evidence and reasonable explanations, will emerge from reviews and debates that this inquiry should provoke.

Controversies in suicide studies often arise from an opposition between claims of insight and expressions of doubt. For guidance, it is wise to list major questions that fall out from this state, beginning with philosophical ones. First, should suicide be considered a single act – namely, self-destruction – or does the introduction of assorted motives as well as mixed intentions compel a more nuanced understanding? Motives and intentions, moreover, are not synonyms; motives are reasons for an action, but intentions satisfy motives. Motives are "because of," and intentions are "in order to."[4] As we will see, this crucial separation complicates any study of the act of suicide. Second, how long before the fatal deed had a person begun to commit suicide? This question reminds us that we are dealing with personal histories, including some burdened with decades of anguish. When did motives form, and when did intention take over from motives? Or, to put it another way, when and how did a socially or medically based crisis evolve into an existential decision? These related questions should be asked whenever there is a time-series discussion of suicide rates, because for some individuals there will have been a lag between crises and action, motive and intention. No time series can really capture such subtlety, which is, after all, an assertion of the individuality of the act. A third question, following upon the previous series: Is suicide best understood as a social act or acts or as an individual matter more readily comprehended by psychologists and psychiatrists? Since the publication of Émile Durkheim's *Suicide* (1897) there has been interest among sociologists in testing for social integration on the assumption that integrated societies, where people may find emotional support, will have lower rates. The stress here is on looking at social forms in terms of their damping effect. Other sociological approaches search for motives for suicide in social dislocations: economic depressions, war's aftermath, and deracination. The accent here is on the stoking effect of social factors.

A fourth question: If suicide is many acts, what implications does that have for the theories and methods of sociology, which, as just mentioned, has long been a field for suicide studies? An atomized approach to suicide and a focus on intentions relegates social factors to a secondary position, particularly in light of the next question. Fifth, what characteristics separate individuals who commit suicide from those who do not? This troublesome question typically strikes when a researcher lists the hardships that have pressed upon suicidal individuals, because he or she must then acknowledge that many latter-day Jobs have bent under the same burdens but carried on. Psychiatrist Karl Menninger made this point another way when he remarked in *Man against Himself* that "for some persons no reality, however terrible, is unbearable."[5] For other people, though, a terrible reality is unbearable. A sixth issue is that mental illness features in many suicide cases. What are the implications of this fact for evaluating suicide as an act of will or as an act that is logical to the individual committing it? Controversy about determinism and free will prevailed around nineteenth-century studies because some asserted that suicide expressed a compulsion of the insane and others rejected that idea because it seemed an act freely undertaken. In the late twentieth century, eminent and sensitive psychiatrists, dedicated to helping suicidal people, have claimed that *almost* all suicides or attempted suicides must be accepted, at the very least, as logical acts to the individuals committing them. "Almost" is a strategic word.[6] Its appearance means that uncertainty persists among the most experienced about whether suicides are always carried out by people acting logically. If there is a spectrum of rationality or logic, then we have returned to the first question: Is suicide a single act? The evidence compiled for this book suggests it is many acts, although, it must be acknowledged, there are seasoned arguments that favour compressing it into a single phenomenon which expresses a particular trajectory of morbid and constrained self-reflection.

Apart from these philosophical questions and enduring controversies, empirical issues are encountered in suicide studies and recounted in the coming chapters. First, why do suicide rates seem fairly consistent over long time periods for particular populations but vary from population to population? To put it concretely, why have Australia, Canada, New Zealand, and the United States had more or less moderate rates for decades, while Greece has had a stunningly low rate and Hungary a remarkably high one? Second, are official statistics ever trustworthy? The collection of data by bureaucracies is a topic worth exploring in itself, and so too is the manipulation of that data by the clerks and statisticians who prepared the tables for official publications. Both collection and manipulation have been intrinsic to suicide studies, and they are discussed critically here. Third, what explains the fact that in most jurisdictions around the world, more men than women take their own lives, but women have a higher rate for attempted suicide? A fourth issue is that there is a puzzling but long-standing and almost worldwide pattern of more suicides in spring and early summer than at other times. What might account for it? Fifth, how can we explain the decline in suicides during wartime, when we would expect plenty of inconsolable grief and stress, and a rise in suicides especially among returned soldiers after a conflict? Finally, for a long time experts claimed that suicide rates increased with age, but increases in rates among adolescents were noticed in the 1960s; the observations figured in a near international panic in the 1970s and 1980s about the troubles of youth. Recently, in many of the same countries that witnessed increases in youth suicide rates from the 1960s to the 1990s, older men have again become the leading population at risk. Do these alterations in the rank order of age cohorts embody historic changes in cultures and economies?

The philosophical and empirical questions remind us of the trouble that people have gone to in order to make sense of human situations exposed in the extreme by suicides. Such situations involve the mystery of human motivation, the disquieting recognition of failure at work and at home, the blend of nurture and nature that make up a life history, the range of burdens carried daily by individuals, the miscellany of individual resistance to adversity, and the inevitable course of life, with its seasons from youth to old age. These human-interest issues are best exposed – certainly, most absorbingly considered – at the level of individual cases, but suicide is frequently discussed in aggregates. Numbers and proportions flow in suicide studies by sociologists; tables and charts adorn national and international health agency reports. The current book also has many quantitative moments, but they function as reference points, opening paths to rough generalizations which in turn prepare the way for deeper discussion based on what people wrote and said. Still, numbers matter, for quantity is a quality. Over seven hundred illustrative cases are mentioned in this study; nearly seven thousand constitute the data sets that guided analysis. Suicide is often studied in terms of variations among rates for specific populations, with the rate usually cited as the number of incidents per 100,000 people. To write about patterns as well as about individuals is challenging, but demonstrating the feasibility and benefit of such integration is an objective of this book.

DATA AND DOCUMENTATION

For a hundred and fifty years the authors of suicide studies have marshalled data to express the scale of self-destruction and to identify patterns in the hope of discovering explanations. Meanwhile, governments have discouraged media coverage of suicides for fear that public awareness might promote a contagion, that reporting might publicize material from specific cases and add to survivors' trauma, or that public awareness might play into media critiques of war, economic depressions, or health care. Public information on suicide therefore oscillates between accounts of celebrity cases that cannot be stifled and reports on rising rates or a rash of instances that prompt panic warnings of alleged new societal crises. There is a consequent lack of comprehension about the scale of suicides and especially about the intimate motives and intentions behind them. At least half of A Sadly Troubled History discusses motives and intentions; however, since this is not a book about suicide globally, the international scale of this mode of death is not discussed, and national comparisons are restricted to a few examples. Thus a few preparatory words about magnitude are in order.

More people die by suicide each year than are killed by homicide, wars, and terrorist attacks combined. It is deemed one of the largest forms of preventable deaths. The World Health Organization estimates the number per year at roughly one million. *A Sadly Troubled History* tracks the evolution of statistical analysis, explains pitfalls, and applies a few basic statistical practices. It also relies on short personal narratives. Data furnish the categories that organize the vignettes of life.

Suicide is a category of death that joins violent crime and war as a topic for historians, who have discovered that it readily works into and amplifies cultural and social history. The potential for cultural history has two parts. First, suicide case files contain intimate information seldom otherwise attainable on work and identity, relations between the sexes, attitudes toward welfare and charity, medical treatment for mental illness, popular impressions about medical treatment, folk notions about an afterlife, the activities of charitable organizations, and some modes of sociability – for example, among work gangs and at hotel bars. Second, cultural history deserves a place in suicide studies because different societies have interpreted suicide's significance in keeping with trends in contemporary affairs and current cultural biases. Suicide studies have plenty to say about the times and societies in which they were written.

I have not attempted an exhaustive intellectual history of suicide studies but have selected landmark books and pertinent articles to achieve two things. First, I use them to illustrate the evolution of research techniques and theories in relation to political and intellectual culture. Second, I employ them to present common findings as a backdrop to my discoveries and conjectures. The opening chapters warn that suicide studies should be appraised in relation to a changeable international zeitgeist, national cultural particularities, and advances in research techniques, including statistics and neurosciences. Many political, cultural, and scientific trends that had an influence on suicide studies shifted concurrently and internationally; the growth of particular fields, including sociology, psychology, psychiatry, statistics, the neurosciences, and the study of history, had their own momentum, which affected their forays into suicide studies. Not every aspect of a major suicide study simply mirrors the time, place, and academic discipline of its composition. There were some solid research findings, and these developments will be pointed out, along with the principal changes in research methods. The isolationism of disciplines dedicated to the investigation of suicide has been remarked upon by others. A few writers ignored barriers and endeavoured – somewhat – to learn from other fields.

All things considered, suicide is a fit subject for a multifaceted historical inquiry. I attempt that here. Note the strengths and weaknesses of historical writing, and consider how they play out. In suicide studies there are places where historical inquiry can tread with confidence. Historical studies are peerless at the discovery of pertinent documents, marking the distinctiveness of time and place, and pursuing motives in biography. The last art occasionally overlaps with psychiatry. When mentioned at all by suicide specialists, time and place enter their inquiries as afterthoughts deserving more study.[7] There are places where historical inquiry can go only gingerly. Errors and adjustments made in other fields serve as warnings to historians who career down the same path. Statistical analysis, for example, is a tricky essential. There are also places where history cannot go at all. It is impossible to find control groups from the past and thus impossible to test hypotheses with the rigour of probabilistic statistics. Biochemical factors fall far outside the scope of historical inquiry.

The bulk of this book ventures beyond a synopsis and critique of prior studies; it summarizes an analysis of nearly seven thousand suicides found in the coroners' inquest files of two jurisdictions – New Zealand and Queensland, Australia. These jurisdictions likely have the most complete and accessible sets of inquest records for any large areas in the world; the territories involved include cities, towns, and countryside. I have searched for and found no better records. In 1900 the population of New Zealand was three-quarters of a million and Queensland's was around half a million; fifty years later their populations were almost two million and one and a quarter million respectively. Their social relations, standards of living, and medical facilities were comparable to those of western Europe and North America. Consequently, the methods of investigation and the empirically based conclusions found in this book may assist generally with the understanding of suicide in prosperous Western societies. Confirmation of the excellence of the records will materialize in the course of the book, but it is worth noting that the New Zealand coroners' files attracted the attention of American sociologist Jack Gibbs in 1946. Looking for data "not usually covered in published reports," he encountered a treasure.[8] The inquest files contained personal information about the individual who committed suicide, attempts by family and friends to find the motive for the action, and sometimes pertinent words spoken or written by the deceased.

In at least two major respects, the extraordinary root documentation transcends the aggregated information from government reports that has sustained numerous, perhaps most, suicide studies for more than a century. First, personal information and circumstances are united in the same records. As a result, the dubious practice of inferring explanations from statistical correlations between suicide rates and other sets of aggregate data is avoided. A so-called ecological fallacy is thus eliminated, because individuals and social attributes are directly linked at the case level. Questions about evidence will always remain, but in the current study they can at least be focused on the shortcomings and benefits of a single root source: case files. The great advantage of the case file over other sources is that it directly unites a deed with a constellation of social facts. Motive and age, motive and occupation, or motive and marital status can be considered together directly. Second, if we assume that suicide is an individual action best understood from first-person statements, inquest files offer choice opportunities for collecting the subjective meanings of suicide because, in addition to suicide notes, many inquest files contain the testimony of witnesses who paraphrased the deceased's words. Second-hand reports have problems, but they provide words to be weighed, and some depositions impart the subjective meaning of suicide to the person who later committed the act because witnesses who heard an individual's laments or last words recounted them to a constable or at an inquest. A few files contained deathbed statements.

Testimony scattered throughout several hundred metres of inquests into all forms of violent or unexpected death offer clues about the states of mind and reasoning processes of individuals who, at least by the imperfect gaze of the outsider, had proceeded from motives to intention with discernable logic. Some authors have maintained that suicide notes are disappointingly mundane and poorly composed.[9] Notes perhaps failed to disclose riveting universal truths, but many of those read for this book were nevertheless composed by thoughtful people who exercised a concluding assertion of their existence. The ordinary statement eloquently levels the grand ambitions of the scientists of suicide, since ordinary people committed suicide for reasons of their own, not those created for them by theory. Some expressed their motives in a very few words that embodied unfortunate lives. Not every society supported the literacy that enabled written testaments from all walks of life, but education allowed the composition of notes from all social orders. In Australia and New Zealand the communities' relative wealth and commitment to extensive basic education sustained state surveillance and a dedication to reviewing and retaining documents. On account of general education, records and letters survive that enable us to witness hardships. The crises of the past are better known on account of literacy, which, while widespread in these two societies and the homelands of immigrants, was still rare among the world's populations. The modern state fostered mass education to support its administrative requirements, loyalty, and economic development; however, literacy in the hands of individuals had alternative uses, including the preparation or recording of intensely personal messages. Notes and depositions remind us about reversals of fortune, disappointments, faults, and grief. While the state directed and inspected, people wrote for reasons of their own.

In addition to the remarkable quantity and intimate quality of documentation, this study is notable because it considers two jurisdictions which, although they resembled western Europe and North America in some ways, had distinctive environmental, settlement, and political histories. Through the comparison of two locales, more is learned about the human condition than would have been the case with the study of a single jurisdiction. For example, at several junctures, New Zealand governments innovated with social and economic policies intended to increase security and optimism. In depressions these measures sustained some men and women who in other places would have been bereft of support or hope. Queensland and Australia generally were less innovative. At the same time, however, the comparison of jurisdictions with different political cultures suggests that, while suicide rates varied at the margins on account of social and economic welfare, motives such as romantic disappointment, grave physical illnesses, and severe mental illnesses persisted in all times and contributed to a core set of suicides.

The book's three parts mark narrowing circles in a discussion that moves from an international setting, to a comparison of suicide rates in the two large, diverse, and often contrasting jurisdictions, and finally to an investigation of individuals' thoughts about their predicaments and expressions of pain. The structure of narrowing circles evokes a progression toward sharper resolution and greater immediacy.

Part 1 (Theory, Conjecture, and Politics), consisting of chapters 1 and 2, exposes themes in the cultural and intellectual history of suicide studies during the nineteenth and twentieth centuries. These chapters also highlight a few findings that pave the way for analysis in later chapters. The three chapters in Part 2 (Rates, Society, and Motives) form an extensive comparative study of suicide in New Zealand and Queensland. Chapter 3 looks at the big picture: changes in suicide rates over a half-century; the seasonality of suicide; the relationship of age to motives. The attention paid to suicide rates places this chapter in the company of numerous studies conducted by sociologists, except that it provides a critical explanation of how the data used for calculating suicide rates have been collected and thus how imprecision creeps into suicide rates. Chapter 3 also introduces the main categories of motives for suicide that emerged from the New Zealand and Queensland inquests, and it summarizes statistical observations about age, gender, and motives; the patterns identified help to sequence the more detailed and personalized revelations that follow in chapters 4, 5, and 6.

In chapter 4 attention is concentrated on cases involving men, while in chapter 5 it turns to women and a tangential exploration of homicide followed by suicide. The gendered features of waged work and household work, of courting and sexual encounters, and of gender-specific aging and illness issues figure prominently in these chapters. More than that, they bring us into contact with people in pain – emotional as well as physical. The intention is not to sensationalize but to personalize and thereby keep in sight the idea that, while suicides may have a social context, they are acts of individuals who have reflected upon the options for dealing with what for them is a crisis situation. In Part 3 (Rationality, Psyche, and Treatment) attention shifts into the mental realm: first to the reasoning leading to suicide and then to the responses of society to contain or prevent acts of self-destruction through psychiatry. Thus chapter 6 looks at the reasoning of suicidal people and at the acts themselves, while chapter 7 considers the development of psychiatric care in association with the attention that people in all walks of life paid to the distress faced by loved ones. Throughout the twentieth century, people sought medical attention for family members who appeared in great mental torment. Chapters 4 through 7 are immersed in anguish – the emotional burdens of suicidal individuals and the people around them. These authentic events from common lives transport the tearful realities of the human condition into social history.

PART ONE

Theory, Conjecture, and Politics

1

Suicide as a Gauge for the Times: The Nineteenth Century

In an off-the-cuff remark, Thomas Szasz suggested that "the main bogeys of the nineteenth-century psychiatrists were self-abuse and self-murder.[1] Suicide has been analyzed incessantly in the West since the early nineteenth century. National libraries list hundreds of titles. Emilio Motta's bibliography on suicide (1890) recorded 647 publications from the sixteenth century to the end of nineteenth; 419 appeared after 1850.[2] Swedish suicide scholar Karl Dahlgren estimated in 1945 that there had been four thousand publications up to that year.[3] Norman Farberow's *Bibliography on Suicide and Suicide Prevention, 1897–1967* listed approximately thirty-five hundred titles.[4] Libraries today hold an astonishing number of recent titles. Waves of publications have been common. Writing in 1868, Alexander von Oettingen (1827–1905) introduced his analysis of *Selbstmord* by remarking that "there was no area of moral statistics that had so much basic groundwork as statistical studies of suicide."[5] A century later Anthony Giddens described suicide as possibly the most thoroughly discussed social problem in the nineteenth century, judging from the volume of publications.[6] His statement triggers a two-part question: Should suicide be conceptualized as a single problem? Is it a social matter?

The thousands of cases discussed in later chapters disclose personal motives and calculations behind self-destruction. Many individuals looked to suicide as an escape; some hoped for a rescue; others wanted to terminate physical suffering; still others desired revenge; a number had committed capital crimes and intended to escape the gallows. Some acted impulsively, and others deliberated for a long time. If suicide is many acts, then theorizing becomes awkward unless it can be shown that diversity reflects special cases of a more general phenomenon or that some so-called suicides deserve another label. If it is a special case of a wider phenomenon – for example, insanity – then that assessment waters down the object of study. In two steps Émile Durkheim adopted the second remedy and rescued suicide for analysis as a single phenomenon. First, he defined suicide to exclude people with impaired reason. Suicide exists "when the victim at the moment he commits the act destined to be fatal, knows the normal result with certainty."[7] Second, he made suicide a sociological "fact" by proposing that suicides were not separate occurrences, "unrelated and to be separately studied."[8] By attempting to wipe murky intentionality from the slate – a brash stroke that would long infuriate or baffle medical specialists – his theory could be predicated upon an act of undifferentiated rationality; he could then mobilize the summary data collected by state bureaucracies.

CATEGORIZING THE ACTS

Many suicides, however, look like means to an end, not just an end. Once intention is introduced, suicide fractures into many acts, and the clean definition that would serve a theory becomes harder to frame.[9] As for the idea that suicide is a social problem, sociologist Anthony Giddens appraised the extensive nineteenth-century literature from the perspective of his discipline; beginning early in that century, however, French, German, and English authors approached suicide from a stance that combined medical and social observations and conjectures. At the end of the century, Durkheim drove a wedge between sociology and medical psychology by insisting that suicide was a social problem. To do so is to bypass a controversy at the very heart of suicide studies and to elide the diversity of motives.

In his review of nineteenth-century French publications, Giddens mentioned the prescience of early writers who identified social factors behind suicides. According to Giddens, these authors pursued social betterment; however, he neglected to stress that most of them incorporated far more than just social circumstances into their understandings of the causes of suicide. They considered mental illness as a motive and discussed religion as a preventative force. Durkheim toiled to separate sociology from psychology, but from the 1820s to the 1870s references in suicide studies to social factors usually originated with medical doctors. These commentators did not coalesce around a common position and more commonly proposed how their comprehension improved on or challenged someone else's. Disagreements fragmented the proto-

psychiatrists of the nineteenth century. Contrary to Giddens's characterization, moreover, they referenced far too much information of a
psychological nature to be considered sociologists. Suicide was not
regarded by the first waves of investigators as purely a social problem.

A short history of evidence, motives, and preventative strategies provides an epistemological study of a significant sub-field of social science
inquiry. This initiative is essential because this book includes an assessment of thousands of case histories. To find meaning in them without
exaggerating the authority of the findings, it is best to prepare the way
with a critical assessment of theories and evidence. To be forewarned is
to be forearmed. Previous studies remind us that this topic is bursting
with philosophical questions and strong associations with intellectual
and political history, and a few nineteenth-century authors even cautioned their contemporaries in ways that are meaningful today. Complexity and confusion, insisted a few of them, characterized suicide
studies. "It is absolutely impossible," wrote Samuel Strahan in 1893,
"accurately to classify suicides as to the causes which prompt them to
the act. In the majority of cases there is more than one influence at
work, and very often the secondary cause is set down as the true one."[10]
Category mistakes were seldom acknowledged in the nineteenth century as an impediment to research, but Strahan's remarks indicate a real
problem that must be confronted when case-file information is distilled
into motives. It is one thing to suggest that there are multiple motives in
any one case but quite another to propose that some suicides are not
*sui*cides, not self-murder. Since the Roman Catholic Church continued
to condemn suicide as a sin, former magistrate turned sociologist
Gabriel Tarde, when writing about moral responsibility in 1890, went
so far as to suggest that some suicides were indirect murders. "How
many unfortunates who kill themselves are killed as well by treacherous
competitors or able swindling speculators who have ruined them, by
slanderers who have disgraced them, by all those honest contemporary
assassins who from a distance, unseen and unpunished, strike down
their victims."[11]

The combination of factors, the inscrutable nature of motives, and
the challenge of defining a suicidal act did not trouble most authors
who mingled curiosity and presumptions with state-collected data. The
subject attracted interest because it seemed to offer the possibility of
exposing truths about life's burdens and the mystery of how people
overcame the fear of death. In 1822 Jean-Pierre Falret (1794–1870), a
shrewd observer of mental illness and later credited with being one of

the first to describe bipolar disorder (Falret's syndrome), opened his investigation of suicide by wondering why people would take their own lives when fear of death drives most of humanity into battles to prolong life.[12] Author after author strayed into a maze when attempting to answer some variation of this question.

Despite the lack of facilities and technical knowledge, a few authors hit upon insights, discerned core problems, or framed theories that stimulated later inquiries. The best writers identified challenges facing anyone who attempted a systematic understanding of suicide. Zealous statistician Adolph Wagner introduced his 1864 study of suicide by admitting limitations. Reluctantly he broke off searching for more data. One had to accept imperfection and take the risk of analyzing what was at hand. Many suicide specialists ignored their own caveats when they drew conclusions, while a few, like Wagner, thrust dilemmas into their central discussions. For sociologists and their forerunners, the big problem has always been to explain, by recourse to a discussion of social forces, an act that seems to follow an individual decision.

Beyond exposing thorny conceptual matters, other rationales exist for reviewing antiquated publications. Such a review serves to impress upon us the idea that suicide's importance has a culturally constructed element. Writer after writer made it into an epic crisis of Western civilization. The great majority of authors proposed remedies consistent with reactionary ideologies. Liberals and socialists commented on suicide, but conservatives dominated the field.

Ideas about suicide's moral standing and its causes were of more than passing literary or political interest. Ideas affected people. Statements by witnesses at inquests, examined later in this book, indicate that there were folkways which influenced the interior discourses people had with themselves about remedies for their troubles and sorrows. Medical information, especially theories about mental illness, reached people through local medical practitioners, popular publications, rumour, and first-hand experience acquired by committal to asylums. Perceptions of mental illness and its alleged connections with suicide affected how a few people burdened by woes thought about life and death and about their prospects for recovery. The cultural construction of suicide's importance in different times and places means that personal crises and the status of suicide do not everywhere in all respects resemble what was found in Western societies where suicide studies originated. Yet there were similarities, and although ideas about suicide in this chapter originated in western Europe, key notions made their way around the world, and in the mid-twentieth century American researchers would take the lead. By the late twentieth century, a global epistemic community of suicidologists was working on causes and suicide prevention.

STATISTICS AND AGENDAS

Suicide and the modern Western world are linked through intellectual, medical, and social history. By the mid-nineteenth century, in Europe and the United States, secular perspectives had more or less displaced theological condemnation. However, organized religion's enduring appeal for many intellectuals who wrote about suicide meant that spiritual considerations still infused leading scholarly attempts to make sense of the deed and to prevent it. Nevertheless, most nineteenth-century commentators did not indict suicide as a sin. Lay commentaries were bolstered by an emerging intellectual passion for collecting and analyzing statistics in the hope of reducing societal ills. What had been treated as a sin or crime was now to be understood and prevented. Especially in France but not exclusively there, the study of suicide, assisted by fledgling psychiatry and moral statistics, took wings. Studies and prophylaxis were crude. Moral reproaches persisted. Well into the twentieth century, moral disapproval of suicide, evicted through the front door of public discourse, re-entered by the back. For example, the act was not immoral, but in a theory of ecological influences, high rates of suicide were associated with urban districts characterized by elevated rates of transience, and thus social disorganization. Mobility suggested disorderly lives.[13]

Statistically minded commentators, especially from the 1830s to the 1890s, decried apparent increases in suicide rates. Typically, they assembled aggregate data from the European states and cities that had begun to publish tables on population, crime, and suicide. What is fascinating about this commitment to use data to get at the truth is the disjuncture between the data and the conclusions. It is not just that statistical information was stretched to support hypotheses but that pages upon pages of statistical findings could be entirely unrelated to an author's conclusions and the inevitable list of suicide-prevention measures. Numbers conveyed near-scriptural authority; so studies typically opened with tables for credibility. Later in this chapter we will encounter instances of spurious analysis, but let us now consider two authors writing twenty years apart who dressed their publications in the fashionable raiment of statistics and then paraded unproven conclusions.

Pierre-Egiste Lisle, like most French suicide authors, was a physician at a mental hospital. His thoughts about suicide demonstrate just how full of twists and turns a single study could be. In *Du suicide* (1856) he attacked the notion that suicide could be understood as a mental illness; he considered it a social and cultural issue. The mental illness explanation, which had had great support around 1845, was under critical pressure ten years later. Lisle remarked intelligently on the likely under-reporting of suicide in many European states, criticized the absence in the published data of stated causes, and remarked on the supreme challenge of discerning people's motives. He churned out obligatory tables and claimed that statistical studies could clarify why people committed suicide. Suicide might be under-reported, but what was reported would be representative of the whole. Lisle's discussion was remarkable because he suggested that suicide had both deep general causes – a malaise of the times afflicting many – and specific short-term causes unique to individuals. The split into predisposing causes and immediate causes would recur in publications throughout the century.

Lisle jettisoned caution as he advanced. It was impossible to enter an individual's mind, he conceded, yet enough information appeared in state almanacs – age, gender, occupation, means of suicide, date of suicide – to form generalizations.[14] Suicide studies from the 1830s to 1890s described statistical patterns comparable to Lisle's: suicide rates mostly increase with age; more men than women commit suicide; suicides are more numerous in spring and summer; suicides are more prominent in growing urban areas than in rural regions. Lisle believed that individuals struggled against suicidal forces but that they needed help.[15] Something curious entered his thinking at this point, because he added that suicide could not be stemmed by a liberal education since suicide increased with education. Whereas the great thinkers of the Enlightenment had proposed that education could surmount social ills, Lisle pointed out that those regions of France with high levels of literacy also had high suicide rates, while locales with poor literacy had fewer suicides.

He did not return to his initial criticisms of published data when deducing what his findings meant. Nor did he propose that many who committed suicide in places with good educational facilities may not themselves have been beneficiaries of an education. Like numerous commentators, Lisle had wandered into the ecological fallacy, an important problem facing sociologists that will be explained in more detail later. What matters now is that he condemned the presumed perils of education. If education was at best ineffectual and at worst a contributing cause of suicide, then the best hope for deterrence was the re-establishment of canon law. Put the fear of God into people.[16]

The second representative of the a priori habit was Enrico Morselli, professor of psychological medicine at the Royal University of Turin and physician-in-chief to the Royal Asylum for the Insane. He introduced his 1879 masterwork, a publication celebrated by contemporaries, with a pan-European analysis of the number of suicides controlled by population increases and compared to homicides and accidents.[17] Statistical analysis had advanced since the middle of the century, but the discussion of statistics still depended on aggregate data, and authors continued to tuck their tables away as soon they got down to the real business of condemning modern society.[18] Morselli found that suicide had essentially increased from the early nineteenth century. This growth, he concluded, proved that "the subjective activity of the human mind" was really not subjective; there was unity and underlying logic in human society, just as there was in nature.

Morselli joined the many intellectuals who followed Charles Darwin in dethroning *Homo sapiens*. The laws of nature governed life, although these laws had yet to be precisely articulated in the case of suicide. Proposing that increases in suicide followed social laws, Morselli concluded that European civilization had stumbled into deep crisis. Suicide was symptomatic. For the "well-being of the whole race," there had to be scientific guidance for legislation that could deal with ignorance, greed, poverty, and dissoluteness.[19] It is one of the curiosities of nineteenth-century suicide studies that in order to strengthen the contention that European civilization was in crisis as a result of its material progress and freedoms, numerous authors remarked that "savages" seldom committed suicide.[20] None proposed that indigenous peoples should be applauded for this achievement.[21] Morselli assembled an enormous amount of fascinating data, but he built no robust bridges from his observations to his contention that latent laws of human behaviour were waiting to be discovered. That is not to dispute the proposition that laws could be developed but, rather, to claim that his handling of state-based aggregate data did not advance that effort. The aggregate data were themselves a problem, because they could not reach personal traits. Crude data sanctioned preconceived ideological positions. Lisle wanted to restore the power of the church; Morselli hoped state measures would help humanity to cope with its struggles.

Morselli and other moral statisticians collected data and calculated national contrasts in suicide rates during an age of state and imperial competition, and they advanced disquieting information. Alleged increases in self-destruction were attributed to rising insanity, race degeneracy, or the decay of culture. Suicides among soldiers were a particular interest, partly because armies kept records, but partly because there were debates about whether or not military service strengthened a nation's men.[22] Soldier suicides intimated problems with the army. Disclosures about such suicides ended during World War I, and secretiveness continued for years. Another subpopulation that came under regular and extensive analysis comprised patients in mental hospitals. Medical professionals who directed asylums debated whether suicides amounted to acts of insanity or sane actions by weak individuals.

. Early in the nineteenth century it was widely believed that mental illness originated from inherited personality traits, although a full history of the study of mental illness would show a discourse that considered inherited factors and predisposing social conditions as well as precipitating causes. Debate arose over the relative proportions. If mental illness had firm roots in inherited traits, then not only was there little scope for the causative role of social factors but individuals could not avoid their destinies. Specialists argued over whether men and women who committed suicide acted with free will. If they did, this factor could put the moral and even religious censure of suicide back into play, as could commentaries that associated suicides with cultural decline. Proponents of free-will interpretations classified suicide with criminal behaviour or the acquisition of a vice because in each category of action people made choices harmful not only to themselves but to others. Efforts to comprehend suicide's roots embraced everything that mattered to nineteenth-century European intellectuals: race, religion, morality, free will, republicanism, the army, industry, natural selection, mental illness, social engineering, national character, medical science, and progress. Many who tackled the suicide mystery concluded with schemes for suicide prevention.

Despite their interest in the future, most French writers discussed suicides from mythology and literary classics or mentioned how religious and secular authorities had dealt with the issue during the Middle Ages. What French scholars knew well, including their prejudices, they applied to the problem at hand. The habitual recourse to the classics set French writers apart from north German contemporaries. Economist Adolph Wagner in 1864 dismissed the French doctors' interest in

Lucretia, Cato, and other "illustrious persons." These insignificant examples, he complained, merely served a priori arguments, and the implication was that statistics did not.[23]

Nineteenth-century social commentators had a new intellectual tool. Statistics beckoned as both a fresh source of knowledge and a new-found technique of argumentation, but most pioneering authors had no training in mathematics and tended to confuse statistical probability with certainty or determinism. They had had a liberal arts education, and they ransacked the classics, history, literature, and religious texts to find arresting examples and gain what we might call psychological insights. Criminologist Louis Proal (1843–1900) based a massive *fin de siècle* tome about crimes of passion and suicide wholly on ancient classics, literature, theatre, and philosophy.[24] Suicide studies from the 1830s to the 1890s rambled as authors drifted into philosophical musings. Nineteenth-century specialists revealed their time, culture, and training; however, that limitation does not foreclose the possibility that they had insights. On the one hand, French studies followed the course of nineteenth-century politics, so that many authors disparaged democratic revolutions and personal independence and denounced secularism, self-interest, ambition, and material acquisitions. Reactionary intellectuals found suicide a convenient subject. On the other hand, some of the same scholars collected and discuss interesting data and a few remarked *sotto voce* on their data's imperfections. As well, some who worked in public or private mental hospitals were sharp observers of individual cases.

Nineteenth-century France was remarkable for the abundance of academic works on suicide (see tables 1.1 and 1.2). In mid-2006 the Bibliothèque nationale held 265 publications with suicide in the title that had appeared in print between 1730 and 1950; these referred to human suicide, not assorted metaphorical uses of the word such as, for example, the suicide of the Second Empire, the Ottoman Empire, the Weimar Republic, Republican Spain, or the race. By topic, the books and pamphlets in the Bibliothèque nationale included 55 of a literary nature, 23 pertaining to legislation or the criminal code, 18 in the form of true stories or sensational court cases, and 18 treating methods and forensic issues. Several more dealt with miscellaneous subjects, such as consoling survivors. Medical, psychiatric, or sociological publications accounted for 102 titles. The first of these, an essay on suicide as an expression of mental illness, was printed in 1816; a second study in 1822 considered the interplay of mental illness and social phenomena.

Table 1.1
Subject distribution of suicide titles in national libraries or consortia of libraries: French, British, and German titles

Years	French moral	British moral	German moral	French medical, sociological	British medical, psychological, sociological	German medical, psychological, sociological	French literary	British literary	German literary
1730–79	1	11	12	0	0	2	1	6	4
1780–1829	7	17	12	3	3	7	13	16	5
1830–79	9	6	9	49	24	12	23	8	1
1880–1929	5	9	10	32	18	51	14	9	3
1930–49	0	0	0	9	6	32	9	14	1
Total	22	34	43	93	51	105	60	53	14

SOURCE: Electronic search of the British Library; the Common Library Network of the German Federal States of Bremen, Hamburg, Mecklenburg, Niedersachsen, Sachsen-Anhalt, Schleswig-Holstein, and Thüringen and the Prussian Cultural Heritage Foundation; and the Bibliothèque nationale.

NOTE: The classification was based on the title and, in some cases, the description of the contents. The term "moral" that is used here has the modern meaning; the publications condemned suicide as a sin or crime. There were few original titles published in Spanish.

Table 1.2
Authors mentioned in chapter 1: their backgrounds and main positions on the suicide puzzle

Year	Author mentioned in text	Culture	Profession	Free-will or determinist	Remedy
1822	Falret	French	Doctor/alienist	Free-will; suicide is not a mental illness	Treatment of mentally ill; avoid publicity of cases
1840	Cazauvieilh	French	Doctor/alienist	Mainly determinist; suicide originates in monomania, but risk is increased by bad passions	Religion and moral education
1840	Winslow	English	Doctor	Determinist; suicide results from mental illness	Religion and moral education

Table 1.2 continued

Year	Name	Nationality	Profession	Position	Prescription
1844	Étoc-Demazy	French	Doctor/alienist	Free-will; suicide is not a mental illness	Moral education for society
1845	Bourdin	French	Doctor	Determinist; suicide originates in mental illness	
1845	Esquirol	French	Doctor/alienist	Determinism; suicide originates in mental illness	Treatment of mentally ill
1856 and 1865	Brierre	French	Doctor/alienist	Some insane; some rational	Treatment of mentally ill and moral education for society
1856	Lisle	French	Doctor/alienist	Some insane; some rational	Return to canon law and frighten people with damnation
1864	Wagner	German	Economist/statistician	Rational; he dismissed the French doctors	Felt it was not the task of the statistician to direct policy, but believed spiritual uplift would help deter suicides
1870	Douay	French	Educator and author	Free-will	Greater personal freedom for greater self-fulfillment
1879	Morselli	Italian	Doctor/alienist	Social Darwinian; statistical determinist	Moral education for society
1880	Buckle	English	Historian	Statistical determinist	
1881	Legoyt	French	Statistician	Free-will	Moral education and censorship
1881	Masaryk	Czech; Austro-Hungarian	Professor/sociologist	Statistical determinist	Moral education for society; religious revival
1893	Strahan	English	Barrister	Social Darwinian Determinist	Let suicides remove themselves and the race will improve
1897	Durkheim	French	Professor/sociologist	Statistical determinist; suicidogenic current	Social reorganization to achieve ideal balance of individual freedom and social integration
1900	Proal	French	Criminologist	Heredity determinist but also moralist	Laws to restrict alcohol, pornography, and divorce; a so-called responsible press; restraint by realist novelists

From 1830 onward, books and articles with medical connotations regularly appeared in print. Research had advanced to such a degree of sophistication that in 1844 Gustave-François Étoc-Demazy (1806–93) suggested the time had come to break from the tradition of studying suicide in Paris and other great capital cities and look at a rural area. For his monograph, he selected Sarthe, where he was medical director at an asylum.[25]

The holdings of the British Library and a consortium of German libraries differ from those at the Bibliothèque nationale, and the variations imply distinct intellectual cultures. British titles of a medical, psychiatric, or sociological nature were comparatively scarce, and German publications in those areas only appeared in considerable numbers toward the late nineteenth century. Forbes Winslow claimed, probably correctly, that his *The Anatomy of Suicide* (1840) was the first English book devoted exclusively to suicide from a medical standpoint.[26]

European scholars read widely to build data sets, to dispute findings, and to argue about implications. Winslow, a member of the Royal College of Surgeons, used French data and expressed his indebtedness to French alienists Pinel, Esquirol, and Falret.[27] Von Oettingen in 1868 cited Quételet, Dufau, Cazauvieilh, Guerry, d'Espine, Boudin, Lisle, and Legoyt, as well as German works by Casper, Oesterlen, Löwenhardt, Salomon, Wappäus, Frantz, Engel, and Wagner. Years later Émile Durkheim cited these same writers. German publications increased substantially during the Weimar Republic, when Germans contemplated the suffering of World War I, its ongoing social costs, and the economic trauma of the peace settlement.[28] During the Third Reich, publications dealt largely with forensic medicine and techniques for determining if a violent death was suicide or homicide. Motta's suicide bibliography mentioned 113 Italian publications from 1850 to 1890, including articles.[29] Holdings in the National Library of Spain suggest that literary works dominated in every decade from the 1830s to the 1940s in that country. Explorations in moral statistics and early psychological medicine were rare.[30] Susan Morrissey discovered that in nineteenth-century Russia, there were few original treatises but during the 1860s and 1870s "a steady stream of translations, compilations, and reviews of Western publications." Statistics on suicide were popularized in newspapers, as they were throughout Europe.[31]

Despite the continent-wide interest, suicide was a French problem, or at least a French academic problem. There was Gallic sensitivity on this point. Falret felt obliged to dispose of an Englishman's assertion that the French had a greater proclivity for suicides than the English.[32] Not only did French alienists debate free will ánd determinism in connection with whether suicide was a mental illness, but French moral statisticians launched an additional controversy about free will. German-speaking academics joined in. Systematic collection of data had been well established in France during the 1820s; however, as Ian Hacking has remarked, "gathering numerical data was not enough to make statistical laws rise to the surface."[33]

Adolphe Quételet (1796–1874) contributed to rising hopes for social laws by proposing a social physics to discover regularities and ultimately to unveil laws. Quételet, who was astronomer royal of Belgium, conceived of applying the astronomers' management of variation in measurement to human statistics extending from physical attributes to behaviour. Observational astronomers and meteorologists had encountered variations in measurements and responded with computations to shape aberrant observations into a single reading approximating a true value. In an 1835 treatise Quételet proposed that the mean of large aggregates of population data could yield a real type, an "average man," just as astronomers could calculate a true value: "It was as if nature were shooting at the average man as a target and deviations from this target were errors."[34] The physical target, or average man, was an ideal physical type. Quételet started by considering height and weight and then proceeded to additional ways of extracting more silhouettes of the average man from state-collected numbers. He went still further, proposing that the propensity of the average man to commit a crime or to commit suicide could be calculated from the crime rates or suicide rates for a particular population. In human affairs, as with astronomical observation, he had assumed, stable patterns resided in the numbers and simply awaited discovery.[35] In 1846 Quételet returned to human physical measurements, but this time rather than dwelling on the average, he emphasized that variations tended to be normally distributed. His concepts both of an ideal type and of a normal distribution entered social analysis as contributions to the emerging idea that if individual acts such as suicide or crime could not be understood because of psychological diversity, then the average and normal distribution might make sense of things. This conjecture launched the social sciences.

Successive leaps from astronomy to physical attributes to social character were required for new studies of crime and suicide. Criminals and individuals who took their own lives deviated from the norm, and it became the objective of the social sciences to comprehend the forces causing deviations or to prepare profiles of deviants. Something else was happening as moral statistics found their way into discourses on social questions. The stability in large numbers at the heart of Quételet's social physics challenged free will: "The greater the number of individuals observed, the more do individual peculiarities, whether physical or moral, become effaced, and allow the general facts to predominate, by which society exists and is preserved."[36] But Quételet was a long way from perfecting his physics because he "showed no inclination toward a simultaneous unwinding of multiply categorized data."[37] He only had the statistical tools to compute many separate average men, and the average man's behaviour followed a probability based on one variable at a time with all other things held equal.

Probabilistic laws in statistics seem to threaten free will, especially when early social scientists assumed that laws were deterministic rather than just ways to comprehend chance. Quételet went a long way toward advancing that misunderstanding. Adolph Wagner went further and created a stir in 1864 with the publication of *Statische-anthropologische Untersuchung der Gestzmässigkeit in der shienbar menschlichen Handlungen,* in which he argued that statistical regularities of the type Quételet had found could not be accidental but must originate from causation and must capture a phenomenon in nature.[38] He concluded that each society directs the rate of suicides "by a causality that we do not yet grasp."[39]

"German reaction to Wagner," states Ian Hacking, "was almost uniformly hostile."[40] From the conservative Lutheran stronghold of Dorpat in czarist Russia (now Tartu in Estonia), Alexander von Oettingen ingeniously picked apart Wagner's thesis. Primarily a theologian, exceptional among the great nineteenth-century commentators on suicide, von Oettingen embraced statistics to attack theories that marshalled data to argue for the existence of socially determined behavior but disregarded ethics or God. Discussions with his colleague Wagner, briefly a professor at Dorpat, led him to write his important work *Die Moralstatistik* (1868). In a treatise that bridged philosophy and statistics, von Oettingen disputed the notion that apparent patterns in social statistics showed regularities with a basis in nature; rather, patterns emerged from the combined workings of powerful ideas and ideals, social forces, and individual traits. Besides, the patterns found in suicide data were tangential to understanding suicides. In 1870 Wagner admitted that he had been extreme in believing that data would reveal social laws, and he expressed great respect for von Oettingen's work on suicide.[41] Wagner's statistical study contained intelligent observations: he felt that, as more data was assessed, errors would stand out and collection practices would improve; he remarked that discussions of suicide numbers should be controlled for population; he thought that researchers should be sensitive to local circumstances such as crop failures. He dismissed French studies of suicide, which he felt abused statistics.[42]

Von Oettingen's reply to Wagner proposed a down-to-earth interpretation of social statistics which, he perceived, captured variation as well as regularity. His position became the more typical one for German social statisticians, who emphasized variation within the human community.[43] Regularity existed because, by living together, people influenced one another. At the same time, the individual's freedom of action and unique experiences endured. Thus regularity in social conduct could never be absolute, and ethics or religion could uplift individuals and change society. Regarding suicide, von Oettingen said that most handy data used in commentaries exposed interesting but extraneous details. There was a seasonal pattern. Summer was a high-risk time, but only conjecture existed about what this meant. Patterns in age cohorts, gender, and marital status also emerged. This absorbing information stimulated speculation; however, there were insufficient statistics bearing on a cascade of immediate motives, such as vice, sorrows, financial loss, loss of a loved one, remorse, shame, fear of disgrace, and pangs of conscience.[44] Von Oettingen questioned the meaningfulness of what Ian Hacking calls "the avalanche of numbers." He recognized that Wagner, following Quételet, had not really solved the problem of how to combine into one analysis many measurements taken in a variety of conditions.

Convictions about social laws determining human behaviour took a lambasting from von Oettingen, but misguided or inattentive authors continued to conflate the idea of laws with determinism. English historian Henry Thomas Buckle (1821–62) wrote that suicide statistics proved the existence of social laws: "In a given state of society, a certain number of persons must put an end to their own life. This is the general law." Individuals, he continued, "must obey the larger social law to which they are all subordinate."[45] Buckle was no fringe intellectual; however, serious statisticians were aghast.[46] A statistical law did not dictate conduct to individuals but, rather, indicated regularity of conduct among free agents. The distinction was subtle enough that even the director of the Australian census in 1911, a fellow of the Royal Statistical

Society and disciple of renowned English statistician Karl Pearson
(1857–1936), made a slip and held that suicide statistics were of special
importance "inasmuch as they disclose the regularity of human conduct
even in matters which might be thought to be peculiarly under individual control." He recovered his wisdom somewhat by stating in the next
sentence that "suicide [not the individual] follows well-defined laws."[47]

Despite weighty treatises from Wagner and von Oettingen and a volume or two from England, French writers dominated European nineteenth-century studies. The persistence and abundance of suicide
debates in France require an explanation. Losses from a succession of
conflicts during the revolutionary era (1789–1815) may well have traumatized many French citizens and precipitated such an exceptional
number of suicides that the topic begged for discussion. It is impossible
to anchor that proposition in data because the necessary statistics were
not collected. However, when classifying suicides, Falret cited examples
of so-called suicide epidemics. He claimed, improbably, that in 1793 in
the town of Versaille alone there had been 1,300. In 1806, during June
and July, there were 60 in Rouen; in 1813 a suicide epidemic swept the
tiny village of Saint-Pierre-Monau.[48] Although chaotic and filled with
contradictions, the revolutionary era fostered an enthusiasm for rational government and state action to remedy social ills. That attitude survived the restoration. A minister of justice in the bourgeois monarchy of
Louis-Philippe reported to the king in 1835 that he would improve government statistics on suicide because he deemed it an illness of modern
societies.[49] Rarely did a French suicide study express dissatisfaction
with a current regime, but it often condemned modernity.[50]

Enthusiasm for moral statistics led to an ostensibly secular analysis of
suicide; specialists in mental illness came at the question from another
direction. Government investment in the medicalization of insanity
began during the revolution and continued through the nineteenth century, and that support sustained a cadre of doctors who wrote about life's
trials and aspired to see experts integrated into state service.[51] As well,
the restoration of the monarchy heartened enemies of social and political
reformation, who hunted for crises to blame on the evils of change. The
warring political perspectives on social issues – trust in improvement versus fear of turbulence – kept suicide studies in play. On the one hand,
several authors of leading suicide studies lamented the demise of an old
order sustained by religion and aristocracy, obligation and deference. On
the other hand, by at least 1830, the bourgeois political nation based in
Paris looked to social statistics to guide governments.

Profound connections tied French medicine to suicide studies. In 1795 the leading specialist in insanity, Philippe Pinel, became chief physician at the Salpêtrière asylum, where he took on students. One of them, Jean-Étienne-Dominique Esquirol (1772–1840), emerged as a forceful self-promoter and the organizer of a circle of alienists. Esquirol championed a theory that lodged "mental life solely in the nervous system." This replaced the humoral theory, which proposed that fluids from various organs affected the brain.[52] Thus a fresh classification of mental illnesses was required. Esquirol supplied five varieties: lypemania, or melancholy, in which there was a delirium with respect to one or a small number of objects and a sorrowful passion; monomania, in which delirium was limited to one or a small number of objects and an expansive passion; mania, in which delirium extended to many objects and was accompanied by excitement; dementia, in which there was complete folly; and imbecility, in which reason was never present.[53]

Suicide, Esquirol proposed, belonged entirely to mental illnesses. There were diverse, sudden, and unexpected personal crises that precipitated "a delirium of the passions" which did not allow an individual time to reflect. Passion extinguished the free will of the sane. Winslow thought that English coroners' juries failed to pay enough attention to the overpowering force of emotions which clouded judgment and guaranteed insanity behind every instance of suicide.[54] For Equirol, there could also be mental illnesses of long duration that led to suicide. A single pathological obsession in an otherwise sound mind was suicidal monomania. Whatever the nature or time span of mental trouble, suicide itself by definition had to be an act of madness of one type or another.[55] This stance attracted support since it undermined moral condemnation by putting the act beyond an individual's will.[56] In instances of lingering mental illnesses, evidence might support the suicide-insanity equation. However, to maintain that all suicide victims were not responsible for their actions, it had to be further accepted that men and women who appeared rational could have been seized by an uncontrollable impulse seconds before a fatal act. Individuals could be brought to this state by life's troubles, heredity, and even secular education, which raised material expectations unrealistically. Much could harm the brain; the connection between crises and insanity was packaged as a somatic condition.[57] These ideas lacked universal support because, as Ian Dowbiggin observed in his history of nineteenth-century French psychiatry, without proof that insanity had somatic causes, doubt formed at mid-century that certain mental states constituted objects for medical scrutiny.[58] The absence of a ruling paradigm in psychiatry led to insecurity, defensiveness, and debates that encompassed suicide.[59]

In 1854 Jean-Pierre Falret, who worked with Esquirol at the Salpêtrière, would demolish his mentor's monomania concept with a treatise on the non-existence of instinctive monomanias.[60] However, long before that critique, Falret had published an essay which undermined the notion that suicide expressed a monomania or any other form of mental illness; rather, he allowed that the deed could originate in a myriad of preconditioning factors. In radical opposition to Esquirol, Falret defined suicide as an act requiring free will. In *De hypochondrie et du suicide* (1822), he conceded that some forms of delusional madness could drive individuals to kill themselves, but this behaviour did not constitute real suicide because the individual acted under a compulsion.[61] Besides, delusional people were too rare to account for variations in the suicide rates among different groups.[62] Variation could only be explained by external causes connected to how people lived. There were predisposing causes (*causes prédisposantes*), such as heredity, age, gender, temperament, and education. Falret explained how each predisposing cause could affect suicides. Gender was significant because women were prone to melancholy. Temperament played a part since some people were rash, excitable, or quick-tempered. He also specified short-term direct causes (*causes occasionnelles directes*), which included romantic entanglements that could foster unease, suspicion, and jealously. Additional precipitating events comprised honour, pride, domestic disputes, debauchery, reversals of fortune, terminal illnesses, and syphilis.[63]

Two-part divisions into background forces and proximate causes characterized suicide studies for most of the century. Another former intern at the Salpêtrière, Jean-Baptiste Cazauvieilh (1801–49), published a study of suicide in Liancourt-Oise between 1804 and 1833. His analysis (1840) mirrored Falret's two-part division. He remarked on deep common predispositions to crime and suicide; foremost was heredity. Shallower predispositions could be acquired and could thus be corrected by religious organizations or other agencies of moral education.[64] Cazauvieilh incorporated more determinism into his explanation for suicide than Falret, but he joined other suicide specialists in angling for a middle position. Étoc-Demazy in 1844 likewise dismissed Esquirol's theory that most suicides expressed insanity. In his study of judicial inquests for Sarthe, Étoc-Demazy also outlined two sets of causes: *causes prédisposantes* and *causes déterminantes*.[65] Shrewd analysts over the years connected the rough regularity of suicide rates across time to deeper causes – *causes prédisposantes* – whether these were social or psychological. Next they associated fluctuations – the tip of an iceberg – with the vicissitudes of *causes déterminantes* or *causes occasionnelles directes*. A separation of types of suicide was useful for those who inclined toward determinism yet wanted to promote moral education. By incorporating heredity and mental illnesses as well as proximate causes into their model, specialists could remain determinists but open wiggle room for moral improvement. In 1900, when hereditary and degeneracy explanations for crime and suicide were extremely popular and many decades after Falret had proposed a two-part explanation, criminologist Proal wrote that, while heredity was important in determining temperament, governments could do more to restrain passions.[66] In sum, for decades writers wanted to have their determinism and beat it too.

Not only had Falret innovated by proposing duality in causation, but he moved in the vanguard in another respect. He inserted a handful of tables using statistics from the Département de la Seine and the London borough of Westminster.[67] He could not find much else, because the routine publication of suicide statistics for all of France began only in 1827.[68]

The first proto-sociological challenge to proto-psychiatric interpretations came from another member of Esquirol's circle. In a landmark study first published in 1856 and revised and republished in 1865, Alexandre-Jacques-François Brierre de Boismont claimed adherence to an empirical medical research method. Put the *maladie* at the centre of the investigation, multiply the observations, and generalize.[69] On the surface, *De suicide et de la folie suicide* applied social-statistical as well as medical approaches, for Brierre (he added de Boismont to the family name) compiled and analyzed suicide data from juridical inquests. In a separate section, he summarized his notes on asylum inmates. To bind his diffuse observations, he introduced moral criticisms that extended beyond France to Western civilization. In a long book packed with observations, Brierre seldom unfurled moralizing banners, but when he did, he blamed modern times for suicide.

In what Brierre termed advanced civilizations, there had been an accelerated progress of individualism, egoism, skepticism, and excessive appeals to democracy.[70] In overwrought, conservative prose, he asserted that the unlatching of restraint tempted people to overextend and isolate themselves. In despair, they committed suicide. Cities hosted

a disproportionate share of corrosive changes; urban areas consequently had higher suicide rates than the countryside.[71] A true Gallican,
Brierre accorded Catholicism an honoured place in the ideal society, not
as a powerful moralizing institution, but as a gentle, comforting, and
learned moralizing institution that should yield to the state in matters of
health. Render unto Caesar, he advised.

Born into an affluent Rouen family in 1797, Brierre became a member
of Esquirol's circle of alienists in 1825. At Sunday gatherings he would
not only have discussed medical topics but would have observed
Esquirol's climb though the state's medical hierarchy.[72] Brierre knew how
to navigate his way to the top. He came of age as a public figure in the
Second Empire. By 1865 he was a *chevalier des ordres de la Légion
d'honneur* and *lauréat de l'Institut et de l'Académie impériale de médecine*. There was substance behind these tributes and a string of international honours. Through cleverness, experience, connections, and hard
work, Brierre produced a remarkable book. In the course of three years,
he read 4,595 files of investigations into suicides by prosecutorial judges.
To establish if a death involved a criminal offence, the police investigated
all violent deaths in France; in the United Kingdom, its settlement colonies, and the United States, coroners or magistrates performed the same
investigative function. Inquests produced the death certificates that provided data for annual reports on causes of death. Some original reports
remained in government archives; some were destroyed.

Brierre recognized the value of the suicide case files; as an esteemed
alienist and author of books and articles about mental illness, he had
access to archives. In addition to judicial files, he examined notes on
862 individuals whom he had admitted to mental hospitals over a
period of twelve years. Of these, 115 had contemplated suicide and 150
had made an attempt. Part pioneer sociologist, part doctor, part moralist, part apologist for social stability, Brierre equivocated about the
power of *la statistique morale*. Numbers deserved respect when they
addressed material conditions, but he conceded that they had less
authority in areas of morals and conscience. Suicide victims, the mentally ill, and criminals would always be with us, but exact figures for
each were not preordained. Variability endured as a troubling fact.
Along with other commentators, Brierre alleged that statistics indicated
increases in social ills. The roots of trouble had to be found among
social circumstances because the only alternative agents, as he saw
them, were God and the law of progress. Good things such as these
could not be held responsible for bad things such as mounting insanity,

crime, and suicide. Even though statistics had limitations, he emphasized that their study must never be abandoned. Here was a scholar,
doctor, and moralist dancing in circles at the crossroads of social science, religion, and politics.[73]

Brierre respected the faith of his fathers and social order, and he
mixed nostalgic reactions with a medical professional's desire to save
lives, to reduce suicide rather than condemn it as a sin or treat it as
insanity. From his experience as an alienist and from reading case files,
he concluded that few people who committed suicide were clinically
insane. If you had seen as many cases of mania and hallucination as I
have, he argued, you would not make rash judgments. Lisle in his book,
also published in 1856, had likewise used his medical case notes to dismiss the association of suicide with insanity. He had asked why suicides
were not more widespread, given abundant instances of insanity.[74]
Early in his book, Brierre divided people at risk of committing suicide
into two groups: the small minority who had mental illnesses that carried a suicide risk and who could be treated medically in various ways,
depending on the severity of the illness, and the sane, who could be
instructed gently by reason and example. As much as he appreciated the
role of the church in helping to prevent suicides by contributing to
moral life, Brierre felt that doctors, not priests, should treat the mentally ill and that compulsory secular education by trained teachers, not
priests, could instill morally fit ways of life.[75] He assigned separate but
complementary duties for the French state and Catholicism in a campaign against suicide.

Brierre extended his analysis to a review of suicide rates in Europe
and the United States, from which he concluded that the number of
incidents had escalated as a result of social factors. The good news
was that suicide could be reduced by remedial measures. While he dismissed God and the law of progress as incapable of capriciously introducing variation into suicide rates, he instead introduced social forces
as agents of fluctuations and diversity. These forces could best be discerned through statistics. Brierre found the evidence in the case files;
they connected suicides to the great social questions of the day, which
he listed as liberty, education, poverty, work, wages, and family life.
Witnesses ventured links between the rash acts and social questions, but
Brierre remained skeptical about measuring the strength of assumed
connections. Statistics could be of service in sorting and ranking
motives for suicide by the frequency of explanations mentioned in judicial inquests.

Without the benefit of a computer to cross-tabulate variables extracted from the files, Brierre reviewed one variable at a time, compiling tables on age, gender, marital status, method, and time of year. The bulk of his study rested on a frequency distribution of twenty motives for 4,595 suicides. Madness, alcoholism, illnesses, domestic troubles, romantic disappointments, general disaffection with life, and poverty were leading categories. In the composition of these motives and the creation of less significant ones – fear of dishonour, laziness, vanity and pride, and jealousy – he betrayed his time, place, and social station. His discussion of most *causes déterminantes* opened with classical or historical examples, considered constituent parts of a general category, remarked on individual cases, and finally summarized. Brierre shifted his analysis without presenting case evidence in depth. He slipped from the general and constituent causes of suicides to explanations that stressed passions such as grief, jealousy, remorse, pride, boredom, and immoderation, including debauchery and ambition. These expressions of unbalanced behaviour led straight to his conclusions about the perils of the modern age. An account of suicide in antiquity, the Middle Ages, and other countries likewise prepared the way for a condemnation of the modern. The subordination of the individual to a divine plan in the Middle Ages had reined in self-destruction. During a long conversation about ennui, Brierre criticized conduct that he deemed excessive and leading to suicidal thoughts. All wild living fostered great unhappiness, because dissipation fed disgust with work and a shunning of family. Since work and family were rewarding states in the creative life, their disappearance drained purpose from life. To avoid risk, Brierre recommended the advice of St John Chrysostom: Don't open a door to troubles; rather, act with moderation. Marry, have children, and thereby avoid emotional isolation. Find an occupation and stick to it. Idleness is not in Providence's plan for humanity.[76] These pearls were not pulled from a sea of tears but from church doctrine and the Second Empire's unwritten code.

Moderation may never go amiss – fair enough. But for many men long hours of labour recommended seizing off-hours for drinks with friends. The suggestion to follow an occupation for a lifetime presumed that people controlled their employment. The assumption that marriage necessarily promoted happiness and prevented emotional isolation deserves interrogation. Marriage worked for some people, probably the great majority, but the case files surely held dark domestic tales. *Du suicide* has interest today as a witness to a period, place, and class. It was a reconnaissance into case files that lost its way because of the author's unfamiliarity with the economic and psychological burdens borne by contemporaries.

PUTTING THE MORAL INTO MORAL STATISTICS

Early alienists suggested treatments for suicidal patients but did not comment at length on suicide prevention. Falret listed several treatments connected with the humoral theory; interventions were intended to stimulate particular organs and thus restore humoral balance. Remedies included drinking abundant cold water and bleeding. Falret himself was skeptical.[77] The measures he urged in 1822 remained popular in Europe and neo-Europes for a century: pursue work as a means of distraction, travel, and take long tepid baths. He also advised restraints if necessary. Laws against suicide, he believed, were pointless, but newspapers could help by refraining from publicizing self-destruction. In the early 1840s, authors had also begun to promote religion and moral education.[78] For example, Cazauvieilh alleged that a monomania for suicide and monomanias for crime originated in hereditary weaknesses that affected the brain in ways currently unknown, but the monomanias grew on account of passions such as jealousy, cupidity, pride, debauchery, and libertinism. The spirit of independence from religion and morality intoxicated people, and religious instruction was urgently needed now to check crime and suicide.[79]

Étoc-Demazy thought that it was insufficient to watch over people in order to prevent self-destruction. As an asylum doctor, he practised surveillance but hoped for prevention. Moral education fortified by religion, he maintained, could prepare people to accept setbacks.[80] Remarks such as these from the 1840s marked the beginning of a recurrent trend, persisting to the present day, of psychiatrists suggesting social prophylaxis. Invariably, the major suicide studies that began with Brierre had a set format: they opened with a discussion of data, remarked on social or individual ills, and concluded with proposals for social reforms to reduce suicides. The preferred remedies were conservative and in France directed against anti-clericalism and liberalism. Proal's *Le crime et le suicide passionnels* (1900) demanded press censorship, restrictions to alcohol consumption, elimination of pornography, and tighter divorce laws.[81]

European intellectuals wrestled with the role of churches in suicide prevention. For a few commentators, the church should remind people that suicide brought damnation. Most writers preferred a gentler faith and a tamer clergy. Winslow in 1840 expressed a wide sentiment when he wrote that "religion must be made the basis of all secular knowledge."[82] The semantics here were bizarre and perhaps uniquely English, but continental writers shared Winslow's assumptions that suicide was increasing and people needed to be educated to bear life's troubles. Economist Wagner remarked that a gradual spiritual improvement in a society was its best hope for reducing suicides.[83] This too was the position of Tomáš (Thomas) Masaryk, who published *Der Sebstmord als sociale Massenerscheinung der modernen Civilisation (Suicide and the Meaning of Civilization)* in 1881. While the book brought Masaryk recognition outside the Austro-Hungarian Empire and was read and cited by Durkheim, fame came years later when he championed Czech independence and achieved an immense respect as a European democrat. As a suicide scholar, his thinking was largely conventional. He arranged his explanation of suicide into proximate causes – what he called effective causes – and an ultimate cause, which was the decline of religious life. The effective causes included poverty, aging, alcohol abuse, marital disintegration, loss of loved ones, and mental illness.

What set Masaryk's ideas slightly apart from those of his contemporaries was the path he recommended for moral reform. To reduce suicide, according to him, it was necessary to stem the malaise left when institutional Christianity became dogmatic and lost influence. A convert to Protestantism, Masaryk did not believe Catholicism or the state could pull society out of a moral slough. To lift people above self-interest and strengthen them to face inevitable adversity, he advocated moral education. A few superbly educated people, like himself, might achieve a safe reconciliation of secularism, personal freedom, altruism, and self-preservation, but such a refined intelligence, achieved through a splendid education, would elude most of society. Irreligiosity had deprived the masses of a common, inexpensive means of attaining what Masaryk called a whole education. It made the life of Job "unbearable with the first blow."[84] Failed morality dominated Masaryk's account of an ultimate cause, but it was the failed morality of society, not the failed morality of individuals. He wished to put moral healing on a scientific footing, and for this reason he considered himself a pioneer of sociology, despite the ostensible backward-looking character of his repeated theme that "the modern suicide tendency is ultimately the product of increasing irreligiosity."[85]

Although Masaryk accepted the common moral panic position, his claim to have undertaken a sociological inquiry had foundation too. First, he presumed that his discussion of a host of demographic variables pertaining to men and women who committed suicide captured the scientific method for studying society. Like most predecessors and many successors, he coaxed meaning from aggregate data. Second, he felt he made an unassailable case – "we know" was his immodest way of introducing a hypothesis – that social and political progress had left people morally unprepared to take hard blows. Great freedom had been achieved, but crime, violence, war, poverty, and suicide endured. Third, he argued that psychoses mainly derived from social ordeals; this relationship was "more important than the fact that psychosis is an effective cause of the suicide tendency."[86] Masaryk shunted mental illness into a secondary position. Finally, he based his claim to eminence as a sociologist on his belief that he had identified a path to alleviating "the evils of modern society." However, his dismissal of economic and political reforms and his appeal for a regenerated Christianity put his sociology at odds with the secularism of French sociology's founding spirit, Auguste Comte.[87]

More than a decade after his massive *Socialethik* had appeared, Alexander von Oettingen returned to write about moral statistics. While preparing a popular lecture series, he read Masaryk's book and greeted it with a mix of admiration and consternation.[88] Although he agreed that raw statistics suggested suicide was on the increase in Europe, he emphasized that numbers say nothing about causes; to comprehend suicide properly, one had to probe for psychological motives hidden from state officials, who, with varying degrees of diligence, collected only summary statistics. Psychological observation and experience in life were required for a better understanding of suicide.[89] Astonishingly modern in spirit, von Oettingen's critiques foreshadowed mid-twentieth-century challenges to a statistical turn in sociology that flourished in the United States after World War II.

In contradistinction to the moral statisticians' recourse to compressed summary data and their quest for social laws, von Oettingen insisted that each case had a unique history.[90] That salient point made, he conceded that there were similarities among histories that allowed investigators to cluster cases. These thoughts essentially duplicated his 1868 position. But whereas he had left a theory of suicide underdeveloped in 1868, in 1881 he tried to contribute to systematic study. He built on the medical distinction between acute and chronic illnesses. Like acute illnesses, acute suicides appeared with devastating suddenness and often were rash responses to actions by other parties. In contrast, chronic suicides originated in lingering personality traits. They were rooted in people's sentiments and feelings, which could be affected by cultural factors. German culture, he proposed, fostered an overly sensitive character, which helped explain the high suicide rates reported by German states. Saxony led all European jurisdictions.[91] More broadly, Europeans suffered from diminishing attachment to community as a result of materialism and partisan politics. This common conservative lament predictably led von Oettingen to promote moral education, organic community-building, and religion. It was nice, he mocked, that Masaryk wanted men to be decent and to embrace a popular *Volksreligion*. An idealist's dream! A firm church-based religion with educated clergy would truly be effective.[92]

From roughly the mid-1850s until the early-1890s, European writers who applied moral statistics to the problem of suicide combined their statistical analyses with statements on how some organized religions might heal society. They differed over details. French ultramontane Catholics favoured a revival of canon law; Brierre and moderate Catholics looked to church and state to share moral education duties. During the Second Empire (1852–70), the government and compliant intellectuals brooded about the size and moral fibre of the France's population, supported moral instruction, embraced the idea that true civil liberty required subordination to a higher spiritual law, accepted censorship, and encouraged religion so long as priests evinced loyalty.[93] The Third Republic (1871–1940) liberalized education and relaxed censorship, but France remained distinct among modern states at the time in that its intellectuals and politicians worried about both "a decline in national power and perplexing problems resulting from the advent of a democratic and economically highly developed society."[94] The abundant suicide literature responded to this perceived double crisis. But intellectuals elsewhere shared some of the French intellectuals' concerns and remedies. Masaryk, too, appealed for religious renewal. Von Oettingen insisted on the moral force of a trained clergy. In opposition to moral statistics, he proposed what he called social ethics, which had a substantial influence on Lutheran ideas on pastoral care. Socialists and liberals had little to say about suicide.

Karl Marx wrote once on the topic. For an article in *Gesellschaftsspiegel* in 1846, he modified excerpts from the memoirs of a Parisian police official, Jacques Peuchet, to expose women's inequality within the family. Marx translated Peuchet's recollections of suicide cases, but he altered wording to stress any social inequality in a suicide case and changed phrasing when Peuchet, a centrist, mildly approved of church-led moral education.[95] Years passed before another commentary emerged on the left. In a critique of the Second Empire, disguised as a philosophical treatise on suicide, republican publicist and educator Edmond Douay denounced the belief that Christian values could suppress suicidal impulses. The rising number of suicides originated in the lack of fulfillment that people felt when they endured life in a corrupted political environment which satisfied material needs but stifled conscience. As for Christianity, it was a religion of resignation that could serve to promote either a longing for life or an acceptance of death. Personal freedom alone could give people a reason to love life. In 1879 August Bebel (1840–1913), founder of the Germany Social Democratic Party, wrote *Women in the Past, Present and Future*. In this remarkable treatise on women's rights, he commented on German reports of a large number of female suicides between the ages of sixteen and twenty-one. The relatively high rate for this age cohort, he argued, was "proof enough that the causes are chiefly ungratified sexual instincts, disappointed love, concealed pregnancy and desertion on the part of men."[96] The claim supported Bebel's advocacy for reforms to the legal status of women and the extension of the voting franchise. It is doubtful that these measures alone could have minimized the suicidal motives of young women, although the case files examined for *A Sadly Troubled History* disclosed events exactly like those he listed. However, men were not the only culpable parties. Mothers occasionally had a role in their daughters' crises, and there were other motives.

Émile Durkheim's *Le suicide* (1897) swept around politics and especially the predominant conservative moralizing of the previous half-century. Instead he promoted sociology as a neutral science. If Masaryk wanted to be recognized as a sociologist, Durkheim wanted sociology recognized. The book long held interest in Europe because of Durkheim's mustering of logic and data to dispose of prior analyses and to establish a wholly original comprehension of suicide. He achieved a theoretical tour de force. Brierre had advanced the course of thinking about suicide by establishing the merit of analyzing social surroundings; Masaryk claimed to be the first author to attempt "a definitive explanation of suicide from the sociological point of view."[97] Both prescribed a moral education. Durkheim applied theoretical rigour to social analysis and dispensed with explicit appeals to organized religion. Anthony Giddens felt that there were "a number of broad theoretical similarities" between Durkheim and Masaryk. The similarities were broad, and Durkheim moved radically beyond his predecessors.

DURKHEIM AND *LE COURANT SUICIDOGÈNE*

Émile Durkheim (1858–1917) was remarkably creative and incredibly ambitious. He packed the text of *Le suicide* with adamantine claims, statistics, and an original theory.[98] As well, he enlisted his classical education from the École normale supérieure, where he had studied from 1879 to 1882. A pupil of noted classicist Fustel de Coulanges, Durkheim, like his contemporary Sigmund Freud, illustrated arguments with literary references.[99] He also synthesized the abundant German, Austrian, Italian, English, French, and Belgian work on suicide from the previous decades.[100] His borrowing has been the subject of assertions that he plagiarized; however, his core theory was distinctive.[101] Wagner and Morselli had collected the data that Durkheim cited and applied more sophisticated statistical techniques. What distinguished Durkheim's book was its obsessive privileging of theory as truth and sociological theory as superior truth. Unlike predecessors, he aimed to bypass the morass of insanity and free-will debates and avoid reactionary moralizing. Adept at tearing down received wisdom by applying militant logic-chopping and marshalling plenty of data, Durkheim tried to demolish psychological explanations.

Theories of insanity could not explain suicide because the suicides of the clinically insane were at best only a small subset of all suicides, and once exceptions were allowed into a theory, it lost its value.[102] However, if suicides were not exceptions but the rule, then Durkheim had another complaint: "If suicide can be shown to be a mental disease with its own characteristics and distinct evolution, the question is settled; every suicide is a madman."[103] But of course not every suicide was mad. According to Durkheim, light mental illness – neurasthenia – could not be a cause since more women than men suffered from mental illness yet, paradoxically, more men than women committed suicide.[104] He disposed of alcoholism by looking at alcohol consumption and suicide rates in regions of France and discovering they were unconnected. A third of the book criticized the work of others, a circumstance that compelled him to apologize. "The results of the preceding book," he asserted, "are not wholly negative." He proceeded to affirm the need for sociology.[105]

Despite his assaults on psychology, Durkheim recognized that the individual was not easily removed from the scene. Like many researchers since, he encountered the puzzle that cannot be ignored. "No unhappiness in life," he summarized, "necessarily causes a man to kill himself unless he is otherwise so inclined."[106] That remains a powerful assertion. If troubles alone do not explain suicide, what does? How could he ignore the life history of an individual? He responded ingeniously by radically altering the angle of attack so that suicide was not a puzzling solution to an individual's crisis, but a collective inclination that he called a suicidogenic current. The motives for an individual's suicide indicated "the individual's weak points, where the outside current bearing the impulse to self-destruction finds introduction."[107]

Durkheim's hypothesis of a current may have been inspired by his reading of Masaryk, who proposed that "the nature of the suicide tendency has been the same in all times, and that the same fundamental causes that have always generated this morbid tendency." "Men are what men always were."[108] A more plausible and statistically centred inspiration for the current was the statistician's normal distribution curve; both the mean at the curve's centre and outliers at its tails entered moral statistics by way of astronomy, thanks to Quételet. Durkheim's conception of the suicidogenic current included the idea of a hypothetical essential rate analogous to Quételet's proposition that individual measurements of men revealed an average man. The suicidogenic current was also analogous to Quételet's later observations about outliers – non-conforming behaviour – on a frequency distribution curve. According to Quételet, deviants taken collectively exhibited stable statistical attributes that amounted to an archetypal deviant or criminal personality.

Like the measurements that produced the average man or those that yielded the essential qualities of the archetypal deviant, suicide rates, in Durkheim's theory, indicated a suicidogenic current which was more real than real. It was an essence. The diversity of suicide rates across many populations could be charted as a distribution displaying disorderly chance, but Durkheim regarded the many rates, which were not remarkably different among western European jurisdictions and were rising slightly over time, as points scattered around an essence.[109] Jack Douglas, the mid-twentieth-century sociologist whose own contribution to suicide studies figures in chapter 2, suggested that Durkheim's work expressed an Aristotelian essentialism. Durkheim's classical education could have played a part, but developments in human and social statistics were influential too. Statistics guided him toward proposing that observable rates were spread around an archetype which did not express the rate in any one country, for example, but embodied an essential rate for all countries in the set being studied.

Like several earlier social scientists – Wagner, for example – who flirted with the concept of statistically revealed essences, Durkheim confused probability with a real entity. Working with government data published on cities, states, and nations, he detected steadiness or parallel increases over time among the annual suicide rates for populations and subpopulations. The fact that suicide rates for countries or members of religious groups, if represented by dots along a frequency distribution curve, would have produced much the same pattern year after year seemed a monumental finding. Furthermore, any variations occurred within a narrow band. For Durkheim, these observations were enough to denote the existence of something real underlying the patterns.[110] Thus he went beyond statistical observation and probability arguments to concoct the theory of a suicidogenic current. It was fine-tuned by social forces. As he expressed it, he would "disregard the individual" and explain variations in suicide rates in terms of the social environment, which included "religious confessions, family, political society, occupational groups, etc."[111]

The accent on the collective (the current) and modulators (the elements of the social environment, social forces) conformed to an axiom in Durkheim's sociology. He maintained that "the social fact is a thing distinct from its individual manifestations."[112] Therefore he did not assemble an impulse to suicide by aggregating individual observations. By contrast, Brierre had attempted to establish from case histories a set of social forces leading to suicide; however, he deviated from empiricism to reach his moral viewpoints. Durkheim avoided making a similar mistake, although his denunciation of working with individual cases originated from an additional contention. How, he asked, can it be possible to create a strong foundation for sociology if its materials are borrowed from psychology, which is the study of the individual? His ambition in writing Le suicide was not primarily to unravel the mystery of suicide but to demonstrate the independent value of sociology.[113] But he did not close his discussion with the mere discovery of the current, because sociology had to have some rationale. Social factors modulated the essential suicide rate, and that effect produced a distinct rate for each population or subpopulation. Sociology would prove its worth by demonstrating how distinct societies affected the current.

For the collective impulse, as we have noted, Durkheim conjured "the suicidogenic current." It bore a resemblance to electric current. Energy and the control of energy fascinated contemporary scientists and analysts of the human condition as well. Vital energy figured in Freud's idea of the libido. For Durkheim, there was "for each people a collective force of a definite amount of energy, impelling men to self destruction."[114] "Each people has collectively an inclination of its own to suicide, on which the size of its contribution to voluntary death depends."[115] Support for this proposition, he believed, arose from the fact that suicide statistics showed distinct national rates that remained relatively regular over time.[116] Suicide might never be eliminated, according to Durkheim's conceptualization, but rates could be altered. Societies with high rates could have those rates pulled back to the balance point that expressed the essence of the current. Social forces in combinations unique to each country or region subjected the suicidogenic current to adjustments that shaped their distinctive national, regional, or group rates. Social forces – conducive to low or high social integration – shaped more than rates; they produced distinctive types of suicide. Durkheim's apologists ignored the fundamental importance of the suicidogenic current and tailored his cloth to suit impressions of what they thought he wrote. Anthony Giddens, for example, characterized Durkheim's social forces as "producing high rates of suicide." That is an imprecise characterization.[117]

Social forces, according to Durkheim, tempered the suicidogenic current but did not produce it. This distinction has been muddled by his champions and critics alike.[118] But Durkheim had not completed his theory; he went further and devised a scheme to abstract the social forces. It was incomplete to say that religious confessions, family, political society, and occupational groups affected suicide rates. He grouped the social forces in four clusters, which he then arranged in pairs: egoistic and anomic; altruistic and fatalistic. These terms had specific theory-driven meanings; the pairs also embodied opposing attributes for an individual's connections with society, with the first pair accenting space for individual development and the second highlighting the individual's integration into society. If one component in a pair was too strongly represented in the social environment, then it failed to counter the suicidogenic current in a particular manner. When the pairs were neither too strong nor too weak, when the egoistic and anomic pair (individualism) was balanced by the altruistic and fatalistic pair (immersion in society), "the moral agent is in a state of equilibrium."[119] Not too hot, not too cold, but just right.

Disequilibrium elevated suicide rates, and Durkheim labelled the types of suicide in relation to where disequilibrium originated. When individuals were dissociated from their groups, they were prone to egoistic suicides. If they lived in communities that had no adequate beliefs to meet current social realities, then conditions conduced to anomic suicide. The subtle difference between egoistic and anomic suicide was that in the egoistic the social force lacking was collective activity, while in the anomic what was missing was society's cultural influence over individual passions, which left the individual adrift and deprived of meaning.[120] Too much cohesion weakened individuality and led to altruistic suicide.[121] Fatalistic suicide exited the theory in a footnote, but Durkheim conceived of it as occurring in oppressive societies.[122] Whereas Masaryk had proposed that an irreligiosity-religiosity mix affected a suicide tendency, Durkheim imagined a set of grand-scale secular modifiers that modulated the suicidogenic current. Just as nature ordained stability and scientists could detect order in distribution curves, so nature produced stability in human conduct and social scientists could identify the determining social forces. A national suicide rate over many years seemingly expressed a stable pattern unique to that country and dependant upon the intensity of egoism, anomie, altruism, and fatalism or actually upon how the pairs balanced each other. Historical circumstances determined the strength of these four qualities.

Only near the end of his study did Durkheim allow personality traits to enter his theory; he classified conduct according to melancholy, apathy, irritation, and anger. These emotions characterized the types of suicide, but the emotions of individuals did not produce these types of suicide. To maintain the primacy of sociology, he positioned suicide's several emotional guises as derivative of a society's inclination toward egoism, anomie, altruism, and fatalism. Durkheim dogmatically insisted that sociology precede psychology; moreover, history, ethnography, and statistics were relegated to "auxiliary disciplines."[123] His defensiveness about sociology – what he called "the emancipation of sociology" – was not his sole justification for privileging social forces.[124] The scarcity of and limitations to personal-level information, he alleged, contributed to this priority. He could not proceed empirically to classify like types of suicides "morphologically" because of "the almost total lack of requisite evidence."[125] He had read Brierre and knew about case files. On the grounds that even these investigations would have lacked sufficient information for reconstructing individual lives, he rejected them in favour of the aggregate data distilled from these same investigations. Argumentative, logical, and single-minded when knocking down obstacles to his views, he simply dismissed case files. Durkheim claimed that he distrusted individual case information because the publications that had used them were connected with projects of "moral casuistry," and he wanted more attention paid to "the social concomitants" of suicide as a means of breaking away from the biases of past studies.[126] People who took their own lives were neither sinners nor insane; society had some responsibility.

What struck Durkheim as abnormal were not suicidal people but apparent rises in suicide rates across Europe, which he identified as troubling and getting worse since the mid-nineteenth century. Suicidal individuals were not to be thought of as deviants but as products of society. He thus joined the queue of doomsayers and attributed the crisis to the decline of guilds, family life, and religious communities that attended industrialization and urbanization. Since social forces not only branded types of suicide but, more importantly, modulated the rates, amelioration of suicide required the rectification of a faulty social and cultural grounding, and the means for the makeover that he favoured resembled syndicalism. He recommended democratic organizations based on occupational affiliations. That was novel. The state he dismissed as intrusive and impotent, hence more likely to weaken social integration than to improve it.[127] Whereas many academics prior to Durkheim had already conceived of social changes as disruptions that contributed to suicides, he differed from many of them by disapproving of clerically driven morality to counteract modern life. He condemned clericalism with as much force as his forerunners had recommended it. Their moralizing was unscientific, and he intended to establish a secular science. The great problem with this ambition was that his selection of historical attributes which impinged on the anomic and egoistic or altruistic and fatalistic social forces was not anchored in any testable theory. In the incisive critique of Jack Douglas, Durkheim failed to "provide any guidelines for operationalizing the theoretical concepts, while nevertheless operationalizing them."[128] He insisted on the validity of his meta-history of Europe. He presumed to know how religion and families functioned, how men and women thought, and how they related to one another. Nowhere did he explain how these assertions could be tested.

When they compared suicide rates in countries over time, Durkheim and the commentators who preceded him uncovered what they believed were trends. Some predecessors explained contrasts in terms of national character, race, or climate; others blamed a county's political and economic traditions. National differences piqued Durkheim's curiosity. "Each society," he wrote, "is predisposed to contribute a definite quota of voluntary deaths. This predisposition may therefore be the subject of a special study belonging to sociology."[129] The quotas of suicides, as we have seen, resemble Quételet's normal distributions, and Durkheim insisted that sociology could explain them. Using simple comparative analysis – for example, by looking at religious denominations and so-called races within countries – he found that religious communities revealed more variation than races. This statistical finding, he argued, proved that social factors trumped others, but at heart he shared with his predecessors an assumption about cultures and their consequences for suicide rates. Catholicism and Judaism integrated people into communities more effectively than Protestantism. Durkheim felt that he had demonstrated a social fact rather than a moral benefit of religion. Religion "has a prophylactic effect upon suicide ... not as has sometimes been said because it condemns more unhesitatingly than secular morality ... but because it is a society."[130]

With his mix of classicism, statistics, science, and interest in religion, Durkheim was a quintessential European academic except for his rejection of insanity as an explanation, his avoidance of moral judgment, and his emphatic commitment to theory. While academics in Europe's modernizing states had agreed for decades that urbanization and industrialization explained a presumed rise in suicide rates, they had not intended that such rates should then be enlisted as a gauge of progress. Nevertheless, the claim that higher suicide rates were not an entirely bad thing but evidence of an advanced economy was consistent with Durkheim's theory. By the turn of the century, a few commentators had proclaimed that silver lining. Susan Morrissey suggests, for example, that the increased reports of suicides in Russian newspapers promised modernization: "To the regret of the populists and the delight of the Marxists, Russia's path into the (European) future seemed assured."[131]

BEDS OF SAND: THE ECOLOGICAL FALLACY

Whether good or bad data was involved, whether or not an author's conclusions were supported by the data, statistically grounded argumentation shaped the knowledge structure of suicide studies by the 1850s. History and literature still provided material for late nineteen-century studies, but they lacked the authority they had exercised at the century's start. Falret in 1822 filled pages with incidents from the classics as if they carried the authenticity of medical or forensic case histories. By century's end, however, Durkheim cited examples from literature merely to illustrate a point associated with the data. Statistical analysis increasingly shaped texts after the 1820s. Tables imposed rigour. The categories that defined the columns and rows which disciplined the numbers also provided the headings and subheadings for the text. By the end of the century, the structure of suicide discussions demonstrated a cookie-cutter uniformity. Authors went through considerations of climate, seasons, ages, gender, marital status, occupations, and methods and conjectured about the patterns' meanings. Earlier writers, especially the many physicians, had narrated case histories, but the pursuit of statistical breakdowns for the sake of statistical authority hemmed in discursive possibilities in later works.

There were problems with government suicide statistics, problems that persisted through the twentieth century. Across Europe, the presence and diligence of civil servants varied, so that the collection and quality of death certificates was uneven. From local knowledge, Étoc-Demazy supposed that between 1830 and 1841 many suicides in his area had escaped notice or been mistaken for accidents.[132] Samuel Strahan, whose legal credentials gave him credibility on this point, noted in 1893 that in England the suicide's effort to disguise his or her act was too often successful.[133] Magistrates or police officials who determined official causes of death could and did report some suicides as accidents. Occasionally, this was an honest mistake. Whether investigators gave the benefit of the doubt to help a grieving family depended on how detached they could remain from the community, on their probity, on central government inspection, and most of all on the plausibility of an accidental death. Some governments improved their collection services faster than others.

As far as I could judge, mistakes and deception were uncommon among the thousands of violent deaths examined for this study. Just slightly over 10 per cent of suicide cases analyzed in this book had been wrongly categorized as other than suicides by coroners, juries, or magistrates. It is impossible, of course, to prove that error and deception did not happen often, but the ones I encountered were readily exposed by reading the evidence. All the same, well into the twentieth century, uncertainties lingered about the composition of suicide statistics because of the possibility that a social stigma might inhibit functionaries from recording suicide as a cause of death if an accidental death were plausible. Maurice Halbwachs opened his classic study, *The Causes of Suicide* (1932), with a critical survey on suicide reporting practices across Europe.[134]

More than other forms of violent death, drowning allowed for the honest mistake of recording an accident and for sympathetic officials or juries to evade a suicide verdict. Henry Thomas Buckle, who relied on official data, still admitted that drowning complicated the discussions of suicide rates.[135] Wagner doubted the accuracy of Russian suicide statistics because of the ease of disguising a drowning as an accident.[136] On rare occasions, magistrates who examined bodies and witnesses in the cases that are related later in this book reported "death by drowning, but whether such drowning was suicidal or accidental there is no evidence to determine." In fact, the evidence was usually quite clear, and the death was a suicide.

Not only are the aggregate statistics used in the nineteenth century of questionable quality, but there are problems with how moral statisticians interpreted them and with how researchers continue to use aggregate data in suicide studies. Until the late nineteenth century, authors rarely related the distribution of suicides by age cohorts to that of age cohorts in the general population. That oversight led to early mistaken claims that suicide was rare among the elderly.[137] In relative terms, this conclusion was wrong: the elderly were at considerable risk relative to their proportion of the population. Controlling for features in the general population improved statistical discussions and was a practice widely adopted in the late nineteenth century. The perils of aggregate data continue, however, because an illogical state of affairs is arrived at if a researcher imposes a limiting definition of suicide – as Durkheim did – and then works with state-collected aggregate data without showing that public officials everywhere applied this same definition.

There was a practical consideration behind a reliance on aggregate data. The individual was and is difficult to recover from a research standpoint because of the timeless challenge of finding a deep enough set of biographical details and because of the daunting prospect of working systematically through any raw information that exists. The image of Brierre sorting for years through thousands of case files sent scholars racing for published summaries. Today computation of case-file information removes an obstacle, but access to confidential records is a challenge that did not impede the asylum doctors who wrote many of the nineteenth-century studies.

Since very few writers in the nineteenth century extracted information from case files, comparisons of suicide rates by religious denominations, levels of education, alcohol consumption, insanity, proportion of urban residents, and other variables had to be done in the aggregate. Recourse to data in this form was legitimated by the assumption that if a region was largely Protestant, or if excise records revealed heavy alcohol consumption, or if the census disclosed relatively high literacy, or if asylum reports indicated fairly large numbers of mentally ill, or if the region was mainly urban, then one could assume that the distributional patterns corresponded to the traits of individuals who had committed suicide in that same region.

The practice of linking attributes at the aggregate level has, since 1950, been branded the "ecological fallacy." Durkheim fell into the error often, but he was not alone. In retrospect, it is difficult to understand how an open-minded investigator would not have seen the problem, but then Durkheim was not open-minded.[138] Late nineteenth-century suicide studies associated sets of aggregate data collected for the same geographic areas. Thus suicide rates in regions of France or in German principalities were compared by distributions of religious affiliations, alcohol consumption, asylum committals, literacy, urban residents, and other variables. The object of collecting and aligning data was to demonstrate a relationship. When Durkheim reported that suicide rates were higher in largely Protestant locales than in predominantly Catholic ones, he drew the inference that suicide was promoted by the social conditions of Protestantism. Such presumptions about the nature of individuals, when based solely upon statistics collected for the group to which those individuals belong, express the erroneous assumption that all members of a group exhibit characteristics of that particular group at large.

Analytic interest was in one kind of grouping – religion, alcohol abuse, insanity, education – whereas the data were in a geographic grouping. To restate the matter, the problem with ecological relationships is that the causes and effects they measure are for groups rather than individuals, but individuals are the proper nexus for relating cause and effect. An example is helpful. When Lisle observed that regions with more-educated people tended to have higher suicide rates, he jumped to the conclusion that the intelligentsia must be at a greater risk to commit suicide than other people. Two considerations comprise the fallacy in this example. In the first place, there is an obvious aggregation bias. Only individual-level data safely allow exploration of associations between factors. A second error is a confounding bias: literate individuals are not only literate but much else besides, and the other features could be determining with respect to suicide. The moral statisticians worked with unreliable data and slipped into fallacious inferences.

RESTORING THE INDIVIDUAL

Not only was Durkheim guilty of the ecological fallacy, but he insisted on a barrier between social and psychological analyses of suicide. His aggressive dismissal of psychology – there is no other description for what he did – put considerable space between sociology and the emerging field of psychiatry. By introducing an energy that impelled people to suicide, he could ignore particular situations, although suicide strikes most people as an individual motivated act arising out of and perhaps intended to affect a situation. The suicidogenic current passed over the human psyche. Individuals with severe depression and alcoholism were recognized in the late nineteenth century as having an increased risk of death by suicide, but Durkheim claimed that the potentiality for suicide by the mentally ill and alcoholics became effective only through social factors.[139]

Maurice Halbwachs (1877–1945), one of Durkheim's disciples, remarked that the master was guilty of "blocking consideration of this question [mental illness] a little too quickly."[140] Halbwachs found the division of social and psychological explanations "undoubtedly too sharp."[141] The individual's mental state could not be ignored. Witnesses who observed an individual prior to a suicide or an attempted suicide saw these occurrences as a matter of life histories and choices. Social factors undeniably affected the troubles and sorrows encountered by individuals, but understanding how they coped requires examining lives as shaped "by personal circumstances and by the possibilities offered in the larger world."[142] Most individuals have found ways to manage anger, disappointment, loss, and guilt that avoid self-destruction. As Durkheim noted, individuals do not commit suicide just because of troubles. He could have made more of that observation and looked at the objective and subjective compensations available to people in trouble, but he was focused on precluding from discussion the individual's ability or inability to cope.

To harmonize Durkheim's social theory with one which included the motives of individuals and to treat him generously, Halbwachs suggested that Durkheim's social forces only amounted to deep forces of deterrence and that he had taken for granted the sources of the suicidogenic current; a host of sociological factors – family sentiments, religious practices, and economic activities – were connected to suicides. To pursue research on them "would really be going further than Durkheim along the route he committed himself to since we would be explaining by social causes not only the major forces that are deterrents to suicide but also the particular events which are not only its pretexts but its motives."[143] This attempt to rescue Durkheim from himself was sensible, and it brings to our attention a trend among other nineteenth-century commentators. They inquired into suicide, not into suicides; they discussed an act, not acts. From this casual narrowing, a slide into tidy theoretical compactness followed. Alienists represented the act as madness. Sociologists produced their own extreme distillations. Masaryk insisted on a human tendency modulated by irreligiosity-religiosity, while Durkheim proposed the suicidogenic current modulated by four archetypal societies. Reductionism was an enduring temptation; in the nineteenth century early sociologists and doctors attempted to release the individual from moral responsibility but then overshot and disregarded the whole person in his or her setting.

One of the most widely cited late nineteenth-century suicide authors mingled the perspectives of alientists and sociologists. Enrico Morselli subtitled his book "An Essay on Comparative Moral Statistics." This physician played sociologist, and possibly the best outcome of this fusion came in a single sentence which followed his claim that people who used their brains to get along in life could experience a specific form of injury when defeated. "It is, therefore, obvious that the first and evil effect of defeat is on the organ which is destined to be the instrument of battle, and as the instrument is destroyed in weak and inexperienced hands, so the brain decays and breaks down under the excessive weight of struggle to which its forces and faculties are unequal."[144] Without today's knowledge of biochemistry and brain physiology, Morselli could not carry this idea further, but he anticipated a relationship between stress and mental illness. Praise for an advanced insight may be reading into his text too much of what we now know, because he ultimately retreated to a familiar position. As a social Darwinist, Morselli insisted on the unavoidability of struggle that produced losers. He framed suicide in terms of nature but held out hope for nurture. The cure for suicide was prevention, and for that, it was necessary "to develop in man the power of well-ordering sentiments and ideas by which to reach a certain aim in life; in short to give force to the moral character."[145] Moral education in some form ran as a theme through suicide studies by Catholics, Protestants, secular conservatives, and even a social Darwinist such as Morselli.

There were exceptions to the pattern of moral-education interventionists. The French republican Edmond Douay, already mentioned as an arch advocate of personal freedom, applauded the collapse of the Second Empire and with it the demise of state collaboration with clericalism. There was another type of secular non-interventionist. London barrister and fervent social Darwinist Samuel Strahan split "self-destroyers" into those parties who had undertaken quasi-suicides and those who committed true suicides.[146] The century-long tendency to propose two forms of suicide was again apparent. Quasi-suicides were acts in which death was pursued by a rational being for reasons that had made death preferable to life: to follow friends or family into the hereafter, to obey some presumed religious dictate, to gain notoriety, to assist others, to avoid physical suffering, or to escape slavery, persecution, punishment, disgrace, or poverty. These allegedly sane acts did not qualify as pure suicides. Prior to *Suicide and Insanity*, Strahan had published *Marriage and Disease: A Study of Heredity and the More Important Degenerations*. The subtitle tips us off about how he contextualized true suicide, which could only be the act of a person "drawn instinctively to death just as the normal creature is prompted to live on at any cost."[147] Morselli appears as a soft-hearted social Darwinist compared to Strahan, who disavowed positive social measures to prevent suicide but, rather, trusted natural selection and a winnowing of the insane and unfit by suicide along with other natural factors. "Only by increasing the vital energy of the people can self-destruction be reduced."[148] With the forethought used in breeding lower animals, the human race could propagate itself intelligently.[149] Quasi-suicides would continue, however, because there was nothing mentally defective about the individuals who committed them since the motives, in Strachan's estimation, could be noble. Durkheim's determination to steer clear of representing suicide as a sin or as insanity has to be seen in relation to idiosyncratic and conflicting moral, medical, and social Darwinian ideas.

CONCLUSION

Long before Durkheim, intellectuals had turned to suicide rates to gauge social changes. They attributed reports of increases to transformations in the organization of work and to urban growth. "The rising tide of suicide," wrote Durkheim, "originates in a pathological state just now accompanying the march of civilization without being its necessary condition."[150] In this synopsis of grand-historical motion, he was careful to avoid rigid determinism. For most commentators, a presumed relationship between modernization and suicide was an unfortunate connection that could be remedied; they followed up with hand-wringing and solutions. A few perverse optimists in less economically advanced societies, however, proposed that increasing suicide rates signalled their society had begun to modernize.[151] Fanatic social Darwinists, meanwhile, could cheer on Samuel Strahan's suicides in a twisted belief that these deeds purified the race. In many political programs, suicide operated as a gauge for the times. Writers perceived what they wanted to find. Furthermore, many states in the first decades of the century had insufficient means to collect social data with regularity, and some local agents had reasons for attributing suicides to accidents when such judgments defied physical evidence. Suicide was surely under-reported, but it is difficult to be sure by how much, for how long, and where. The often-reported upward curve of suicide rates should have been suspected as an artifact of the growing capacity of states to collect data, but it suited conservative hobby horses. Reactionaries perceived moral crises. It helped if their jeremiads had scientific sanction.

The leading suicide studies marked differences among French, English, and German cultures, but there were convergences. Wagner thought of himself as a statistical scientist and of French doctors as dilettantes besotted with irrelevant knowledge. French writers were abundant, but from the 1820s to the 1850s they cited cases from England and Germany. Alienists in the United States were aware of the European developments and cited them in their publications. From the 1860s to the 1890s, suicide scholars assembled data from many states, speculated about societies other than their own, and debated propositions from books published in other languages. The suicide investigations of the nineteenth century identify tensions between religion and secularism, between free will and determinism, between nascent psychiatry and sociology. They capture an era's enthusiasm for and naïveté about statistics.

Inquiries from across Europe betrayed a persistent belief in religion's importance. Except in a few contrary instances that highlight the general pattern, commentators did not recommend a revival of an unflinching condemnation of putative sinners who committed suicide. Interest in religion had shifted from the hard position of suicide as a sin to a soft enthusiasm for the consolations that clergy and faith might bring to people in despair. Other healing professions – general practitioners and alienists – were only capable of decisively challenging the clergy's healing services after 1900. Physicians and alienists had engaged in a long intermittent dispute about whether or not suicide was a sane act; consequently they detracted from their observations about individual cases and from their attention to social circumstances. Beneath rivalries and disagreements, astute and subtle interpretations entered the literature.

Durkheim downplayed religion as a restorative. His project had little to do with healing individuals. At war with psychology, he pilloried the already heavily criticized notion of suicide as insanity. This critical positioning of Durkheim matters. His focused argument diminished the standing of observers who sensed that suicide involved the soul, psyche, or mind. We too might judge the ideas of earlier writers as retrograde, but their thinking about prevention loosely agreed with the goals of medical practitioners during the twentieth century. Any lasting connection of suicide with sin was, of course, at odds with psychotherapy, but moral statisticians generally were not proposing the hard theological position of sin and perdition, and they were sensitive to healing. By 1920 the medical profession was poised to contribute to areas of mental health that impinged on suicide and suicide studies. Body and soul were both objects for healing. By 1950 psychiatry had extended its reach toward fields of social reformation to stem mental illnesses, delinquency, and crime. In suicide studies an interplay of psychiatry and sociology that had begun by the mid-nineteenth century persisted into the late twentieth century and the new millennium.

Although nineteenth-century authors could not free themselves from their education, ambitions, and politics, they were observant and inventive. Their publications and our reactions to them supply a number of points to keep in mind when we analyze suicide data. Straining to resolve the suicide puzzle, the best writers put into play issues and problems that must be taken seriously. What can we learn from them?

First, moral statistics and psychiatry broached philosophical considerations of free will and determinism. It remains important today to consider the reasoning processes of individuals who commit suicide, not by resorting to the naked choices of the protracted sanity-insanity debate, but by paying attention to what some people thought they were doing when they took their own lives and by considering what might have impaired the judgment of some others. When Durkheim defined suicide as "a positive or negative act of the victim himself," he remarked that the act is "performed advisedly."[152] This declaration should be kept in mind because I will demonstrate in chapter 6 that there are many modes of deliberation respecting suicide but also clouded and impaired deliberation. Second, the issue of deliberation impinges on the question of whether suicide is an act or many acts. Third, the abuse of data to validate a favoured interpretation without exploring alternate hypotheses was a hazard of early suicide studies, and it continued in the twentieth century. The language describing the presumed traits of men and women at risk may come from a vocabulary of conformist prejudices that support such superficialities as modernism's evils, the alienation of city dwellers, and the protective harmony of the family. We must be wary of these assumptions. A fourth observation is that the introduction of statistics occurred without a vigorous debate about the meaning of probability; consequently, ideas about a suicidal social type or about factors which could insulate against risk must be considered carefully to make certain that causality has not crept into an argument which really calls for a probabilistic statement. Fifth, the preference for aggregate data over case-based data leaves many studies open to the criticism that their authors have been guilty of the ecological fallacy.

Finally, the great body of nineteenth-century suicide literature contributed the idea that there could be both deep or chronic causes and proximate or acute causes. Social and psychiatric causes were frequently discussed together by doctors, advocates of moral statistics, and theologians. The pursuit of interconnections between society and psyche was renounced by Durkheim, however. By intellectual sleights of hand, the magician of sociology transformed an act by individuals into a social phenomenon. Nearly a century of studies on suicide ended with the publication of a work that, despite departures from stale arguments and hermeneutic brilliance, was constraining and lopsided.

2

Epistemic Communities and the Suicide Problem: The Twentieth Century

The pre-eminence of French suicide studies waned after World War I. Momentum shifted to American social scientists, who wrote about suicide in relation to their country's brief but explosive history. During the 1920s and 1930s American sociologists regarded cities as laboratories for comprehending deviance. Anxiety over nonconformity and all forms of violence spilled over into suicide studies. Suicide and homicide rates were discussed as reciprocal phenomena drawing on a fixed pool of violence; if homicide rates were low, suicide rates would be high.[1] Race and suicide became particularly topical in the 1960s, following urban rioting. Race, racism, and the historical burden of slavery persisted as topics in suicide studies long after the 1960s.[2] Also starting around 1960, suicide studies in the United States and abroad expanded to include systematic investigations to aid suicide prevention efforts. In a short time, suicidology showed up as a specific field of research promoted by a global epistemic community that included the World Health Organization.[3] A few prolific American suicidologists contributed to an unprecedented public awareness that grew appreciably in the 1960s and continues today.[4] Contemporary political, academic, and medical research currents in the United States furthered an abundance of innovative studies, but a perceived shift in the historic pattern of age cohorts also added urgency and complexity to investigations. Age distribution of suicides in many countries began to change during the 1960s and 1970s; adolescent suicides increased, and that development upset assertions that the suicide rate of white males increased with age.[5] Also, age rates appeared more volatile than previously assumed.[6]

Authors on suicide in the twentieth century could not disentangle themselves from politics in the widest sense. By the late 1960s, more-

Table 2.1
Books published in New York that dealt with suicide, 1800–2000

Years	Moral, ethical, philosophical, and bereavement	Legal	Medical, psychological, psychiatric	Social sciences, sociology	Literary	Total
1800–29	1					1
1830–79		1				1
1880–1929	5	1			3	9
1930–49	1			1		2
1950–69	5	1	5	7	5	23
1970–89	31		32	40	47	150
1990–2000	49	4	15	15	40	123
Total	92	7	52	63	95	309

SOURCE: Library of Congress, electronic search of books by subject and published in New York.

over, drug company sponsorship of studies and conferences supplied a further reason to suspect that intellectual autonomy was now an illusion.[7] At the time, however, experts and readers were credulous, particularly since American scholars claimed competence in the pursuit of testable social theorems to explain deviance. They were aided by the surge of statistical manuals.[8] During subsequent decades and into the new millennium, quantification grew in sophistication, and research questions widened to include parasuicide and suicide ideation.[9]

A social science focus on variation among populations was ascendant in American suicide studies from the 1920s to the 1960s, although psychiatry contributed with an almost equal outpouring of literature (see table 2.1). Publications from both disciplines left many nineteenth-century assumptions in place. Some academics still condemned the city as unhealthy and blamed modern living for social, and thus personal, disintegration. Well past mid-century, sociologists continued to use aggregate data to pursue a general theory to explain variations in suicide rates among different populations; some still hypothesized that suicide was a unified phenomenon and proceeded to discuss variations in rates without sustained discussion of motives or intent.

The methodological divide between sociological and psychological interpretations of suicide endured from the nineteenth century, although on occasion sociologists, on one side, and psychologists and psychiatrists, on the other, took an interest in one another's perspectives and findings and often employed similar statistical tools. However, nowhere in the world did Freud's influence on psychiatry "express itself so dynamically and fruitfully as in America." And Freud's American disciples were ardent defenders of a border between psychiatry and sociology.[10] That endured long after the decline of Freudianism itself. When noted Columbia University psychiatrist David Shaffer addressed the press in Auckland, New Zealand, following a symposium at the height of a youth suicide panic in that country in 1989, he asserted that youth suicides had little to do with social pressure and everything to do with individual histories of mental illness.[11]

To an astonishing degree, indicative of the gender profile of university faculty members, suicide studies, whether by sociologists or psychiatrists, were the domain of white males. That bias could account for the abundant arguments that modern civilization uniquely burdened white males and hence accounted for their higher suicide rates. The white males who dominated the social sciences lacked an appreciation for critical self-awareness and assumed, without a blush of embarrassment, that white males generally advanced and sustained high living standards for everyone's benefit and, moreover, did so at a low psychic cost to everyone except themselves. Other races and women, it was proposed by some writers, were conditioned to taking direction, and consequently they escaped the trials of leadership that could push white males to suicidal angst.

THE RISE OF AMERICAN SCHOLARSHIP: THEORIES OF SOCIAL DISORGANIZATION

World War I had had an ambiguous influence on the study of suicide in France. Official secrecy about soldier suicides prevented forthright analysis of war trauma and self-destruction; yet, as in other combatant countries, veterans' groups lobbied for pensions for men with war-related mental illnesses that could lead to suicide. Public concern for the mental well-being of soldiers and veterans elevated psychiatry's prominence and marked growing public sympathy for the mentally ill. Maurice de Fleury's powerfully eloquent *L'angoisse humaine* (1926) could not have been written without the author's exposure to war and the variability in soldiers' emotional reactions to crises. De Fleury (1860–1931) empathized with men who had endured a dreadful state that soldiers labelled *le cafard* (cockroach), an anguish or depression that laid them as low as a roach.[12] However, if crises caused suicides, then the war's privation, fear, gore, and futility should have precipitated an epidemic of self-destruction. *Le cafard* gripped many men in the trenches, but only a few escaped by suicide.[13] Looking at society more generally and building on what he had witnessed about privation and endurance in the trenches, de Fleury resurrected an old question in suicide studies. He doubted whether social burdens alone could explain self-destruction. Over eight thousand suicides had been committed in France during 1920, and the motives assigned by the Ministry of Justice seemed remarkably unexceptional: mental illness, physical ailments, family troubles, loss of work or money, and unhappy romances. As de Fleury saw it, the people who endured comparable distress were five thousand times more numerous than those who succumbed.[14] The entire citizenry of France had problems; however, not many suffered such deep mental torment that death appealed as a remedy.[15] There had to be something else at work. Psychiatrists henceforth never relented on this point.

De Fleury and his supporters among doctors had as much use for sociology as Durkheim had for psychology. De Fleury justified contempt for sociological theory by reminding readers about his treatment of psychiatric patients, some of whom had attempted or committed suicide. He wrote scornfully that "nothing at all resembled the suicides which Durkheim, a pure theoretician who worked out of an office, labelled egoistic and anomic."[16] Except for the passionate intensity of his prose, de Fleury said little that was new. He restated the alienists' claims of the nineteenth century: suicide was associated with mental illness. He arrived at this generalization without self-awareness about his own limited field of vision. From his professional experience (*notre métier*), which he invoked as his authority, 90 per cent of suicides suffered from melancholy anxiety (*la melancholique anxieux*), and the remainder had comparable ailments.[17] De Fleury had studied with Jean-Martin Charcot, who established the first neurology clinic in Europe in 1882 and whose reputation as an instructor attracted Sigmund Freud. By one estimate, de Fleury had seen 60,000 patients in forty-five years of a career devoted to mental illness.[18] He had a right to parade his *métier*.

According to de Fleury, suicides were caused by the fit of anguish produced during the period of depression in recurrent manic-depressive psychoses.[19] The contemporary sociologist Maurice Halbwachs believed that de Fleury's opinion was unfortunate but "rather common among physicians."[20] Medical professionals would long insist on a high percentage of the mentally ill among suicides and in France rally to defend de Fleury.[21] Furthermore, because they had seen tormented men and women, they had a low opinion of the detachment from flesh and blood unavoidably apparent in sociological publications. Decades after de Fleury and Halbwachs, American psychiatrist Edwin Shneidman condemned all labels, whether taken from Durkehim's *Le suicide* or from psychiatric questionnaires: "None of the classifications of suicide that I know of has an urgent usefulness."[22]

De Fleury supposed that his suicidal patients represented all suicidal individuals. His strong feelings and his literary style contrasted with the asceticism and scientism of American studies that had started to appear around the time of *L'angoisse humaine*. In countries that suffered heavy casualties in World War I, the psychiatric understanding of suicide had renewed significance, while in the United States, which had avoided the long war, disturbing observations about poverty and deviance in the midst of plenty and growth called for made-in-America explanations of the phenomenon. Sociology answered that need and held a pre-eminent standing in suicide studies until psychiatry powered back into the arena in the 1930s.[23]

Whereas late nineteenth-century European sociological publications worked with national or international data, books in the first wave of pioneering American publications concentrated, with good reasons, on an individual city. One of the great historical developments in the United States was the swift rise of its world-class cities. The term "shock city" is the evocative label for an urban area that emerged suddenly and embodied physical and economic innovations which set trends for other centres. Chicago was a shock city and appropriately the home to a system for analyzing urban society and a purported urban pathology. The Chicago school of sociology, sometimes described as the ecological school, produced the first major body of works that shared a method for research into urban society. The sociologists and geographers associated with the school were influenced by biologist Frederic E. Clements (1874–1945), who had proposed that a community of vegetation – a forest, for example – was a super-organism. These communities developed in a pattern of successive stages from inception through to a climax or, in other words, to a self-regulating state of equilibrium. By analogy, the human urban community, as it grew, expressed stages. Academics associated with the Chicago school regarded urban society as a super-organism affected by physical surroundings that operated on it, just as soil, rain, and sunlight – the environment – affected a forest. The physical layout of urban space and the built environment of the city were major factors in shaping human behaviour. Scholars who adopted this outlook refined a research technique. They collected data from civic authorities on specific phenomena, including poverty, juvenile delinquency, homicide, and suicide; then after computing rates based on federal census data, they mapped findings to identify by visual comparison where spatial variation occurred. To achieve real understanding, they were advised to observe with sympathy. The Chicago race riot of 1919 galvanized the school's teamwork approach to understanding the city.[24]

To explain areas with elevated pathologies, some social ecologists applied what became known as social disorganization theory. They attributed deviance to the failure of social organizations, including family, church, school, and political institutions; they perceived the failure of neighbourhoods or social relationships that they believed traditionally encouraged co-operation or restraint. Researchers left an impression of the city as a place of superficial relationships where residents risked anonymity, where friendships were transitory and family bonds weak. It is instructive to compare these conclusions with similar ones from late nineteenth-century European authors. Americans added a proficiency in method, yet they maintained anti-urbanism in common with their European forerunners.

Ruth Shonle Cavan's *Suicide* (1928) deserves to open a discussion of American sociology and suicide for several reasons. First, Cavan (1896–1993) jeopardized theoretical coherence in favour of a refreshingly transparent struggle with methodological problems. She admitted the limits of her information and methods. Second, she was the first woman to publish a major study on suicide; her perspective as a woman showed in the occasional descriptions of men's cruelty and in her appreciation that it was not the family per se that protected against suicide, as Durkheim had claimed, but the "well-adjusted family," which provided companionship, praise, security, and wider recognition in the community.[25] The distinction is meaningful. Third, it is evident that she accepted psychology's importance. In reference to a suicidal woman who left a diary, she wrote that "her entire personality was organized around the need for constant and intensive response and love from someone."[26] Cavan recommended the establishment of agencies with trained psychologists and sociologists to diagnose trouble.[27] Finally, the book carried many of the Chicago school's hallmarks and has been assessed by Jack Douglas and Howard Kushner as an exemplar of that influential school.[28]

On maps that delineated Chicago's four highest suicide districts, Cavan overlaid symbols to show areas with an exceptional number of deaths by alcoholism, areas with high divorce rates, the city's pawn shop centres, the vice district, the drug-peddling centres, and the rooming-house streets. She attached social disorganization theory to these overlapping indicators.[29] In her estimation, rooming-house occupants were people without neighbourhood life and without families. Social disorganization of the type seen in the rooming-house areas happened when institutions that taught "rules of right and wrong" disintegrated.[30] "Cities," she asserted, "tend to be in a perpetual state of disorganization."[31] Even if her claims about disorganization were true, they did not explain why some areas apparently suffered more disorganization than others. When it came to supplying details for an ecological analysis, Cavan seemed comfortable with a colourful description of "cheap hotels for men and sooty flats over stores" and streets with "hundreds of men who drift in aimless, bleary-eyed abandon."[32] The Chicago school sociologists were encouraged to put the immediacy of the best journalism into their publications.

Cavan avoided asking two essential questions. First, how did specific local physical surroundings, the immediate ecology, produce social disintegration? Or, to put it another way, did the physical attributes of a neighbourhood affect the social or vice versa? Second, by what social processes did certain individuals – presumably those most harmed by social disintegration – come to reside in a particular part of the city? Neighbourhoods seemed to be not so much factors in social disintegration as containers for defective or missing social processes. From the social data collected for city blocks, Cavan had gone on to assume that a disintegration of the institutions vital for pointing out right and wrong had produced socially impoverished individuals; however, she needed evidence to operationalize this hypothesis. She had to tie together aggregate social data, the disintegration of institutions, and the individuals who committed suicide, and she seized upon a partial solution.

From the outset, Cavan insisted that her book would be "a study of suicide in its relation to social and personal disorganization."[33] That claim foretold her interest in life histories. The latter provided "vastly more insight into, and understanding of human nature" than statistics, and they also disclosed the presence of "some mental abnormality."[34] This was an extremely interesting concession from a sociologist, and it intimates that not all sociologists were insensitive to psychology and psychiatry. Cavan had more surprises in store.

Life histories featured in the Chicago school's repertoire of research methods. A few Chicago school studies incorporated them to bring subjective balance to the analysis. Cavan went further and claimed that "the bulk of the study consists of an analysis of individual cases of suicide."[35] Over fifty profiles came from the files of the United Charities of Chicago and the Jewish Social Services Bureau (cases of attempted suicide) and the records of the Cook County coroner. Cavan also circulated 201 questionnaires to extract statements in support of her thesis that "suicide is partly dependant upon the existence of attitudes favourable to the act of suicide which show themselves in the form of wishes, day dreams, and vague plans, and that such attitudes are extremely widespread in the United States today."[36] On account of attitudes favourable to suicide, vulnerable, socially disorganized people turned to suicide rather than to making adjustments that allowed them to go on living. A flirtation with a cultural analysis of suicide thrived in America, as it had earlier in Europe, because of a belief that "the old religious attitude that the individual belonged to a divine creator had broken down. The newly advocated attitude that the individual owes a duty to society is not widespread."[37] The resemblance to Morselli and Durkheim could not have been accidental. Suicide scholarship had crossed the Atlantic.

Cavan realized that, in order to confirm that social and cultural disorganization exacerbated personal disorganization, she had to probe deeper than the aggregate data which backed the symbols dotting her maps.[38] The ecological fallacy had not yet been exposed and labelled by statisticians, yet she understood the value of case histories for linking events and motives. "Only a study of actual cases," she wrote relative to a clash between Morselli and Durkheim on alcohol abuse, "can determine whether alcoholism and suicide are linked together."[39] To provide an evidentiary connection between individuals and social processes, she turned to case files and questionnaires. However, since she never demonstrated that her cases were representative of society, she had not solved the problem of connecting the one and the many.[40] For example, she could have selected only cases that fit her theory.

Psychiatrist de Fleury had committed a related error when he reasoned that his suicidal patients were sufficient evidence to show that mental illness explained suicide. The social sciences and psychiatry were struggling in the 1920s to connect the experiences of the one with those of the many, a problem that requires a holistic understanding of suicide if it is to be resolved. The sociologist started with *population* and backed into individual cases, because the discipline had a commitment to social entities that were greater than the sum of their parts. This preference had its purest expression in Durkheim's *Suicide*. The psychiatrist began with the individual and generalized about *self*, because medical sciences and early experimental psychology accepted that individual cases could illuminate a universal truth because of the commonality of cerebral physiology or because of the practice in psychiatric literature of analyzing a case to establish a syndrome.[41] Theorizing from a small number of cases exposed psychiatry to objections that it was unscientific.[42] This, too, was one of Cavan's problems; she reasoned from a few score of cases. But her book had other problems.

The ecological element in Cavan's work was in jeopardy because, unlike trees, people move. If individuals took their own lives because they were not steeped in the right values, how could she be sure that the social disintegration, supposedly responsible for an absence of adequate social control mechanisms, originated in the disorganization of the shock city? Chicago pulled in immigrants and migrants who had spent their formative years in other countries, perhaps in rural or small-town settings. Cavan countered this objection by showing that newcomers from Europe had a higher rate of suicide in the United States than did citizens in the home countries. "In all cases the rates for immigrants in this country are two to three times as high as the rates for their brethren in Europe."[43] Was the American urban ecology or something else at work?

Subsequent research partly corroborated Cavan's findings on immigrants, but a gap remained between facts observed and a theory that blamed urban-based social disorganization. The ecological fallacy bars easy acceptance of a causal relationship between the city as disruptive agent and the higher suicide rates of immigrants relative to compatriots at home. Without individual-level information, there was no firm evidence of a connection. Further, not all European groups had higher rates in the United States than at home. Howard Kushner found that high rates among newcomers concentrated among Danes and Germans, who, he explained, had less effective mourning practices than Italians and Irish.[44] It would require an incredible research effort – assembling case files, interviews, and control groups – to discern what explains the different rates for some immigrant groups and for counterparts who had not emigrated.

In addition to immigrants, the shock city housed migrants. William Cronon demonstrates in *Nature's Metropolis* that Chicago businesses so effectively covered the interdependencies between city and hinterland that it was easy to forget that both were implicated in a common economic and spatial system; the features of the hinterland were removed from consideration.[45] A seasonal migration of labourers was forgotten as well, in the sense that the Chicago school imagined people currently in the city were city dwellers. Cavan's rooming-house districts sheltered some of the transient labour force for an enormous region. The labourers' work experiences on western farms, ranches, and public works and in northern forests may have been at least as significant as time spent in the city.[46] Cavan's *Suicide* did not solve mysteries about suicide. As an intelligent quest, however, it deserves admiration.

Other ecological studies that considered suicide were written by sociologists who, lacking her likeable inquisitiveness, pressed the template into their material. In a study of suicide in Seattle (1928) and in his social survey of Minneapolis and St Paul (1937), Calvin Schmid produced maps and references to social disorganization. He found an area in each of his subject cities that had the highest mobility and the greatest incidence of crime, vice, alcoholism, and suicides. "Our investigations," he wrote in 1937, "have shown a definite correlation between a high incidence in these large American cities and a high rate of population mobility."[47] Schmid gave the impression that mobility caused social disorganization and thus higher suicide rates, and he came to an identical conclusion in an ecological study of Seattle in 1948.[48] Significantly, he left open the possibility that mobility and suicide may simply have attracted the same type of people, "the unconventional types, those who have revolted against the prevailing folkways and mores and who want 'to get away from their neighbours.'"[49] Schmid innovated in one respect, because more zealously than anyone since Brierre de Boismont, he read primary documents to develop a statistical profile of motives. Altogether, he reviewed 901 Seattle death certificates covering the years from 1914 to 1925.[50] Social ecologists – Schmid and Cavan, for certain – abhorred nonconformity and an anonymous milieu. They could not determine whether the people who actually committed suicide were nonconformists, so they floated an innuendo that agreed with the country's political temperament. In the long run, the ecologists had an impact, because social workers and suicide crisis centres formed after mid-century would eventually concentrate on urban "suicide belts."[51]

Despite Cavan's feebly justified preference for conformity and social control, her work was a cut above other social ecology studies of suicide because she appreciated individual motives.[52] Astonishingly for a sociologist, she wrote that personal disorganization "involves different emotions, and is subject to different personal interpretations."[53]

Individuals reacted to their material plight and lack of social adjustment in personal ways.[54] At almost the same time that Cavan published her study, Durkheim's fault-finding but loyal supporter Maurice Halbwachs articulated an extension of Cavan's unspoken but unmistakable urge to harmonize sociology and psychology. Halbwachs was perturbed that medical practitioners made exclusive claims, that Durkheim had also made such claims on behalf of sociology, and that other writers occupied a middle position by accepting two categories of suicide, one associated with the mentally ill and the other comprised of normal persons.[55] Insisting that a suicide was a suicide and always a unique genus of death, Halbwachs upheld a unified approach, although he assumed, too, that "at the moment any individual commits suicide, and perhaps for some hours and even some days preceding, we would find some trouble of the nervous and cerebral functions, more or less deep-seated but always real."[56] He segmented the decision-making process temporally. However, if suicide involved different thought processes and varying degrees of nervous disorder, then Halbwachs had inadvertently weakened his own stricture that suicide was a single genus of death. The challenge of reconciling the individual and the collective, the one and the many, persisted.

A blend of sociology and psychology in suicide studies guided a report in 1955 by London psychiatrist Peter Sainsbury, who subtitled his book *An Ecological Study*. Sainsbury followed to the letter the American ecological model with maps and a social disorganization argument, and he proposed that the differences between the psychoanalytic and sociological viewpoints were "more apparent than real."[57] He distinguished himself by trying more precisely than Cavan to connect suicide, society, and personality, but he chose ultimately to privilege medical connections. It will be remembered that Durkheim had asked why some people with burdens persevered and others did not. He answered idiosyncratically by dismissing the idea that suicides were acts by individuals and postulating a suicidogenic current regulated by social forces. Now Sainsbury asked "why is it that though many have to face the problem of living in a socially disorganized locality, and everyone has to adjust to disrupting situations, only some commit suicide?"[58] Personality made a difference. Using information extracted from 409 coroners' inquests for North London in 1936–38, Sainsbury concluded that suicide occurred to a great degree in areas of mobility, decreased with poverty, rose with a sudden fall in the standard of living regardless of class, and involved an unusually large number of people with mental illness or personality abnormalities.[59] When *Suicide in London* appeared in print, research in the United States was poised for a major controversial change.

PUTTING SCIENCE INTO SOCIAL SCIENCE: AMERICAN SOCIOLOGY AND STATUS INTEGRATION

The publication of an English translation of Durkheim's *Suicide* in 1951 contributed to a revival of interest in his theory of deep socio-cultural controls on a suicidogenic current. Jack Porter Gibbs resurrected Durkheim for a bold attempt at a general theory (1957). Taking a sociological position that ad hoc explanations were unworthy of consideration, he moved to a four-stage preparatory argument that paved the way for his theory. First, Gibbs insisted that all general theories of suicide had to explain the well-known fact that rates varied from jurisdiction to jurisdiction. Second, a general theory had to be testable, and he accordingly eliminated a handful of theories, including the ecological.[60] Third, on the basis of abundant data which suggested that suicide rates rose according to age, he maintained that suicidal risk intensified with people's longer exposure to some as-yet-undefined social factor.[61] Gibbs's age data predated the surge in adolescent suicides and ignored the likelihood that suicides among the elderly included euthanasia, which had little to do with social – or, as Gibbs called it, status – integration. Fourth, the theory he had in mind would be highly abstract and controversial. That had to be accepted because "abstract theories ... abound in any science."[62] Gibbs was keen to put sociology on a scientific footing, to become a latter-day Durkheim.

Durkheim's theory looked reducible to a testable proposition: the greater the strength of social relations in a population, the lower the suicide rate.[63] The absence of a census category that measured the strength of social relations precluded a direct test of the hypothesis. Therefore, in a classic postwar social sciences move extremely popular among economists, Gibbs devised a surrogate measure following a series of questionable assumptions. First, he suggested that the strength of social relations was equivalent to how well members of a population conformed to the socially sanctioned expectations of behaviour or, to use the emerging specialized vocabulary of sociology, how well they conformed to the roles of their several statuses. The idea of conformity or integration shared ground with the ecological school; however, Gibbs wanted to distance himself from unscientific sociology, and so linking himself to a newer trend in sociology that focused on integration, he labelled his theory "status integration."[64] Status integration is best summarized as the overall cohesiveness of social ties. Gibbs set out to measure this cohesiveness.

Further, he assumed that if a population contained abundant status conflicts, it would have high suicide rates. The idea of status conflicts was problematic. A status was a social identification such as age, marital situation, or occupation. A conflict, Gibbs proposed, could occur when a person occupied statuses that were statistically rare for a given population, but he avoided a psychological explanation for these conflicts. Presumably, misfits destroyed themselves with greater frequency than others because they felt at odds with the population's expectations. The idea of an average person harkened back to Quételet and the moral statisticians. Moreover, because Gibbs did not have data on individuals, he operated at the level of a population and tested for status integration in assorted state populations. In effect, he proposed that status integration was equivalent to the degree of probability of predicting an unknown status from data on a number of other statuses. If a person's gender, religion, race, and occupation made it possible to predict his or her marital status, then marital status in that society was at a maximum.[65] The chain of hypotheses looked like this: societies with a lot of predictability were nicely integrated; therefore citizens were pleasantly compliant with social mores, and suicide rates were relatively low.

Nineteenth-century moral statisticians had worked with one variable at a time, but Gibbs could take a multivariate approach, which was necessary because, as he put it, "a person is never simply a carpenter and nothing more. He is a single, married, widowed, or divorced carpenter."[66] Statistical exercises produced scores that summarized the degree of status integration for a particular subpopulation: for example, the residents of New Jersey. When these scores for a number of states were correlated with suicide rates for the same states, Gibbs found a negative association (a Pearson's r score of -57 with P less than .01), which allowed him to state that the greater the status integration, the lower the suicide rate. The data set could also be used to examine status integration for race and occupation for all states in the study. In other words, Gibbs could consider status integration within states or within socially defined subpopulations (see table 2.2). His theory was suggestive rather than conclusive, but he proposed that it could stand until falsified.[67] In a later book (1964), Gibbs and Walter Martin extended the

Table 2.2
Examples of status integration and suicide using United States census data for 1950

Race-sex status configuration	Occupational integration measure	Occupational integration rank	Suicide rate	Suicide rank
African American female	.2473	1	1.5	6
White female	.1828	2	5.3	5
Other female	.1416	4	5.9	4
African American male	.1588	3	6.1	3
White male	.1295	5	18.5	2
Other male	.1243	6	21.3	1

SOURCE: Jack P. Gibbs and Walter T. Martin, *Status Integration and Suicide* (Eugene: University of Oregon Books, 1964), table 10.

computations from the original thirty states to thirty-two countries, a number of European cities and regions, and districts in West Bengal. They also conducted a case study of New Zealand using cases files from coroners' inquests. Suicide studies had gone global and statistical. Gibbs's theory hypothesized that suicide rates would vary inversely with status integration; he and Martin had 676 observations, and the theory predicted 58 per cent, considerably better than distribution by chance.[68]

The innovation of status-integration scores required ingenuity that deserves description, because the technique was emblematic of a methodological leap. Taking the census data for age, gender, race, and occupation for each of thirty states, Gibbs first performed a cross-tabulation of occupation by age, gender, and race for each state. Next he took the sum of squares for the values in each column and called the result an integration measure; the sum of the integration measures became the state's total integration measure. Summing squares was a standard statistical manoeuvre for the study of variance; variance itself had been pursued by social scientists and mathematicians who followed the nineteenth-century moral statisticians and who shifted attention from the latter's interest in the mean to an exploration of variance. In other words, the social science quest had moved from characterizing the average person to the study of differences in a population. Gibbs enlisted the significant proposition that the sum of squares for any set of scores varies directly with the sum of the forces which led to the variation. The total integration measure, however, was flawed. It did not take into account the possibility that a high status-integration score for a particular group (for example, white, male managers aged thirty to fifty-four) which was only a small proportion of a state's population could elevate the total and give a false impression of status integration. In a final step, he used all groups' proportions in the state's population to compute a weighted total status-integration measure.[69] It is a tribute to Gibbs's striving for objectivity that when he later edited a collection of essays, he included several that emphasized individual motives rather than rate variation.[70]

Status integration's legacy consists chiefly of demonstrating an austere scientific turn in sociology. The empathetic eye of the Chicago school had been displaced by testable hypotheses explored from sterile computer centres. Crucially, Gibbs insisted on a doctrine of conjecture and refutation which stipulated that no theory deserved attention unless it presented well-formulated theorems which could be exposed to tests. Experimental sciences had largely adopted a principle attributed to Karl Popper that, although it was impossible to prove a theory conclusively because there were always too many unknowns, the theory endured as long as it withstood attempts to falsify it. Gibbs adopted an identical position. Since earlier theories about the variation of suicide rates in populations, such as the ecological and social disorganization explanations, failed to present a testable hypothesis, he dismissed them. Likewise, he set aside psychology and psychiatry because their amorphous tenets resisted clear conjectures and tests that could falsify them. Durkheim, he felt, at least presented ideas that supplied a testable hypothesis. Gibbs marched by austere postulates punctuated with reminders that everything he concluded was tentative; he purged his text of human interest and the anecdotal. His modernist social science technique was as clear of adornment as a Mies van der Rohe office tower. The numerate research aesthetic predominated in suicide studies for decades, but it should be pointed out that in addition to Popper's falsification theorem, systems of statistical inference offered techniques for calculating the probability of events, and these too have been marshalled by suicide researchers to estimate risk.[71]

Durkheim inspired Gibbs, but *Le suicide* perplexed Ronald Maris, who eventually would write an exceeding important case-based study. Maris had studied philosophy and religion before turning to sociology, and he came to suicide studies with less commitment than Gibbs to a single strand of inquiry. In his doctoral thesis on suicide in Chicago (1965) he combated the Durkheim tradition in sociology when he questioned the value of aggregate data and suicide rates. "Unfortunately," he concluded, "the suicide rate of a community can be explained [in theories] without shedding much light on the causes of suicide in subgroups or individuals of that community."[72] Maris followed Cavan and used the Cook County coroners' inquests to secure information on individuals. City-centred studies remained a staple of American suicidology long after the salad days of the ecological school; Los Angeles, Houston, Seattle, and New Orleans figured in publications during the 1960s.[73] On the strength of what he saw in coroners' records and in the possibility of learning more by interviewing witnesses, Maris proposed that, thanks to advanced statistical practices such as factor analysis, one could now study multiple partial causes of suicide. He challenged trust in a focused theory, a fixation on variations in rates, and reliance on aggregate data. However, he was in the family of statistical researchers.

By the late 1960s, status integration had fallen by the wayside. The status-integration measure was criticized as a static snapshot of a society that did not capture relations among individuals over time. This criticism touched on the perpetual concern that, whether sociologists from the Durkheim mould liked it or not, a suicide really looked like an act by an individual with a distinct history. Gibbs acknowledged as much in a latter account of his theory when he wrote that "the decisive factor in a particular case of suicide may be a disruption that occurred several years in the past and is not reflected in the present status integration of the individual." Taking a quintessentially American example, he mentioned that Ernest Hemingway, married at the time of his suicide, had a high degree of marital status integration, but he had been divorced three times.[74] Jack Douglas questioned whether the state had been an appropriate level of study for Gibbs. American states blended rural and urban life, when almost everyone who had written on suicide believed there were distinctions between country and city.[75] This issue made it difficult to affirm that a population's expectations were unified enough to set up role conflicts.

THE RESURGENCE OF PSYCHIATRY AND PSYCHOLOGY

In the estimation of Howard Kushner, "psychiatric thinking about the etiology of suicide" in the United States relied for decades on foundation texts by three authors: "Mourning and Melancholia" (1917) by Freud, a series of articles (1936–37) by Gregory Zilboorg, and Karl Menninger's *Man against Himself* (1938).[76]

Gregory Zilboorg (1890–1951), who had been analyzed by one of Freud's inner circle, Hans Sachs, took much the same position as de

Fleury concerning sociology and the lamentable distance that statistical analysis placed between the researcher and the individual. However, the Americans Zilboorg and Menninger went much further than de Fleury in articulating theories of suicide. Kushner notes that Zilboorg broke with Freudian orthodoxy over suicide and, based on his clinical cases, proposed that the individuals who were at most risk had lost a close family member in childhood. That loss made them vulnerable when they experienced a later psychological trauma. This theory was no better than sociological ones at explaining why some persons committed suicide and others did not, because many men and women had experienced childhood losses. If the critical variable was the degree of neurotic distress later in life, then the theory ran into uncertainties and could not explain suicide any better than a sociological theory.[77]

Karl Menninger (1893–1990) was a professional colleague and friend of Zilboorg, but also a scheming writer with an ambition to reach a mass audience. His smoothly written psychoanalytic account of suicide, *Man against Himself* (1938), opened with the claim that although actuaries and sociologists had paid attention to suicide, a taboo had descended over the subject. It had "attracted surprisingly little attention from physicians."[78] While the rare investigation resorted to "barren statistical analyses," the public naively believed that suicide was merely "the logical consequence of circumstances, particularly ill health, discouragement, financial reverses, humiliation, frustration, and unrequited love."[79] In light of what he claimed was the indifference of the medical profession, the useless statistical aggregations of the sociologists, and the short-sightedness of the public, Menninger set out to strengthen the will to live by popularizing Freudian theories. A skilful propagandist for complex Freudian ideas, he projected unwavering certainty about the power of psychoanalysis to achieve victories over the will to die. Rival accounts of suicide he dismissed as seductive in their incompleteness.

By incompleteness, Menninger meant their failure to solve the classic problem of why most persons could endure hardship and disappointment and a very few others could not. He turned to "the unconscious purposes," which are "of more significance in understanding suicide than the apparently simple, inevitable external realities."[80] Freudian theory, which was at maturity when Menninger contemplated writing about suicide, made concepts available that could be applied to individual cases. Sociology aggregated toward the articulation of social laws, but psychiatry functioned dialogically, working down from laws to clinical cases and then back to adjust those laws. Its applied and interactive qualities made Freudian psychoanalysis not only difficult to articulate but agile. Like quicksilver, it was difficult to contain or pick up.

Menninger had arrived at his conversion to Freudian psychoanalysis in 1920. Until that time, he considered himself a mental hygienist; in his case this meant an interest in tertiary syphilis, shell shock, and dementia following cases of influenza in 1918–19.[81] All three syndromes were believed to have somatic origins and associations with suicide. To leap from neuropsychiatry to Freudian psychiatry was a considerable task, but Menninger became a complete convert. Although he had had a brief exposure to analysis in 1920, he completed his education in Freudian techniques only after undergoing analysis for eighteen months in Chicago in 1930–31.[82]

To understand Menninger's explanation of suicide in *Man against Himself*, several of Freud's more important terms must be described. The id is the reservoir of unorganized instinctual drives such as love (Eros) and destruction (Thanatos); it has an unconscious dimension. The ego has the tasks of self-preservation, gaining control of the id, and mediating between the id and the external world. The superego scrutinizes behaviour and thoughts and acts as an agency of moral conscience.[83] The id and ego had major roles in Menninger's explanations for suicide. He attributed acts of suicide to psychodynamic churning under the capacious authority of the wish to kill, the wish to be killed, and the wish to die. The last of the three, he thought, was still "only a hypothesis in comparison to the demonstrated facts of the existence of the other two elements."[84] Confidence suffused Menninger's writing. However, the wish to kill and the wish to be killed were not demonstrated facts in the sense that they could be exposed to tests that might falsify them; the evidence – dreams, repetitive acts, behaviour patterns, slips of the tongue – could be contorted to conform to theory. If it seemed that a claim had been falsified, the psychiatrist might reply with a reinterpretation or by alleging that patients were resisting psychoanalysis and suppressing deep truths. More patience was needed.

Let us go along with Menninger to better understand a Freudian's comprehension of suicide. Menninger drew heavily from Freud's short essay "Mourning and Melancholia."[85] "Psychoanalytic investigations have established beyond any doubt," Menninger pronounced, the existence of love as well as murderous, destructive wishes.[86] How could the latter drive from the id be turned against the self? The answer was introjection, another Freudian concept. If there could be projection outward, then why not projection inward? Introjection was the inter-

nalizing of the qualities of an object (a close person). In psychoanalysis
an object of hate that escapes the ego can be regained by the shift of
emotions from the original object onto a person within the person. The
object of hate within could be destroyed by destroying the self. Many
things can thwart the destructive impulses, and each blockage can foster a particular mental illness. Take, for instance, the death of a loved
one. Since love and hate "have alternating expression," the death
disperses the erotic and the hostile components of the id. Hate has to be
directed inward since otherwise it will be directed against the whole
world, but love is also directed inward. This dual introjection produces a conflict expressed in melancholia, which is "the condition in
which suicide most often happens." The individual engages in bitter
reproaches as well as narcissism. "Were it not for the protection of the
narcissism every melancholic would be determined to commit suicide."[87] The variability in the relative strength of hostility and narcissism went unexplained by Menninger. We are no closer to understanding suicide. As for the wish to be killed, it was an extreme form of
submission. The murderous impulse provokes a desire in some individuals for extreme punishment. An overly tyrannical superego produces a
compulsive neurotic.[88]

In a recent critique of psychoanalysis, Joel Paris conclude that it
failed "to meet the test of empiricism, leading to its replacement by biological psychiatry."[89] The Freudians fell far because they had set themselves up with an arrogant confidence that Menninger epitomized: "It
is quite evident" or "strikingly apparent."[90] "Such cases," he would
report, "could be multiplied by any psychiatrist," and there were also
"the less conclusive" but colourful examples.[91] He insinuated the con-
clusiveness of any psychiatrist. Other claims were "well known," and
"scientific studies have been made." Supporting footnotes proved
empty.[92] With respect to psychiatrists, who were "not psychoanalytically oriented" and consequently in the dark about inner motivating
factors, Freudians condescendingly granted that they made helpful clinical observations.[93]

While it is tempting to dismiss *Man against Himself* as an intriguing
time capsule, we should keep in mind that it had a following among
psychoanalysts and other suicide specialists for at least forty years.[94]
Menninger wrote about more than the motives for what he called acute
suicide. Interested in a range of self-destructive practices, he analyzed
chronic or slow suicides, by which he meant the conduct of individuals
who brought disaster and drawn-out martyrdom upon themselves. As

well, he discussed chronic invalidism, alcoholism, psychosis, self-mutilation, purposeful accidents, frigidity, and impotence in terms of struggles that engaged the id, ego, or superego in distinct combinations.[95] Going even further than that, he advocated the idea that self-destructive processes could be focused on an organ. He wanted to destroy "the comfortable illusion of the separation of mind from matter."[96] The book resembled French medical tracts from Falret to de Fleury because of the scope of subjects covered and the use of case histories and illustrations from literature. However, the overlay of Freudianism distinguished it, as did one other feature. Whereas French doctors during the nineteenth century tried often to explain mental illness in terms of somatic causes, Menninger reversed causation and suggested that emotional factors could contribute to somatic disease.[97] He had no scientific evidence. Little wonder that psychoanalysis seemed closer to the humanities than to medical science. However, in a way that no critic of psychoanalysis could have expected, Menninger anticipated the medical science of the late twentieth century. Emotional stress and trauma damage brain cells as well as inhibit healing.[98]

Well before the collapse of Freudian psychoanalysis, several psychiatrists added to the analysis of suicide. Studies of attempted suicide by Edwin Stengel and colleagues in England during the 1950s provided information on the number of persons who attempted suicide and the number who succeeded. To diagnose suicidal conditions and to attempt to prevent suicides, the International Study Group for the Prevention of Suicide was organized in Vienna in 1960 under the direction of Viennese psychiatrist Erwin Ringel and Berlin psychotherapist Klaus Thomas; simultaneously, Edwin Shneidman and Norman Farberow introduced a campaign against suicide in the United States and established the Los Angeles Suicide Prevention Center. These initiatives re-energized a mental health approach to suicide. "For me as a physician," wrote Ringel, "suicide is primarily a psychological problem … From the medical standpoint we are dealing with a disease – above all with neurosis."[99] The emphasis on disease was a riposte to Thomas Szasz in *The Myth of Mental Illness* (1961), for Szasz insisted that when physicians in the late nineteenth century ran out of physical ailments to classify, they invented mental illness to enhance their influence and prestige. The notion of a disease changed from the "physicochemical derangement of the body to the disability and suffering of the person." This redefinition allowed medical doctors, psychologists, lawyers, and journalists to expand the scope of mental illness.[100] Szasz put forward a hostage to fortune, for, in effect, he predicted that "science would never show disorders of thought or emotion to be characterized by anatomical pathology."[101]

In the 1920s and 1930s, psychiatry was sometimes described as medical psychology. Experimental psychology, meanwhile, had been unfolding as a distinct field. American psychology, by the middle of the twentieth century, affected suicide studies because the field had subtly changed. At the end of the nineteenth century, psychology had had several research strategies to explore consciousness through the study of the individual. The intention of experimental psychologists was to move clear of philosophical introspection, from which the field had originated. From its philosophical roots, psychology maintained a tie to suicide studies through a connection with consciousness and ultimately with personality. Initial experimental psychology in Europe, meanwhile, concentrated on sensory physiology; experiments involved an individual testing himself or someone else with stimulation to learn about intensity, spatial location, and duration. The inveterate explorer of human capabilities Francis Galton (1822–1911) added a dimension to experimental psychology in 1884 when he collected observations on the abilities of thousands of people to perform a set of tasks. He had introduced the notion that psychological information could be statistical and could ultimately promote a science to inform public policy. Psychology was set once again on a track to intersect with suicide studies on account of the scientific interest in consciousness, the statistical study of personal attributes, and social policy.

In an insightful treatment of epistemology and psychology, Kurt Danziger traced the steps by which a handful of psychologists founded an applied dimension to psychology that considered the propensities of groups rather than individuals. Group attributes were conceptualized as the sum of individual characteristics because the traditions of the discipline as a whole revolved around the individual, and now the hypothetical individual. Some studies of suicide by psychologists stayed close to this latter conception and tried to examine the motives and personality of "the suicidal person" from data collected from living people who had attempted suicide, from accounts of people who knew the deceased, or from coroners' reports.[102] Individual types could be deduced, not by anything transpiring in their minds, but by assembling traits and comparing them with a statistical norm.[103]

This way of thinking led to psychological portraits of "normal people" found in control groups and to a pastiche of "the suicidal personality" based on assorted research innovations. Whereas statistical discussions of suicide data could identify particular populations at risk, such as older, single farmers or traumatized soldiers or adolescents or indigenous people, the ambition of a few psychologists was to go deeper and describe a personality type at risk that cut across occupational or ethnic identities. Some researchers obtained the personality factors of individuals who had attempted suicide from Rorschach tests and compared the results with outcomes from a control group. Others examined suicide notes or abundant hospital records of suicidal patients and deduced suicidal types such as the "dependant-dissatisfied" person, who was "continually complaining, demanding, insisting and controlling."[104] By the turn of the millennium, the assessment instruments had expanded, the populations studied had widened to include school students, and a substantial portion of new research initiatives dealt with suicide ideation.[105] Underlying these approaches was the supposition that suicidal individuals had personality properties deep within that caused them to act differently from other individuals. The conformity issue in American suicide studies transcended sociology to include psychology; however, the authors of personality reports could not agree upon a common bundle of defining traits. Compared to the normal control group, suicidal people were more aggressive, less aggressive, or no different.[106]

Jack Douglas wrote *The Social Meanings of Suicide* (1967) partly as an attack on several currents in sociology, on "simple-minded positivism," and on "the vast prestige of Durkheim's *Suicide*."[107] Suicide had figured often in sociology's evolution; however, because Douglas's arguments originated in a philosophical critique of positivism, they struck not only at sociology but at psychology as well. For that reason, he has been held over for discussion here. Douglas wielded a two-edged blade. One edge exposed specific flaws with a set of individual theories that he characterized collectively as statistical-hypothetical.[108] The other edge opened a discussion of what he called social meanings, by which he meant the message that suicidal individuals, affected by social circumstances, intended to compose with their act, as well as how that message was taken in by intended recipients. This second edge cut sharply and uncompromisingly to the core of many sociological and psychological studies from the 1920s to the 1960s and beyond, because Douglas pointed out that suicide had to be considered from several perspectives which could not be extracted from mere data. Beginning with the idea that it was a meaningful act, he worked out probable scenarios in which the act would be consequential to persons who committed it and to others designated to receive its message. What mattered, according to Douglas, were the following: situations communicated in the act of suicide; the fact that statistical-hypothetical theories could never recover these situations, which were thick with meanings; and that authors of statistical-hypothetical studies had imposed their own meanings.

There were implications. First, suicide rates could never be explained in terms of the modulating social forces attributed by Cavan to cultural values and by Gibbs to social integration; Durkheim, Cavan and the ecologists, and Gibbs had laboured in vain. Second, it was impossible to infer concrete situations from any research that abstracted the participants from the deed. In other words, questionnaires and laboratory experiments were unhelpful because they had absolutely no contact with the act and the actors.[109] The social sciences and certain modes of psychology needed more "careful, detailed descriptions of real world events."[110]

Douglas worked with a handful of cases reported in prior studies to furnish examples of what he meant by concrete situations, the act's message, and the intended impact on recipients. In his methodology, the basic principle was that suicide should not be seen as odd but as rational to the persons contemplating it.[111] From that position it followed that when a few men and women attempted or completed suicide, they mentally separated their bodily self from their situational self; they saw suicide as a means of escaping a situation and still experiencing things after death. For that reason, Douglas rejected the definition of suicide as self-destruction.[112] It was not necessarily self-destruction from the vantage point of the principal actor, and that was the correct perspective from which to work. There were also religious suicides: the individual believed that it was possible not only to survive death but to go home to peace with God.[113] A few individuals used suicide to communicate an important message; the suicide note or words spoken at a last meeting could express atonement, an appeal to improve a situation, or revenge. The last message could be expressed by subtle means in the not-so-subtle act of suicide. A suicide note, for example, could deliberately excuse someone from responsibility, while simultaneously calling attention to him or her.[114] Douglas regarded a suicide as a dramatic exchange worthy of qualitative analysis.

Sociologists who used aggregate data or who aggregated individual case data to explain variations in rates were "locked into the assumption that social meaning is the same for everyone."[115] But in Douglas's judgment, although cultures can influence how people internalized the impact of social events – unemployment, bankruptcy, divorce, and so forth – social meaning is not a stand-alone factor but is determined largely by the interpretations that individuals place on those events. That outlook is congenial to the way historians think, for it accents time, place, and individual action. It strongly influences chapter 6 in this book. Howard Kushner saw that Douglas posed a serious challenge for the social sciences by questioning the assumption that "each unit of datum (the individual suicide) acts just like every other unit in response to external force."[116] Douglas's challenge to the social sciences paradoxically came from a sociologist. More commonly, appeals to make the individual the centre of attention have come from psychiatrists and clinical psychologists. At the conclusion of a critical testing of theories against the contents of suicide notes, psychologist Antoon Leenaars remarked that the theorist and the clinician have only their formulations, but persons killing themselves are the ones who alone experience the motives and the reasoning. We cannot construe all the vital circumstances in their lives, but we can strive to get closer by working with personal documents.[117]

BLURRING THE DISCIPLINARY BOUNDARIES?

Ronald Maris wrote *Pathways to Suicide* (1981) with the stated aim of avoiding disciplinary bias and enmity. "Although I was trained in sociology and a little in psychiatry and psychology, this is not a book about the sociology, psychiatry, or psychology of suicide."[118] Biographies were important because "no one suicides in a historical vacuum."[119] Notwithstanding his praise of openness in the quest for useful ideas, Maris conveyed likes and dislikes. He was not attracted to clinical case studies; he had a firm social science perspective and insisted that theory and a scientific method were indispensable. Biographies would bring intellectual collapse from an overload of facts. In an earlier book, *Social Forces in Urban Suicide*, he wrote that "there is a need for a much more rigorously constructed theory of suicide than Durkheim envisaged," and "any systematic theory of suicide will probably be modified by the development of new empirical generalizations."[120] In that first book, Maris adapted Durkheim in a standard way and proposed that a single postulate, external constraint, could regulate variation in suicide rates.[121] By external constraint, he meant the influence of other people, so that the array of associates in a person's life could temper any impulse toward suicide. He was thinking ahead, because he regarded external constraint only as a component variable in a future systematic theory based on observations and a rigorous methodology.[122] *Pathways* was his stimulating and ambitious follow-up.

Although Maris claimed an open mind, he was a spirited partisan for the statistical-hypothetical approach and followed in a lineage from Quételet to Durkheim to advanced statistics that dealt with variance and probability. He was interested in ideal types but realized they relied on probability statements and would have error terms.[123] Maris dealt with Douglas's ·critique of number crunching without addressing his challenge directly. Instead, he countered in two ways. First, he designed a remarkable research project that built upon individual case data by structured questionnaires which collected information on a substantial number of cases. Second, he marginalized Douglas's idea that suicidal acts had meanings. Of course they did, but for the purposes of understanding why people brought an abrupt end to their biological existence, these meanings were finite: most involved escape, and the remainder aimed at vengeance. Besides, social meanings were not the nub of the matter. "Most emphatically the main problem in understanding suicide lies not in its meanings but rather why some individuals use this radical means [to escape or get revenge] and under what specific circumstances."[124] While Douglas believed it essential to consider the meanings that men and women adduced for their pending act, Maris wanted to get at the reasons for that reasoning. He asked a variant of the old question: Why did this person succumb and many others did not? In his rendering, he questioned why this deed and not some other coping response had been selected? His answer was the existence of pathways to suicide.

The pathways were life courses or, as he named them, "the suicide careers" of people who reasoned ultimately that there was no alternative to suicide and that "the real problem was life."[125] The pathway consisted of personal traits and circumstances that led to suicide. Many, if not most, suicides, according to Maris, "did not spring full-blown out of some acute life crisis."[126] Some of the variables along pathways are readily understood: age, gender, and the number of previous suicide attempts. Others are fairly straightforward: drug use, transience, depression, and alcoholism. And still others are conceptual: lethal contingencies, such as the availability of a gun; negative interaction, such as violent domestic relations; early traumatizing relationships, such as disruptions in the family; and abortive life-stage transitions, such as a failure to mature or accept one's stage in life.[127] He deduced that these were the important variables after he had analyzed three data sets. First, he drew a sample of Chicago suicides (1966–68) from death certificates (n=725). Interviews were conducted with roughly two informants for each of just over half the cases (n=401). Second, interviews were conducted with a sample of non-fatal suicide attempters (1970) from Baltimore (n=64). Third, more interviews were held with informants who knew individuals who had recently died of natural causes (1969–70). The second and third data sets were intended as controls to provide points of comparison with the suicides in order to coax out differences.[128] Historians, alas, cannot conjure up control groups from the past.

For reasons of economy, Maris excluded African Americans and had to draw second and third data sets from a city other than Chicago. These expedients, as Howard Kushner has commented, weakened the study and put a shadow over a group of controversial findings. According to Maris, non-fatal suicide attempters and suicide completers had quite different pathways; non-fatal attempters used low-lethality methods. Since most completers die quickly as a consequence of their first attempt, Maris contended that how others reacted to the attempt is irrelevant to prevention. This assertion put him at odds with clinical psychologists.[129] Critics jumped on his conclusion that suicide is directly related to unhappiness with the human condition.[130] Such an obvious truth was less impressive than the research design that had led there. Where an explanation for suicide is almost anything, it risks becoming nothing. Scratch the surface, and similar reduction is seen in other studies.

For example, summarizing several investigations, Herbert Hendin remarked that older individuals with depression were vulnerable to suicide because their "expectations for the future were not bright."[131] Hendin was too seasoned to accept that suicide could be distilled to the inevitability of growing old. Instead, he wrote that the individual's capacity to deal with the trials of aging depended "on the meaning and personal significance they have for him."[132] To be fair to Maris as well, he published abundant specific observations about suicidal pathways and their long-term development. Many of my observations in chapters 4 through 6 concur with his findings.

Even though Maris dismissed Douglas's social meanings of suicide, a concept that I have found valuable, I think highly of *Pathways*. I prefer to ignore the oppositional tone in both works and regard their viewpoints as complementary. Objective stresses (Maris) and the subjective management of them (Douglas) have to be part and parcel of any effort to comprehend suicide.

NEUROSCIENCES AND PHARMACOLOGY

The French alientists and later psychiatrists who examined the men and women who attempted or committed suicide had mainly assembled their portraits of people at risk from therapeutic interviews with patients at asylums. Looking retrospectively into patients' records after suicides or attempted suicides, they prepared summary profiles. In a few instances they dissected the brains of the deceased and searched for lesions that could provide a somatic explanation for suicidal mania; however, only when Paul Pierre Broca (1824–80) began to systematize the study of the regions of the brain did cerebral anatomy acquire vigour. Broca launched modern physiological work on the mechanics of the brain, and his heirs established neurology.

More directly significant for suicide research were the efforts of Emil Kraepelin (1856–1926) to reorganize the classification of mental illnesses and establish their causes in brain physiology and functions. His observations of patients at the university hospital in Dorpat (Tartu), von Oettingen's hometown, persuaded him that particular mental illnesses were not characterized by any one symptom but by a pattern; so his system of classification proceeded by pattern recognition. Thus he split the previously unified concept of psychosis into schizophrenia, which he called dementia praecox, and manic depression. He believed that schizophrenia had a deteriorating course with a decline in mental function, while manic-depressive patients were relatively symptom-free during intervals separating acute episodes. Later, at mental hospitals and clinics in Heidelberg and Munich, Kraepelin systematically recorded patients' symptoms as a basis for frequent reclassifications of mental disorders for his *Lehrbuch der Psychiatrie*.[133] Detecting that more schizophrenics appeared among the relatives of schizophrenic patients than in the general population and more manic-depressives among the relatives of manic-depressives, he claimed biological origins traceable to brain pathology. Although he and a colleague, Alois Alzheimer, succeeded in establishing the pathological basis of what became known as Alzheimer's disease, he could not do the same for depression and suicide.[134] Eventually, in the late nineteenth century, the psychological research path to understanding mental illness would yield to Freudian psychoanalysis.

For Kraepelin and his followers, according to Howard Kushner, Durkheimian and Freudian explanations of suicide were "no more convincing or scientific than late medieval pronouncements that Satan's temptations underlay suicidal impulses."[135] But from the early 1920s to the mid-1970s Kraepelin's influence in psychiatry was marginalized. His writing lacked the literary quality, cultural appeal, and paradigm-shifting impact of Freud's. Besides, as a textbook writer, he formulated no grand therapeutic solution, while Freud had. Since the early 1980s, however, a biological orientation has dominated psychiatry, and Kraepelin's theories on the etiology and diagnosis of psychiatric disorders have inspired major diagnostic systems, such as the later editions of the American Psychiatric Association's Diagnostic and Statistical Manual of Mental Disorders (DSM), which has gone through four revisions since its first publication in 1952.[136] Edwin Stengel, the British psychiatrist who had initiated research on attempted suicides, chaired a committee of the World Health Organization to standardize classifications in other countries.[137] Crucially, DSM III, published in 1980, introduced "a scheme that was based on lists of explicit criteria rather than speculations about underlying psychological processes."[138] Standardized tests and definitions – an algorithmic approach – may be expected to be used in both research and clinical settings; in daily practice, however, guidelines may not be meticulously applied on account of the intricacy of individual cases and questions about the validity of DSM definitions.[139]

Durkheim mounted statistical attacks on tracts which postulated that alcoholism and mental illnesses promoted suicide, but medical practitioners had an intimate perspective, as they inevitably reminded everyone, and were less skeptical about the impact of alcoholism and mental illness. Although psychotherapy assumed that unconscious urges and conflicts could lead people to destructive conduct, hope for recovery was based on enabling the conscious self. For those who could afford it, psychotherapy, whether Freudian or based on other schools, was a leading method from roughly the 1920s to the 1950s for treating suicidal conditions by assisting the conscious self. To treat suicidal tendencies, psychotherapy was supplemented by convulsive chemotherapy in the late 1930s and electroconvulsive (shock) therapy in the early 1940s. Barbiturates came into general use in the late 1940s.

All these treatments contributed to another phase in the ongoing medicalization of suicide, because the shared idea of addressing suicidal symptoms with physical intervention or pharmacological treatments set the course for the introduction of antidepressants to treat conditions that carried risks of suicide. By the 1970s, pragmatism was highly valued by suicide clinicians, and by the following decade, practitioners could refer to risk estimator scales.[140] Even with respect to schizophrenia, the pharmacological assault, in conjunction with psychotherapy, scored successes. In her memoir of enduring schizophrenia, Elyn Saks unequivocally praised medication. "Thanks to the new chemicals coursing through my body," she recounted, "I experienced long periods of time in which I lived as other people did – with no psychotic thinking at all."[141] Schizophrenia was long recognized as an illness that carried a high risk of self-destruction. Meanwhile, the most experienced and influential suicidologist, Edwin Shneidman, recommended modes of psychotherapy that bought time and tried to show options other than self-destruction. Convincing the patient to consider a variety of coping tactics ran straight into something that Shneidman detected in most suicides: "a tunnelling of the thought processes, a narrowing of the mind's content, a truncating of the capacity to see viable options which would ordinarily occur to the mind."[142]

Successive therapeutic developments and reports on their efficacy were not the only ways that medical science contributed to suicide studies. By the beginning of the twenty-first century, genetic and biochemical explanations centred on the likely presence of congenital mental fragility. Traumatic experiences grievously affected the already vulnerable, and some mechanisms that specifically contributed to depression, for example, were becoming better understood through research and reasoned conjecture concerning the stress hormone pathway. Depression is not the sole motive or sole contributing factor for suicide, but it has been claimed that "even at the subsyndromal state, even the merest hint of depression, confers a suicide risk three or four times that of the general population."[143] Thus theories about depression are important for suicide studies. Genetic fragility and subsequent neuronal cell damage caused by stress offer one promising theory; it is general enough that it accommodates rival hypotheses involving a variety of neurotransmitters and hormones. Peter Kramer, a psychiatrist who moved in his own practice from psychotherapy to psychotherapy and the prescription of antidepressants, proposed an eclectic approach: "any viable account [of depression] will include attention to genetic predisposition, early-life trauma, later adversity, varied insults to brain cells, anatomical damage, neuronal pruning and sprouting, and new cell growth."[144]

For our purposes, the details of current research that upholds each element in this statement are less important than its melding of social, genetic, physiological, biochemical, and neurological factors. Kramer essentially echoed Howard Kushner's concluding arguments in *Self-Destruction in the Promised Land*: "If I have insisted on anything in the preceding pages, it is that we can only begin to understand suicide by integrating social, psychological, and biological factors."[145] Suicide studies had become three-dimensional.

But had biomedical discoveries achieved a breakthrough in understanding suicide? Not a complete one. Genes, DNA, and neurochemicals have roles in anger, aggression, anxiety, and depression, "but how the person actually behaves depends just as much on emotional and cognitive habits – habits learned by exercise and repetition."[146] These are lifetime processes. Questions arise about the types of stress that affect the mechanisms which bring about neuronal damage and weaken individuals' capacities to take in stressful experiences differently. Identical twins may share an environment, but how they absorb common events may be a subjective matter, a question of personality, an experience of the self.[147] On the one hand, to classify motives is to sacrifice some of this vital individuality; on the other, to proceed purely on a case-by-case basis is to forego theory, summary, and categories. The analysis of case histories in the current book acknowledges this dilemma and proceeds pragmatically. To comprehend suicide, many individual instances should be examined to ensure that an array of personality issues and circumstances can be covered. When this approach is attempted, the abject inadequacy of aggregate data is exposed, but another difficulty surfaces. How can the chaos of raw information be reduced and the loss of individuality from compression be minimized? In the chapters that follow, this problem appears often and is handled by selecting statistics to summarize patterns and then citing witnesses' statements and suicide notes to recover the individual. As the next pages show, the case documents that sustain my quantitative and qualitative analysis have had a mixed reception from historians.

THE SUICIDE YEARS AND THE ARRIVAL OF HISTORIANS

From approximately 1970 to 1990, to judge from the volume of books published, suicide exploded onto the American public scene. The number of titles was not surpassed the next decade. Classics were translated: Mazaryk (1970), Morselli (1975), Halbwachs (1975). Cavan's *Suicide* had been reprinted in 1965; Menninger's *Man against Himself* was reissued in 1966, and a paperback edition appeared in 1985. Several factors explain this phenomenon. From the late 1950s to the early 1970s, approximately 120 suicide prevention centres were established in the United States and received federal support.[148] In 1968, a decade after he became co-director of the Los Angeles Suicide Prevention Center, Edwin S. Shneidman founded the American Association of Suicidology to promote public awareness, and several years later the association established the journal *Suicide and Life-Threatening Behavior*. At approximately the same time, annual reports by national and international agencies showed a rise in adolescent suicide rates. A euthanasia debate contributed to publicity, and so too did the mass suicide (or murder-suicide) of 912 Americans at Jonestown, Guyana, in 1978.

Academic publications increased, and suicidologists expanded their field to include indirect self-destructive behaviour: uncooperative patients, unhealthy living, self-mutilation, delinquency, and high-risk sports.[149] Qualitatively, something was happening too. Fiction poured forth and played up the youth suicide theme emerging from scholarly investigations and publications on prevention, self-help, and bereavement. In fiction meant for teens, suicidal young people confronted family breakup, school troubles, abuse, and the suicide of a sibling, parent, or friend. The tone of many fiction and non-fiction publications could be summarized using the title of the 1993 publication *Help Your Child Cope with Depression and Suicidal Thoughts*.[150] By the end of the millennium, the articles in *Suicide and Life-Threatening Behavior* covered all continents and most research traditions, although psychology and psychiatry predominated.

Historians arrived late to suicide studies and promptly took conflicting positions on what could be known and what should be the proper focus of inquiry. In the 1970s, in the wake of the quantification revolution in social history, suicide statistics attracted initial interest. Roger Lane, in *Violent Death in the City* (1975), theorized about relationships among the rates of accidents, homicides, and suicides in Philadelphia.[151] Lane opted for a theory that inversely related suicide and homicide rates. Other historians, far less enthusiastic about quantification, let alone theory, scrutinized the institutions responsible for investigating suicides and collecting suicide data for official publications; these probes jibed with historians' long-standing interest in institutions and ideas. From the perspective of political, intellectual, and cultural history, studying suicide meant concentrating on what Kenneth Pinnow describes as "the historically and culturally contingent nature of suicide's significance."[152] Cultural-historical accounts that position suicide studies in particular places and times have consequences for global suicide studies. The hard position is that they can subvert empirical and theoretical generalizations by shaking the idea of the uncompromised observer.[153] The soft position is that historical criticism may remove flawed studies from the canon and warn against arrogance, without erecting an insurmountable barrier to discoveries about suicidal people. Of course, the controversy over what historians can bring to the social sciences begs a question that always concerns historians. What sources will be used?

A few historians heartily repeated the warnings of Jack Douglas, who insisted that it was futile to try to learn about the motives for suicides from official records, because of administrative inefficiency and varying definitions of suicide.[154] Georges Minois agreed that "the testimony of witnesses, when it exists, is seldom very enlightening."[155] Douglas intended to disabuse his colleagues of their trust in official aggregate data as capturing the real incidence of suicide, but his warning dismissed official records prematurely. Social historians rejected advice to ignore official records. They were not about to discard potential clues to the past; they had long gleaned meaning from offbeat fragmentary evidence and squeezed clues from potentially duplicitous and certainly posthumous witnesses. For some researchers, suicide notes were an authentic source, but since they existed for perhaps only 10 to 20 per cent of cases, they were not representative.[156] However, they had value as communications of a special kind from people who found themselves in a situation that they perceived as traumatic, although it may have seemed trivial to others.[157] What made the situation unbearable rather than trivial were events from the person's history. Suicide was an irresistible subject for social history.

For Olive Anderson, who pioneered a cautious acceptance of official records, "doubts and criticism did not seem particularly disconcerting."[158] With care and appropriate methods, she proposed, historians who used official statistical returns could discover much about relationships among people, the significance of aging, and the different crises faced by men and women.[159] Simon Cooke, writing about suicide in the Australian state of Victoria, went further than Anderson in pulling evidence from the original coroners' documentation. By exemplifying what could be achieved through actually reading the testimony that clerks distilled into official statistics, he demonstrated the virtue of looking at archival holdings rather than assuming that relevant documents would be scarce, mute, or tainted. Cooke documented the importance of the interaction of the social and the biological; aging brought dependence, and differences between the life courses of men and women were embodied in the distinct methods of suicide.[160] Historians have begun to show that in various times and places in the past, physical illness and injury made suicide "an option at least worthy of consideration."[161]

Carrying on an aggressive defence of social history's exploration of suicide from documentary sources, Victor Bailey made reasonable concessions to the problems with officially generated records. As well, he acknowledged the hubris of attempting to fathom the motives of men and women who took their own lives, because "the real motives that impel a person to suicide are ultimately unfathomable."[162] Learning something, anything, counted as an advance. Responding to exponents of literary theory who would deny that an objective reality could be reached from texts, Bailey reported that witnesses' depositions "were grounded in the interlocking reality of socioeconomic structures and subjective experiences."[163] Friends, neighbours, family, and co-workers of the deceased had a fair knowledge of daily life. We should credit their agency and intelligence; we should learn from what they said and not dismiss the evidence out of stubborn conviction.

Bailey's exploration of suicide in Victorian Hull, England, required a compression of hundreds of motives into a handful, which he discussed in relation to the course of life for men and women. Women were by no means immune to suicide, although Bailey proposed that older men faired far worse than women essentially as a result of domesticity. Ironically, one of the best possible defences of Durkheim's poor claim that marriage protected women came from individual case records, which he denounced. Men, thought Bailey, were the more privatized partner in the marriage, and women kept in touch with family and friends and cultivated and maintained the support of neighbourhood networks. For women, the routines of housework and the circumstances of penury were not much affected by losing a spouse.[164] Gender has been and will remain a productive topic in suicide studies. Indeed, differences between men and women are sharply delineated in the special instance of murder-suicide, a heavily researched area of criminology. Women in these cases have taken the lives of their children more commonly than men, at least in part because the closeness of mothers to their young children meant the children's involvement in their mothers' distress. Men in murder-suicides have often killed women and then themselves from motives of morbid jealousy. [165]

Historians have shown serious interest in the sociological and psychological studies of suicide, but for conflicting purposes. While historians of culture and anthropologists have scrutinized discourses to coax out biases and to censure confidence in social science empiricism, social historians have adapted some of the very observations that are under critical scrutiny. By nature, all historians remain suspicious of the timeless present that prevails in disciplines which have long taken on suicide studies. This suspicion is history's common ground.

It is paradoxical but feasible to investigate life through death. Several historians also have stretched this opportunity to contribute to suicide studies generally by emphasizing the merit of setting theory against evidence and by taking advantage of the fact that without a rigid disciplinary tradition in the field of suicide studies, they can advocate holistic approaches. Admittedly, this latter ambition is extremely difficult to achieve. The pioneer historian in this respect, Howard Kushner, had participated in psychoanalysis study groups and collaborated with neurobiologists.[166] The evidence from the New Zealand and Queensland coroners' inquests examined in this study does not supply any clues about biochemical or genetic elements, but there is a surprising amount of information about mental illness and its treatment.

CONCLUSION

Twentieth-century suicide scholarship captured intellectual trends and followed fashions in the social sciences. Just as the leading nineteenth-century studies expressed currents in European culture, especially French anxieties, prominent books now reflected main currents in American culture. American leadership in twentieth-century suicide studies – the city-based ecological investigations, the Freudian perspectives, the statistical-hypothetical inquiries, and the revised psychiatric approaches – mirrored that culture's liberal and patriotic trends. Suicide investigations maintained an overall positivist faith in deliverance from unnecessary deaths, deliverance through the intervention of secular agencies employing trained social workers and medical professionals who worked with individuals. Researchers from the ecological school initiated the idea of neighbourhood studies and supported intervention at the civic level; the local-agency approach to prevention

persisted long after the school's investigative techniques ceded pre-
eminence to other methods of inquiry.

The availability of federal funding for post–World War II nation-
building improvements aligned liberalism with abundance, since prosperity supported suburban development, higher education, and hospital
construction. Spending on psychiatry soared too, and roughly 80 per
cent of all psychiatric units built in the United States were constructed
after the war.[167] A focus on understanding the individual pathway to
suicide and on healing the person characterized a renewed psychiatric
thrust in American suicide studies; emphasis on the troubled client coincided with the long-standing medicalization of suicide, but it also har-
monized with the liberal ideal of enabling the rational individual. The
subjective rationality of the suicidal individual, a keystone in American-
inspired suicidiology, maintained the liberal ideal of rational citizens.
Suicidal individuals were presumed rational parties whom a psychiatrist or psychologist could reason with, persuade, and ultimately save.
Concurrent with this singling out of the individual, American liberals
shed some mistrust of big business during and after World War II. The
medical revolution of wonder drugs, which had begun during the war,
smoothed the path for collaboration between doctors and drug com-
panies to treat mental illnesses pharmacologically.

A trace of nationalism channelled the major American studies, for they
placed a mental health premium on conformity, assimilation, and adjustment. Each of these related values made Durkheim's notion of social balance, achieved though integration, a beacon for American sociological
studies. In a self-styled land of freedom, conformity might have been a
pejorative word; not so, however, because a democratic majority rule
required and imposed a degree of self-control and acceptance. Conformity also had cultural and normative aspects that were conveyed to
immigrants by the pressures of Americanization. An assumption that
nonconformity was dangerous artlessly steered leading suicide studies.
Ruth Cavan and Calvin Schmid believed misfits were at high risk, and
Jack Gibbs attributed elevated suicide rates to weak status integration. A
moderate suicide rate in the United States during the Cold War sustained
American crowing about the superiority of a free- enterprise society relative to socialist societies. Sweden was a favourite target.[168]

Popular commentaries on suicide and suicide researchers did more
than follow the strong currents of American culture, because the topic
of self-destruction raised core questions mentioned in this book's introduction, and from the early 1970s onward, suicide research acquired

substantial international scope. Studies of suicide were not and are not simply bragging points or cultural constructs that ignore the fundamental existential crisis. Earnest researchers in the United States and elsewhere have struggled to understand what separates suicidal individuals from people with like problems who endure their troubles. As well, they have wondered whether suicide was one or many acts, and they looked to the life course for answers. Important themes in suicide studies transcended the specifically American undercurrent of conformity.

Suicide literature from the 1920 and into the new millennium reveals a persistence of transnational issues as well as the opening of new controversies. First, a rift between sociology and psychology, opened by Durkheim, persisted. Clinicians by the 1920s had emerged as the hardliners; they dismissed sociologists as desk-bound theorists. Second, some sociologists accepted the value of psychology but never quite arranged a meeting of the methods. Third, new splits in suicide studies appeared when Jack Douglas introduced his social-meanings interpretation of suicide to challenge the statistical-hypothetical methods. Fourth, developments in the biomedical sciences revolutionized suicide studies by pushing the origins of a suicidal life back to genetic predispositions for conditions that allegedly contributed to risk. Fifth, controversy in suicide studies expanded with the entry of historians and their craft debates. With no disciplinary roots in suicide studies, they have been free to rummage about and to propose, as Howard Kushner did, holistic versions of the causes of suicide. Sixth, by the 1970s, suicide studies in sociology attained a remarkable abundance; specific topics such as the relationship of suicide to marital breakup, alcoholism, and unemployment were heavily researched. Seventh, youth suicide joined the list of matters studied internationally and placed a potentially inconvenient fact in the pathway. Maris's theory conveyed the idea of a long development behind suicide. A redefinition of "long" would be required for the pathway to accommodate adolescents.

More was intended with this chapter than a cultural and intellectual history of a field of study. A few investigations made suggestions that can help with the interpretation of material in the next section of this book. Neither the evidence I gathered nor the theories that I favour satisfactorily dispel the mysteries of suicide. However, they teach us something. Historians routinely work with incomplete or conflicting information, often seek guidance from other fields, and balance doubt with plausibility. These qualities influence how social historians have written about suicide. *This Rash Act* (1998), by Victor Bailey, is exemplary and draws attention to the usefulness of analyzing motives by age and gender; however, his was a city-based study, and Victorian inquests apparently lacked commentary on mental illness.

Historians are accustomed to gaps in evidence and thus accept an odd mix of skepticism and confidence; they acknowledge imperfection and still venture observations. In that spirit, I propose that social meaning and pathways together promote fruitful thinking about the suicidal life in a sequence that leads from the evolution of personality to precipitating crisis to awareness of opportunity and to the social meaning of the act for that individual. This schema immediately runs into problems. There are always going to be imperfections in knowledge about individual lives, and suicide certainly appears to be an individual act. A question of typicality naturally arises if a few cases are studied intensively, but to collect thousands of cases, as this study does, presents the additional but contrary problem of retaining intimacy and credibility while striving for summary compression. The issue is illustrated by the example of Ronald Maris's *Pathways* because he sacrificed intimacy in favour of data-derived conclusions. He lists over 120 concluding observations, and some cannot be related to a discussion of suicide in New Zealand and Queensland because they invoke control groups and historical inquiry lacks them. It is possible to note the strengths in Maris's research design and to take his findings seriously, regarding them as plausible for a specific population in distinct time and place. However, *Pathways* offers no glimpses into the subjective quality of suicide.

The following selected conclusions from *Pathways* should be kept in mind because they are confirmed, modified, or challenged in the next three chapters. First, Maris found a strong positive association between age and suicide, which is most pronounced for white American males. Second, the rate for white women peaks between ages forty-five and fifty and then declines modestly. Third, individuals who commit suicide tend to have life structures in disarray to the point of collapse. Fourth, they tend to be socially isolated. Fifth, they are more likely than other people to have been divorced or never married. Sixth, often the people closest to suicidal persons are resigned to the act. Seventh, individuals who commit suicide have more work problems. Eighth, many are unemployed shortly before the suicide. Ninth, for males, blocked aspirations are significant for all age groups. Tenth, for many women, the life changes wished for are related to marriage. Eleventh, suicide completers are more likely to be alcoholics than drinkers in the general population. Twelfth, they are more likely to have had a major mental illness than individuals who die a natural death, and many more are in poor mental health. Thirteenth, the predominant mental disorder is neurosis, including anxiety and reactive depression.[169] Fourteenth, escape and revenge are prominent motives. And fifteenth, the acute or immediate triggering situations for acts of suicide are similar to the more long-term chronic causes.[170]

Guidance from a social-meanings understanding of suicide boils down to following an inclination. Recall that Douglas revolted against the statistical tradition in the social sciences, which attempted to comprehend the meaning of a phenomenon by looking at its frequency and correlating that to some attributes in the population and then imputing meanings to the population that would account for the correlation. In effect, the researcher invented meanings to explain the data, when it should have been the individuals involved who gave the act its meanings.[171] The meanings of suicide would ideally come from good descriptions of actual events; from these incidents and related biographies, more abstract theories might someday be attempted. Douglas felt blocked by "the serious shortage of good descriptions."[172] To overcome the dearth of case histories, he reached back and borrowed primary material from Cavan. Good descriptions were also valued by psychiatrist Herbert Hendin, who drew upon case histories from his own practice to put more information in the public domain. His *Suicide in America* (1995) situated these histories immediately after reviews of current literature on suicide and the young, the old, the violent, alcoholics, and homosexuals. The New Zealand and Queensland inquests furnish abundant events and the words of participants, although the life histories are not comparable in their depth to the clinical cases narrated by Hendin, which originated in protracted psychoanalysis and psychotherapy.

The summing-up of major twentieth-century theories of suicide could leave us with a collection of erudite and abstruse methodological conflicts, the detritus of turf wars among academic disciplines. We could retire from this particular battlefield of academe by declaring that knowledge is socially constructed; we could move on to explore other seemingly constructed topics. However, because no construction of knowledge that seeks to explain real-life events can be formed from blithe musings, because there are facts in the foreground, we should join the quest to understand but move warily, explain our steps, reveal our doubts, point to gaps in the core evidence, and identify where socially constructed knowledge informed witnesses. Many discipline-based studies of suicide cleaved to theories that were analytically convenient but may have been and likely were inaccurate in terms of real-life experiences composed of people's material realities and their individual reflections upon these verities. Victor Bailey described the blend of social circumstances and individual deliberations that I seek when looking at society and psyche. "Suicide," he wrote, "is decipherable only through a reconstruction of the complex setting and social meaning of the action."[173] The threefold challenge is to collect and prepare these reconstructions, to interpret them so that they leave memorable and defendable patterns which can inform our humanity, and to retain modesty and reticence when we encounter and seek to explain the thoughts of others.

Before specific cases in context are encountered, reconstructed, and interpreted historically, some statistical patterns need to be explored in the next chapter, not to frame statistical correlations – like those relished by Gibbs and distrusted by Douglas – but as an introduction to the role of historical analysis, problems of interpretation, curious statistical patterns, the importance of the life course, and differences in the lives of men and women. Social scientists try to avoid selection bias or choosing cases that support their arguments and ignoring those that do not. The statistical breakdowns of cases by gender, age, and occasionally by occupational groups help to check selection basis.

"Here's hopin'." Promotional literature for New Zealand and Queensland accentuated myths of wealth. Queensland continued into the 1930s to appeal to prospectors. Older men who had pursued the mineral rainbow beginning in the 1870s were prominent among the state's suicides decades later. Image 191956. Courtesy John Oxley Library, State Library of Queensland.

MORE MONEY FROM
YOUR DAIRY HERD

A dairy farm in New Zealand, ca. 1918. Dairy farming had its ups and downs in the first half of the twentieth century. All agriculture pursuits depended on cheap labour, while employers themselves suffered assorted stresses. Image Eph-A-DAIRY-FARM-EQUIPMENT-1918–01. Courtesy Alexander Turnbull Library, National Library of New Zealand, Te Puna Mātauranga o Aotearoa.

Farm of William Coombridge, ca 1910. Rural life in New Zealand was far from glamorous, although high commodity prices from roughly 1900 to 1920 encouraged expansion and the opening of new farms. Rural suicide rates exceeded urban rates. Image 1/2–024176–9. Courtesy Alexander Turnbull Library, National Library of New Zealand, Te Puna Mātauranga o Aotearoa.

A shearing crew, ca.1910. Sheep shearing was a leading form of itinerant rural labour in both New Zealand and Australia. Image 1/1–016378–G. Courtesy Alexander Turnbull Library, National Library of New Zealand, Te Puna Mātauranga o Aotearoa.

A "swagger" on the trail in New Zealand, ca. 1910.
Image1/2–020418–9. Courtesy Alexander Turnbull Library,
National Library of New Zealand, Te Puna Mātauranga o
Aotearoa.

Cattle mustering in Queensland, date unknown. Isolated male work camps
disrupted family life and contributed to heavy drinking before 1920. Image
75431. Courtesy John Oxley Library, State Library of Queensland.

Young men on their bunks on a farm at Scotchy Pocket, Queensland, ca. 1910–20. Young itinerant labourers on Queensland farms could cope with the hardships, but some who continued in this way of life had fewer prospects for marriage. Rural labourers often faced their declining years alone. Image 93398. Courtesy John Oxley Library, State Library of Queensland.

Publican at Dannevirke, ca. 1900. The prominence of alcohol in the lives of suicidal men meant that publicans were often called as witnesses at inquests. They regularly testified that "the deceased was a man who could hold his liquor," or "the last time I saw the deceased, he looked sober to me." Image 1/1–007929–G. Courtesy Alexander Turnbull Library, National Library of New Zealand, Te Puna Mātauranga o Aotearoa.

The bar of the Quilpie Hotel, Queensland, ca. 1921. Like many hotel bars in outback Queensland, this one mainly served itinerate labourers who worked in intensely hot and dusty conditions far from amenities. Image 76024. Courtesy John Oxley Library, State Library of Queensland.

Tree foliage cut in desperation for horse feed, ca. 1920. Queensland's severe periodic droughts, as well as the stress of debt and fluctuating commodity prices, adversely affected the physical and mental health of farm families. Image APE – 056 – 0001–0007p. Courtesy John Oxley Library, State Library of Queensland.

PART TWO

Rates, Society, and Motives

3

Bearings on a Temporal Compass: Rates, Seasons, Cohorts, and Motives

For inquiries into health, crime, suicide, wealth, class, race, and much else, social historians rely on data collected by modern bureaucracies. Routinely generated statistics are essential, but investigators who enlist government data must proceed cautiously, conscious of bureaucratic error, bias, and informants' reticence.[1] Transparency about the generation, collection, and publication of sources is essential, and so too is transparency about the methods of compression and restatement applied by researchers to temptingly accessible but tainted published tables. This chapter reviews the sources for and modes of collection of official suicide data; it also remarks on standard techniques for restating them, and it advances guarded conclusions about variations in suicide rates from one society to another and about seasonal patterns. Further, it introduces a preliminary account of trends in motives for different age cohorts for men and women, an exercise that prepares the way for the detailed scrutiny of gender and the course of life in subsequent chapters. The current chapter raises questions of universal importance about sources and methods of analysis, demonstrates how national or state trends may be explained historically, and sets up a framework for later discussions of case-file information.

Statistical conventions govern how scholars today present data. Thus the annual suicide rate per 100,000 people remains indispensable for sociological and historical investigations. Something like it – suicides per 1,000 or 10,000 – anchored the late nineteenth-century analyses by Enrico Morselli, Tomáš Masaryk, and Émile Durkheim, and rates remain a favoured descriptor for authors of national and international reports.[2] When calculated annually, they enable comparison over time.

A rate is derived by dividing the number of suicides in a given population during a year by the number of individuals in that population, ideally during the same year; however, annual population data is not always available. The selected population is referred to as a population at risk. In arithmetical terms, it acts as the denominator in a simple formula. Division would place a decimal point and string of zeros before the final number, so to avoid this awkward outcome, the division is multiplied by 100,000. Although the procedure is uncomplicated, the notion of a rate is tricky, because behind it is the concept of a population at risk. Identifying appropriate populations at risk requires a grasp of propositions in the fields of suicide studies and social history; there must be logic behind requisitioning particular denominators to embody populations at risk. But issues that currently excite interest, and thus seem logical, in one era may not necessarily retain enduring merit. For example, analyses relying on aggregate data frequently depended on rates stated in terms of national populations.

Nineteenth-century writers concerned themselves with national comparisons and then compiled suicide rates for particular subpopulations, notably religious groups. Durkheim famously compared Catholics, Protestants, and Jews to support his idea that some cultures insulated people better than others by integrating them into a network of supportive social relations. National rates remain commonplace in publications about suicide. The discussion of religious affiliations seemingly led into blind alleys because identity extends beyond any single category; however, in recent years religious affiliation has surfaced in epidemiological studies, and since religion is a mainstay of culture, its study can contribute to cultural interpretations of variations in suicide rates.[3] Other subpopulations have attracted attention as a consequence of changing intellectual fashions. These include but are not confined to class, race, age cohorts, and marital status. A quest for patterns underlies the social sciences and social history; that pursuit drives a search for appropriate population data. In this chapter, rates are calculated for subpopulations across a series of years to identify changes over time.

Suicide studies often dwell on rates, but suicide is also about individuals. Paying attention to rates and social circumstances as well as cultivating sensitivity toward individual meaning poses a basic challenge of analysis, although the prior challenge is to locate the best data and report on their weaknesses and gaps.

CALCULATING "RELIABLE" RATES

Representative questions about suicide illustrate why the calculation of suicide rates for subpopulations remains essential. After World War II, as we have seen, social scientists began to apply sophisticated statistical techniques to investigate the impact of age, class, race, and marital status. Researchers layered inquiries by cross-tabulating variables in order to look into these variables singly or in combinations.[4] A number of questions involving subpopulations originated in monumental historical events. Did World War I create a cadre of men so traumatized that they were at greater risk of committing suicide than other men of their generation? Were farmers in the Great Depression more likely to commit suicide than urban labourers? Some subpopulations are recommended as fit subjects because social scientists and social historians paid attention to the life courses of men and women. A handful of nineteenth-century topics linger on the agenda. Have married women been at greater risk than single women? Are men or women who separated after marriage more at risk than married people?

To investigate each question, subsets of suicides must be extracted from the principal data set; other data sets must be scoured for denominators to complete a calculation of rates. Extractions proceeded easily in this project because the core data consisted of individual cases. Through the selection of an appropriate value from a variable – for example, all unmarried folk from the martial status variable – cases could be reassigned to a newly defined file. Subpopulations could also be computed using several defining variables. If required, a very narrow subpopulation – for example, single, female domestic servants who had been seduced and abandoned – could be selected and occupy a separate file. Researchers who have depended on aggregate data have lacked the flexibility to form their own subpopulations and have accepted those provided by government publications. When they survive in nearly complete runs, inquest files are valuable to social history and suicide studies. The volume and frequency of individual observations in this study (4,220 cases for New Zealand from 1900 to 1950; 2,402 for Queensland from 1890 to 1940; and 255 for Brisbane from 1942 to 1950) offer opportunities to reconstruct aspects of private lives and to investigate suicide. The collection of hundreds of cases in alternate years over a long period means that short-term as well as long-term trends can be picked up.

The inquest process began with the discovery of a body or bones and scraps of clothing. Anyone who died violently or suddenly while not under a doctor's care was subject to an inquest. Eventually, someone had to summon a constable. Bodies are conspicuous. Burials required documentation, and few inhabitants could escape the requirements, although remote first peoples long evaded this paper net, and authorities were less concerned about their welfare than they were about settler populations. Consequently the history of life's troubles is more difficult to recover for Maori and Aboriginal people. Perhaps in exceptional instances individuals from the settler populations disappeared without a trace, but perfect isolation was rare. Even highly reclusive men – lonely prospectors, shepherds, and hunters – turned up in the inquest files when mere bones were discovered years after a disappearance. More typically, a constable was summoned to examine a body by a family member, co-worker, or passerby; the officer examined the surroundings, interviewed witnesses, made notes, and reported to a coroner, who in most instances immediately convened an inquest. In cities later in the period under study, a heavy case load could delay inquests. Since coroners were rarely appointed in Australia or New Zealand except in cities, the duty of holding a public inquiry in rural areas and towns fell to either a stipendiary magistrate or unpaid justices of the peace.[5]

In recent decades, to get around the hazards of aggregate data, a few suicide researchers conducted so-called forensic interviews or psychological autopsies that involve questioning family members or friends of the deceased.[6] The magistrates or coroners who conducted inquests asked questions too, within hours of the death, not days or weeks later. Theirs was a solemn fact-finding exercise to establish the cause and circumstances of death and to name a suspect in the event of foul play. Coroners could instruct a physician to conduct an autopsy to secure evidence. Rare in 1930, autopsies were commonplace by 1950. Poison remnants went to government laboratories for identification. Witnesses' depositions were not extensive responses to well-designed research questionnaires. Besides, as psychologist Jerome Kagan remarked about questionnaires, "words, like the wrapping of a package, do not reveal all of the contents hidden inside the speaker's mind."[7] Swiss psychiatrist Walter Morganthaler reported in 1945 that about one in three suicide notes he reviewed falsely stated motives.[8] The shortcomings of recent inquests in the United Kingdom have been catalogued, and the most serious omission seems to be the absence of routine questions about a psychiatric diagnosis or contact with a general practitioner.[9] Notwithstanding problems discerned in the case files and in other studies, a surprising number of witnesses in New Zealand and Queensland stated details about intimate matters and psychiatric treatment. Furthermore, the attribution of motives in this book depended on a weighing of notes and witnesses' statements.

Magistrates or coroners who conducted inquests asked simple questions about the deceased, the relationship to witnesses, the deceased's last hours, and potential motives for self-destruction. A clerk or magistrate read the witnesses' statements back to them before they signed them. Answers were brief and by no means universally revealing; there was no standard set of questions required for all inquests. In New Zealand no plausible motive could be discerned for a suicide in 341 cases (8.1 per cent), and in Queensland complete mystery extended to 284 cases (11.8 per cent). Jack Gibbs, who examined 955 New Zealand inquests in 1946, found many verdicts unreliable but discovered that the evidence in the files was ample enough to make an independent evaluation.[10] That was our experience too.

Until the 1930s coroners took little interest in the age of the deceased. Often, witnesses volunteered that information, but age was still missing in one in five Queensland suicide inquests (20.1 per cent) and in one in six New Zealand inquests (16.6 per cent). Imputing distributions is a feasible but complicated process, since the percentage of missing ages varied by gender from year to year. Crucially for the success of this study, the office of the Registrar General of New Zealand provided assistance by locating missing ages from death certificates, a measure that reduced missing ages to one file in about forty (2.4 per cent). The New Zealand findings on age are reliable; those for Queensland useful but incomplete. This flaw weakens the credibility of age normalization procedures, which would have been useful for testing the impact of demographic discrepancies between the two jurisdictions. Instead, conclusions on this topic are especially provisional.

In Queensland and New Zealand the coroner or magistrate sent each inquest file, consisting of witnesses' depositions and a form with a determination, to the Department of Justice for review. In both jurisdictions roughly one in ten of all inquests into violent deaths pertained to suicide. A file received a sequential registration number when it arrived at the department. Only a handful of missing files, identified by gaps in numbering, were encountered during research, too few to affect the calculation of suicide rates. For most years in this study, coroners and magistrates would have been rebuked as negligent by their respective justice departments if they issued a death certificate without an inquest, but around 1920 expanding duties forced changes in some jurisdictions. Coroners' inquests were subjected to legislative reformation. In England, following a review in 1938, inquests ceased being mandatory for suspected suicides. The government of Queensland reviewed this development. Magistrates welcomed any relaxation in duties because the state had saddled them with also investigating auto fires for the state insurance office. From roughly 1922 to 1930, magistrates informally excused themselves from investigating all suspected suicides and only proceeded when the police requested a full inquest.[11] In late 1929 a scandal erupted over a magistrate's failure to hold an inquest into the suspicious suicide of a former Queensland beauty queen who had died in the office of an avuncular barrister. Parliamentary ructions forced the drafting of an act compelling magistrates to resume inquests for all suspected suicides.[12] However, a 1943 act granted magistrates statutory discretion, weakening some of the research value of ensuing inquest files.[13] The Queensland inquest files from 1890 to 1920 and from 1932 to 1940 probably include the vast majority of suicides, but the number of files for intervening years fell below official counts based on death certificates.

Rare among common-law countries, New Zealand insisted until 2006 on mandatory inquests for all suspected suicides. They are now discretionary. Inquests continue to be held in public places and in theory are open to the public, but restrictions may be imposed on access and publication. In New Zealand throughout the period under review, coroners or magistrates who acted in their place could require a jury of four to six jurors. They did so for some suicide inquests, although the practice diminished over time.[14] In Queensland there were no juries after July 1866.[15] Family members of the deceased occasionally attempted to hush up suicides; magistrates in both jurisdictions reported meddling to their superiors.

A coroner or magistrate who wished to evade a verdict of suicide could report that the intent of an individual found drowned or shot or poisoned was unknown. A stock finding for a so-called open verdict read: "how or by what means the deceased became so drowned sufficient evidence did not appear to the Coroner."[16] There never can be a sure count of suicides because of the potential for disguising a few as accidents. Perhaps some barbiturate overdoses and auto collisions – both rare until the late 1940s – were erroneously judged accidental. In instances when the means of death could have pointed to an accident,

Graph 3.1
Three counts of suicides: New Zealand, 1900–50

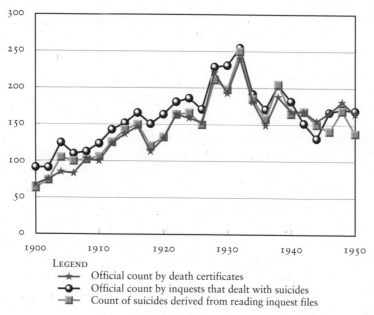

LEGEND
★ Official count by death certificates
○ Official count by inquests that dealt with suicides
■ Count of suicides derived from reading inquest files

testimony, suicide notes, or a constable's observations usually indicated whether or not a suicide had occurred. A review of evidence in the case files of deaths officially ruled of undetermined intent seldom leaves doubt about whether or not the individuals took their own lives. The suicide count based on New Zealand inquests is likely as good as any series anywhere anytime, and it has the further advantage of covering all manner of communities in a national jurisdiction. In some years, inquests yielded more suicides than the official count based on death certificates and published annually in *New Zealand Official Year-Book*.[17] A separate section of this publication devoted to law and order cited statistics on inquests, including the number deemed "suicide inquests." These inquests generally exceeded the number of suicides reported from death certificates (see graph 3.1). Thus there are discrepancies among separate official counts. Significantly, the counts compiled by reading the actual inquests produced the largest numbers for many years under consideration.

The ability to examine cases enabled a check on the attributions of motives in all reported instances of sudden and violent death. When cases that looked like suicides were added to officially determined suicides, the sum exceeded the official count by 11.9 per cent in New Zealand and 11.7 per cent in Queensland. Most open verdicts that truly were suicides involved deaths by drowning. In Queensland 175 open verdicts were added to the suicide data set. Drowning accounted for 101, or 57.7 per cent; in New Zealand, out of 492 additions, 367, or 74.6 per cent, were by drowning. The true cause of the death was revealed by farewells, telltale threats, previous attempts, pockets filled with rocks, weights tied to legs or neck, bricks in a bag, a rope around the legs or hands, or a coat pulled over arms. In other jurisdictions around the world, deaths by drowning created classification problems too.[18]

Open verdicts occasionally applied to deaths by rifle shot or coal-gas poisoning. New Zealand inquest files read for this study included thirteen open-verdict rifle cases and ten coal-gas incidents. Queensland experienced few coal-gas poisonings; seven open-verdict cases were read that involved rifles. Many deaths by a rifle in the bush could have passed as accidental except for the removal of a boot and sock to free a toe to depress the trigger or the presence of a string and stick to do the same. When police reports on coal-gas poisoning mentioned rags stuffed under doors, a pillow on the floor near an open oven, or a hose running from outlet to bedroom, the case was deemed a suicide for the purposes of this study. Jack Douglas maintained, in *The Social Meanings of Suicide,* that official statistics had to err because judgment criteria as to whether an act was a suicide or not would vary according to different observers and because even coroners did not adhere to a strict definition of suicide.[19] His objections, challenged later in studies of coroners' practices in assorted jurisdictions, are handily overcome by reading the evidence.[20] The vast majority of cases are not tricky; however, he was right to suggest that at a deeper philosophical level, suicide becomes more than one act once intent and deliberation are introduced. Moreover, Douglas's criticisms about judgment and labelling legitimately apply to studies that employ aggregate data, for their authors may not have been able to appreciate the diversity of acts bundled together to arrive at a total and hence a rate. When case files are studied, the fact of self-destruction is seldom in doubt, but the motives and intentions are astonishingly diverse, and thus suicide is readily disaggregated into many acts, rather than seen as an act that responds to social variables. In New Zealand the reassignment of many open verdicts into suicides translated into a higher suicide rate than the official one. The additional cases in Queensland produced a rate that was

Graph 3.2
The variation between an official crude suicide rate and an inquest-based rate: Queensland, 1890–50

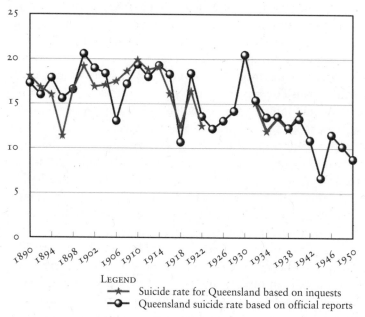

LEGEND
—★— Suicide rate for Queensland based on inquests
—⊖— Queensland suicide rate based on official reports

extremely close to but not generally higher than the official rate based on death certificates.

The New Zealand suicide counts determined on the basis of reading the inquests files generally exceeded rates calculated from official published data (see graph 3.1), but only slightly. The conduct of Queensland's magistrates compromised the inquest count for some years (see graph 3.2). As a result of these differences in reliability between the New Zealand and Queensland counts, the highest potential suicide rate for New Zealand is one based on a case-by-case review of inquests; in Queensland the highest rate is based on the official count derived from death certificates, which in turn originated from both inquests and police investigations. The survival of police investigations into violent deaths in the Brisbane police district permitted the formation of a data set of suicides (255 cases) in the metropolitan region from 1942 to 1950.

To finish the preparatory work required for the calculation of suicide rates, reliable suites of data that relate to well-founded research questions must be found to serve as denominators. Counts for some populations at risk are readily located. Census tables invariably provide age distributions by gender. Adolescent suicide, to take a prominent example, can be studied over time by employing a series of rates calculated with denominators taken from age cohort tables for selected years. However, the numbers of individuals in an age cohort may be based on slightly outdated counts. New Zealand normally held censuses every five years but did not conduct them in 1931 and 1941. Australia held census enumerations in 1910, 1911, 1921, 1933, and 1947. To fill in missing information, population estimates can be interpolated with statistical software. Flaws in annual suicide counts and imperfections with population tallies for denominators mean that rates are approximations, although trends over time seem reliable and conform to historical expectations. Thus the Queensland rates were high during the era of the shearers' strike (1891) and the eight-year "federation drought" (1894–1902), rose during the Great Depression, and fell during the prosperity of the 1940s.

At least eight plausible crude rates can be calculated for New Zealand. There are four suicide counts: the official death certificate count, the official suicide inquest count, the count of inquest case files with a suicide verdict, and a count of the case files that include many but not all open verdicts. There is more than one national population. A variety of annual estimates could be computed from census data by different methods of interpolation; however, the main reason for considering more than one national population at risk relates to the fact that, for demographic purposes, a national population could either include or exclude Maori. It should include Maori. Yet the suicides of rural Maori were under-counted, and so the problem is whether to attempt a calculation of a national rate that includes Maori or focus on a Pakeha rate. On the one hand, to include the Maori population would pull the national rate below a hypothetically correct one. On the other, to exclude the Maori population would reduce the divisor and increase the rate. Some Maori suicides appeared among the inquests files, and more were committed by Maori not identified as such at the inquest but possibly counted as Maori during a census enumeration. Four of eight possible rates are shown in graph 3.3. One rate was selected for discussion. The count based on reading the inquest files and using the total population, including Maori, produces a realistic, though marginally low, rate. If different rates can be calculated in New Zealand, a country that prided itself on the quality of its social statistics, then rates elsewhere deserve unremitting scrutiny.[21] It is likely that suicide data

Graph 3.3
Diverse potential suicide rates for New Zealand, 1900–50

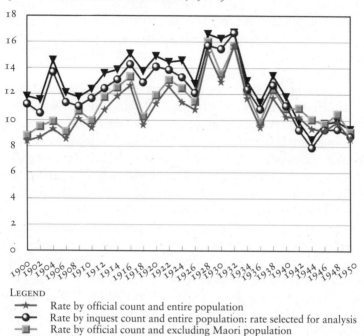

LEGEND
—★— Rate by official count and entire population
—○— Rate by inquest count and entire population: rate selected for analysis
—■— Rate by official count and excluding Maori population
—▼— Rate by inquest count and excluding Maori population

became progressively more accurate. In New Zealand the gap between the highest and lowest plausible rates, widest in the early twentieth century, had closed by the 1920s (see graph 3.3).

Statistics for some populations at risk are presented in cumbersome ways, are missing from government publications, were collected at a different period from the occurrences of the suicides, or were organized by labels that differed from those used by witnesses at inquests. Consequently, the cohorts of persons who actually supply the suicides are never precisely coeval with the cohorts who contribute the population. While New Zealand and Queensland bureaucrats kept watch on local affairs to a remarkable degree, their information-collecting practices never anticipated future research needs. When they summarized census information on occupations, they reported on economic sectors: professional, domestic, commerce, transportation, industry, primary producers. Some classification schemes followed the logic of materials: work on land, in the forests, on the sea, or with metals, wood, leather, clay, and paper. Officials preparing the explanatory introduction to the complexities of industrial and occupational statistics for the 1933 Australian census noted that the taxonomy problem could not be solved and was "complicated by the development of new fields of industrial enterprise and by the splitting and overlapping of fields previously conventionally definable."[22] As well, the scarcity of census tables that break down the working population by disparities in wealth complicates but does not preclude assessing risk by class. Case-file data suggest that farmers, farm labourers, and unskilled urban workers faced great risk. To confirm that impression, it is vital to know the proportion of the population for each group, but that figure is going to be inexact.

For New Zealand, but not for Queensland currently, several fairly sound means exist for looking into risk by class. In 1926, 1936, and 1945 the New Zealand census reported on incomes, and Erik Olssen with colleagues reconfigured the published returns to organize occupations hierarchically for 1901, 1926, and 1936.[23] Miles Fairburn compiled occupational information for household heads for ten major population centres; he organized this data according to a simplified class scheme. The government of New Zealand also published the occupations of men of military age during World War 1.[24] Data helpful for assessing classes at risk exist in New Zealand but not in Queensland, where data on occupation can play only a supporting role in a discussion of class. Reference to occupational data compiled during World War 1 brings attention to missing data for returned soldiers, a specific subpopulation that, judging from inquest statements about shell shock and horrific wounds, seemed at high risk. Information about these men after they returned to civilian life is scarce. In 1930 a New Zealand government commission estimated that five thousand veterans in distressed circumstances required assistance and recommended that a census question should be posed to establish the scale of need.[25] Depositions from inquests and extant military files described diverse forms of physical and mental distress; only by estimating the annual numbers of living veterans at a particular time, however, can a rate be calculated with the objective in mind of detecting whether or not returned soldiers were at greater risk than other men of their generation.

Additional gaps drive home the point that studies employing official aggregate data must be unreliable in key places. Agencies that collected information did not and could not effectively probe interpersonal relationships; people did not volunteer important private or unconventional information during census enumerations. Martial status, by way of illustration, was not a straightforward affair. Whether men or women lived in common-law relationships or were divorced or separated is significant for any discussion of stress, but while governments collected data on marriages and divorces, they did not pull together information on common-law arrangements and informal separations. New Zealand collected data on divorce petitions and legal separations, but informal arrangements stayed beyond the state's ken. When separation was mentioned in a suicide case file, there was often no indication of legality. Official records simply do not allow the preparation of an accurate suicide rate for people whose unions failed. Outright abandonment cropped up in the suicide case files of men as well as women. A suicide rate for all abandoned, separated, legally separated, and divorced individuals cannot be calculated as a reliable series because of the limitations in published information relating to domestic states; a rate merely based on divorce would drastically underestimate the scale and significance of marital failure. In Queensland especially, it seems, itinerant labourers kept silent about marital status. One witness's statement from among many similar ones demonstrates the point. A stock drover who rode with Olof Pearson for eighteen month told the magistrate that Pearson "was a single man as far as I know."[26] Judging from Queensland inquests, vagueness about personal histories was a habit. Nevertheless, case files yield raw numbers about whether men acted as though single, and many files held rich qualitative evidence about family relations. Marriage breakdown was a major risk on its own, as well as a flare signalling the presence of other personal situations, principally debt and unemployment, alcoholism, and temper. Episodes of discord were plentiful and well described.

CONTRAST AND CONVERGENCE

Often, international reports publish suicide rates from scores of countries. Assuming that rates are imperfect but loosely embody trends, credible explanations for variation over time and between jurisdictions ought to be attempted. Sociologists, beginning with Durkheim, have tried often in their search for a general theory of variability.[27] The following discussion works as an explanation of differences and similarities in the rates for New Zealand and Queensland; it works, too, as an entreaty to embrace complexity in suicide studies. Historical inquiry stirs doubts and questions but also provides plausible interpretations.

No matter how the crude suicide rates for Queensland and New Zealand are calculated, the rates for New Zealand were lower until around

Graph 3.4
Crude suicide rates for New Zealand and Queensland selected for comparison

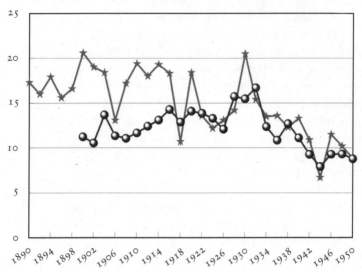

LEGEND
——★—— New Zealand rate by inquest count and entire population: rate selected for analysis
——●—— Queensland suicide rate based on official reports: rate selected for analysis

1930 (see graph 3.4). What explains the considerable early divergence? The lower rate for New Zealand may merely be an artifact of how governments collected data or maintained case files. That unlikely possibility can never be discarded. Demographic factors could have contributed somewhat to the higher rate for Queensland. Age distribution can influence suicide rates; some age cohorts in different eras have been at greater risk than others. At times, adolescents have been the troubled cohort; at other moments, the elderly. A population distribution skewed toward high-risk age cohorts would show a higher crude suicide rate. An adjustment to the data, a so-called direct standardization or normalization, is used by epidemiologists to iron out this distortion so that rates from different places can be compared.

Age normalization employs as a control an arbitrary external age distribution, and it serves to correct distortion. However, unlike diseases, where the relationship of risk to age is often clear – rising with chronic illnesses; declining with others, such as measles – suicide involves social as well as physiological circumstances. Cohorts with the highest risk do not necessarily remain at the top decade after decade. Nevertheless, many suicide studies compute age-normalized rates to demonstrate how the age structure can trip up analysis.

Several widely accepted tables of worldwide normal age distributions provide tools to fine-tune comparisons. Age-specific suicide rates, especially from the mid-twentieth century forward, have been normalized by the Segi World Standard Population Table. Epidemiologist Matsuo Segi's table, based on the structure of the population of Japan in 1950, entered wide use. There are rival Scandinavian-European and World Health Organization tables.[28] On account of missing ages in the Queensland data, normalization cannot be pursued with confidence in the results. Yet normalization is too significant to dismiss. As an initial step, the computation of both crude and normalized age rates for Queenslanders required reapportioning the cases that had missing ages.[29]

Since the Queensland data has many missing ages, normalization is unreliable; it requires a distribution of the missing-age cases according to the allotment of known ages. Inaccuracy could creep in since missing ages will not necessarily follow the distribution of known ages. Gender is a pertinent demographic factor because, globally, men have a higher rate than women, although women attempt suicide more often than men. In New Zealand and Queensland, the crude suicide rates for men were three to six times greater than those for women (see graph 3.5).[30] An imbalanced population with an abundance of men will produce additional suicides. Both New Zealand and Queensland had more men than women, and Queensland had a slightly larger proportion than New Zealand. Gender, too, must be normalized (see graph 3.6). The gender normalized rates were similar to the crude rates (see graphs 3.5 and 3.6). The overall normalized rates expressed in graph 3.7 take both age and gender into account. The estimated normalized rates for Queensland and the far more reliable normalized rates for New Zealand (see graph 3.7) roughly parallel the crude rates. An intriguing pattern of wide divergence followed by parallel downward trends toward a convergence survived adjustments.

To account for the divergence and later convergence between suicide rates, whether crude or normalized, I propose economic, social, and political-culture differences.[31] These jurisdictions differed with respect to politics in ways that enable us to consider how economic and sociopolitical factors could foster or temper despair. It is conceivable that for long periods aspiring men and women of moderate means found New Zealand stable, supportive, and congenial. During the 1890s the government began borrowing in the United Kingdom at low interest rates

Graph 3.5
Crude suicide rates for New Zealand and Queensland men and women based on official data

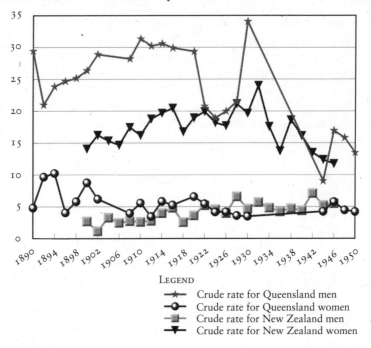

Graph 3.6
Gender-normalized suicide rates for males and females: New Zealand and Queensland inquest data

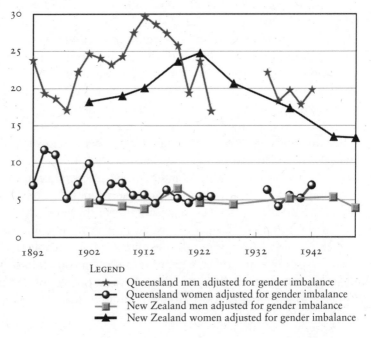

Graph 3.7
Estimated normalized (by gender and age) suicide rates for New Zealand and Queensland for
selected years

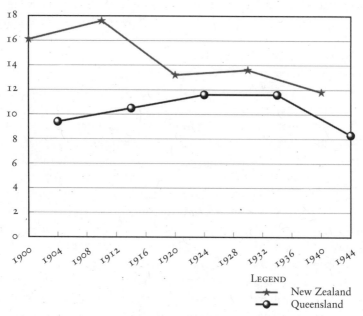

LEGEND
—★— New Zealand
—●— Queensland

to lend to farmers, home buyers, and local authorities; concurrent
cornerstone labour measures included fair wages legislation and dispute
arbitration.[32] The 1890s in Queensland were grim years for working
men. The decade opened with a massive, bitter labour dispute, and
then a protracted drought struck. Labourers could not have expected
relief from a government with an appointed Legislative Council controlled by moneyed interests. Migration from Queensland to New
Zealand increased.

New Zealanders appreciated that collective action and democracy
could aid self-advancement. Early feminists campaigned for voting rights
and succeeded in 1894. A means-tested old age pension, funded from
general revenues, was launched in 1898, expanded from time to time,
and greatly liberalized in the 1930s. Pensions for the aged and
disadvantaged, "a complex maze," in the words of Michael Bassett,
were available earlier than in any other country. However, a few eligible
men refused to apply. For them, such support was tantamount to charity,
and collecting the sum at the post office was a public ordeal. Mary
McCormack proudly described her drowned seventy-one-year-old

husband: "He was a labourer. He was not a pensioner."[33] Later, after Australia introduced old age pensions, some men refused them. Police Sergeant Patrick Murphy tried to get John Ryan to apply. Ryan protested, "I have a few quid left." But when those resources were gone, he ended his life.[34] Despite some individuals' reluctance to apply for pensions, New Zealand's early provision of old age pensions likely made a difference. Contemporary research on suicide, public policy, and the elderly in the United States found that state-level support for the low-income elderly "may not only relieve financial stress on elderly households but foster [through assisting mobility] social interaction among the elderly and between the elderly and various helping professionals."[35]

At the turn of the century, an insulated economy, considerable state employment, a modest but unique welfare safety net, and political talk about fairness contributed to security and satisfaction. Outside commentators who visited New Zealand and Australia in the early twentieth century felt the former had gone further to promote the spirit of equality in the face of individualism.[36] David Hamer detected political calculation in every move but conceded that "the Liberal reforms became the first major means of defining a distinctive national identity and purpose for New Zealand."[37] Leaders of the reforming Liberal Party may have claimed more credit than they deserved and benefited from market forces that sustained farm and national prosperity, but Peter Coleman noted an important point about Liberal rule from 1893 to 1912: "Thereafter, no party could win office without being responsible to electoral needs."[38] At the village level by 1910, a significant number of residents were employed by the state on railways, on public works, and as community workers, post office officials, schoolmasters, and policemen. And there were abundant villages with public employment.

Queensland was aligned with male individualism; it was a jurisdiction superior for anonymity and full of hazards. Several cases can convey an impression of the society's deracination well into the twentieth century. Under oath, brush clearer William Hibbins commented about his work partner, James King, that "during the two and a half years he was with me he never disclosed his proper name."[39] The only person who knew much about labourer Bob Lynn was a fellow worker of no fixed address who remarked at an inquest in July 1924 that Bob was so reserved he did not even reveal his surname: "I cannot say if the deceased was ever married. I cannot say what regiment he served with at the front. The deceased never told me his age." A publican testified that "he never spoke to me of his relatives or of his friends." Witnesses did know that Bob suffered from drink.[40] Labourer Charles Phillips appeared to have constant work, but he drifted, "living in lonely places with one mate only, coming into town about once in 12 months."[41] Anonymity seemed a feature of Queensland masculine bush culture. Additionally, many country Queenslanders lived in a cycle of working, drinking, sleeping, and working. Available employment was gruelling. A transient male workforce sweated on sheep and cattle grazing stations, on sugar cane plantations, in mines and forests, at public works, and on wharves.[42] Periodic droughts could ruin rural men toiling on their own account. The high ratio of men to women in many foreboding places contributed to masculine realms that prized independence, toughness, and mateship. Immoderate drinking thrived, because towns had few amenities beyond licensed hotels and on sheep and cattle stations there was little to do outside of work. Voters elected the Labor Party to office in 1915, and it dominated for forty years, but Queensland still had a lacklustre reform record when compared to New Zealand. More fundamentally, to benefit working men, Queensland Labor's conservative leadership looked chiefly to the progress of primary industry rather than social programs. All Queensland governments warmed to talk of development.[43]

Relief for worn-out inebriates and aged men and women in Queensland was basic to the threshold of punitive. Desperate people appeared before a magistrate, pleaded destitution, subjected themselves to a police investigation, and petitioned for admission to the Dunwich Asylum on North Stradbroke Island. The data set contains twelve cases of people who committed suicide there. A self-styled poet of the bush leapt to his death from Brisbane's Storey Bridge in 1944, hoping to publicize conditions at Dunwich. For thirty years, this former Scottish footballer had travelled around reciting his poems in camps and hotels. When he lost his pension, likely for alcohol abuse, he entered Dunwich. In a suicide note he alleged sexual abuse of the feeble-minded and blind. "So, I, Adam Morrow, shall die gratified in trying to help those aged and blind men residing in Dunwich, earthly purgatory."[44] Dunwich concentrated the poor elderly, imposed regulations, maintained a detention ward, and had a frightful reputation.[45] However, the burdens of the elderly transcended welfare regimes. Much of their distress originated in ailments, senility, and uncaring families. Elements of even New Zealand's welfare system, moreover, were inadequate. A few elderly folk residing in New Zealand charitable homes – inmates, as they were known in the early twentieth century – complained of poor food and maltreatment.[46]

Old pensioner John Chorley of New Plymouth drowned himself in December 1900. "They gave me the life of a dog and I could not stand it no longer." Cold draughts and poor food wore him down. He and a friend at the home had been begging briskets from a friendly butcher.[47]

Despite social policy differences, New Zealand and Queensland shared some labour practices and related social attributes. Rural employers in both societies exploited swagmen, whose entire lives followed a succession of dead-end seasonal jobs.[48] Wellington magistrate and philanthropist Edwin Arnold compared "swaggies" to "sea dogs" because of their wanderings and love of a spree. He worried especially about the gap between the fifties, when "they are not able to do a day's work as when they were strong," and the age of sixty-five, when they were eligibility for the state pension. Not many manual labourers could work until sixty-five, and, observed Arnold, "in many cases their own children don't want them."[49] His impressions, born from his experiences as an inspector of jails and asylums, were confirmed in numerous suicide inquests. Few cared about the men who lived rough in tents, barns, and huts. For example, when he was asked to identify a casual labourer who had hanged himself, New Zealand farmer William Trail, who had hired him, said, "I did not ask him for his name and he did not tell me."[50] A Queensland constable in 1924 failed to discover a dead man's identity, but the setting for the suicide is instructive: "The place where the body was found was a camping ground for swagmen."[51] Into the early twentieth century, both New Zealand and Queensland possessed a camp culture of heavy drinking and relatively lean kin structures; however, New Zealand also had features that contradicted the picture of deracinated males, because it had experienced the group migration of Anglicans to Canterbury and Presbyterians to Otago. These organized settlements and other compact coastal communities contributed to identity and social management. Small towns proliferated in New Zealand. In Michael King's estimation, the lower middle class in these places established the climate of opinion. "They formed and staffed a web of social, sectarian, cultural, and recreational organizations designed to promulgate their social attitudes."[52] By contrast, in Queensland, according to Ross Fitzgerald, the emphasis on farming, mining, and manual labour "worked against the growth of manufacturing, the influence of Brisbane and the existence of a politically powerful middle-class."[53]

New Zealand labourers worked seasonally on grazing stations like their Queensland counterparts, although from roughly 1900 forward a population of small farmers grew into a more significant element than in Queensland. Refrigerated shipping and the related growth of the frozen meat industry had already commenced an optimistic rural diversification; this expansion was accompanied by the subdivision of many large grazing stations and the purchase of Maori land for Pakeha farmers. Entrepreneurs at the turn of the century built freezing works up and down country.[54] Government land distribution, finance measures, and promotional literature accented a hoped-for conversion of casual labourers into a property-holding yeomanry spread across green acres under a smiling sun. The author of an article on agriculture in *The New Zealand Official Year-Book* (1902) remarked that "in the near future, we shall have a thrifty and numerous body of yeomanry settled throughout the country."[55] This prediction was almost borne out. A sizable dairy industry emerged in the first decade of the twentieth century, and by the 1920s it accounted for over a third of the value of the country's farm production, a proportion close to that of pastoral production. By 1933, 534 cheese factories or butter creameries received milk from nearly 70,000 milk producers.[56] Many families did not own land or herds but lived on someone else's farm and milked cows on shares.[57] Nevertheless, average real income per working household head surpassed Australia's and fell only slightly behind that of Canada or the United States.[58] "Farming," wrote Tom Brooking, "enjoyed a 'golden age' from the recovery of the late 1890s to the depression of 1921."[59] Surpluses could be earned from a few hundred sheep or a score of cows. Marginal farms appeared in the bush, and for a while their increase promoted village growth.[60]

World prices for cheese and butter fat started falling after 1920, when European countries resumed exporting dairy products after the war. Constant increases in the efficiency of production, a source of stress to farmers, enabled New Zealand producers to remain solvent. The fall in prices for other farm produce was worse, so suffering farmers moved into dairying exactly when profit margins narrowed (see graph 3.8). When farms failed, farm labourers and villages suffered. Little wonder that witnesses at inquests into suicides on farms and in rural villages commented on the stresses and fears of failure that ground men down.[61] In New Zealand four out of ten suicides (419 cases, or 39.8 per cent) committed by men working in agricultural production were farmers; in Queensland, three out of ten (183 cases, or 30.0 per cent). In Queensland far more workers who took their own lives laboured on grazing stations (see table 3.1).

Graph 3.8
Agricultural production and dairy capacity in New Zealand, 1921–50

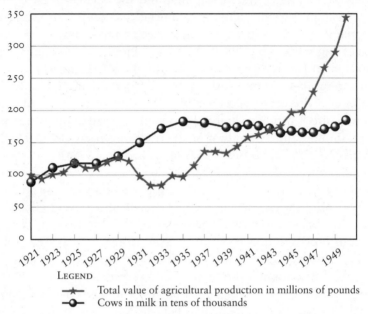

LEGEND
—★— Total value of agricultural production in millions of pounds
—⊙— Cows in milk in tens of thousands

The Queensland crude suicide rate, based on the official number of suicides, spiked in 1930; the rate for men exceeded anything witnessed before (see graphs 3.2 and 3.5). Worry afflicted rural producers during the double crisis of drought and depression in the early 1930s. Lambing failures were the norm, and pastoralists cut scrub to feed breeding stock.[62] But it was not only the rural conditions that had deteriorated; in fact, as we will see in chapter 4, the suicide rate among men dependant on agricultural income had actually peaked during the postwar recession in 1920. The Great Depression struck all economic sectors; in July 1933 over a quarter (27.9 per cent) of all waged or salaried Australian men were unemployed.[63] The first years of the depression were the worst. In an effort to prevent the unemployed from congregating in camps, the conservatives who ousted the Labor Party in 1929 required single men to travel from centre to centre to draw ration coupons. In rural Queensland, wages were cut, and the government removed half the workforce from the jurisdiction of labour courts, which had normally arbitrated between rural unions and employers.[64] When Labor returned to office in 1932, it initiated a moderate inflationary program of spend-

Table 3.1
Leading agricultural-sector occupations represented among suicide inquests: New Zealand and Queensland males

New Zealand	N	%	Queensland	N	%
Farm worker/rural labourer	429	40.7	Farmer/selector	183	30.0
Farmer	419	39.8	Rural labourer	163	26.6
Farmer partly retired	30	2.8	Jackeroo/cowboy	30	4.9
Shepherd	17	1.6	Grazier	30	4.9
Farm manager	16	1.5	Shearer	28	4.6
Rabbiter	10	.9	Stockman	18	2.9
Well driller	9	.9	Station manager	11	1.8
Horse trainer	8	.8	Kangaroo shooter	7	1.1
Share milker	7	.7	Cane cutter	6	1.0
Grazier	6	.6	Cane farmer	6	1.0
Orchardist	6	.6	Cotton farmer	6	1.0
Jockey	6	.6	Bushman	6	1.0
Shearer	5	.5	Dairyman	5	.9
Groom	5	.5	Stock dealer	4	.7
Bushman	4	.4	Horse trainer	4	.7
Caretaker on rural property	4	.4	Boundary rider	4	.7
Market gardener	4	.4	Wool presser	4	.7
Drover	3	.3	Station cook	3	.6
Apiarist	3	.3	Prickly pear cutter	3	.6
Jackeroo/cowboy	2	.2	Shepherd	3	.6
Stockman	2	.2	Caretaker	3	.6
Station cook	2	.2	Ploughman	2	.4
Orchard worker	2	.2	Shearer and butcher	2	.4
Dairy factory hand	2	.2	Groom	2	.4
Flax cutter	2	.2	Cattle dealer	2	.4
Other agricultural occupations	55	5.2	Other agricultural occupations	76	12.4
Total agricultural sector	1,058	100.0	Total agricultural sector	611	100.0
Agricultural: percentage of all men		31.7	Agricultural: percentage of all men		30.7
Other occupations and pensioners	2,283	68.3	Other occupations and pensioners	1,381	69.3
Total	3,336	100.0	Total	1,992	100.0

ing and granted relief workers a full basic wage. Thereafter, according to Raymond Evans, "state politics moved inexorably rightward."[65]

The New Zealand suicide rate peaked in 1928 and again in 1932. Rural New Zealand was hit very hard by the Great Depression; typically, the incomes of large farmers with employees, farmers on their own account, and farm labourers plummeted by 50 per cent from 1926 to 1936. Some costs eased, but debts were not subject to deflation. Witnesses' comments expose the conversion of material hardships into psychological tragedy. Inquests relate how people's economic circumstances affected mental states. Financial worry precipitated nervous breakdowns; men overwhelmed by loss of employment or debt sought medical treatment for chronic insomnia and depressed spirits. Material hardship had psychological consequences, and men and women of the time recognized the association.

In the early twentieth century, New Zealand experienced demographic shifts associated with a transformation from a frontier to an urban society. By the 1870s natural increase had become more important than immigration as a source of population growth. The government's initiatives to combat infant mortality affected natural increase and reduced the emotional strain that, according to the suicide data, particularly affected women when their children died.[66] By 1900 the male-female ratio had become balanced in urban centres, which from the 1890s to the 1920s grew in size and number.[67] Demography cannot explain everything; a more balanced sex ratio is only part of the story of gender and troubles. Charlotte Macdonald has insisted that cultural and political values bear on lives; gender analysis must "encompass the social organization of sexual difference."[68]

New Zealand's first Labour government, elected in 1935, reached out to the countryside to alleviate rural stress. Legislation provided mortgage relief that reduced farm foreclosures; a primary products marketing act guaranteed a fixed price for dairy products.[69] A sharp drop in the suicide rate for the rural sector in 1936 could have stemmed from these measures. There was hope. "People seemed to have more choices," wrote Tim Frank. Hugh Somerset compiled his remarkable sociological study of life in rural Canterbury in 1938, just when these measures were having an effect. He detected a shift in mood; farmers could make some headway. "The general outlook," Somerset wrote, "is one of optimism."[70] As a consequence of social legislation, women and children at the end of the 1930s were less dependent on male breadwinners; "it seemed less imperative for males, especially the old and the very young, to work."[71] World War II restored rural commodity prices (see graph 3.8). The shockingly high casualty rates of World War I were not matched in this conflict.[72] Many women found wartime employment, and although governments attempted to restore domesticity after the war, that inclination was watered down by the need to hire teachers, nurses, and civil servants. Melanie Nolan sees a flourishing diversity of lifestyles in postwar New Zealand.[73] In their study of occupational stratification in New Zealand's ten largest centres, Miles Fairburn and S.J. Haslett discovered that from 1946 to 1951 the proportion of semi-skilled and unskilled labourers among household heads dropped considerably. Full employment and rising wages made this an unusually good time for young adults, who could now afford to establish households.[74] Comparable trends affected Australia; unemployment for men, according to the 1947 census taken in June, had dropped to a mere one in thirty (3.6 per cent) and real wages were rising.[75] It is understandable that suicide rates in New Zealand and Queensland during and after World War II fell to roughly half what they had been at the start of the Great Depression. Notice that the slide in suicide rates after the Depression is mainly attributable to declines in the male rates (see graphs 3.5 and 3.6).[76]

Therapies for the treatment of mental illness were similar in the two societies, although New Zealand provided more resources earlier for mental health. It established a separate Mental Health Department in 1908; by then the government was already operating seven regional hospitals for mental illness: Auckland, Porirua, Wellington, Nelson, Hokitika, Christchurch, and Seacliff.[77] Facilities were added, closed, and expanded over the next fifty years. The regional principle remained in place. A private hospital, Ashburn Hall near Dunedin, opened in 1882 and treated affluent patients throughout the period under study. A special facility prepared for shell-shocked solders at Hanmer Springs adapted to peacetime and began accepting neurasthenic men and women in 1922.

Queensland concentrated its facilities in the southeast; regional care came late. Private hospitals or clinics did not open until after 1920. New Zealand permitted voluntary admissions – "voluntary borders" – to mental hospitals in 1912; Queensland waited until 1940.[78] New Zealand's Social Security Act of 1938 initiated free health benefits that included mental health treatment.[79] New Zealand doctors facilitated a higher admission rate to mental hospitals than counterparts in Queensland (see graph 3.9). However, no relationship appears between these initiatives in psychiatric care and suicide rates; greater accessibility did not necessarily translate into a lower suicide rate since New Zealand's rate was already below Queensland's years before the surge in hospital admissions. Furthermore, the sustained drop in Queensland's suicide rate transpired without a rise in psychiatric admissions. Therapies may have been more effective earlier in New Zealand than Queensland, but

Graph 3.9
Patients admitted to mental hospitals per 100,000 people: New Zealand and Queensland, 1890–1950

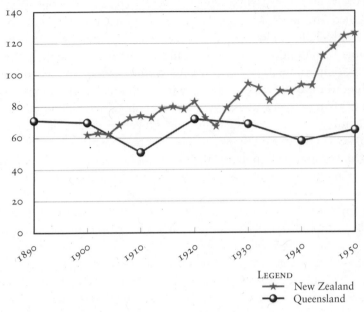

LEGEND
New Zealand
Queensland

SOURCES: Reports on asylums or mental hospitals in *Appendix to the Journals of the House of Representatives of New Zealand*; *Queensland Statistical Yearbooks*.

that hypothesis can be neither proven nor dismissed. One mental health issue cannot be discerned from admissions data or the history of psychiatry, and that is alcohol abuse. Heavy consumption of spirits declined after 1920 as a result of the continuation of wartime temperance efforts. Coincidently, witnesses at inquests gave fewer harrowing descriptions of delirium tremens.[80]

New Zealand seems the more caring society. The divergence in the suicide rates of the two jurisdictions from the early 1900 to the 1920s could thus owe something to differences between their rural economies and to Queensland's relatively "hard" and New Zealand's relatively "soft" political culture. Progressive innovation characterized New Zealand in two periods – 1890 to 1912 and 1935 to 1949; social caution and flat-out resource exploitation concurrently gripped Queensland. Historians Michael Bassett and William Oliver have accented decency behind

New Zealand's ever-closer embrace of the welfare state. As Oliver put it, "when external circumstances defeated the self-reliance of even the most deserving … it was hard to resist the argument that self- reliance had to be supplemented by a greater reliance upon the resources of society as a whole."[81] Comparable shocks rattled Queensland, but they failed to inspire remarkable reform passions. In Bassett's estimation, vague egalitarianism rather than ideologies drove New Zealand reformers. Such egalitarianism did not suffuse Queensland's political life. For much of the first half of the twentieth century, New Zealand sustained a good standard of living and fostered hope. A dyed-in-the-wool adherent of Durkheim might claim that New Zealand had achieved the greater degree of integration, but interest in such a distillation pales when placed against details from an inquiry set amidst real lives.

So far, so good. But there is a problem with any attempt to link suicide rates tightly with socio-economic history. Even if the impact of social legislation reduced distress, it would have had modest importance for suicide rates. Beneath the peaks and valleys of rates, there was an enduring stratum of self-destructive events that may not have been responsive to macro-economic trends or social policies. This observation concurs with recent findings by Bijou Yang Lester, who noticed that the several theories on a relationship between the economy and suicide rates all assumed that other factors played a role and that there was a natural suicide rate which, in the United States, was roughly 6 per 100,000.[82] Durkheim's similar observation about the stability of suicide rates in specific countries served his claim to have found a suicidogenic current. Lester ventures no such claim, although the very idea of a natural suicide rate is a retrograde step toward Durkheim since it can lead us away from the motives and intentions of the individuals committing the act and into the superficiality of analysis based on aggregate data.

If there is a *natural* rate, it should not be construed as *natural* and should not be attributed to an abstraction like Durkheim's current but related to the aggregate of real-life circumstances, some of which endure as motives for suicide year after year. In the case of New Zealand and Queensland, there are good historical reasons for a so-called natural rate or core set of suicides with common motives persisting across jurisdictions and over a long time. The two jurisdictions had commonalities as young settler societies. There was "a porous industrial environment" between New Zealand and Australia. People, ideas, institutions, and capital drifted back and forth across the Tasman Sea.[83]

Common problems, connected with the normal course of events, over which people could impose little control, afflicted men and women in both societies; arguably, these problems comprised the bulk of events adding stress below the peaks and valleys. Marital troubles, physical ailments, mental illnesses, and other difficulties transcended place and time; these motives arose from eternal human concerns. Severe economic catastrophes could exacerbate these motives and foster suicide motives of their own. As well, hard times have long-term psychological consequences and a lagged impact on people, making it difficult neatly to correlate periods of economic distress with trends in suicide rates. In chapter 4 the difficulties of linking an economic slump to suicide rates are explained, with examples from the case files.

Ronald Maris proposed that many, if not most, suicides result from long-term, rather than sudden, life crises.[84] The idea of crises encountered and accumulated across the life course helps to explain the relative steadiness over time of suicide rates in given jurisdictions, because rates only partly reflect short-term changes or good or ill political and economic events; a lot can be transpiring in a life. State benefits and medical assistance, for example, could not have checked every emotional tide that washed over each individual suffering a crisis brought on by work, debt, ill health, aging, or combinations of these difficulties. Societal, political, and medical factors lose some pertinence in view of the fact that suicide rates for Queensland and New Zealand essentially converged in the 1930s, moving first upward and then downward together (see graph 3.7).

The decline of suicide rates that began in the late 1930s and continued during and after World War II marks a historic conjuncture. Economic circumstances started to improve in the late 1930s, and the better economic times persisted, reducing for many individuals the accumulation of shocks over the life course. Postwar prosperity, decent opportunities for work, and a surge of consumer rewards after a miserable twenty years of deprivation likely contributed to less abject despair for a while. It is conceivable, too, that medical care and a diffusion of information about physical and mental health tempered cases of emotional and mental anguish. From the 1920s to the 1950s, psychiatrists worked beyond the walls of feared mental hospitals and reached more people. Private psychiatric practices expanded appreciably in the 1930s and 1940s. So much progressed on the economic, social, and medical fronts that it would be wrong to attribute falling suicide rates to a couple of separate ameliorative factors. Suicide studies and social history should not be distilled into a handful of decontextualized variables. A *natural* suicide rate is not natural in the sense of being a biological function that drives a few people lemming-like; rather, it expresses a sum of personal circumstances. The picture is compounded, too, by the blending in everyone's life of such diverse sources of stress as romantic trials, short-term economic shocks and crises, the intrusions of wars and epidemics, and the aging process in relation to available social support and much else. Apart from the philosophical challenge that real-life events pose for a concept such as a natural suicide rate, the diversity of setbacks challenges attempts to isolate a single master motive for suicide in each case.

There is another conclusion to draw at the end of this discussion of rates and jurisdictions. In the introduction I observed that variations in suicide rates among countries have puzzled writers for more than a century. I asked why Australia, Canada, New Zealand, and the United States have had more or less moderate rates over a long time, while Greece has had a stunningly low rate and Hungary a remarkably high one also over many decades. The variations in rates among countries likely include an error factor that is more pronounced in some countries, but they may also express relatively short-term economic conditions and social policy. As well, variation may put across the idea that truly distinctive cultures treat the crisis events of the life course in importantly distinct ways. Courtship, marriage, martial troubles, childbirth, child-rearing, work, unemployment, menopause, aging, and terminal illnesses are regarded differently. Suicide itself is subject to cultural sanctions or approval in particular circumstances. While the data set is limited to two jurisdictions, the case-file information helps explain a mainstay of suicide studies – the presence of distinct national suicide rates – with multiple arguments. Moreover, these arguments are backed by evidence on errors in data generation, on how motives are fostered or eased by political and economic events, and on how cultural practices may assuage crises in the life course.

Besides rates, data in other easily understood formats pilot suicide research and, like the exploration of rates, leave behind awkward questions. Two examples of other data formats complete this chapter. Percentages of suicides by month and the distribution of suicides by age cohorts divulge striking facts about nature's seasons and seasons in the lives of men and women.

SEASONALITY

Analysts of suicide from the mid-nineteenth century to the late twenti-eth have puzzled over a seasonal pattern that continues to perplex scholars.[85] Whether in the Northern or the Southern Hemisphere, sui-cides have peaked in spring or summer and tapered off in winter.[86] The fact that an identical seasonal pattern exists in both hemispheres inti-mates a natural rhythm which could originate in physiology, the eco-nomics of horticulture and animal husbandry, or some combination (see graphs 3.10–3.15).

Perhaps the seasonal pattern expresses neurobiological functions traceable to abnormal levels of particular biochemicals in the brains of individuals who completed or attempted suicide. Among the bio-chemicals considered in conjunction with suicide are cortisol, serotonin (5-HT), and norepinephrine. The stress hormone cortisol could be con-nected with seasonality. The increased production of this hormone dur-ing reactions to anxiety and fear has been associated with neuronal cell damage, depression, and higher suicide risk. Cortisol in blood serum also undergoes diurnal variation. The highest levels occur in early morning, lower levels in the evening, and the lowest several hours after the onset of sleep. Daylight and darkness affect cortisol production through information transmitted from retina to hypothalamus.[87] Cor-tisol is subject to a seasonal fluctuation on account of variation in daylight. If the seasonal pattern of suicides partly expresses hormonal fluctuation, we should see summer spikes at high latitudes, with their white nights, and a progressive flattening of the curve until seasonality vanishes altogether in equatorial regions. Nothing about society and psyche is ever so simple. Data from nineteenth- and twentieth-century studies do not show progressive flattening toward the equator. Pearson correlation tests indicate strong associations between several jurisdic-tions at different latitudes. It is not helpful for the theory that the curves for Norway in 1866–73 and Italy in 1869–73 produced a Pearson's r of .864 at the 0.01 level (see table 3.2).

The absence of a neat incremental relationship between latitude and the seasonal pattern may express a bias in reporting. The universal under-reporting of suicides by drowning may have pulled down the spring and summer counts in cold-winter jurisdictions. In these coun-tries suicide by drowning was more difficult in winter, and that charac-teristic produced more deaths by hanging, shooting, cutting, and poisoning, which could seldom be mistaken for accidents. When ponds,

Graph 3.10
Nordic countries and Russia: main population centres at 55 to 60 degrees north

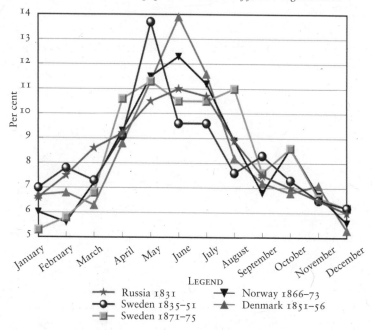

SOURCES: Enrico Morselli, *Suicide: An Essay on Comparative Moral Statistics* (New York: A. Appleton and Co., 1882), passim; S.A.K Strahan, *Suicide and Insanity: A Physiological and Sociological Study* (London: Swan & Sonnenschein, 1893), 156.

Graph 3.11
North European jurisdictions: main population centres at 50 to 53 degrees north

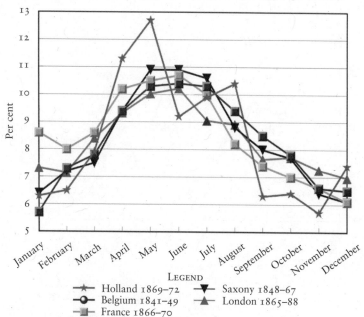

SOURCES: See graph 3.10.

Graph 3.12
Middle European jurisdictions: main population centres at 45 to 48 degrees north

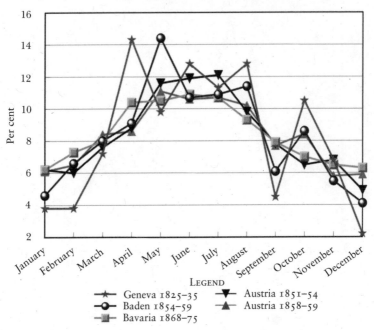

SOURCES: See graph 3.10.

Graph 3.13
Number of suicides per diem in a population of 1,000,000 persons: Australia, 1900–15

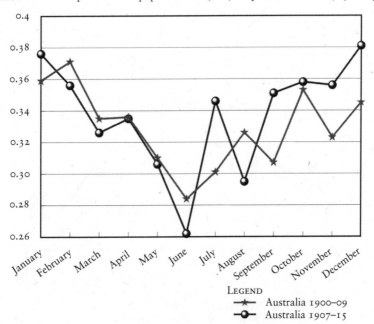

SOURCE: G.H. Knibbs, "Mortality," Appendix A, in Australia, Bureau of Census and Statistics, *Census of the Commonwealth of Australia…*1911, vol. 1, *Statistician's Report* (Melbourne: McCarron, Bird, and Co., 1917), 428.

Graph 3.14
Monthly distribution of suicides in Southern Hemisphere jurisdictions: main population centres at 27 to 45 degrees south

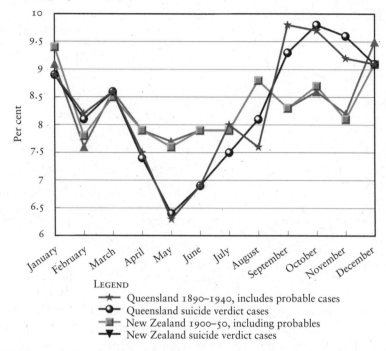

LEGEND
—★— Queensland 1890–1940, includes probable cases
—○— Queensland suicide verdict cases
—■— New Zealand 1900–50, including probables
—▼— New Zealand suicide verdict cases

SOURCES: See graph 3.10.

Graph 3.15
Monthly distribution of New Zealand suicides: urban and rural locales, 1900–50

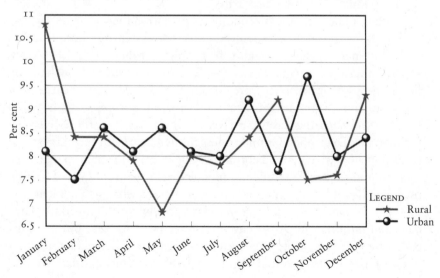

LEGEND
—★— Rural
—○— Urban

Table 3.2
Correlations of monthly distributions of suicides for selected places and years

County and period	Italy 1869–73	Spain 1906–55	Mexico 1930–39	Queensland all cases 1890–1940	New Zealand all cases 1900–40
Russia 1831	.963**	.959**	.308	-.823**	-.678*
Sweden 1871–75	.807**	.873**	.063	-.705*	-.582*
Norway 1866–73	.864**	.919**	.237	-.730**	-.551
Denmark 1851–56	.871**	.891**	.194	–.758**	–.618*
Holland 1869–72	.807**	.778**	.126	–.869**	–.561
London 1865–88	.913**	.944**	.271	–852*	–599*

SOURCES: See graph 3.10.

* Correlation is significant at the 0.05 level (2-tailed).
** Correlation is significant at the 0.01 level (2-tailed).

lakes, and rivers were ice-free, death by drowning beckoned and could be deemed accidental by honest mistake or friendly misjudgment. More summer than winter suicides were wrongly attributed to accidents in hard-winter regions. In Southern Hemisphere jurisdictions, with their relatively warm winters, deaths by drowning wrongly reported as accidental were apt to be spread across the year. A latitude effect on bureaucratic conduct cannot be discounted.

There is a plausible socio-economic explanation for seasonality. Farmers and farm labourers experienced greater stress during the spring and early summer. By then, roughly from mid-October to mid-February, grazers and grain farmers in New Zealand and Queensland had run down their savings from the previous harvest, wool clip, or cattle sale; credit was important at this juncture. For sheep grazers, costs began to peak when shearing crews arrived, mainly from early November through late December. Grain farmers needed help with the harvest and threshing in January and February.[88] Sugar cane farmers in northern Queensland required credit early in a new year before they had harvest revenue. Rural producers spent money before earning payments on their staple. Dairy farmers received payment on a different basis. They collected monthly advances based on milk fat delivered, but at year's end, often in late June, the butter creamery or cheese factory paid bonuses based on profit.[89] Agrarian operators faced financial and climate stresses from mid-October to mid-February and received their largest payments from March to July. The cycle of stressful and good times helps explain a seasonality of suicide for owners and operators.

Slightly different seasonal factors affected farm labourers. They were stretched for cash while waiting for the busy period of the summer and fall. They could expect wages to begin late in the year. Their income resumed before that of employers.[90] Spring and summer should have heralded good times, and possibly for younger men, all other things being equal, they did. Calvin Schmid suggested that, since spring was the mating season, it left shattered romances in its wake. The New Zealand data, with its good age material, shows, however, that young single males encountered romantic problems throughout the year.[91] There was no seasonal special on broken hearts, but it seems likely that spring forewarned older men of hard work ahead, and they had little hope of anything better. In the late nineteenth and early twentieth centuries a rural itinerate labourer in New Zealand worked about 160 days a year.[92] Conditions had improved by 1936, when farm labourers reported losing around seven weeks of employment.[93] The ages of rural labourers who committed suicide, as well as the qualitative evidence from witnesses and from suicide notes, indicate debilities and aging.[94] With the return of shearing or harvesting, older rural labourers realized that they could eventually face destitution, vagrancy, or charity. When they left boarding houses and rooming houses and headed into the countryside, they felt the indignities of age.[95] It was not just toil that drained men; they had to trek by "shanks' mare," competing for jobs when they arrived at a farm or sheep or cattle station.

The living conditions described by one young labourer must have been devastating to older men who had known little else. In his diary he confided that he was "wet, weary, hungry, grubby, and homeless."[96] He lay awake at times in filthy shacks, overcome with alcoholic nightmares, bitter repentance, and physical wretchedness.[97] Older men could look back and wonder what might have been. At the age of seventy-four, Fred Williams was poor, single, and could work no more. According to a sergeant of police, "he was a labourer and went to the country to work and would return to the city." He bequeathed his pawn tickets to a barman and his belongings to the boarding house.[98]

In New Zealand, shearers during the early 1900s would start in coastal Hawke's Bay in early October and move southward, finishing in late February at the high-country stations of the lower South Island. A few workers might pick up haymaking work in December. Threshing mills could extend the employment of some men from March until June. In his history of rural New Zealand labour, John Martin cited observations from the late nineteenth century to the effect that only 30 per cent of the unskilled labouring population could find work for the entire year; the rest were found on the road.[99] This impression may exaggerate underemployment, but it recorded a struggle that left casualties. Calvin Schmid was shocked to discover that in the city of Seattle during the years 1914–25 the highest suicide rate among all occupational groups (143.8 per 100,000) belonged to agricultural and forestry workers, who, as he put it, were mainly single, homeless, and mobile – "a group in which personal demoralization is very high."[100] This subpopulation of transient but essential rural workers appears to have been at risk in other jurisdictions around the world as well.

The rural-stress hypothesis can be tested by looking at the character of the communities where suicides were committed and by considering occupations (see graphs 3.15–3.18). If suicides in rural areas and among rural occupations had a more pronounced seasonality than in urban centres and occupations, the rural-stress hypothesis is plausible. New Zealand, with its dairy farms, may have been slightly less reliant upon itinerate labourers; urban-based labourers may have been more rooted in their trades and places than were their counterparts in Queensland. As well, New Zealand dairying did not call upon seasonal labour as commonly as the wool, meat, and sugar industries that predominated in Queensland. The young men who typically made up New Zealand's dairy labour force originated in the community where they worked. If they migrated into towns and cities, they remained there. They did not leave farm employment on account of the seasonality of work but for better prospects.[101] Transient occupations connected with cattle and sheep stations were more numerous among men who committed suicide in Queensland than in New Zealand. There are reasons to think that the careers of rural and urban labourers were likely more compartmentalized in New Zealand than in Queensland.

Farmers appeared prominently among New Zealand suicides. In our data set for that jurisdiction, 431 farmers, or 12.5 per cent of all male suicides, killed themselves. The comparable figure for Queensland was 171 farmers, or 8.6 per cent of all male suicides (see table 3.1). Seasonal rural crises affected both societies because of their substantial agricultural sectors, but the movement of itinerant labour between countryside and city may not have been as great in New Zealand. Consequently, the country had an urban as well as a rural seasonal distribution.

Graph 3.16
New Zealand suicides: rural and urban occupations, 1900–50

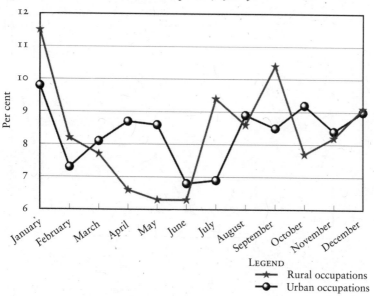

LEGEND
Rural occupations
Urban occupations

Graph 3.17
Queensland suicides: urban and rural locales, 1890–1940

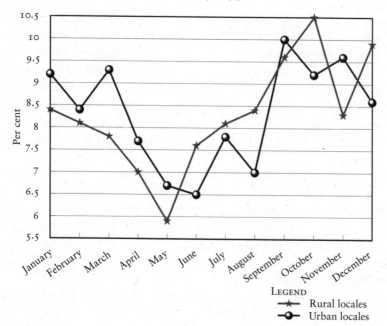

LEGEND
Rural locales
Urban locales

Graph 3.18
Monthly distribution of Queensland suicides: rural and urban occupations, 1890–1940

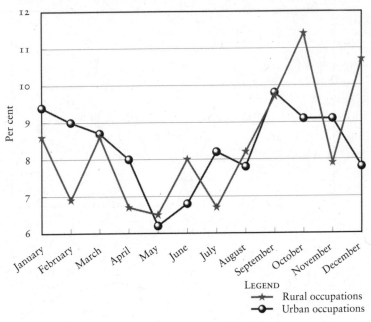

Seasonality in suicide opens a rich but inconclusive discussion of physiology and society. A bounty of daylight hours could have intensified the restlessness, insomnia, and anxiety of beleaguered individuals. Seasonal variation in suicides intimates an interaction of biochemical and socio-economic processes, especially among rural workers and farmers; however, it serves, too, as a reminder that even when we see a pattern in suicide data, even when we can meld diverse pieces of information into theories, uncertainty and contestation linger.

THE CRISES IN LIFE'S SEASONS

In the late twentieth century, suicide studies pointed to a youth crisis. Reports for many countries from the 1960s to the 1990s highlighted increases in suicide rates among fifteen- to nineteen-year-olds. To judge by media attention, wrote Ronald Maris in 1985, "adolescent suicide is probably *the* issue in suicidology right now."[102] During the late 1980s teen suicides in New Zealand cornered enormous media and political attention.[103] International reports confirmed that the suicide rates of the young were rising, but not everywhere. David Lester noted in 1991 that some countries experienced a decline in youth suicides.[104] For example, in Italy rates for a century pointed toward a decline of youth suicides and an increase among the elderly.[105] Nevertheless, the increases among the young – if official data are to be trusted – occurred in enough countries that youth suicides were tracked by the United Nations publication *The Progress of Nations* and scrutinized by the World Health Organization.[106] New Zealand, Australia, and Canada had rising rates for adolescents. Adolescents from first peoples had shockingly high rates in several jurisdictions. Suicide rates among fifteen- to nineteen-year-old New Zealanders increased from 5.8 in 1970 to 31.1 in 1990. From 1987 to 1997 young people aged fifteen to twenty-four had the highest rate in New Zealand. In Australia the rate for people aged fifteen to nineteen rose from 4.1 in the period 1921–25 to 11.5 in 1996–98; the rate for people twenty to twenty-four increased from 7.7 to 22.2.[107] Since young adults have longer to live than older adults, the rising rates for young people have been particularly alarming. As well, governments in many societies – certainly those in Australia and New Zealand – assume that their communities have nurtured youth.

The startling jump in youth suicide rates in New Zealand and Australia dinted self-assurance that these societies were glorious places for raising children. It also ran counter to a long-prevailing maxim in suicide studies. Until the 1960s, suicide studies routinely reported a positive and almost axiomatic association between age and suicide rates, particularly for men. For women, the suicide rate peaked at somewhat younger cohorts (see graphs 3.19 and 3.20). Ronald Maris pronounced the positive association between rates and ages for white males in Chicago in 1964, a major research result along with the observation that suicide rates for white females peaked earlier.[108] The New Zealand and Queensland data covering roughly the same half-century as the American studies showed similar relationships between age and rates. Elderly New Zealand men had extremely high suicide rates for the first three decades of the twentieth century, as did Queensland men (see graphs 3.21 and 3.22). The normalized age rates for New Zealand and the crude rate for Queensland men reaffirm that the elderly were at high risk until almost mid-century. The high crude rates for Queensland men from thirty to fifty in the first decade of the twentieth century captures the hardships of the "federation drought," a related depression, and a depression after the South African (Boer) War (1899–1902). In New

Graph 3.19
Suicide rates for age cohorts of Chicago and Seattle men, American (white) men, and men in thirty-nine countries

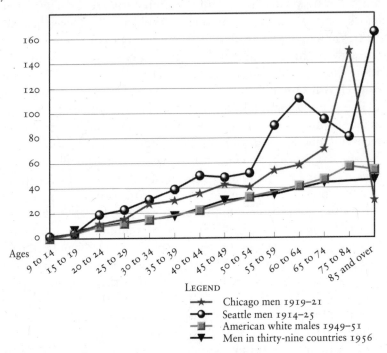

LEGEND

    ★   Chicago men 1919–21
    ○   Seattle men 1914–25
    ■   American white males 1949–51
    ▼   Men in thirty-nine countries 1956

SOURCES: Ruth Shonle Cavan, *Suicide* (New York: Russell & Russell, 1965; reprint of 1928 ed.), 313; Calvin F. Schmid, *Suicide in Seattle, 1914 to 1925* (Seattle: University of Washington Press, 1928), 31; Jack Porter Gibbs and Walter T. Martin, *Status Integration and Suicide: A Sociological Study* (Eugene: University of Oregon Books, 1964), 70; André Haim, *Adolescent Suicide,* trans. A.M. Sheridan Smith (New York: International Universities Press, 1970), 100.

Zealand and Queensland women's age rates contrast slightly with men's rates. For women, the middle-age years were high-risk (see graphs 3.23 and 3.24).[109] But the small numbers for women and missing ages meant limited estimates for Queensland.

No sooner had adolescent suicide become a familiar concept or new orthodoxy at the end of the millennium than the suicide rate of middle-aged men attracted notice.[110] "Grim reaper suicide now moves through generations," reported a leading New Zealand newspaper in late 2006. "Suicide isn't just a youth tragedy. Almost half the New Zealanders who take their own lives are men in their middle years."[111] American suicide data in early 2008 indicated an identical shift toward mid-life suicides.[112] These reports and the earlier ones on youth suicides make

Graph 3.20

Suicide rates for age cohorts of Chicago and Seattle women, American (white) women, and women in thirty-nine countries

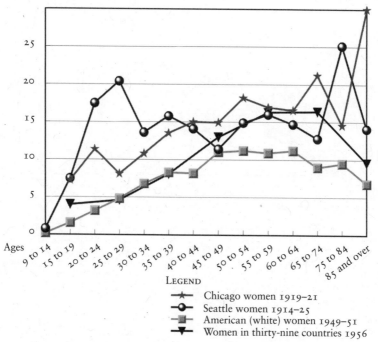

LEGEND

—★— Chicago women 1919–21
—○— Seattle women 1914–25
—■— American (white) women 1949–51
—▼— Women in thirty-nine countries 1956

SOURCES: See graph 3.19.

use of age cohorts which, as we are about to see, are vital for investigating the motives for suicide. The suicide rate for age cohorts is an invaluable measure for detecting shifts in the patterns of suicide over long periods, and when these age cohort rates are scrutinized in conjunction with the motives for suicide, they show that, roughly speaking, the troubles for which men and women seek a final end change through the life course.

A few words must be said about motives. In *This Rash Act* Victor Bailey avoided the word "cause," preferring "motive." "Cause," "motive," or "explanation" all suit, but they convey subtlety different meanings. I work, as Bailey did, with witnesses' explanations. "Motive" implies choice and creates a space for doubt about an ultimate factor; "cause" connotes a circumstance urging itself decisively upon individuals. These slight distinctions deserve attention because they recall an intellectual history of tensions between deterministic and free-will interpretations of suicide; they also require comment because

Graph 3.21
Age-normalized suicide rates for age cohorts for New Zealand men

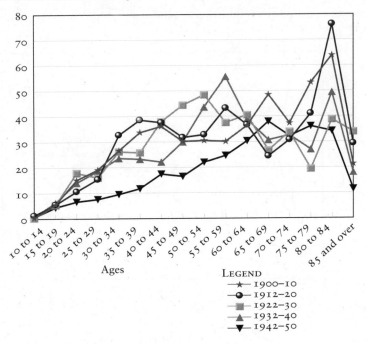

Ages

LEGEND
★ 1900–10
● 1912–20
■ 1922–30
▲ 1932–40
▼ 1942–50

Graph 3.22
Estimated crude suicide rates for age cohorts for Queensland men

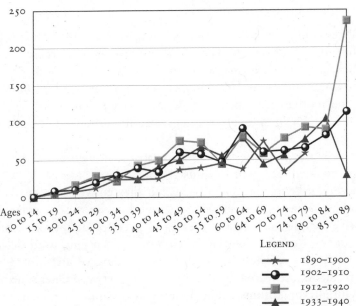

Ages

LEGEND
★ 1890–1900
● 1902–1910
■ 1912–1920
▲ 1933–1940

Graph 3.23
Age-normalized suicide rates for age cohorts for New Zealand women

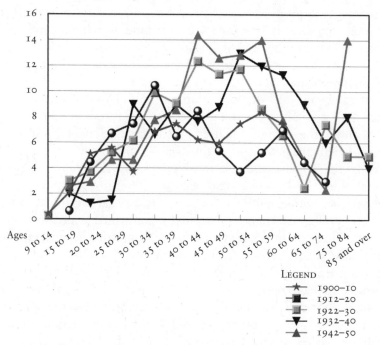

Graph 3.24
Estimated crude suicide rates for age cohorts for Queensland women: all cases for 1933–40

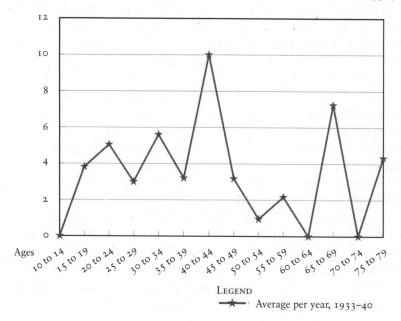

witnesses at inquests spoke about calm deliberation in a number of instances, impulsiveness in others, clouded judgment and mental illness in others. In light of their assigning interpretations of consciousness and deliberation, it seemed best to avoid the idea of cause, with its implication of compulsion. Many rational men and women were not caused to commit suicide. Most did have motives. This claim has greater significance than it would seem at a glance, because it revives an old controversy about the complex matter of suicide, rationality, and mental illness. Briefly, near the end of this chapter and in chapters 6 and 7, I take up the problematic relationships among rationality, self-harm, mental illness, and medical treatment.

When attributing motives, witnesses by and large agreed with one another; police investigations normally confirmed witnesses' conclusions because constables seldom extended inquiries beyond talking to people whom they recommended should attend the inquest. Coroners and magistrates followed police advice. A few times an enterprising constable spoke to more people, reported on common local knowledge, or checked for police and military records pertaining to the individual. The witnesses' words often depicted sets of connected troubles; in about one in ten cases, a suicide note helped. Deceased parties frequently endured more than one problem. They carried the burdens of alcoholism and unemployment; they were separated and suffered from high blood pressure; they had just been jilted and had long been ordered about by a domineering parent; they were ailing, poor, and on their own. Each person discussed at an inquest was a member of more than one category and had more than one motive. All judgment is based on categories that necessarily constrain understanding. Yet the sheer diversity of tragedy forces compression before analysis can go forward.

Many discussions in the chapters that follow rely on a sequence of inquiry: individual instances, when accumulated, supply an underlying pattern; the pattern guides the selection of instances exemplifying it. To get at the pattern requires categorization, and some critics will correctly remark on the impropriety of sacrificing diversity and note the real possibility of a priori categorization. Meaningful activity in most lines of endeavour, alas, requires the ordering of information. The 6,877 cases for New Zealand and Queensland contained roughly 1,000 specific motives. In accordance with a golden rule of data-set creation, as much original information as possible was retained in the data sets and referenced through a research codebook and notes on cases. The insurmountable problem with respect to compressing motives is restraining preconceptions about the categories of motives and assigning the specific motives that should go into each. In the process of reading case files and coding the contents for later statistical analysis, my research assistants and I placed new motives, as we encountered them, under headings that became the basis for a new variable: namely, a compressed statement of motives. The clusters that comprised the new variable were revealed in the dynamic of research, although how we read the statements of witnesses is certain to have been influenced by our biases and remoteness from the individuals.

Ten clusters emerged: alcohol abuse, work or financial problems, romantic misadventures or marital difficulties, physical ailments, mental illnesses, character and adjustment problems, the death of someone close, the impact of war, civil or criminal law problems, and cases in which motives remained mysterious. Victor Bailey employed seven clusters; in a crucial decision, he treated physical and mental illness jointly but mentioned instances of both. We can split physical and mental illness more precisely, show their intrinsic differences, and remark on the medicalization of suicide in the twentieth century. Unquestionably, some cases could have been assigned to several clusters. Alcohol abuse, for example, carried over into work and marital problems. A root motive was sought when assigning a case to a general motive. An urge to condense likely led to an inflation of the alcohol and mental illness categories because these problems were mentioned often in association with other matters. To cite but one example, Clarice Swift of Allora, Queensland, stated that her husband's drinking was the cause of marital strain, but also that "he was in difficulties with his money," and they had been forced to move.[113] By and large, however, across several decades, alcoholism, mental illnesses, and unemployment persisted as motives with tragic clarity, and the occasional witness described conduct in startling detail. The cluster of motives labelled "character and adjustment" serves as a catch-all for personal difficulties that do not quite cross into mental illness. Into this vague category went unhelpful statements that the deceased was "tired of life," "cruel," "a perfectionist," and so forth. There are bound to be overlaps and errors in setting boundaries.[114] Percentages of cases assigned to motives are expressed to the first decimal place as a statistical convention, but it would be wrong to maintain any pretence of such accuracy. However, the rank order of motives is plausible since the patterns have the backing of large numbers in two jurisdictions. The distribution of cases across the ten clusters varies slightly from New Zealand to Queensland, and these narrow differences strengthen credibility. Congruence would be suspicious, and great variation worrisome (see graphs 3.25 and 3.26).[115]

The excellent information on ages for New Zealand sustains age cohort analysis, which is vital to this book. A discussion of motives and age begins with adolescents. In New Zealand the suicides of young men aged fifteen to nineteen were disproportionately attributed to romantic misadventures and disappointments. Almost one in five of these young men (18.6 per cent) had been jilted or otherwise experienced a rejection by a girlfriend or abandonment by a wife, usually with good self-evident reasons that imply other background problems affecting the young men. In a few instances, parents obstructed a romance. Romantic and marital difficulties formed either the second or the most prominent cluster of problems cited for men into their thirties. The percentages for relevant age cohorts were as follows: twenty to twenty-four: 13.8 per cent; twenty-five to twenty-nine: 16.2 per cent; and thirty to thirty-four: 18.6 per cent. By contrast, among all male New Zealanders, romantic or marital troubles surfaced in only one in fifteen instances of suicide (6.9 per cent). For the adolescent cohort in New Zealand, character and adjustment problems (18.6 per cent) were as prominent motives as the romantic for young men; this omnibus cluster included for young men problems such as a violent temper, strange anti-social conduct, rejection of a step-parent, and flight from a harsh father. Work and money problems were not especially significant as motives of suicide for young men; they appeared in 15.4 per cent of all male cases but accounted for just 11.9 per cent of motives in the fifteen-to-nineteen cohort. Adolescent males were slightly more likely than older men to commit suicide as a result of a brush with the law. Physical illness, mental illness, the death of a loved one, war-related issues, and trouble with the law merit mention but were not leading motives.

Queensland presents an identical impression of impetuous young men flushed by rejection. Witnesses mentioned the salience of romantic troubles in roughly one out of thirteen cases (7.9 per cent) of all male suicides, but greater percentages for men aged fifteen to nineteen (11.9 per cent), twenty to twenty-four (14.8 per cent), twenty-five to twenty-nine (16.7 per cent), and thirty to thirty-four (11.1 per cent). In both jurisdictions, romantic and marital problems waned as motives in early middle age. After the age of thirty-five, the ravages of alcohol abuse, occurrences of mental illness, and work and money worries assumed prominence.

Graph 3.25
Distribution of ten major clusters of motives by gender: New Zealand, 1900–50

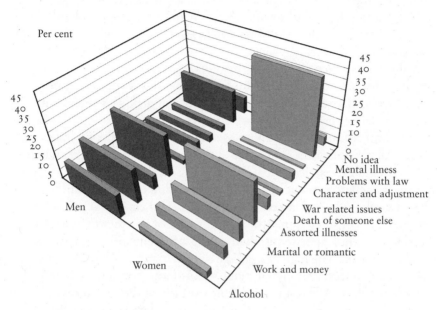

Graph 3.26
Distribution of ten major clusters of motives by gender: Queensland, 1890–1940

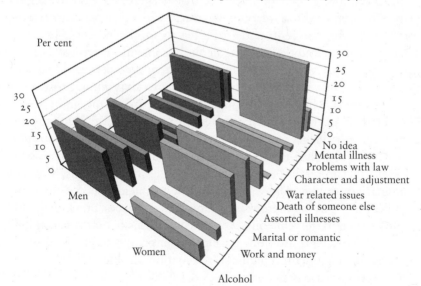

Of the 3,243 New Zealand men for whom ages are recorded in the data set, slightly more than one in ten (11.8 per cent) were deemed by friends and relatives to have suffered alcohol-related problems. Commencing with the thiry-to-thirty-four age cohort, alcohol-related troubles assumed mounting prominence (12.6 per cent). The significance of alcohol abuse then increased: thirty-five to thirty-nine, 17.7 per cent; forty to forty-four, 17.1 per cent; forty-five to forty-nine, 13.4 per cent; and fifty to fifty-four, 15.0 per cent. The proportion of suicides attributed to alcohol eased in later age cohorts.

The scale of the alcohol abuse as a motive is breathtaking in Queensland. Alcohol played a major role in the crises of middle-aged and older Queenslanders, particularly before the 1920s, during decades when the state attracted nomadic men. Of the 1,545 men for whom ages are known, alcohol was blamed in over one in eight cases (12.5 per cent); if all men are considered (n=1,993), regardless of whether their ages were known, alcohol appears as the leading problem in one in five cases (19.2 per cent). The high percentage of heavy drinkers whose ages were unknown suggests anonymity and isolation among alcoholic suicidal Queenslanders. Alcohol persisted as a source of distress across several seasons in the lives of these men. Alcohol-related disasters hit them from their late thirties into their seventies. For those cases where age is known, over one in six men aged thirty to thirty-four (15.3 per cent) were reported with alcohol problems; from that age cohort onward, the picture becomes darker: thirty-five to thirty-nine, 22.1 per cent; forty to forty-four, 27.4 per cent; and forty-five to forty-nine, 25.4 per cent. Then as men entered their fifties, alcohol problems tapered off: fifty to fifty-four, 23.5 per cent; fifty-five to fifty-nine, 19.0 per cent; and sixty to sixty-four, 18.7 per cent. From sixty-five to sixty-nine it rose again (23.9 per cent). The controls on alcohol in New Zealand and Queensland during World War II reduced alcohol abuse as a motive for suicides among men. It surfaced in only 2.1 per cent of suicide cases in wartime New Zealand. Police reports for Brisbane during the war mentioned alcohol as a motive in 9.3 per cent of suicide investigations, a far cry from earlier decades. The wartime decline in suicides, noted for many jurisdictions, has numerous interconnected causes, including full employment and the removal to overseas locations of many men at high risk. Additionally, restrictions on alcohol improved public health and "reduced the supply for a high risk population on skid row."[116]

The age-related pattern of motives for New Zealand women differs from that of men in ways that summon divergent interpretations about gender and power, about women's emotional states, and about their circumstances in male-dominated societies. Crises frequently originated in women's domestic standing as potential mothers, as mothers, and as family caregivers. Alcohol, legal problems, and war trauma rarely entered the picture. Work and money problems first appeared as a significant motive among widows aged fifty to fifty-nine. Only in widowhood did women have an economic identity, and an onerous one at that. Witnesses portrayed women as emotional, swayed by romantic urges, devastated by the deaths of others, and susceptible to depression and mood swings. Socially constructed or historically determined expectations for women and biologically influenced life-course stages coalesced. Operating in the lives of individuals, society and psyche engendered age-specific risks. Unwanted pregnancies and parental outrage overwhelmed many adolescents. For women from their teens through to their twenties, romantic rejection and failed marriages came in diverse forms, but each inflicted feelings of failure and low self-worth; the setbacks also intensified worry over material security. This latter anxiety may have been acute in rural locales since country living held few options for young women except marriage and extensive domestic labour.

The case files overflow with statements about love affairs broken off by the other party or by parents. "Families," reports New Zealand historian Kate Hunter, "could be crucial in determining whether or not love blossomed at all between young women and men."[117] Mothers hoped for sons-in-law who could provide comfort for daughters. Romantic disappointments dominated the age cohorts of the young: fifteen to nineteen, 32.4 per cent; twenty to twenty-four, 39.0 per cent; and twenty-five to twenty-nine, 23.2 per cent. These crises plummeted with maturity (thirty to thirty-four, 6.7 per cent). Women from forty to forty-four (12.5 per cent), fifty-five to fifty-nine (10.0 per cent), and sixty to sixty-four (10.3 per cent) were touched by family deaths with marginally greater force than men.

Out of 871 New Zealand women, witnesses reported 351 (40.3 per cent) as having suffered some form of mental illness. By contrast, witnesses reported that 572 men (17.6 per cent of all men) had mental illnesses. Women in their late forties and early fifties were slightly more inclined than women in other age cohorts to have experienced a nervous breakdown, depression, or another problem related to this cluster: forty-five to forty-nine, 49.6 per cent, and fifty to fifty-four, 47.5 per cent. Between a third and a half of the men and women in their sixties and seventies who committed suicide had faced the challenges of living with serious physical ailments.

There were statements about profound lingering sadness over the death of a spouse, children, and parents. There were abundant reports on treatment for nervous breakdowns and mental illnesses. These findings are significant because of the scarcity of information on neuroses and rural life; farm women "rarely had their breakdowns discussed outside the country women's organizations."[118] The data on mental illness deserves preliminary discussion because an assessment of mental illness and suicide will recur in all subsequent chapters as a motive, as a consideration when looking at the intent to commit suicide, as something from which men and women sought relief, and as a label applied by families, judicial authorities, and medical practioners for manipulative purposes of their own.

At inquests, witnesses were forthcoming about the symptoms and treatments of mental illnesses. The shame of being thought an accessory to a person's demise may have pushed a few witnesses to embroider the facts or to open up with frank and true admissions about a problem that threw the balance of blame on a condition, mental illness, not on harsh deeds by employers, erstwhile friends, or family. The evidence about mental illness was occasionally graphic and corroborated; still, it was always evidence from lay and medical people who had Western cultural perceptions as to what constituted mental illness at roughly that moment. Unlike physical illnesses, most mental illnesses have no physiological signs; psychiatrists have no battery of blood tests or X-rays to determine their nature. Mental illness remains today determined by the social conduct and expression of feelings by the sufferer. These socially or subjectively defined symptoms have contributed to rounds of controversy about whether or not mental illness is illness. At one extreme, schizophrenia is widely and transculturally accepted as an illness, while at another extreme, the boundary between normal distress over setbacks and clinical depression has been hotly contested.[119] The inquests show that in many instances social circumstances were important to the origins, courses, and outcomes of neuroses. A diagnosis of depression as a mental illness *qua* illness was and still is treacherous ground, but the suffering that men and women experienced, occasionally described in their own compelling words, was real and could be crushing.

Depression, nerves, nervous breakdown, and neurasthenic were labels for debilitating realities. Because of the authenticity of the anguish and a desire to retain as far as possible the motives as proposed by witnesses, mental illness has been discussed as a motive here and will be again in later chapters. It must also be recognized as a stigmatizing and problematic concept.[120] Mental illness lacks a bright-line boundary marker that separates it definitively from everyday sadness and emotional distress. That fact does not mean that there are no criteria for judging the likelihood of a mental illness. The following considerations singly or in combinations helped determine if mental illness was a plausible motive, given the evidence from suicide notes and witnesses' depositions: loss of self-control, psychological disorder that made functioning difficult, incapacitation, probable diminished responsibility, expressions by the individual of mental suffering, irrationality that tainted a great deal of an individual's judgment, disruptive conduct, and self-harm. In many instances, there were recurrences of these related and mainly socially defined criteria. The fact that they are socially defined makes them no less markers of illness, and furthermore, the quest for cerebral-physiological expressions is far from over.[121] The indictment of the expression "mental illness" comes from the fact that the very term has precipitated damaging fear, stigma, and therapeutic blunders. More will be said about these points in chapter 7.

CONCLUSIONS

What may we conclude from this survey of suicide rates? First, historical data have shortcomings that constrain the statistical elegance of analysis and point to potential snags in studies which rely on published government data. Suicide counts are imperfect and, to highlight a single crucial flaw, de facto marital states are not readily established. Second, although national suicide rates should be treated with care, they provide useful approximations. For Queensland, the fact that official rates and my calculations are close means that the inquest case files represent most known and possible suicides. For New Zealand, the situation is even better, and the files likely constitute just about all known and suspected incidents. Inevitable errors in the count arise from our inability to distinguish accidental deaths from suicides in a handful of deaths by drowning, by poison, and at mid-century by barbiturates. Third, national suicide rates can vary from one another and change over time on account of divergences in age structure and gender distributions. For the jurisdictions compared here, any demographic complications are minor, and so the crude and normalized rates are best explained by socio-economic circumstances, although the evidence is inferential. Fourth, psychiatry may have had an ameliorative influence, although the impact of medical intervention is difficult to disentangle from concurrent socio-economic developments. Society and psyche blend too well to make firm claims for medicine's impact during the decades studied.

A fifth conclusion is that the post–World War II era opened opportunities; if declining suicide rates provide any measure, the quality of life exceeded that of earlier decades. The awfulness of the previous fifteen years had kept suicide rates relatively high, particularly for men. Though excessive weight should not be placed on claims about suicide and society, the inferences from a comparison allow tentative points about the ameliorative impact of a sense of security that can originate in a welfare state or the sense of optimism that can effloresce in prosperous times. Sixth, on balance, the shift from a rural to an urban society inched along without evidence that suicide rates rose on account of a presumed urban alienation. Rural life as experienced in these new societies offered no bed of roses, and it possibly lacked the benefits of extended families that may have prevailed in the old-world countryside. Seventh, the long search by some sociologists for a general theory of variability in suicide rates is up against history that can add the specificity of time and place to social analysis. Eighth, even if social and economic circumstances improved, there were continuities among the rates and motives for suicides. Self-destruction declined somewhat but remained a significant cause of preventable death. Beneath the peaks and in the valleys of fluctuating rates, life's tears flowed. An interest in variability is fine, but the bedrock of life's enduring problems remains. A ninth conclusion is that data from New Zealand and Queensland confirm long-standing perplexing observations about suicide's seasonality. No simple explanation exists, although physiological and social forces likely acted together. Tenth, crises change with life's seasons. Eleventh, in different eras there have been different leading age cohorts; for a long time older men had the highest normalized rate, then adolescents, and most recently middle-aged men. Data from the inquests only extend to 1950, so a thorough investigation of these shifts is not feasible here. However, most of the changes in the leading age groups at risk concern men, suggesting that work and career expectations and related male cultural outlooks figure in the phenomenon. Across the life cycle, men and women have experienced some gender-specific troubles and sorrows. Finally, however, men experienced comparable, as well as disparate, difficulties from women. Among the crises they shared – although with gendered inflections – were illness and aging.

With a temporal compass and hypotheses, we can now explore life's harder realities and the meanings of suicide.

4

Work and Troubles: Men and Motives

At the end of the previous chapter, alterations across the life course came up for discussion. As men and women aged, motives changed. Young men tended to have romantic and character motives; middle-aged men typically experienced unemployment, money shortages, and alcoholism. The elderly had medical complaints. Although exceptions drifted into all age groups, trends remained unmistakable. Several patterns changed with the decades. Alcohol abuse fell off before the mid-century; unemployment and money problems waned remarkably during the 1940s. To some extent, the drop in suicide rates during wartime in a few countries may reflect the good economic times; Australia and New Zealand experienced economic boosts during the South African (Boer) War and both world wars. Increasing incidents of adolescent suicide occurred just beyond the end of this study in the 1960s. Global events in the first half of the twentieth century put men through terrible trials. As some physically and emotionally bruised men aged, failed to find a mate, formed habits that fed and deepened their depression, and isolated themselves, life became a burden. There are plausible age-related patterns to motives, but exceptional cases and encroachments by historical events preclude any dogmatic assertions.

With respect to the recurrent question "Why do a few select death when so many do not?" the statistics on motives given in the previous chapter suggest that unbearable pain originates in crises shaped by experiences which are traceable to the circumstances of age and gender. Perhaps the question will forever elude an answer, but this chapter is dedicated to achieving a better understanding of what brought men to the brink. The next chapter attempts to do the same for women. Movement toward greater comprehension requires both a composed statistical analysis and a passionate visceral understanding of suicide's meaning to those who took the fatal step. The statistics are necessary for the maintenance of proportions. It is essential to know if an episode is representative. Psychiatrists used to quip, "One case is not sufficient for a theory; two are needed." Quantity matters. However, while history, science, and the social sciences search for trends and gain confidence for their propositions, an intuitive emotional understanding is crucial for a subject that reaches into the human condition. There is no better demonstration of this claim than the vignettes that follow in this chapter – indeed, that appear in all the remaining chapters.

We can try to understand how individuals felt by paying attention to their words and noting social and cultural pressures and the physical torments. To a large degree, this chapter situates the difficulties of men in the material world familiar to the sociologists who studied suicide. In chapter 6 I will turn to the mental realm and appraise psychological pain and decision-making. For this chapter, I have selected excerpts from witnesses' depositions and suicide notes and organized them along the lines of a progression through the course of life. The chapter starts with young men and their romantic longings, misadventures, and troubles with parents. The narratives move from youth to matrimony, a state that in suicide studies has often been presented as a protective coating against a hostile social environment. Alcohol abuse, attacking and corroding that coating, comes next. An advance of urban waged work and the reciprocal decline of gangs of itinerant labour possibly moderated overall consumption and helped to sober up society.

World War 1 killed for decades; soldiers with physical and mental trauma shocked their families when they returned home worse in body and mind. Injured workers also suffered in body and mind, because to miss work for months was catastrophic. Men needed to work; the necessity was not only material but emotional too. Work denoted purpose, achievement, and a future. What these intangibles meant will be heard in the voices of despondent labourers, farmers, managers, and merchants. Nevertheless, it is important to avoid gendered assumptions about work by observing that men in their prime (ages twenty to fifty-five) had a variety of motives for suicide. In New Zealand only 17.6 per cent of these men were presumed to have work or money motives, but significantly, 40.2 per cent were struggling financially. In Queensland the figures are 15.3 and 35.6 per cent respectively.

The chapter begins with the nearly wed and terminates with the nearly dead. On occasion, elderly and infirm men chose the moment of their passing, some with a tear and others with a rant. In each section, New Zealand and Queensland are considered separately to allow analysis by theme while retaining a sense of place.

IMPETUOUS YOUNG MEN AND OTHERS

Parental disapproval devastated fragile young people, and there is evidence of physical abuse in a few instances. Seventeen-year-old meat packer William Tretheway left his job and quarrelled with his father, who remarked that "you must expect to do something. I can't keep you doing nothing at all."[1] At the inquest into the suicide of his fifteen-year-old son, Robert Morse admitted, "I beat the boy with a rope."[2] George Hurkett wrote: "Dear Dad, You have driven me to it, I am sorry if I cause any one worry but I will feel pretty sure you will be glad to see the last of me."[3] A girlfriend's rejection left many young men badly shaken. When James Crombie asked his girlfriend for a dance at the New Year's Ball, she reported, "I had a partner. He did not ask me for any more that night."[4] "Your words have severed every cord in my heart," wrote Anthony Paterson in a vengeance note to an ex-girlfriend, "and I hope to have a long quiet rest."[5] A co-worker reported that when Ernest Villens, a quiet young baker, received a letter from his finacée breaking off their engagement, Villens "stood as though he was riveted to the floor for about five minutes."[6] At twenty-six, farm labourer Francis O'Connell was no longer a youth; however, his disappointment with life was shared with younger men: "Life's no good without a beautiful sweet affectionate girl and I have been craving for one for a long time."[7]

Young men disagreed with parents and girlfriends over matters that meant a lot to them. On the morning of his death William Walsh was scolded for writing to a girl who was enticing him to stay with her family. William's mother threatened that if he left home, she would have the police return him.[8] Robert Lewis wrote his girlfriend, "Sorry that I struck you that night but can't be helped but if you will make it up this time I swore by the god above I will never lay my hand on you again." In the same note he threatened to "hunt you wherever you go." To his parents he wrote, "Maud and me have had a row and she says she will never speak to me again."[9] A barmaid who gave evidence at the inquest into the death of George McIntyre recalled an argument when he discovered that she was "keeping company with another young man."[10] Charles Whalen left a revenge note: "I am committing this deed through failure of a love affair but the least said easiest mended. I leave the woman to her own thoughts."[11] Deep in denial, Walter Cobb refused to accept that his son had shot himself over a girl. "The quarrel he had with Marie Luxton that afternoon had no bearing on his death."[12] For sheer loneliness, Leslie Palmer had no rival: "I have only loved two girls in my life and they have both turned me down." He told a witness that "he had no home, no father, no mother."[13]

The first peoples of New Zealand and Australia were undercounted in early twentieth-century suicide statistics. Decades later, in the 1990s, in Queensland and across Australia, there was a broad consensus that Aboriginal suicides comprised a serious crisis. There appeared to be a contagion of suicides in particular communities.[14] Suicide inquests for Aboriginal people in the years covered in this study were extremely rare and confined to individuals living among the white population. However, many Aboriginals lived beyond state surveillance in northern Queensland, a situation that may have concurrently been to the liking of these Aboriginal communities as well as an expression of government indifference to their well-being. Almost all Aboriginal suicide cases involved men (ten of eleven), and a good portion were relatively young labourers caught up in domestic problems or the motives were unknown. Maori were not nearly so neglected. Ninety-four Maori male (2.8 per cent of all men) suicides surfaced, and the cases differed from other New Zealand men. First, most of the deceased lived in the country or in small farm towns (85.1 per cent) and worked as farm labourers (36.1 per cent) or farmers (18.1 per cent). Second, in general, these men were young; over half were under thirty (52.8 per cent), and one in six (17.4 per cent) was under twenty. One in five or six men (17.9 per cent) of other nationalities was under thirty. Third, youthfulness was associated with a concentration of romantic misadventures and marital disputes. About a quarter (26.8 per cent) of the Maori cases involved such motives, but these motives were not so prominent (7.0 per cent) in the male population at large. Jealous men in a number of Maori cases attacked another party, felt remorse, and then took their own life, usually with a firearm.[15] Grief overwhelmed a few men.[16] "I think my son shot himself because he felt his wife's death very much. My son was twenty years old."[17] Maori will be mentioned throughout the chapter.

A set of murder-suicides concerned Japanese men residing in Queensland. While no Japanese residents were found among the New Zealand suicide inquests, fifteen cases (fourteen men) emerged from the Queensland files. Many had come to Australia to work with the pearl fleet, and their cases exemplify the importance of historical and cultural contingencies. Suicide was not absolutely condemned in Japan, where the double suicide of lovers was an established literary and artistic trope. Some men could not persuade a woman to join them voluntarily in a double suicide. Japanese diver Yoosuke Yosuke fatally wounded widow Shina Nakogawa and boarding-house keeper Fugita Tatsu before turning his revolver on himself on Thursday Island.[18] Before she died, Shina Nakogawa gave a statement. He had broken into her bedroom and demanded that she go outside with him. "I do not know why he shot me. He never asked me to marry him." Yosuke "was at this time under bond to keep the peace."[19] In the confines of the mostly male pearl-diving community on tiny Thursday Island, jealousies, gambling, and debts prompted numerous assaults. Some who shed blood accepted their fate as putative criminals and wanted to save their honour through suicide. The island's peculiar society had little in common with mainland communities, but murder-suicides by Japanese men were not confined to Thursday Island.

Tomosabro Shintani, cook at a Townsville hotel, shot himself after killing waitress Margaret Gallagher. His brother testified that the deceased had deserted from the Japanese army. Following the receipt of a letter, he said that "he did not care what he did now and that he would kill two or three before he died." According to a third witness, the letter from Japan advised that he would be shot as a deserter if he returned. He said, "I don't care now. I want to die. I will kill all you girls before I die." He had previously threatened girls working at the hotel with murder and was jealous if they spoke to other men.[20] Another Japanese male, Hayashi, killed his countryman Tokozo Takaki and then committed suicide at Mackay. Hayashi suffered from tuberculosis. He held a grudge against Takaki, who had complained about his spitting habits.[21] Iwamatsu Kohara, a laundryman, shot and stabbed his wife, set their house on fire, and then killed himself.[22] A witness said that Mrs Kohara was afraid of her husband and until recently had been living with another man on Thursday Island. Her lover had written saying that he was coming to get her. It was assumed that her husband read it.[23] Placing these murder-suicides here underlines the theme of cultural differences and suicide.

Both New Zealand and Queensland had a small number of Chinese residents, some of whom had arrived during gold rushes and later operated market gardens, retail businesses, and laundries.[24] In both jurisdictions a few committed suicide: thirty in New Zealand and forty-two in

Queensland. Almost all were older, single men. Prominent motives included illness and money and work problems. At the age of fifty-six, New Zealand prospector-miner Ah Lie was "sick lately and unable to work."[25] Gardiner Ah Man "came in for tucker and said he was not strong enough for work."[26] Blind for forty-five years and very ill for a fortnight, Queenslander Tommy Lew told a friend, "I want to die."[27] There were remarkably few youthful passionate episodes. The striking contrast between Japanese and Chinese residents of New Zealand and Queensland accords with an American study that explained the distinction in relation to a modern Japanese acceptance of suicide as a solution to some problems, but among the Chinese there was "an expectation of troubles as fate that must be borne."[28]

Dozens of other national and ethnic groups appeared among the case files, and close study might identify cultural and historical elements in suicides, but there is a barrier. Asians were readily identified; however, inquests files did not routinely include information on cultural identity, and that fact precludes deeper study of culture and suicide. Maori, Japanese, and Chinese cases suggest that culture influenced how younger men handled adversity and anger.[29] This observation reminds us of a significant claim made in chapter 3. Different cultures contribute to variations in suicide rates among a number of countries. This point could only have had a sound grounding in research based on case files; it will be re-examined in the book's conclusion.

THE MANY FACES OF MARRIAGE

Aggregate data assembled from many jurisdictions for over a century show a lower risk for married men.[30] Without information on the circumstances of individual cases, the meaning of this observation is unclear; besides, marital status is complicated by the failure of censuses to collect accurate data on informal separations, which often turned up in inquest files. Some men kept their status to themselves. The head of a survey crew commented on his morbid chainman. "I knew the deceased well," said John McFarlane. "I don't know if he was married or single."[31] This inconsistency in testimony likely expressed a commonplace situation in Queensland's deracinated male society. Men knew other men as workmates and chums at the bar, but not their life histories. Unaware of faults in the aggregate data they employed, many writers from the mid-nineteenth century onward jumped to conclusions about marriage's benefits, never able to delve deeper than superficial public

Table 4.1
The under-representation of suicide among married men in New Zealand and Queensland, 1900–50

Census years (even years covered by inquests)	Percentage Queensland men over 15 and married	Percentage of Queensland male suicides by married men over 15	Percentage New Zealand men over 20 and married	Percentage of New Zealand male suicides by married men over 20
1901 (1900–10)	39.2	27.0	52.8	30.5
1911 (1912–20)	50.1	24.4	54.1	30.0
1921 (1922–30)			62.6	39.5
1933 (1922–36)	59.4	34.8		
1936 (1932–40)			63.3	40.6
1951 (1942–50)			70.2	45.3

data on civil states. The superior data from the New Zealand and Queensland inquests show that married men did in fact have a lower rate than unmarried men (see table 4.1). But when the suicide rate is calculated for marital status by age cohort, the marital factor becomes especially fascinating. For example, young single men had a lower rate than middle-aged bachelors (see graphs 4.1 and 4.2).[32] This significant observation would have been impossible to extract from aggregate data. Many cases described later in this chapter capture the isolation of older single men. Information about individuals permits a closer examination of additional factors, since marital status can be cross-tabulated with other variables, the most revealing of which is support. Support was adduced during research on each case and expresses whether or not the deceased had received care and attention from a spouse, child, neighbour, or friend.

A relatively happy marriage with support provided greater insulation against life's hard blows than an unhappy one. In New Zealand the information on age permits a breakdown of the mean age of suicide cross-tabulated by marital status and support. The hypothesis is that with support and marriage, an individual could cope longer with distress. Married men on average committed suicide later than unmarried men, and by the measure of the mean age, married men with support did better. Unmarried men apparently gained only marginal advantage from support, a situation perhaps explained by the possible disappointment of not having had a companion or of enduring poor prospects that diminished chances for marriage (see table 4.2).

Graph 4.1
Suicide rates by marital status and age cohort: New Zealand men, 1902–20

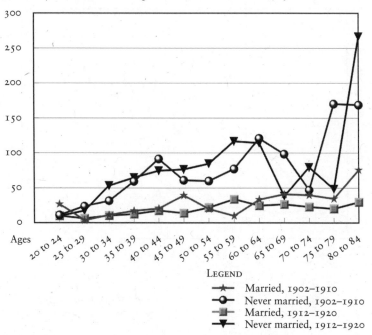

LEGEND
—★— Married, 1902–1910
—○— Never married, 1902–1910
—■— Married, 1912–1920
—▼— Never married, 1912–1920

SOURCES: Population data from *Results of a Census of the Colony of New Zealand Taken for the Night of the 29th April, 1906* (Wellington: Government Printer, 1907), 242; *Results of a Census of the Dominion of New Zealand Taken for the Night of the 17th April, 1921* (Wellington: Government Printer, 1925), 158. Suicide data from inquests and death certificates.

Happy marriages could originate in and contribute to a happy life; unhappy ones could develop out of and exacerbate problems. From his interviews, Ronald Maris concluded that "negative social interaction is at least as powerful as predictor in explaining suicide as are concepts like anomie and egoism."[33] A more recent study supports this view and goes further by stating that "although divorce is a stressful life event, we should recognize that an unhappy marriage is socially and mentally depriving too, implying not only pains but also possible gains from divorce."[34] Alcohol, unemployment, violence, and marital dissolution combined almost seamlessly, and that makes it difficult to disentangle these motives to establish a priority ranking.[35] Unemployed dock worker John King shot himself after a violent attack on his wife, Annie;

Graph 4.2
Suicide rates by marital status and age cohort: New Zealand men, all cases for 1932–40

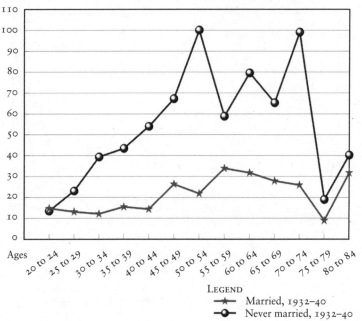

SOURCES: Population data from New Zealand, *Population Census, 1936*, vol. 4, *Ages and Marital Status* (Wellington: Government Printer, 1940), 33. Suicide data from inquests and death certificates.

he had been drinking heavily, and she had fled to her mother's house. Annie described their circumstance: "We were very often pushed for money. On different occasions I was left hungry. That worried my husband very much."[36] Unwilling to acknowledge that his violent behaviour had destroyed their marriage, John Tasker attempted to burden his wife with guilt by killing himself and leaving a revenge note that said, "I hope that to your dying day you will never forget that you took my boys away without me saying goodbye."[37] Women in abusive relationships in New Zealand and Queensland often had the backing of magistrates and pursued husbands for support. From time to time, that attempt enraged husbands, who took perverse revenge by committing suicide to end the line of income. In a note to his son, Henry Millen referred to a separation order and maintenance payments: "That would drive me mad seeing her going about with Dogs breakfast and defying me. So I have made up my mind to end it all."[38] "Let God judge

Table 4.2
The mean age, marital status, and presence of support for New Zealand men who committed suicide, 1900–50

Status and support	Mean age	Number	Standard deviation
Married and supported	51.6	938	12.9
Married and not supported	46.3	142	12.4
Married and support unknown	46.0	134	12.4
Unmarried and supported	38.5	673	16.3
Unmarried and not supported	41.5	478	16.3
Unmarried and support unknown	39.3	117	12.1
Separated and supported	46.7	100	12.5
Separated and not supported	45.2	110	12.5
Widower and supported	64.2	142	12.9
Widower and not supported	59.3	61	17.5
Wife lives abroad and support unknown	49.5	10	15.0
Unknown status and supported	53.3	24	14.9
Unknown atatus and not supported	47.9	79	17.0
Unknown status and support unknown	46.2	62	16.4
Assorted other statuses and support circumstances (fewer than 10 cases)	NA	56	NA
Cases with missing age or individual institutionalized	NA		NA
All cases with ages	48.4	3,216	18.9
Total number of men	NA	3,353	NA

between you and me," wrote Robert Hanna after his wife obtained a separation order, while William Murray fired a full quiver of guilt arrows against his wife:[39]

By the time you get this I will be gone for ever and you will be free to carry on your intrigue with a married man. I only hope his wife (if he has one) knows how he has been the means of breaking a home up and sending a man to his grave. I told you I would not appear in Court against you but don't forget there is a higher tribunal above where we shall meet one of these days and wrongs will be righted. There is one thing I can say and praise God its true. You can put my death down to your stupid infatuation for a damned scoundrel, a lying hypocrite and an habituant [sic] of brothels a thing who would and has said anything at all about you but you would not listen to my warnings. I only hope one thing and that is that my face, the face of a true and devoted lover may haunt you to your dying day.

Revenge suicides mainly involved romantic or marital motives, but not always. Poor Cecil Fowler had never recovered from shell shock and a gas attack. However, what seemed to precipitate his self-destruction was unkindness at work in 1936. To his superior he wrote that "you and you alone are responsible for this. If only you have given me assistance when I asked you."[40]

The wife of Alexander Stewart tried to stop his drinking, and when that failed, she got a separation order and custody of their daughter. Stewart shot himself through one of her handkerchiefs while holding a copy of Robert Burns's poems that she had inscribed.[41] Plenty of men wrote notes that expressed their romantic angst and simultaneously set out to wound the other party emotionally. No one surpassed Stewart's theatricality, but other notes responded to a court order with identical sentiments of romantic self-pity. "I have died for love. Forgive me. You never loved me." This revenge note and a bottle of carbolic acid were Walter Flemingham's responses to a separation order.[42] In 1936 Maori share-milker Ronald Hiko McMaster was treated by a doctor for depression and insomnia. His brother explained that McMaster's wife had left him. "His domestic matters had not been too pleasant recently and his wife was going to get the farm."[43] Some wives were more independent or argumentative than their husbands could stomach. Reports of his wife's infamous conduct got back to William Race and "seemed to be preying on his mind."[44] For a frank portrayal of domestic mayhem – "one perfect day and the next one hell" – Pat Johns's confession-cum-suicide note is matchless: "I am doing this mainly because Jean has driven me to it with constant nagging and fits of temper. I have found lately that I am not mentally strong enough to take it and found myself doing the most horrid things to hurt her [threatened her with a rifle] in return as she was hurting me." The truth about Jean we can never know, but Pat felt that his only escape from perpetrating some terrible deed against her was to kill himself.[45] After a fight with his wife during which she armed herself with a cleaver and he with a frying pan, George Rackley cut his throat to preclude an awful act: "I'll settle myself."[46] Men in these situations justified suicide as a chivalrous act to protect their wives.

Queensland witnessed cheerless situations comparable to those in New Zealand. Time and again, a wife fled an abusive husband, taking the children; the husband pursued them, and the wife refused to return. After his wife left him for drinking and ill-treating her, George Blythe went after her "to find out what sort of life she was leading in Brisbane." She refused to live with him again.[47] Shortly before he took his life, blacksmith George Fairbrother had a dispute with his wife. "I have had enough of being with you," she exclaimed. "I am going back to my mother's at Ipswich."[48] The police had charged Harry Martin with assault because he had wounded his de facto wife, whom he suspected of sleeping with a boarder. Martin was out on bail when he hanged himself.[49] Marital disputes were tangled affairs. Fault for some could be shared by both parties and with in-laws. As he was dying from poison, carpenter Albert Darwen told a friend that "you don't know my wife, she's a real terror."[50] Florence Tindall candidly told the magistrate investigating her husband's death that "his principal worry was me." She had initiated a court case against him.[51] Robert Taylor married a pregnant girl when he was eighteen, but her mother kept her working as a prostitute. As one witness put it, "the only worry the deceased had was about his wife going with the sailor men of the fleet."[52]

For venom in a revenge note, it would be hard to surpass William Brown's remark in a letter to his estranged wife: treat your other men differently and "only have one murder on your mind."[53] Some men hoped to repair their pride. In March 1944 George Fildes learned that his girlfriend had given her door key to five other men. He took it badly. "I can't be played for a sucker."[54] World War II upset relationships.[55] American servicemen in New Zealand and Queensland disrupted a few marriages. David Hayes had been "depressed ever since his wife left him and produced a child of whom an American was the father."[56] Leslie Love wrote that his wife "told me she was in love with an American and wanted a divorce." He feared she would take their son to the United States.[57]

CHRONIC DECLINE BY ALCOHOL

In the previous chapter, I commented on alcohol abuse as a motive in male suicides and noted the risk from early to late middle age. International studies report that the percentage of all suicides – men and women – who were alcoholics has varied from 15 to 27 per cent, and one study estimated that the suicide rate of alcoholics was 270 per 100,000.[58] In Queensland nearly one in five cases of male suicide (19.4 per cent) involved alcohol abuse, and this motive peaked in the period 1900–10, when, astonishingly, a third (32.9 per cent) of all male suicides could be connected to this motive. The case files for these years depict an image of society blighted by the alcoholism of older single men who had come to Queensland during a gold rush, land rush, or on a labour contract. In reference to culture, Queensland historian Ross Fitzgerald claimed that "much more important than pursuit of the arts were sporting activities and, above all, drinking."[59]

The assignment of this motive in individual cases was not difficult. The explanation often came from the deceased. Single labourer Joseph Scholl, who had a lingering death, told his sister he took Lysol because "I am sick of life and drink has got the best of me."[60] Lysol (a mixture of cresols, related to carbolic acid, and soft soap) was a common and corrosive household disinfectant. George Hampson asked to "remember me to everyone and don't worry about me. Drink has brought me to this."[61] One heavy drinker wrote to his wife, "I made a mess of my life and I know only one way left for me. I am not worthy of you and I know only too well that I am no good to anybody else. Don't break your heart over me, because I am not worthy."[62] Men with alcohol-related problems came overwhelmingly from the working class, which accounted for seven out of ten alcohol-abuse cases (71.6 per cent). That proportion was greater than their distribution among all male suicides. Middle-class men accounted for over a fifth; elites and retired men were comparatively scarce. Within the working class, unskilled labourers were prominent; four out of ten (42.2 per cent) working-class alcoholic suicides were committed by unskilled labourers. The case files connect labourers to alcohol, alcohol-related mental illnesses, alcohol-exacerbated domestic ruptures, alcohol-related physical decline, and alcohol-intensified poverty.

In *Be a Man*, Peter Stearns proposed that industrialization challenged men to bolster masculinity in a new environment which minimized their property and reduced their control over work. Men assumed that in return for the burdens of heavy toil, they could claim rewards. For married men, these included the status of breadwinner, control of the household budget, and domestic authority.[63] Another reward was alcohol, although men who defined themselves partly by the bar's sociability disadvantaged themselves as breadwinners and family heads.[64] Empirical studies have verified a connection between male socialization, frequent drinking, and suicide.[65] In New Zealand, over half of male suicides who had alcohol-abuse problems (52.7 per cent) were unemployed or self-employed and having trouble. For Queensland, almost half (44.8 per cent) were in comparable dire situations. A young New Zealand swagman captured a philosophical outlook when he wrote in his diary, "drink, for tomorrow we starve."[66]

Table 4.3
Leading alcohol-related motives for men and women: Queensland, 1890–1940

Motive	Males n (%)	Females n (%)	Total
Serious drinking problem	192 (44.6%)	14 (51.9%)	206
Delirium tremens or the horrors	47 (10.9%)	1 (0.37%)	48
Heavy drinking recently	86 (20.0%)	1 (0.37%)	87
Alcohol abuse and bad health	21 (4.9%)	1 (0.37%)	22
Alcohol abuse and unemployment	27 (6.3%)	0	27
Alcohol abuse, unemployment, and old	14 (3.2%)	0	14
Alcohol and worried about debt	15 (3.3%)	0	15
Assorted alcohol problems	29 (6.8%)	10 (37.0%)	39
Total	431 (94.1% of total)	27 (5.9%)	458 (100.0%)

In New Zealand and Queensland the presence of itinerant labourers on grazing stations, mines, and public works promoted a masculine camp culture that compounded reward-taking. One witness described this sociability. He met up with an old work mate; they then travelled together and drank heavily "for about a week." "We took drink with us to the camp. We drank rum, whiskey, beer, all sorts."[67] Flax cutting and gum digging were unique to New Zealand; sugar plantations added a specific feature to Queensland's manual labour market. Masculinity's standards remained consistent from workplace to workplace, but they collided with one another because excesses of reward-taking undercut work and were self-destructive. Heavy drinkers described at inquests had exhibited the shakes, nervousness, and peculiar behaviour; they had downed gargantuan quantities over many days. John Brennan's niece deposed that "he had been drinking both whiskey and brandy for about a month."[68] For two weeks, Jack Sala had not been eating, yet he downed thirty to forty drinks per day: spirits in the morning, beer in the afternoon.[69] When money ran out, drinking stopped.[70] The intervention of family or authorities both enraged and depressed men. Unemployed veteran Richard Evett, alternately depressed and excitable, could not stand the idea that the supervisor of a scheme for soldier settlements intended placing him under a prohibition order.[71] Witnesses described an assortment of alcohol-related motives (see table 4.3).

Delirium tremens was the principal explanation for suicide in 2 per cent of all male cases and accounted for over 10 per cent of all alcohol-related cases among men. Hallucinations involved animals, insects, and devils.[72] John Blizzard screamed in the night that "there is a big spider on the side of my leg and I can't grab him, and there are snakes on the other side."[73] Physicians diagnosed some alcoholics with dipsomania, a condition described as leading to oversensitivity and an inability to cope with difficulties, humiliations, setbacks, and stress. Still others had chronic alcoholism; the individuals were sociable and emotional at the bar but irritable at home. Men with alcohol-related problems were plagued by unemployment, marital breakdown, and worry about debt. Why did men drink a substance known to be addictive and unhealthy? First, the ambiance of the pub appealed to men who otherwise had no opportunity to entertain and show they belonged. Boarding houses, bunkhouses, and construction camps lacked recreational set-ups. For socializing and entertainment, the countryside offered little other than the pub. A second reason was that anxiety and depression have been associated with drinking. Men may have self-medicated their feelings and thus, in a tragic irony, aggravated their depression.[74]

In 1940 Queensland psychiatrist John Bostock considered chronic alcoholics a risk: "Sometimes acute depressive states with intense anxiety arise and in them the alcoholic is likely to commit suicide."[75] Bostock, a former staff doctor in mental hospitals in Western Australia and New South Wales, claimed that 10 per cent of men admitted to these hospitals suffered from alcoholism.[76] As early as 1900, witnesses at inquests described alcohol-dependant males as depressed; they also used terms such as "confused," "strange," "excited," and "impulsive." Family members saw these men as belligerent, violent, nasty, quarrelsome, and complaining. Marital breakdown figured often in alcohol-associated suicides. Single alcoholic men were more prone to suicide than married counterparts. Nearly six out of ten labourers (58.9 per cent) with alcohol-abuse problems who committed suicide were unmarried. Roughly one in fifteen labourers (7.1 per cent) with a history of alcohol abuse was separated. Some alcoholic labourers were unmarriageable, but others had been married, had fled court-issued support orders, and preferred anonymity. Witnesses at inquests for labourers included fewer family members than at inquests into suicides by middle-class men with alcohol-related problems. Single, divorced, and separated men were at greater risk of suicide than married men.

Table 4.4
Leading alcohol-related motives for men and women: New Zealand, 1900–50

Motive	Males n (%)	Females n (%)	Total
Serious drinking problem	85 (21.4%)	10 (32.2%)	95
Delirium tremens or the horrors	17 (4.3%)	4 (12.9%)	21
Heavy drinking with financial and marital problems	29 (7.3%)	1 (3.1%)	30
Heavy drinking recently	7 (1.8%)	0	7
Assorted alcohol problems	259 (65.2%)	16 (51.6%)	275
Total	397 (92.8% of total)	31 (7.2%)	428

Alcohol abuse among male suicides in New Zealand was less prominent than in Queensland. In New Zealand it appeared as a motive for about one in eight cases (11.9 per cent), and the number of such cases peaked in the years from 1910 to 1920, when alcohol was the attributed motive in a third of the cases (33.5 per cent). In the early twentieth century there were contrasting levels of hard liquor consumption, and arrests for drunkenness in Queensland exceeded those of New Zealand. Drunk and disorderly conduct declined during World War 1 and stayed lower in both jurisdictions (see graph 4.3).

As in Queensland, the most dramatic symptoms of alcohol abuse in New Zealand, well-known to constables and men on pastoral stations, in timber camps, and at public works, deserved to be labelled "the horrors." However, the horrors in New Zealand were not quite so prevalent as in Queensland (see table 4.4). A few witnesses aptly described withdrawal as "suffering a recovery."[77] Recent research on suicide peaks after holidays supports the proposition that withdrawal is a risk-laden period for people with alcohol dependence.[78] The inquest records show that hallucinations drove men to bizarre conduct. A station hand near Gisborne related the conduct of a labourer getting over two weeks' drinking: "He was generally running about with a piece of wood in one hand and his hat in another."[79] First encounters with men suffering the horrors came as a shock. James Gadbury and his mate Charles Schultz left the farm where they worked to go to the races. Schultz drank for seven or eight days, after which he was feeling "the after effects of the liquor." "I had never seen anybody who was suffering from Delerium [sic] Tremens. He had the horrors or very near them."[80] Most witnesses, however, spoke calmly as if they had prior encounters, and this casualness is not surprising in view of the levels of consumption.

Graph 4.3
Charges for drunkenness per 1,000: New Zealand and Queensland, 1898–1941

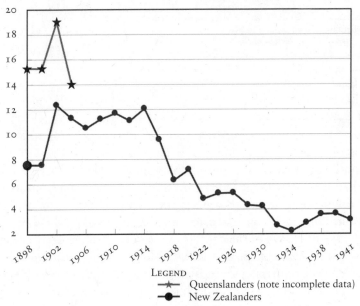

LEGEND
—★— Queenslanders (note incomplete data)
—●— New Zealanders

SOURCE: *New Zealand Official Year-Book*, 1900–50.

Consider Austin Bergan, whose erratic life was not unique. A
co-worker remarked that Bergan "was a man who worked steadily for
a few months at a time and then usually had a drinking bout for a few
weeks, shifting about from district to district."[81]

Witnesses recounted marathon binges. Farm manager Lachlan Cal-
der told a coroner that his cook had been in the habit of overindulging
and had recently gone on a six-week spree. "Since he returned he was
dodging about the hut, suffering recovery."[82] Deckhand Roland Angelo
had known Anthony Gratz, a former Timaru fisher, well enough to say
of him, "I think he suffered a good deal while recovering from drink."[83]
Dr David Johnston treated Alexander Rae for alcoholism over three
weeks in 1914. "Whenever he took alcohol he became an absolute
lunatic."[84] A blacksmith who saw thirty-six-year-old farm labourer
Charles Chandler after a spree "concluded at the time that the deceased
was off his head." Chandler's employer was precise: "I would say the
deceased when I saw him last was suffering from delirium tremens."[85]

A friend of labourer Richard Lynch described him as an excessive drinker whose "mind was perfectly unhinged."[86]

A type of paranoia affected men with the horrors, and it is possible that the delusions were symptomatic of alcoholic psychosis. Such clinical language appeared in only few accounts. One doctor reported that his patient, a heavy drinker, was "suffering from marked depression of spirits and showing signs of delusions of suspicion."[87] Acquaintances described events memorably. Kakatahi farmer Thomas O'Neill drank whisky with nips of Chlorodyne. A farmhand thought O'Neill had "a touch of the delirium tremens" because he imagined "the police were after him and going to arrest him."[88] The men who worked with Walter Scott near Waipiro Bay in 1912 had sleepless nights because from the bunk he screamed that "they are after me." Following a spree five months earlier, phantoms had pursued Scott into the bush. His mates on the most recent occasion tied him to a bunk and told him to shut up.[89] Adelina Carter observed that her carpenter brother "seemed to think that people were watching and following him."[90] Widowed clerk Thomas Manley downed a fatal quantity of carbolic acid in front of a witness, exclaiming, "Thank God, it is all over. The Indians will not chase me any more." He left a note: "I am prepared to suffer by my own hand rather than suffer the tortures I have seen."[91] Mariner Hugo Retowski spent on drink the money he had saved to outfit himself as a gum digger. During withdrawal, he worried "about people looking fiercely at him."[92] When trooper Nelson Colenso went into withdrawal in his tent in early 1916, he believed that other soldiers thought he was a spy.[93]

The horrors drove men mad. Richard Fulton, an unemployed farm labourer, had been drinking for a week. An acquaintance gave him a ride in a gig. Twice on their journey Fulton said he saw men on horseback following him. He jumped out on a bridge and threw himself into a gorge. He often asked, "Who is that?" but there was no one.[94] Fifty-two-year-old Southland farmer Daniel O'Brien would disappear from his home for a week at a time. He spoke of "seeing things at night and even in the daytime." Several days after drinking bouts he became depressed.[95] Maori teamster Matene Kingi, working at Tangihangi Station, was only twenty-six when withdrawal symptoms convinced co-workers that he was "out of his mind." His friend Hata Warakihi stated that Matene woke him about 4:00 a.m. the day before "and asked me to say prayers as he saw a lot of people outside the house."[96] Shortly before he took his life, Edward Vince experienced nightmares.

A co-worker "heard him express wonder why people were going to hang him as he had never committed murder."[97]

Men helped workmates through bad periods. A casual acquaintance of withdrawal sufferer Daniel Doolan fed him steak and put him in a bunk.[98] Fencer William Galbraith noted that his friend Richard Lynch had been unwell with delirium tremens for a week. "As a friend I was looking after him."[99] Police constables arrested drunks but also furnished food and modest medical attention and sometimes contacted family. Blenheim constable Dennis Byrne spoke to James Ford's co-worker Abraham McGuiness, asking that he "keep him off drink." McGuiness complied and scarcely left Ford for a fortnight.[100] Employers could be tolerant. The foreman of a public work near Otira delivered one of his labourers by buggy to the nearest police station because the man had delusions – "they seemed to be in reference to his mother."[101] A justice of the peace recognized delirium tremens and remanded him to Greymouth Prison for medical treatment. Farmer William Barron let one of his men have the day off because "he was slightly the worse of drink." Barron prepared the man's meals while he recovered.[102] William Walker, a licensee at Bluff, dismissed twenty-five-year-old barman James Whittaker for drinking and neglecting work. Unwilling to send the young man packing immediately, Walker gave him a room and helped him through the attack.[103]

The acts of civility are touching contributions to a picture of homosociability, but there were ugly countervailing properties of the drinking culture. The squandering of pay by married men led to neglect of family and much worse. Janet Scott made a disastrous decision when she remarried. Her new husband stole her money, went "drinking about the town and shouting for all who came about with her money." She was "down in the dumps" and gassed herself and her eight-year-old daughter.[104] She was not alone in feeling wronged by a masculine cultural drive to shout a round of drinks. If there was no more money, desperate men sold whatever they could. Returned soldier Andrew McKendry sold his boots and clothes "to by some boose."[105]

The celebration of drink and matesmanship focuses on pub life, but a number of serious drinkers isolated themselves. Their rough, self-destructive behaviour went unseen. Blacksmith Thomas Davidson slashed his throat in a hut filled with bottles. "It smelt of whiskey. Judging from the number of bottles I should say he had been drinking heavily."[106] "When I first went into the kitchen," said Mary Clayon at the inquest into the suicide of her de facto husband, "I saw a lot of empty beer bottles lying on the table."[107] According to his wife, John Clow kept a shed for his retreat and "often retired to this room to do his drinking, and I suspected that he had been drinking and was probably sleeping it off." She added, "I fear my husband when he has been drinking."[108] The constable who investigated the death of Lawrence Blakie found that "some empty and some full bottles of wine were in the deceased's room suggesting that he had been indulging in a drinking bout previously to his death."[109] When farmer George Ironside drank whiskey and kerosene, his wife fled with their children.[110]

The impositions of dependent drinkers constituted at best irritating burdens and at worst terrifying upsets to others. Acquaintances, friends, and employers could berate a noisy sufferer, walk away from the problem, or shunt the man along to the authorities. Managers of institutions that furnished shelter for workers or the destitute tolerated some drinking, but they had to be firm for the sake of others. The overseer of the Lyttleton Seaman's Institute turned out mariner Stephen Guiton "owing to excessive drinking."[111] Wives and children suffered because they could not eject a chief income earner without simultaneously inflicting hardship on themselves. When women did act, it was often after many years of enduring their spouses' drinking. Charles Butler of Auckland recalled that his father had had an attack of delirium tremens, and his mother had taken out a prohibition order against her husband and then finally left him.[112] Lucy Walker refused to go out and fetch more alcohol for her husband; drinking was undermining their stake in a farm. She also could see the effects of drink on his mental health. "At all times, other than when a depression occurred after a drinking bout," she said, "he was most agreeable."[113] Many forgiving wives said the same: "He was all right when he was off drink. He was a good husband."[114] "If he wasn't drinking he was a splendid man."[115] Not every suffering wife would concur. After a drinking binge, Arthur Joy committed suicide and left a note for his estranged wife: "I remain your disobedient Husband."[116] Alcohol, separation, unemployment, and violence were associated. Wives endured a lot.

Males other than husbands could disrupt households. Pensioner and widower William Lane came to his son's house in a drunken state and threatened people. "We tried to pacify him as we had a music teacher in the house giving the girl [his granddaughter] lessons. We had to ask the teacher to leave the house on account of the language."[117] Woman had a distinct perspective on the misconduct of drunken men. Bertha Austin, daughter of a Wellington boarding-house keeper, had to fend off

William Anderson. "I smelt liquor on him. He said would I go out with him? I said no I would not. With that he hit me on the face and head with his fists ... He had said previously that he would do for [kill] me if I did not go out with him."[118]

Abuse of alcohol affected mental health beyond the horrors. During the hours when he was not drinking, the habitual drunkard was ill-tempered, discouraged, depressed, taciturn, and incapable of concentrating. Kathleen Teague recalled her efforts to bring her husband to his senses. "I prevailed upon my husband to leave hotels about six weeks ago in order to save expense, and in an endeavour to keep him away from associating with drinking companions ... During that time my husband was endeavouring to obtain a business, or employment, and his failure to obtain either was worrying him badly. He was drinking heavily, and was wasting his money, and was worried about it."[119] The association between alcohol and depression are complex. Nevertheless, it is striking how frequently witnesses before World War I used the expressions "depressed in spirits," "depressed," and "depression." Boarding-house keeper George Hill noted that Lyttleton wharf labourer Frank Humphrey had been drinking heavily of late and became "more and more depressed."[120] A constable ascertained that Albert Ballard had been "drinking to excess over the past two years and when on these drinking bouts he became very depressed."[121] Whether depression came before or after a pattern of heavy drinking is less important than noting the complicated disruptive relationship.[122]

Licensees were frequently summoned to inquests but wanted to distance themselves from blame. Their accounts of men who knocked back enormous quantities of alcohol and then walked steadily and talked coherently were suspicious, although dependent drinkers could develop a tolerance and consume quantities that would have flattened abstainers. Police constables had generous ideas about what constituted drunkenness. "A man had to be staggering drunk to be drunk."[123] "A drunkard," said constable Charles Woodley, "is a man who is often run in for being drunk."[124] Carterton farmer Martin Kern described neighbour Daniel Murphy as "a man that could go on a spree, occasionally for a few days, but he was not a heavy drinker."[125]

Witnesses described prodigious drinking. William Prior, only twenty-nine when he jumped in front of a train in Wellington, had been drinking heavily for five weeks.[126] Before he threatened to shoot his wife, Alfred Ransley had been "drinking on and off for three weeks."[127] Wellington labourer John Finn, separated from his wife, had "been

drinking heavily for the last fortnight."[128] Blenheim constable Dennis
Byrne knew tailor James Ford well enough to report that he went on
sprees that could last a month.[129] Pipiriki shopkeeper George Manson
went to Wanganui for a five-day binge in 1914 and on his return "was
very excited as a result of drink."[130] August Pederson told a friend that
he could not work because of the effects of drink. Pederson had just
come from a ten-day spree in Christchurch.[131] In early December 1914
Daniel Doolan, employed at a public drainage works on the Hauraki
Plains, took a drink. Unable to stop, he went to Thames, drank for at
least three weeks, and then returned to the project, but could not
resume work. An overseer said that "his only trouble was drink."[132]
Charles Manley claimed that his father "had been drinking from the
beginning of May till about the 4th of August."[133]

A depressed and worried bootmaker, William Hunter, had been
drinking for over two weeks when he killed himself. According to his
brother, "he used to break out on the burst every three months."
Between sprees, he consumed two cases of whiskey every three months.
"My brother got through a good amount of whiskey when he got
going."[134] Unemployed during the postwar recession, Henry McEwen
nevertheless joined his mates for drinking bouts, when "they practically
lost count of days and nights or time."[135] For some men, a craving was
so great that when family or the authorities secured a court order to put
them on the list of prohibited persons or when they had run out of cash
or credit, they descended into abject misery. At age fifty, farm labourer
Richard Hiatt remarked that he was getting too old to follow his usual
line of work, but to make matters worse, the licensee "had stopped his
drink and life was not worth living."[136]

Drinking caused or exacerbated health problems. A patient of Dr
John Paget had an attack of the horrors. Paget worried that heavy
drinking would affect the man's brain and heart. If he was insane when
he committed suicide, said Paget, "it would probably be the result of
chronic alcoholism."[137] Post-mortems occasionally added incidental
information about heavy drinkers. Master mariner Henry Johnson was
forty when he took an overdose of Chlorodyne in Dunedin in 1910; the
post-mortem showed damage to the stomach from alcoholism.[138] The
report for John Roberts, who died in 1914, stated that "the liver
showed old standing and chronic alcohol cirrhosis. The heart was
unhealthy and showed valvular disease of the aorta."[139]

Alcohol-plagued men were more likely than others to be emotionally
isolated; in New Zealand and Queensland they were more likely to be

Table 4.5
Motives and marital status: New Zealand, 1900–50

Motive	Married n (%)		Single n (%)		Separated n (%)		Widowed n (%)		Divorced n (%)		Wife abroad n (%)		Unknown n (%)	
Alcohol abuse	100	(25.2)	178	(44.8)*	61	(15.4)**	16	(4.0)	4	(1.0)	2	(0.5)	36	(9.1)
Work or money	288	(48.8)**	205	(34.7)	22	(3.7)	27	(4.6)	3	(0.5)	5	(0.8)	40	(6.8)
Marital or romantic	62	(26.6)	83	(35.6)	76	(32.6)**	2	(0.9)	3	(1.3)			7	(3.0)
Assorted ailments	305	(41.3)*	265	(35.9)	17	(2.3)	74	(10.0)**	3	(0.4)	6	(0.8)	68	(9.2)
Death of someone close	20	(27.8)	11	(15.3)			39	(54.2)					2	(2.8)
War-related	85	(43.3)*	84	(42.9)*	9	(5.5)	7	(3.6)					11	(5.6)
Character and adjustment	32	(25.2)	68	(53.5)**	7	(5.5)	10	(7.9)	1	(0.8)	2	(1.6)	7	(5.5)
Problems with the law	25	(24.3)	52	(50.5)**	7	(6.8)	1	(1.0)	1	(1.0)	3	(2.9)	14	(13.6)
Mental illnesses	260	(44.4)	223	(38.1)	16	(2.7)	28	(4.8)	1	(0.2)	5	(0.9)	52	(8.9)
Reason unknown	82	(27.7)	132	(44.6)*	4	(1.4)	14	(4.7)	1	(0.3)	6	(2.0)	57	(19.3)
Total	1259	(37.7 % of cases)	1301	(39.0)	219	(6.6)	218	(6.5)	17	(0.5)	29	(0.9)	294	(8.8)

Table 4.6
Motives and marital status: Queensland, 1900–50

Motive	Married N (%)	Single n (%)	Separated n (%)	Widowed n (%)	Divorced n (%)	Wife abroad n (%)	Unknown n (%)
Alcohol abuse	97 (25.3)	202 (52.7)*	33 (8.6)*	14 (3.7)		5 (1.3)	32 (8.4)
Work or money	134 (44.1)**	106 (34.9)	14 (4.6)	15 (4.9)			35 (11.5)
Marital or romantic	51 (34.0)	59 (39.3)	28 (18.7)	3 (2.0)	4 (2.7)	4 (2.7)	1 (0.7)
Assorted ailments	99 (34.3)	125 (43.3)	8 (2.8)	8 (2.8)		6 (2.1)	43 (14.9)
Death of someone close	20 (27.8)	14 (20.3)		29 (42.0)**		1 (1.4)	6 (8.7)
War-related	11 (23.9)	26 (56.5)**	9 (5.5)			3 (6.5)	2 (4.3)
Character and adjustment	12 (11.9)	54 (53.5)**	5 (5.0)	15 (14.9)	1 (1.0)	2 (2.0)	12 (11.9)
Problems with the law	16 (24.6)	37 (56.9)**	2 (3.1)	1 (1.5)			9 (13.8)
Mental illnesses	96 (30.1)	163 (51.1)*	12 (3.8)	17 (5.3)		3 (0.9)	28 (8.8)
No idea	37 (14.8)	144 (57.6)**	6 (2.4)	7 (2.8)		4 (1.6)	52 (20.8)
Total	572 (28.9 % of cases)	930 (47.1)	112 (5.7)	109 (5.5)	5 (0.3)	28 (1.4)	220 (11.1)

* Over-represented.
** Significantly over-represented.

unmarried, divorced, or separated; only men deemed to have character or adjustment problems had a higher proportion unmarried. The unmarried, divorced, and separated had less support than married men (see table 4.5 and 4.6). Men with alcohol-abuse problems were more likely than other men to have committed suicide in hotels, boarding houses, huts, tents, workers' barracks, and bodies of water rather than in a house.[140] Stephen Garton's study of the admissions to asylums (mental hospitals) in New South Wales in the late nineteenth century revealed that many men came from remote locales and may well have been drifters. Garton speculates that their footlessness made them conspicuous and easy for police constables to hold for lunacy assessment.[141] Perhaps, in addition, some of these men suffered from mental illness exacerbated by alcoholism. From 1890 to 1940 in Queensland, there were approximately eight hundred suicides of men who had alcohol problems; from 1900 to 1950 in New Zealand, perhaps a thousand. When it is recalled that unsuccessful suicide attempts today are ten to twenty times suicide deaths, alcohol-related life-threatening acts during a half-century may have reached between ten and twenty thousand in each jurisdiction.

THE GREAT WAR AND THE INFLUENZA PANDEMIC

War scarred New Zealand more deeply than Queensland. The pandemic that immediately followed the conflict also struck Kiwis more severely. It is likely that around six hundred returned soldiers from World War 1 committed suicide in New Zealand and around three hundred in Queensland.[142] Single men were overrepresented (see tables 4.5 and 4.6). In both jurisdictions, half the suicides by returned soldiers occurred in the half-dozen years after the war, but such suicides certainly continued through the 1930s and 1940s. William Ayre survived a long war; he had been away for four years and had been gassed in the last month of the conflict. At home, he endured indifferent health and was expectorating blood for two months before he swallowed potassium cyanide in April 1930.[143] In 1936 house painter Robert Davie, gassed in the war and suffering from paralysis and shaking palsy, worried a good deal about his prolonged illness and the poverty imposed by two years without work.[144] The war killed men long after the Armistice because physical and psychological wounds differed in their healing time and each emotionally scared returned soldier had a unique level of support. The overall situation in New Zealand and Australia probably differed from that of the United

States, where, as Ira Wasserman notes, World War I did not produce great casualties. But he discovered a rise in suicides coincident with the great influenza epidemic. Significantly, he recommended more study of war and suicide using disaggregated data.[145]

Men from New Zealand and Australia had been gassed and wounded; they lost limbs to the enemy at the front and girls to the men at home. Soldiers in Palestine and Mesopotamia contracted malaria.[146] Subject to many operations from his war wounds, Thomas Hanna lamented that "life was a torment."[147] George Faulkner seemed to have adjusted to his wounds. His brother judged him an exceptionally healthy man in possession of all his faculties, but he did have one problem: "His right arm was amputated."[148] In this inquest and a few others, witnesses seemingly wanted or needed maimed and emotionally distraught returned soldiers to be normal and reminders of the war put aside, but the men could not co-operate. Not all those who lived through combat and then took their lives did so because of war alone. Alcoholism and mental illness evident before the war continued afterward, and precisely that claim of prior troubles gave the government a pretext for foot-dragging on disability pension applications. Unemployment during the postwar slump affected a lot of men who had given up several good years. A lot could go wrong in a single life.

Witnesses felt compelled to note that a friend, brother, husband, or son was not the same man who had left home.[149] "He was good until the war," said Thomas Adamson's father.[150] A girlfriend testified that "on his return from the front," Vladimir Valicha "was not in the same state of mind."[151] Friends were shocked that James Mill's hair had turned white; he had aged and now hid from imagined enemies.[152] Philip Connell from Dunedin returned in a peculiar state and suffered through "very depressed periods and has been subject to drinking bouts." In and out of hospital, he threatened suicide several times. James Stenhouse, who knew him from before the war, told the magistrate in a December 1920 inquest that Connell "has been suffering since his return from acute nervous depression. This I believe being due principally to the stress and shock of war."[153] Heroes could deteriorate into drunkards unfit for domestic life.[154] After his return, Herbert Wittner did very little work. "He was addicted to drink and appeared to me to be sometimes queer in the head."[155] After his head wound at Gallipoli, Arthur Best "wanted to be by himself all the time."[156]

Shell shock became a catch-all term among civilians for non-physical trauma. Witnesses used it casually without explanation or depth of understanding. Shrapnel made plumber William Fox's arm useless. He had done very little work in four years, but despite an obvious handicap and grave disappointment, his brother-in-law put his unhappiness down to shell shock.[157] Doctors engaged in guesswork too. "After shell shock," Dr Harry Tressider proposed, "a man may be high spirited one hour and low spirited the next."[158] Another doctor thought that a former pilot was "more or less neurasthenic due to his war services and being in that condition he would more easily be upset by liquor."[159] What was a real motive and what was a pretext could be obfuscated by a shell shock diagnosis. A school headmaster away on active service for five years and wounded in the head allegedly underwent a total mental change; however, according to parents' complaints, he was simply "interfering with the boys." He chose not to be interviewed by authorities.[160]

In some instances, references to shell shock understated conditions. A few men heard voices and imagined they were under attack or would face a firing squad.[161] An older returned soldier, forty-four-year-old Sidney Martin, had no relatives in New Zealand; always quiet, he was even more so after the war. He explained to his boarding-house keeper that he did not know what was coming over him. "He would sooner have come back with a limb off than be in the state of mind he was in."[162] Isaac Taylor had seen too much at Gallipoli and in France. He went through "his trench performances," and if anyone came near, he shouted to "stand back I am speaking to my God." When he first arrived back, he spoke to no one for three months. Finally, relating his experiences at the front, "he would break out in tears, thoroughly break down."[163] For years Fred Tarmery would wake up at night and fight Germans."[164] William Keast heard trumpets and shouted at passersby.[165] Financial troubles in late 1930 exacerbated farmer Harold Leslie's nervous condition, which had originated in the war. Doctors could not remove shrapnel, and Leslie would wake up at night, covered in perspiration, and go over his war experiences.[166]

A handful of men grieved over the death of a son or brother. Poor Charles Hunter. At fifty-eight he was a widower and had lost both sons.[167] Unable to look after his farm alone and under a doctor's care for eighteen months since hearing that his two sons were wounded, William Fawcett sold up. That precipitated a nervous breakdown.[168] After news that his brother had been killed in action, David Sutherland suffered "great depression," and "he could not bear to speak of Frank's name or of the war."[169] Several years later, a young printer whose two brothers were killed in the war shot himself with the rifle that had

Table 4.7
Estimated suicide rate for returned soldiers: New Zealand, 1920–40

Year	Suicide rate for non-combatants who were eligible for service	Suicide rate for returned soldiers based on number of men serving overseas	Suicide rate for returned soldiers based on number of casualties	Suicide rate for returned soldiers based on number of men granted a disability pension in 1920
1920	17.1	42.3	80.4	95.7
1922	30.1	30.8	58.5	69.6
1924	34.5	29.5	56.1	66.6
1926	35.3	19.2	36.6	43.5
1928	44.8	30.8	58.5	69.6
1930	55.3	29.5	56.1	66.6
1932	47.2	38.5	73.1	87.0
1934	42.9	20.5	39.0	46.4
1936	36.7	14.1	26.8	31.9
1938	56.5	26.9	51.1	60.1
1940	39.8	24.4	46.3	55.1

SOURCES: New Zealand, *Population Census, 1936, Appendix B, War Service* (Wellington: Government Printer, 1938), 2–3; Gerald T. Bloomfield, *New Zealand: A Handbook of Historical Statistics* (Boston: G.K. Hall & Co., 1984), 362; Archives New Zealand, Wellington, LE 1 box 754, record 1921/250, House of Representative, Return on the Number of Businesses Carried on by Returned Soldiers, 14 December 1921; suicide data from inquests.

belonged to one of them. "Whenever their names were mentioned in the house he would always get up and walk out." The father had just sailed for England to see his sons' graves.[170] The same devastating circumstances shattered families in Queensland. Labourer John Reeves slashed his throat with a razor shortly after news came that one of his sons was missing. Two sons had already been killed.[171]

Immediately after the war, the suicide rate for returned soldiers in New Zealand was two to four times that of men in same age cohort who had not served, and it remained somewhat higher than for other men for the next twenty years (see table 4.7). Information as to whether a man was a veteran came solely from witnesses' remarks. Whether or not the deceased was a returned soldier was not as obvious or as important to witnesses as the years progressed. Men stopped wearing old uniforms, and witnesses increasingly put the war behind them. The suicide rate of returned soldiers was probably higher than my estimates.

For Queensland, it is only possible to estimate crudely the suicide rate for returned soldiers because we do not have extensive data on those living just in that state. However, in 1933 former soldiers residing in

Queensland likely numbered slightly over 30,000; if it is assumed that there had been 35,000 in 1920, then the suicide rate for veterans was 70 in 1920 and 47 in 1933.[172] These estimates agree with the probable rates in New Zealand. At inquests witnesses said many of the same things about a change in character as came out in New Zealand inquests. Time and again, witnesses mentioned that the deceased had come back a different man, not in the same mental state, had begun drinking, behaved erratically, complained of head pains, and so forth. Friends said of Joseph Conlon that "he took no interest in anything that would tend to his welfare."[173] Men broken by war had started arriving home before the end of the conflict, and a few made symbolic statements about what had happened. John Halligan returned in January 1918 with an arm amputated below the elbow. One day in late April he put on his new civilian suit, walked to the Brisbane River, placed a folded uniform on the bank, and jumped in.[174] Unemployed returned soldier Frederick Marshall, alias Percy von Gombert, wrote to a friend that "when you receive this I shall have passed the Divide ... I wish to be just tumbled in [the grave] like a soldier with my boots ... This world is full of cant and hypocrisy. I am heartily sick of it."[175] Herbert Taylor wrote "Farewell" on the back of his discharge paper. He had been looking for work and was so poor he carried no swag. His mother had been in the asylum (mental hospital) for twenty years, and he had been in foster care since the age of nine.[176] War was a ghastly chapter in a sad tale.

With help from a repatriation program, wounded soldier William Keller opened the Allies Bakery in Toowoomba and soon afterward killed himself. His wife, Martha, stated that "there have been times since he returned from the war that he has been rather depressed."[177] Military Medal recipient Leonard Jarvis, wounded in the right arm, back, and leg, "also had shell shock and had been complaining about his head for past nine months." More had gone wrong in his life. He was unhappy in his domestic relations, and his wife had had two still-born children.[178] To shake bad memories of battles in Palestine, malaria, and a trip home in a straitjacket, David Molloy had gone north to a remote pastoral station. While hunting, he met another returned soldier, and they started talking about the war around a campfire. Later that night Molloy walked into the bush and shot himself.[179] John Reardon committed suicide in 1924. An uncomplaining, silent individual, he had a bullet still lodged in his spine below his neck. He would take periodic turns, sit up in bed, and cry out, "They're coming." According to his brother, "he did not speak much about the war. He never spoke about those turns."[180] Ivan de Grouchy had shrapnel in the head and body; after he had received his discharge, three pieces passed away from his head, and one piece took the sight of his left eye. He suffered great pain and could not sleep for weeks at a stretch. During the last month of his life he was despondent and spoke very little. "He told me many times," reported his brother, "that he was frightened of insanity and would never face an asylum and that he would finish everything before that came to pass."[181]

Shell shock was a common term, and sometimes witnesses elaborated. William Fisherton, secretary of the Returned Sailors and Soldiers League, had acted as trustee for Francis Ryan's military pension for more than a year. "When he arrived back in Queensland he was in a bad case of shell shock. In fact," said Fisherton, "he was the worst case I have seen ... He was not fit to travel himself. When he returned he was drinking and later was admitted as an inebriate to the Dunwich Institution where he was for six months. He complained to me about his head." He wrote to Fisherton, "I think to try to get me on to some quiet place as my head is very queer at times – and often makes me frightened I can tell you and as I do not like to think of Goodna [the state mental hospital] – will get [move on] if I can't get something to do very quickly."[182]

On their return, men craved work. John Hitchcock had enlisted in October 1915, endured two years at front, returned in poor health, and shared a room with his brother. He had had employment for a mere three weeks during the six months before he died. Two days before death he told his brother that "'this is terrible.' I said what is terrible. 'He said not being able to get work.'"[183] Patrick Ryan had been at war for three and a half years and now suffered from "melancholy and nerves" so badly that he had seen two local doctors, and "he then went to Dr. Ross' Mental Hospital in Sydney." His wife remarked that "he had worked for about six weeks of the last eighteen months; worked at the meat works; the remainder of the time he was knocking about at home."[184]

An odd cluster of suicides occurred in New Zealand in late 1918, coinciding with the great influenza pandemic, which struck New Zealand more severely than Queensland. That year witnesses at inquests into seventeen suicides of men placed influenza among the motives. Most men were labourers (ten of the seventeen, or 58.8 per cent). The influenza cluster may be explained by witnesses latching onto a convenient courtesy explanation, because in some instances there were other motives. However, several physicians remarked that influenza had a side effect which increased the risk of suicide. "Influenza is a disease well known to cause sudden impulsive mental aberration."[185] It was linked to depression, low spirits, nervous breakdowns, and unbalanced behaviour on account of fatigue. Wharf worker Harry Barlow explained how influenza undermined his will to live. He survived a self-inflicted pistol shot to the head long enough to say, "I got very weak from the influenza and I didn't think it worthwhile." His suicide note simply read, "I am suffering terribly. I can hardy stand up."[186] A friend of labourer George Hill had seen him a week earlier. "He was then recovering from a severe attack of influenza. He was very much pulled down."[187] As late as 1922, the mother of a poor, unemployed, and melancholy farm labourer mentioned at his inquest that "he had influenza in the epidemic of 1918."[188]

Remarks about influenza and depression had long preceded the 1918 pandemic. In 1902 a farmer's wife stated that after the influenza her husband was not the same man.[189] Herbert Bolwell's cousin reported at a 1904 inquest that "he told me he had been suffering from influenza and became very ill – generally depressed. This was in England. He went from place to place for his health under advice of Dr. Steele of Clifton."[190] Amelia Dunn told the magistrate at a 1910 inquest that her husband had "a very bad case of influenza from which he never properly recovered. He came home in September and has been attended by Drs. Macdonald and Nairn. He complained of severe pains in the head. He thought he was going mad."[191] A witness at the inquest for a young engineer in 1910 reported that "for about five weeks prior to his disappearance he was ill with influenza which left him in an unusually depressed state."[192] Ruby Hunter said that her father "was taken ill with influenza which later developed into insanity."[193] Auckland physician Alfred Knight held influenza responsible after the death of a young man in 1902 without domestic or money problems. "Influenza is responsible for producing mental depression. There are recorded cases leading to suicide."[194] Other physicians remarked on a connection between influenza and suicide. John Edgar of Napier treated shipwright John Northey in 1904. "He had been suffering from influenza. It is just possible that the depression caused by influenza may have made him commit suicide."[195] In 1908 a doctor attending the inquest into the suicide of draper Gilbert Oswald remarked that "influenza often leaves mental depression behind it."[196] Auckland doctor Edwin Milson deposed at a 1910 inquest that "after a severe attack of influenza a period of severe depression may set in often affecting the mental balance."[197]

Perhaps physicians comforted survivors with a courtesy diagnosis. What may have helped doctors reach these assessments were reports of acute confusional psychosis after a global influenza outbreak in 1889–91.[198] A possible tie-in between influenza and mental illnesses prompted Sir William Osler to write in *The Principles and Practice of Medicine* (1912) that "almost every form of disease of the nervous system may follow influenza." Osler stressed that "the most important nervous sequelae are depression of spirits, melancholia, and in some cases dementia."[199] Whatever inspired a doctor's comments at an inquest, the medical profession in the early twentieth century had settled on the idea that influenza disturbed mental stability. The 1918 pandemic inspired an accumulation of data. The surgeon general of the United States army as well as doctors at Manhattan State Hospital, the Brooklyn State Hospital, the Walter Reed Hospital, the Worcester State Hospital and others in North America and Europe investigated patient records to connect mental illnesses to influenza.[200] The question attracted Karl Menninger, then pursuing specialist studies in Boston. During the pandemic, Boston Psychopathic Hospital admitted one hundred cases of "mental disturbance associated with influenza."[201] Going beyond Osler's cautious suggestion that influenza could bring on a nervous breakdown, Menninger claimed to have encountered cases of influenza-induced schizophrenia. The records of patients at a psychiatric hospital provided atypical cases, and years later Menninger accepted the likelihood that the instances of schizophrenia were predisposed. Still, he would not let go of the idea that influenza had a role. "It took only a little pull on the trigger to fire the gun."[202] The little pull was influenza. Even as he converted to Freudianism, Menninger kept open the idea that major infectious diseases could have a toxic impact on the mind.

Back in New Zealand, during influenza outbreaks in 1926 and 1928, physicians continued to connect the flu with mental illness when they testified at suicide inquests. A doctor practising at Taumaranui explained during the inquest of a young farm labourer that "an influenza patient usually suffers more or less from mental depression and the best remedy for such a condition is absolute rest. In the present case I have heard from the evidence given that deceased did not take rest but fought against the trouble; depression in such a case would be more marked than in a severe case when the patient is compelled to stay in bed."[203] Not long afterward, a doctor in Christchurch remarked that his patient, now deceased, "was a bit depressed. He was quite assured that everything would be right in time. It is a common symptom of influenza for the patient to be depressed and melancholy much more so than is any cause for. In that condition he would be likely to exaggerate any worries he has, or be liable to a sudden attack of dementia. I do not think he would be accountable for his actions at the time of his death."[204] The last sentence suggests a courtesy. The most unusual claim came from a wife who deposed that "about twelve or thirteen years ago deceased had a bad attack of influenza. It affected his mind slightly for a time. Ever since then, he has been very easily upset, very nervous."[205]

Influenza weakened men and women struggling with other debilities and worries. At thirty-nine in 1928, farm labourer and widower Victor Macken suffered from heart attacks brought on by the after-effects of being severely gassed during the war. When he contracted influenza, he had had enough.[206] Influenza helped funnel the thinking of people such as Macken; they needed an escape and saw only one sure route. New Zealand doctors continued to relate influenza to depression and suicide into the 1940s. A doctor treating Gerald Dempsey for depression testified in 1940 that "this depression was not wholly post influenzal but dated further back. The actual origin seemed to be with the last war, when he was buried in an explosion, being rescued only at the point of asphyxiation and this left a state describable as shell shock."[207] Even in Queensland, which came through the pandemic of 1918 relatively unscathed, it was commonly assumed that influenza "always seems to induce a suicidal frame of mind."[208] In recent years some research has associated the onset of chronic fatigue syndrome (CFS) with a trauma, stress, toxins, or a severe bout of the flu. Conceivably, the great influenza pandemic left some survivors with a lingering, incapacitating syndrome comparable to CFS.[209]

THE STRUGGLES AND DEFEATS OF WAGE EARNERS

Attempts to correlate business cycles with suicide rates have yielded modest or complex associations. "A business crisis," observed statistician Louis Dublin, "is not always followed by a rise in the suicide rate and the severity of the crisis is no measure of the attendant increase of suicide."[210] Similarly, suicide rates do not necessarily correlate directly with unemployment data, and there is likely a lag effect of many months before a serious economic downturn with significant job losses is reflected in suicide rates.[211] People react to periods of economic adversity differently and can accumulate or absorb a series of blows before feeling defeated. Queensland dairy farmer Farrow Jarvis had strained hard to survive Australia's great turn-of-the-century drought; he made it through that terrible time, but when a dry season struck in 1919–20, he remembered the earlier hard times, lost sleep, felt he was "going silly" from continual worry, and could not face another period of extreme stress.[212] The assumption that wide-scale recessions or depressions are the source of work and money problems and thus set the timing of personal crises is questionable. Depressions do intensify hardship, but businesses can fail in a variety of circumstances. Personal finances have collapsed through weather disasters, accidents, illness, family circumstances that depleted income, a bad investment, living beyond one's means, labour strife, nervous breakdowns, and dismissal. Denied union membership on account of his working as a "scab" during a strike, miner James Brown had been without employment for months. "I have made up my mind to end my life," he wrote, "rather than shift the family about."[213] Elizabeth Harvey blamed a strike for her husband's lack of work and depression.[214] Even during prosperous years, men toiled in low-paying occupations, and misadventures could push them into destitution.

Not only is the relationship between economic cycles and suicide murky and intricate, but so too the relationship between urban class and suicide and between rural producers and suicide. In New Zealand, where there has been research into urban classes, it appears that in towns and cities at the beginning of the twentieth century as many as 40 per cent of working men were semi-skilled or unskilled. The proportion had likely dropped to 25 per cent by mid-century. These men at the margins of the labour market were not overrepresented among suicides, because the proportion of semi-skilled and unskilled men who committed suicide was 40.1 per cent in the early 1900s and 24.6 per cent in the 1940s.[215] Higher socio-economic groups possessed greater material resources, even after bankruptcy, but they may not have had greater emotional resources to deal with life's problems and could have been more fragile after scandal and loss of status.

The large number of men whom witnesses described simply as labourers and who died in rural locations complicates determining how many suicides were committed by men working in agriculture. Furthermore, a number of New Zealand farmers lived close to small towns and died in those places rather on their farms; some farmers and graziers in both jurisdictions took their lives while visiting towns and cities. There is no clean way to calculate rural suicide rates or to reach an exact rate

Graph 4.4
Estimated male suicide rates for rural employment compared with rates for all males: New
Zealand, 1900–50

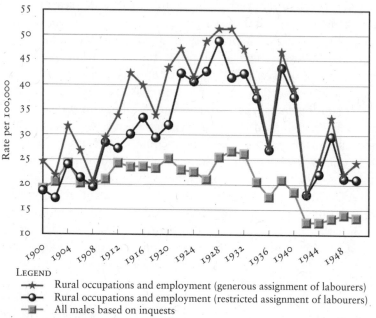

LEGEND

    —★—   Rural occupations and employment (generous assignment of labourers)
    —○—   Rural occupations and employment (restricted assignment of labourers)
    —■—   All males based on inquests

SOURCES: Gerald T. Bloomfield, *New Zealand: A Handbook of Historical Statistics* (Boston: G. K. Hall &
Co., 1984); Australia, Bureau of Census and Statistics, *Census of the Commonwealth of Australia
…1911*, vol. 1, *Statistician's Report Including Appendices* (Melbourne: McCarron, Bird & Co., 1917),
383–7. Suicide data from inquests.

for farmers, as opposed to rural labourers, because many owners of
small farms depended on employment on neighbouring farms or
stations. Interdependency linked the one-horse farmer and the heavily
capitalized sheep farmer.[216] The New Zealand censuses provided good
disaggregated data on occupations, and the suicide data set supplied
slightly more complete information on occupations; thus a range of
rates for men in agriculture was calculated. These estimates suggest that
men reliant on income from agriculture in New Zealand and
Queensland were at a greater risk of suicide than other men, but figures
for both jurisdictions should be treated as approximate. The chronological patterns were different (see graphs 4.4 and 4.5). The suicide rate for
Queensland men in agriculture had several peaks prior to the Great
Depression, possibly on account of the lagged impact of the protracted
"federation drought" (see graph 4.6).[217] A drought in the mid-1920s

Graph 4.5
Estimated male suicide rates for rural employment compared with rates for all males:
Queensland, 1890–1940

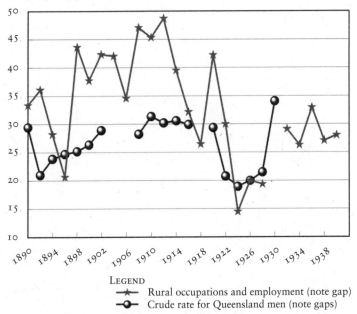

LEGEND
⋆ Rural occupations and employment (note gap)
○ Crude rate for Queensland men (note gaps)

SOURCES: "Employment in the Rural Industries, Colonies, the States, and Territories, 1841–1981," Table
AG-19, in Wray Vamplew, ed., *Australians: Historical Statistics* (Collingwood, Victoria: Fairfax, Syme,
and Weldon Associates, 1987), 72. Suicide data from inquests. The crude rates by gender for Queensland
used data reported in the *Queensland Yearbook*. No data was available from that source for 1904, 1906,
1918, and 1932–42.

put the state economy into recession, and hardest hit were the sectors
where casual labour was common: pastoralism, rail construction, and
mining.[218] It is striking that in New Zealand and Queensland the highest suicide rates for men with rural incomes reached a maximum that
was almost twice that for all men.

The scale of agriculture activity in both jurisdictions ensured a
bounty of detail about the trials and burdens of rural workers, farm
owners working on their own account, share milkers in New Zealand,
and farm and station managers with employees. When suicide is studied
at the case level, the connections between self-destruction and unemployment or economic hardship are restored as significant factors, but
ones that take into account the conjuncture of economic conditions
with other historic circumstances, the compounding effects of chance

Graph 4.6
Impact of federation drought on sheep and cattle: Queensland, 1897–1920 (log10 scale)

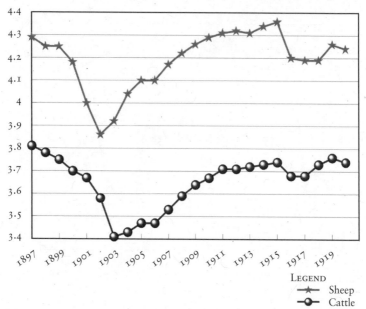

LEGEND
★——★ Sheep
●——● Cattle

SOURCE: "Beef and Dairy Cattle, Colonies, the States, and Territories, 1850–1981," Table AG 55-63, and "Sheep, Colonies, the States, and Territories, 1850–1981," Table AG 64-72, in Vamplew, ed., *Australians: Historical Statistics*, 80–1.

occurrences, the lagged impact of economic crises on individual lives, and in the case of agriculture, many stressful hazards. Moreover, economic stress can affect non-impoverished individuals, and their cases will be discussed alongside the instances of impoverished individuals throughout the rest of this book.[219]

In both New Zealand and Queensland, the worse years from the perspective of men who had work or money-related motives for suicide were the 1920s, which had a slight margin of darkness over the 1930s. Unemployment during the postwar recession was aggravated by returning soldiers. Single and looking for a job, carpenter Herbert Cooper hanged himself in the Auckland Domain in 1922. He wrote on the back of an envelope: "No work. No money. No friends. Nowhere to go."[220] Demobilized men included the able-bodied, who competed for jobs, as well as the injured and disoriented, who found it difficult to hold a job. In over half the New Zealand suicide cases (54.9 per cent) where war was a motive, the men were unemployed or, if self-employed, doing poorly. In Queensland nearly half the returned men (47.7 per cent) who committed suicide were unemployed or not doing well.

In New Zealand, economic or work motives appeared in one in six male suicides (17.7 per cent). If suicides among semi-skilled and unskilled working men and farm labourers are combined, the total accounts for over half the suicides (52.0 per cent) by men with these motives. Shopkeepers and small businessmen were notable among suicides where economic problems were the motive (8.4 per cent). Absolute desperation overtook a few itinerate labourers. William Hubble left South Australia in 1900 to seek employment in New Zealand. "I am in a strange country without friends and cannot get work, have not a penny, have been turned out for not paying my board, and my wardrobe taken so am starving. There is no other course open than taking my life. Please write and tell my wife."[221] Young farm labourer William Brennan, laid low by the influenza pandemic, worked sporadically for several years afterward. His mother recalled that "he said to me that a man might as well be dead as be out of work."[222] One of Tasman Henderson's last diary entries read: "Things are not too good. Haven't had a feed all day. I don't know what is going to happen." He was twenty-two.[223] Young Maori labourer Tui Nicholson, deaf from meningitis, took poison in his sister's yard. He had begged her for money. "I have not got money and mum has got not money either." As he lay dying, he told his sister that he was "worried, worried, no work."[224] It was winter when Charles Gimlett lost his job as a meat worker at a freezer works. He wrote to his sister: "The frosts here are something terrible and I do freeze in the tent every night. I have tried and I can get no work anywhere and things are getting worse."[225]

While men such as Hubble, Brennan, Henderson, Nicholson, and Gimlett never knew job security, other men had had stable careers until retrenchment struck them late in life. Solomon Rowe was sixty-two and without other prospects when Christchurch city council gave him three months' notice in 1928. He had worked twenty years for the city. His wife told the magistrate that "he has never been the same. He seemed to be regularly upset."[226] Commercial traveller Alexander Shaw had had steady employment until he was fired in July 1934. Without an income, he could not marry and so broke off his engagement.[227] Financial crises therefore could precipitate a concatenation of personal setbacks.

Injury or illness kept men from work. As a result of his heart condition, wharf worker Fred Brown looked fifty-five when he was only forty. Single and employed casually, "he complained of his heart and

could not do heavy work."[228] Misfortune crushed labourer John Walsh
in 1908. He had had no earnings for four months because of accidents.
"His being unable to work preyed on his mind and made him despondent." He and his wife had to move house and were talking about their
grim future shortly before he drowned himself.[229] At the age fifty-two,
Maori farm labourer John Moyan had never fully recovered from an
appendectomy. As his doctor expressed it, "this made him gloomy for
the future. He complained that he was only able to do light work and in
consequence was getting hard up."[230] With a large family to support,
railway labourer James Scott had "fits of depression" as a result of a
back injury. "His one anxiety was to get back to work."[231] John
Crawford's wife remarked at her husband's inquest in early 1924, "I
knew he was brooding over losing work owing to his being laid up with
a bad leg."[232] In November 1927 a rail collision threw labourer John
Hill over a viaduct, causing injuries that made him despair about ever
working again.[233] War wounds and a gastric condition confined wharf
worker Edmund Bennett to part-time work.[234] William Beehre was "a
habitual inebriate" with fingers missing on his right hand. His drinking
made it unlikely that he would secure government relief work. His wife
had ejected him and was taking out a maintenance order. In the face of
personal and financial calamity, he had nowhere to go. His options
at forty-six were so scaled down that suicide seemed the only way
out.[235] In a terse but not unusual note, unemployed butcher John
Rowntree wrote, "No Work. No Money. Good buy [sic]."[236] "I am perfectly sane just fed up with poverty and ill-health," wrote returned soldier Andrew Bennie.[237]

A sequence of things could go wrong, and unemployment contributed
to the overall sense of failure and depressed spirits. Steady work that
was not overwhelming could mitigate worry. "When the deceased consulted me for neurasthenia," testified Henry Forsyth's doctor, "there
was nothing to suggest that he would take his life. Brooding over his
loss of employment would have aggravated his condition. Employment
would have been good for his condition."[238] Work fed self-esteem; its
removal blasted confidence. Hector Cole had been out of work for two
months and left a note: "Please take care of my poor dear wife and darling Shirley. I am not worthy of being called their husband and
father."[239] It was not necessarily the loss of income alone that upset
men. For a few, the harm was in the loss of purpose or self-respect.
Retired bootmaker William Johnston, according to his wife, "was at
times depressed in spirits ever since he gave up business."[240] Just out of

hospital, Frederick Wybrott "was pining a lot because he had no work to do at all."[241] According to his wife, carpenter Thomas Glaister "often threatened to do away with himself." "He said it when he could get no work."[242] Skilled tailor and returned soldier William Todd was forced to take on manual relief work when he was fifty-six and had started drinking heavily on account of his loss of self-respect.[243] Bad health and the Depression kept carpenter and builder Ralph Heald from his trade; friends and relatives noticed that he became "very depressed."[244] To make a living after he lost his position as an insurance agent, Ernest Lilly went door to door selling coal in the summer. His wife remarked that "he was always worrying about finding suitable employment."[245] After underestimating a contract, builder George Henry felt that "his prestige had been lowered by the mistake," and his loss of face, as president of a local builders association, precipitated an overwhelming depression.[246]

In a few instances, the difficulty of the work precipitated a breakdown. Constable David Brown, assigned to a remote posting with extensive duties as constable, clerk of court, bailiff, and gaoler, felt overwhelmed. "I have been worrying over my incompetence that I cannot go on, and my dear wife is worrying about me."[247] School headmaster Johann Gloy was concerned about his new appointment and "seemed to think he would not be able to do the work well."[248] In the 1940s the proportion of work and money motives dropped, and rather than economic conditions putting men out of work, illnesses were the chief reason.

In Queensland, witnesses reported work-related difficulties or financial problems in one in seven male suicides (15.3 per cent), and among these work- or money-related suicides, agricultural workers and semi-skilled and unskilled labourers accounted for four out of ten (41.3 per cent). Shopkeepers and small businessmen turned up, but slightly less often than in New Zealand (5.6 per cent). Men out of work, without steady work, on strike, or whose farms and businesses had failed left more complete suicide notes than alcohol-dependant men. Some wrote long, poignant letters with passages touching on work and identity. Breadwinners had to explain why they could not get work. Evincing low self-esteem, they endeavoured to account for themselves, to give meaning to their life and their final act. Accountant Carl Harden suffered from dengue fever, so could not work. "Am only sorry that I have not been able to provide better for my poor wife and children. Am very ill worse every day, and not much good for work now."[249] During a depression that followed the South African (Boer) War, when labourers streamed into Brisbane, Arthur Garlich, an accountant out of work in 1902, wrote to his mother:

> I have nine pawn tickets which includes everything I have in the world, even down to my Gladstone bags and hat box, they amount to eleven pounds odd at 120% a year interest.
>
> You ask why I don't try and get manual labour, that just shows how little you know of what the state of things are in Queensland, there are unemployed meetings held on the street corners here every day, attended by from 1000 to 1500 men all looking for work, and more men coming in from the country every day. I have tried to get a job as lumper on the wharf, and even applied to the Government labour bureau, every hotel in Brisbane to get a job as barman, and the Tramway Co as conductor.
>
> I have borrowed money from everyone I know from 3d up to £1, & have to keep clear of the main street during the day. I walk the streets from early morning till midnight. Every day seems like a week, so if I am desperate, & don't care what happens next, it's hardly to be wondered.[250]

A mission to work persisted among farmers, craftsmen, and professionals, who brooded when they stopped toiling. As a study of suicides in England put it, "the meaning of what it is to be without a job is also important."[251] Men without work denigrated themselves, because work could bring purpose and meaning to their lives. Men at work felt they were contributing value to society; for some, idleness translated into worthlessness. Unemployed meat works employee Albert Poulson, a victim of postwar closures that resulted from the termination of war contracts, told his wife, "I hate hanging about home. People will think I am as bad a loafer as the rest of them." Matthew Brennan confided to a friend, "I am down to my last fifty pounds now, as soon as that's finished there is nothing but the river for me. I couldn't live and not be able to provide for my wife." On account of old age, he had mortgaged the farm and then sold it; he finally had to sell his horse and dray.[252] The mental burden seems particularly pronounced among married men in Queensland, as it was in New Zealand (see tables 4.5 and 4.6). There was a greater probability of work or money motives among the suicides of family men. Wives were often the chief witnesses. Thomas Rumney left a note for his wife that overflows with guilt:

To Mrs Thomas Rumney, Wynnum

It has come to this, my last day on earth is here, and I am in the [city botanic] gardens where we used to sit together and make plans for the future 14 years ago. Alas! How things have changed, I have had no luck in Queensland, in any way, quite the reverse. I am so troubled as having to leave you and my dear little ones to the cruel world, but what am I to do? I cannot get any work that will enable me to keep you in any way fitting to your life, so I am no good, to myself or to you. If ever a man was in torment, I am. It is awfully hot and nearly 12 o'clock. The people will soon be leaving here for dinner, then it <u>must</u> be done. Your talents should have placed you in a very different position, but it's my fault. So now for the grand secret.[253]

If employment failed, men believed they had failed, although few controlled their work. Witnesses described men who had committed suicide because of work or money problems as quiet and worried, reserved and worried, upset and troubled, despondent, glum, sad, and depressed, but never angry or violent. Masculinity's expectations furnished a scorecard. Suicide notes and witnesses' statements conveyed introspection, self-criticism, fatalism, and curtain-call eloquence. Dismissed from employment, accountant William Hallinson wrote to his employer: "This will be the last note you will receive from me, as when you read it, I shall be dead. Far better so – no wife, no home, no work and no money."[254] Unmarried, unemployed miner Thomas Williamson wrote to his family in England: "I am tired of my life. It has been a very unhappy one. I have tried all kind of ways to get one but always failed."[255] "I have tried and failed," wrote businessman Albert Maurice.[256] Only a few men denounced capitalism. Leo Orange, who testified that his brother was demoralized, said that "the whole trouble was he was low down on finances, in very poor circumstances. He was out of employment. I am of the opinion that he took his own life. He had only one enemy, the master class, the worker's only enemy."[257] More typical were the sentiments of shearer William Brown in 1940: "I have tried to live a decent life I cannot work and it has broke my heart because I cannot give you and children what I would like to. Do not think bad of me. I love you and the kids and there is nothing about me that you should be ashamed of on account of my name. I have a clean record. May God Bless you all and help Great Britain and allies to victory."[258]

ENTERPRISE AND TEMPTATIONS

Bad investments and defeated expectations came in an amazing variety. Charles Deane's failed gold-mining speculations caused lasting difficulties.[259] Miner-prospector John Downing realized there would be no more gold rushes.[260] A recession in 1907–08 affected a number of speculators; the suicide rate was on the rise. Commercial traveller Thomas Craig, a childless widower, talked of doing away with himself during that slump because "he lost a good deal of money in shares a few months ago."[261] In June 1908 farmer Lawrence Laurenson went to his doctor for a sedative; the bank had been squeezing him for two years, and he could not sleep. Because of his failed speculations, he remarked that "his was a case for millionaires not doctors."[262]

For runs of bad luck, some life histories were star-crossed beyond fiction. Horse trainer Percy Coffey, a separated father of two, had hoped to cash in on a horse race because he faced a law suit over a debt. "Our separation," said his wife, "was temporary and due to marital problems."[263] The horse died before the race. For twelve months James Nevin operated the Birchwood-to-Nightcaps mail service without a profit. Bad health and depression had dogged him for seven years, ever since he contracted meningitis in an army camp. "During the past two years," reported his wife, "he had been drinking a bottle of whiskey each day."[264] Thomas Johnson, a fifty-year-old insurance agent, worried because he could not get through all his work.[265] Tile manufacturer James Christmas had imported machinery from South Africa that was supposed to have been practically new but was useless. Freight charges and custom duties absorbed his spare cash. He had been negotiating with firms in Australia and New Zealand for the sale of tiles and could not manufacture any.[266] When his brush factory ceased turning a profit, Frederick Peters "could not sleep at night. His nerves appeared to give him trouble."[267]

Great differences separated how men managed their lives and accepted responsibility. Some turned the ethos of the survival of the fittest inward. Commercial traveller Angus Macgregor – single, forty-four, and living at home – left this note: "I did not seem to be a success up the present so I may as well get out."[268] The shame of their name appearing in a newspaper in connection with a debt suit was too much for some men.[269] Accused of peculation, hospital board secretary Nelson Bunting could no longer stand "the wicked, baseless rumours." "Forgive and forget an unworthy and tortured soul," he wrote.[270] Most bankrupts had attempted to make a living, but there were rogues who folded their cards after a losing hand in a deplorably colourful life. Hector Parkman, "who had no other occupation than master of the hounds," squandered or enjoyed his inheritance – take your pick – until "he was pecuniarily embarrassed," at which point his fiancée left him.[271] "My Dear Wife," wrote William Tough, "by the time you receive this I will be no more. Financial trouble. Everybody thinks I have money but it is not the case, went too strong. Horse racing, whiskey, and motor cars is the cause. Weep not for me. Make the best of it."[272] Car salesman William McKernan's fantasy life crumbled when his girlfriend discovered he had a wife and could not secure a grand life for them in America through help from a fictitious friend "who was the editor of the New York Times."[273]

The farm was New Zealand's most common enterprise. Farmers accounted for more than one in ten (12.6 per cent) of male suicides, and along with farm labourers of all kinds, they had an especially high suicide rate in the 1920s and 1930s (see graph 4.4). Farmers working on their own account faced multiple troubles, for they wore the hats of both businessmen and toilers and could be quite lonely. The diaries of Wairarapa middle-aged farmer and widower George Welch, who took his life in 1906, recounted that work left him "dead beat." He recorded setbacks, debts, worries, and sciatica and drew his late wife's picture on the cover of one diary volume. Subject to interludes of insomnia and depression, he took a sleeping draught of Chlorodyne when troubled and feeling unwell.[274] Clifford Hood's wife could have spoken for many rural wives in the 1920s: "The farm had not been paying as well as it should." Her husband was "concerned over the financial position of the farm"[275] The farm, a purpose in life, and domestic trouble occasionally combined, as they did for Ngatai Wanoa, who gave up milking on account of his health, moved to a smaller house, and dealt with a feud between his daughter and his second wife.[276] The realization that work was too much and that the farm might have to be sold conjoined to devastate men. James McAuliffe's wife said that "he might sell the farm and that this seemed like an admission of defeat."[277]

Farmers in Queensland were at considerable risk too. They accounted for more than one in twelve (8.6 per cent) of male suicides. Graziers contributed a few dozen more cases. The trials of life in rural Queensland put men – and women – at risk. Fearful of making wrong decisions regarding stock, crops, or land, farmers and graziers routinely endured stress.[278] French immigrant and dairy farmer Georges Robert wrote despairingly that "seasons, floods, everything has been so much against us that our position is now desperate."[279] Farmers pleaded with creditors, endured injuries, experienced crop failures and livestock diseases, and encountered disastrous markets. Neighbours assisted Jules Lareher, but he could not make a go of it. He apologized to the friendly farmers who staked him: "I have strived very hard to be worthy of your help and have failed." On the outside of an envelope the single, thirty-two-year-old farmer wrote, "Can not get over loneliness."[280] When a grain buyer rejected his wheat, William Palmer "took his hat off his head, threw it on the floor and made five or six jumps in the shed and with a stick he struck the bags of wheat in the shed ... he seemed very excited and troubled."[281] Sugar farmer William McClosky was depressed on account of his cane crop. On the day he shot himself, two buyers from Consolidated Sugar Refiners had inspected his cane, and shortly after that, he complained to his wife about the company and then wrote a will.[282]

Droughts could last years. In the 1930s lack of rain and depressed prices laid many farmers low; during that decade it is likely around one hundred and fifty committed suicide; during the previous decade perhaps a hundred had ended their lives. In his note former farmer Andreas Arntzern apologized for the trouble he would cause, but wrote, "I can not see myself going to live on the dole, and I have just come to the end of my tether."[283] Shortly before he died, farmer Hugh Sim remarked that "it is a worry the way the farm business is mixed up."[284] Farmer Michael Herrigan ran out of horse and cattle feed. A neighbour said that "he wished he was dead. He seemed depressed on account of the failure of his crops."[285] Cattlemen's suicides reached record levels in the 1930s. Grazier William Carvasso wrote to a friend:

> If I try to carry on any longer it will only mean that I will make a mess of things and make it worse for everyone interested so it is far better for me to stand down. Going on my past experience I feel sure that we are in for a bad drought and the job is too much for me. It hurts me to make this admission but age will naturally beat us all. The water is drying up fast and something must be done at once. I have been a sick man for a long time and simply cannot carry on any longer. I intend to go out. It seems a rotten thing to do, but after long consideration [I] think it is the best for all those interested. It is not much use for me to say anymore. The Bank no doubt will do what they think best to protect their interests.[286]

Then there were unexpected disasters. Emma Kachel explained that her husband had assembled a good dairy herd, but "one morning when we got up we found that they had got poisoned on the Railway line, through a poison train going through a few days previous destroying the weeds by poison, of which we were not aware. He lost over 20 cows and was only left with about half a dozen cows. Since then he had not been able to get a herd together and been going back financially all the time."[287] The tragic aspect about many farmer suicides during depressions was the underlying unawareness of market forces, which left men blaming themselves; in earlier decades, hard work had meant prosperity, and poverty implied slackness somewhere. When Hugh Somerset investigated life in rural New Zealand in the 1930s, one informant described how the economic collapse had left his father a broken man. "The depression killed him ... He seemed to take the blame of it all on his shoulders, wondering where he had gone wrong, and what false steps had given him an overdraft instead of a credit balance."[288] Since farmers at least could work, the way out of the depression that came immediately to mind was to work more. So they added to their burdens, increased supply, and further reduced prices.

Middle-class men shared with labourers and farmers the urge to be useful and a common lack of control over the economy. They proceeded on a life trajectory at a time and in a place where the maintenance of social distinctions recommended progress by respectability, careful management of time, and limited frivolity.[289] Individuals broke this code. Businessmen and white-collar employees drank, gambled, maintained mistresses, visited brothels, overspent, and stole. The sporting life of wine, women, and racehorses in the early twentieth century attracted rogues, and the life caught up with them. Clerk Robert Catt managed the accounts of the OK Mine Company, which showed "irregularities." "I cannot balance my books. Cannot find all the mine entries. Think am mad would commit suicide but am too much of a coward. Drink is the cause of it all."[290] Men clinging to respectability might proffer an exculpatory assessment. Storekeeper William James wrote: "Will someone kindly write [to my family in England] and tell them I am dead. My brains seem to have ceased their action. Do not put my death down to drink for my mental and bodily functions caused me to find relief from pain in drink."[291] The fast living caught up with Eugene Gilliard, who had debts, a drinking problem, a wife, and a young girlfriend. "My life was a double life."[292] He was not alone. James Rhodes wrote to his mistress, "My Dearest Jessie, I was between the devil and the deep sea, my lawful wife on one side and the bank on the other."[293] Suicide offered escape from seemingly impossible situations that these men had orchestrated for themselves.

Middle-class men who abided by the rules struggled to hold onto social rank. Married one month, contractor Daniel Smith encountered unexpected responsibilities: "I have tried my best and the more I try the further I get behind. I am in debt ... I told you that I had to borrow money when I married you. I did not marry your father and your damn lazy brother and your mother."[294] Status meant a lot to middle-class men who accepted the code. Contractor Frederick Bunce told acquaintances that he would commit suicide because he was losing money. They suggested that insolvency might be wiser, but he feared losing social position.[295] A few subscribed to self-improvement, but without advancement, they turned on themselves. Daniel Gillespie tried to get a job running equipment on road construction, but he lacked qualifications. He studied for a licence. His wife testified that "the constant studying has affected his brain." He would sit at night with the books in front of him and his head in his hands.[296] It was one thing to feel challenged, another to feel broken.

TIRED OF LIFE

Age, injury, and illness did more than reduce earnings; they assaulted self-respect. Retired or ailing farmers surrendered their mission as providers. For the swagmen in their fifties and sixties, the open road became an uphill climb best accomplished by young bodies. In early 1922, shortly before his fiftieth birthday, single farm labourer William Todd had been hospitalized and released in weak condition. Suffering from "melancholic depression," he told his employer, "I am useless on the farm."[297] When he was fifty-four, George Parker "worried about not being able to work as much as compared to when he was young."[298] Only forty-seven, farm labourer Charles Johnson had to shift for a job. "I paid him off," testified market gardener Ah Kim, "as I had no more work to do." Described as feeble, destitute, and single, Johnson could not continue on the tramp.[299] Sacked, single, and sixty, Patrick Herald feared cancer would return.[300] Middle-class professionals who retired missed their work. The editor of the Auckland *Herald* told journalist George Main that the paper would provide a pension; however, "his great trouble seemed to be that he was unable to render service for the payment."[301] It was the sociability of work he craved, not money. A supportive spouse helped men adjust to reduced earnings and idle time, but in both jurisdictions, single men fifty-five and older and without emotional support were at higher risk. Where could old, single men in the country go when unable to care for themselves? When grazier William George was seventy-two and ailing, he packed his clothes and a revolver and moved in with his generous neighbours, the Coyles. When his health got worse, he told a friend that "he wished he could die as he was getting so weak that he was afraid that he would be an annoyance to the Coyle family."[302]

To qualify for a New Zealand pension, men had to be sixty-five and have resided in the jurisdiction for twenty-five years. At the turn of the century a few who did not qualify ended their years as jailed vagrants.[303] Even if they were recipients of pensions, poor, elderly men often wound up in miserable circumstances. Single and seventy-three, Richard Reid lived with a niece, who sent him to the local hospital with a letter in a sealed envelope: "Dear Sir you will admit and not allow him to leave the place." Reid knew what had been planned.[304] Seventy-five-year-old pensioner Leonard Hindley had never married, and he lived in a hotel until friends took him in. He was confined to his bed, and he shot himself when he learned of arrangements to move him into an old men's home. An investigating constable reported that "he was not destitute but he was very much opposed to going to the Old Man's Home."[305] Thomas McKenzie, a seventy-five-year-old labourer, told his son that "he would sooner die in the Tussock than go back" to the Old Men's Home in Invercargill.[306] Seventy-four-year-old Peter Maskrey of Christchurch said that "he would rather throw himself in front of the Express rather than go into the Old Men's Home."[307] John Crimmons was disabled, old, and poor, but still the Opotiki Charitable Aid Board reduced his assistance. A constable on the board excused himself from guilt: "He did not say to me he was starving."[308] Family members looked after retired axle-turner Sam Bullivant, but he complained about the treatment. The food, he claimed, "was out of the pigs stuff."[309] Growing old, widower William Hale "was much upset by the treatment he received from his sons."[310] In addition to real abuse, senile dementia fed suspicion.

Widowers were vulnerable. Eighty, weak, and lonely, George Moorcroft told friends that "when his time came he hoped he would not have to suffer as she [his late wife] had done."[311] A few men with serious illnesses decided that they had no enjoyment left. Encephalitis made John McDonald bedridden and unable to read.[312] Parkinson's disease was wasting Philip Denham when he wrote, "I am nearly useless and have decided to end it before I become a cot case."[313]

Queensland's destitute elderly and the state's inebriates could appear before a police magistrate and request committal to the Dunwich Asylum on North Stradbroke Island. Aging Queenslanders did not look forward to that trip. "It's a terrible thing when you are getting old," remarked ex-solider George Sweet.[314] At age seventy, labourer John Norton could hear a swish from the Grim Reaper's scythe. He acted oddly and repeated that "old people were better dead."[315] This attitude was shared by George Grayton, described by his children as a very old, sick man who had lost the sight of one eye and could barely walk. "He said he often wished himself dead as he was only a bother to other people."[316] After three spells in the hospital in six months, sixty-eight-year-old Johann Struckmeir told a friend, "I am very unwell and I do not think I'll ever get better."[317] Old age pensioner Walter Palmer took strychnine. Witnesses recalled him saying, "Oh what is the good of being a cripple" and "Oh damn it all the poison is nothing to the pain in my leg."[318] "I have for some time been afflicted with a malady and partial blindness," explained Jesse Dorrington.[319]

Older single men felt their isolation. James Barrett feared he had cancer, but he confided, too, that "he was lonely, and wished he had married as a young man, so that he could have company in his old age. He also said that life was not worth while living for an old man like me, as he had no one to live for."[320] Old, single dingo hunter Robert McSporran, who described himself as an incurable physical wreck, prepared for his death by shooting his sole friend – a dog that no one would want. He then composed a final poem.[321]

> No more in the sun he'll sit
> Among the other wrecks
> His body's cold his soul has flit
> Old Bob's passed in his checks
> Now where the murky shadows creep
> Among the tombstones white
> He lays alone in peaceful sleep
> Through never ending night.

CONCLUSIONS

The words of diverse men recounted journeys that ended abruptly during the worst years of the twentieth century. Residing a world away from battlefields and financial capitals, they were nevertheless affected by decisions made in distant places and left feeling that no choices they could make would give them any life they wanted. Some had travelled a global nightmare. Other men were relatively isolated but decided to live fast and recklessly until time caught up with them. Sara Wilson told her wild boyfriend, Neville Rice, that "he should stop drinking or he would look like 50 at age 30."[322] If we were to judge by their last chapters, these tales of private existence could never be considered typical of individual lives. No method is available for proving or disproving that these troubles were characteristic since there are no comparable narratives from the great majority, no caches of heart-felt words collected from abundant survivors, no control groups. But the personal stories of suicides expose experiences that were part of common knowledge and common fears. We leave these glimpses into personal histories with a better sense of a past society and especially its common burdens.

They reveal no suicidal personality, but they do provide a cross-section of humanity, a mix of the rash, morose, irresponsible, decent, prideful, brittle, dignified, violent, and even roguishly witty. At the same time, the lives of these men show patterns that agree with many of Ronald Maris's observations, although the case files are so rich as to compel elaborations on his conclusions. First, troubles accumulated with age, and this process occurred in an era when medical intervention was far from what it was about to become and in an era when social welfare was rudimentary. No wonder suicide among men correlated with age. Second, marital problems increased risk, as Maris found in Chicago. However, the roots and consequences were varied. Questionnaires and interviews that he used may not have disclosed a husband's violence or subsequent shame and remorse at a violent attack on a spouse. "I must have been mad to have behaved this way," confessed Robert Davis about his violence at home; he ended the abuse by jumping in front of a train.[323] A third observation is that culture affected suicide. It could make the act more acceptable and could influence motives by elevating a value such as honour. Fourth, alcohol abuse was important, and there were compounding effects as a result of accompanying unemployment and marital breakdown. However, alcohol abuse tapered off in the interwar years. Fifth, war trauma was important and is the type of factor that is neglected in some social science analyses which pass over historical contingencies. Social forces occur in historical time, not a timeless present. A sixth conclusion is that class or occupational rank was not a factor, but unemployment certainly was, and farmers, farm labourers, and graziers endured readily identified and diverse difficulties. Seventh, a few men chose the fast life and bowed out when they had no money. Finally, mental illness was significant as a factor on its own and in conjunction with war trauma and alcohol abuse.

5

Sorrows and Burdens: Women and Motives

For as long as suicide statistics have been collected and studied, much has been made of the lower suicide rates for women that prevail in many jurisdictions around the world. In the two studied here, the ratio of men to women was approximately four to one (in New Zealand 79.2 per cent men and 20.8 per cent women; in Queensland 83.0 per cent men and 17.0 per cent women). Writer after writer presumed that there had to be a connection between the low rate and an alleged protective wrap of domesticity. This thesis served the conservative bias of nineteenth-century suicide studies. Durkheim broke slightly from this overt politicization of suicide, but he still accepted the idea that women were sheltered from the worst tensions of commerce and the most acute trials of labour. He presumed that, although marriage shielded women, it did not benefit them quite as much as men, because after marriage, women more often than men saw their illusions take flight. That perspective painted over the uglier scenes of marital discord. Had Durkheim's data enabled him to probe into that "flight of illusions" and had he been less driven to defend marriage as part of healthy social integration, he might have encountered discomfiting information about the hard lives of some women within marriage.[1] Aggregate data conceal the lives of people, and a male-centred comprehension of suicide was ensured by the overwhelming presence of male commentators.

Analysis of gender and suicide remained stalled for a long time at the moment when male writers put the hardships of breadwinning into the open and reported on the benefits of marriage.[2] On its own, the insight that the hazards of commerce and the vulnerability of waged work put men under stress has merit, but not as the basis of a credible contrast between men and women. Weaknesses showed, for example, in the presumption that women at home did not share in the crises and anxieties of their spouses. Conceivably out of masculine pride, men did not convey their anxieties and setbacks. Alfred Penny was silent about his "money troubles" until the end: "I tried to put a good front to you and the children and kept it from you until now."[3] Nevertheless, women could not ignore the consequences following from breadwinners' loss of income. At the psychological level, the spectrum of unhappy relations extended from a husband's brooding silence to explosive rage. At the economic level, women were drawn into their husbands' struggles through household management. The last time anyone spoke to Linda Page, she had tears in her eyes. "I have been in to Mr. Drinnon," she told a friend, "and he has stopped our credit and will not let us have anymore meat."[4] The idea of domestic serenity proposed by Durkheim also ignored an assortment of physical and mental strains associated with reproduction. Finally, there is an empirical flaw with the domesticity thesis. A focus on suicide rates leaves suicide attempts out of the picture. Women have led men in parasuicide. In New Zealand, for example, the number of women hospitalized for self-injury has been roughly twice that for men.[5] The burgeoning literature on this discrepancy sometimes refers to it as the gender paradox.[6]

Unsuccessful suicides are largely invisible in history except when there were prosecutions for attempted suicide, which were exceedingly rare, or memoirs and biographies that brought an attempt to light. More commonly in the period under examination, the police or the family members of the men and women who attempted suicide initiated the process for committal to a mental hospital. Without reliable historical data on attempted suicides for New Zealand and Queensland, the reconstruction of suicides among women must rely on the inquests to disclose the circumstances that led women to contemplate self-destruction and to watch for gender-specific as well as shared motives. Evidence from successful suicides suggests that in some instances during asymmetrical disputes with spouses or parents, women sought empowerment by threatening suicide; a few then moved on to harmful acts but calculated – wrongly – on rescue. Mary Gough argued with her husband about helping her to discipline their children and then ran into the house, poured poison into a cup, and drank it just as he came in. "I though she was trying to frighten me," he said. "'You saw me with the cup in my hand, why didn't you take it away from me?' I answered that I did not know."[7] The complex dynamics of intention and the response of others to an individual's threats, not just the immediate lethality of the method, help explain differences in the suicide rates of women and men. By and large, the men who committed suicide in New Zealand and Queensland wanted "to finish the business" or "get out of it." It was consistent with a cultural conditioning that they would follow a script which represented masculine conduct as decisive, brave, and unequivocal.[8]

Women's motives are best considered in a progression through the life course, in association with biologically and culturally directed phases. Many women in New Zealand and Queensland saw their long-term goals and prospects in relation to procreativity and motherhood; these predispositions and inclinations can undoubtedly be learned and unlearned, but the women presented in the inquests thought these roles natural. Statistics on motives help sort out the stages in these roles, but hundreds of witnesses and scores of suicide notes vividly expose the sets of emotionally charged, high-risk situations, which altered with aging.

In any discussion of men or women that broaches high-risk situations and ailments, the concept of a life course helps to order circumstances. However, life-course theories proposed by psychologists and psychiatrists influenced by Freud have attracted the criticism of sociologists. Psychologists accented the idea that changes in the life course are triggered by biology; they characterized the movement through stages as a progression in autonomy with an enhancement of mental powers. Freudian psychiatrists represented the life course as the evolution of drives and defence measures; the latter reconcile the former to the outside world. Sociologists pointed out that blue-collar families are exposed to trials which can obscure the developmental stages propounded by assorted psychological models. "Identifiable developmental stages," wrote Janet Giele, "appear more likely to occur in some persons and in some social settings than others."[9] The suicide inquests for men point firmly toward the existence of stages: adolescence, young adulthood, the prime work years, the years of physical decline, and old age. Witnessed through the darkness of suicide, stages in the life course do not seem to bring freedom and wisdom but convey a sequence of limitations and frustrations, a sequence latent in the lives of many and manifest in the deaths of a few.

Women have different benchmarks in the life course from men. Germaine Greer suggested that "women's lives are constructed of changes so vivid that they might be called metamorphoses," signalled by "contrasting body states from skinny to curvaceous or pregnant or obese and back again."[10] Greer recommended seven stages: birth and infancy, the stormy passage of adolescence, defloration, childbirth, menopause, widowhood,

Graph 5.1
Suicide rates for women in the United States by marital status, c. 1950

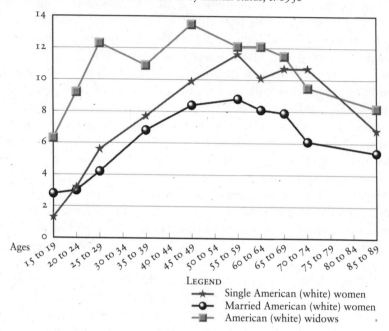

LEGEND
—★— Single American (white) women
—⊙— Married American (white) women
—■— American (white) widows

Graph 5.2
Suicide rates for New Zealand women by marital status, 1902–42

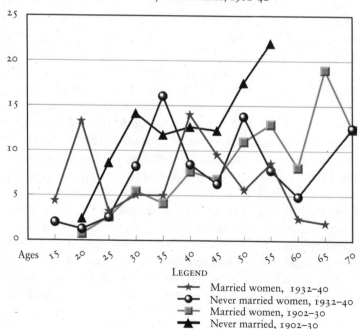

LEGEND
—★— Married women, 1932–40
—⊙— Never married women, 1932–40
—■— Married women, 1902–30
—▲— Never married, 1902–30

and death.[11] Except for birth and infancy, her stages accord with largely age-specific patterns in the motives for suicide.

It has been often remarked that married men have had a significantly lower suicide rate than their unmarried counterparts and that married women have had only a slight advantage over single women; the New Zealand data supports that proposition (see graphs 5.1 and 5.2).[12] The finding for married women is rather surprising given the picture of heavy drinking and domestic discord found in files that dealt with the suicides of both women and men. On the one hand, the risk for young, single women was well described by Victor Bailey when he observed that "the most common experience of suicide for young [single] females was a disturbance in personal relationships, specifically bereavement, romantic disappointment, and family disagreement."[13] On the other hand, explanations for marriage's buffering come to mind. First, women – like men – had a better chance of weathering problems if they could share them. In a summary of research on women and mental illness, Janet Giele noted that marriage in some cases insulated against stressful events that caused depression. She added, however, that a Quality of American Life Survey found that married women may be happiest before they have children and after the children have grown up, because they have more time for themselves.[14] Second, as a number of cases propose, single women who either were pregnant or wanted a family and seemingly had no prospects for one were at risk; they measured themselves against society's expectations and their reproductive potential respectively. Finally, although marriage may have benefited women generally, the benefits for men may have been greater.

BROKEN-HEARTED WITHOUT YOU

Young, single woman appear more likely than their male counterparts to commit suicide over romantic misadventures. In New Zealand the overrepresentation of romantic motives among single young women relative to men was noteworthy but not startling (6.0 per cent of single male suicides versus 16.3 per cent of single female suicides); however, in Queensland the romantic motive was pronounced among single women (6.4 per cent of single male suicides versus 30.5 per cent of single female suicides). The unmarried women with romantic motives had a mean age in New Zealand of twenty-four (23.7), and for cases where age was known in Queensland, twenty-one (20.6). In Queensland almost half (44.4 per cent) were domestic servants, and in New Zealand only one in five (18.3 per cent). Other occupations in Queensland included cook, hotel employee, boarding-house keeper, and nurse; in New Zealand the positions included nurse, store clerk, and dressmaker. Among adolescents, individuals aged seventeen or younger, females had a higher proportion of suicides relative to males than for any other stage in the course of life (in New Zealand 68.8 per cent of the seventeen and younger were males; 31.2 per cent were females).

As the more settled society, New Zealand offered slightly greater possibilities for women. At the same time, commonalities reigned across the two societies in the form of pressure to marry and in the attendant risks, which included rejection, the shame of pregnancy outside marriage, and the financial and emotional crisis of abandonment. Permutations within the general categories of motives were likely complicated by factors falling outside the recollections of witnesses with a limited ken. For example, documents do not speak to childhood abuse, genetic vulnerability to stress, or biochemical conditions that could develop from the interplay of these factors.

Documents also fail to account adequately for the passions that young women everywhere felt for particular men. The stormy passage of adolescence was Greer's apt label, and it transpired across cultural lines. In a firmly Maori region of New Zealand, young Ivy Pomare had exchanged greenstones with Raroa; this, said her grandfather, was an act of engagement. However, Raroa refused to marry Ivy when "she was in trouble." "There is much pain and sorrow within me," Ivy wrote.[15] Wherever there were young women, there was anguish over men on account of harsh results from the mating game. Several broken engagements left Bessie Bunny despondent, and according to her brother, she felt worthless and "could not bear it any longer."[16] We cannot measure the physical appeal of men in the tragedies, cannot watch them apply their charms, cannot dismiss the physical allure, cannot hear their promises, and cannot experience the loneliness or longings of young women. Why would seventeen-year-old Alicia Hintz have liaisons with a much older locomotive engineer when his train was in town? Because she had a paralyzed leg and arm and he paid attention to her, but she did not know he was married. When she learned of his situation, "this seemed to trouble her a great deal."[17] Despite the curtain of time that obscures our view of the past, witnesses' statements and other evidence presented at inquests allow us to see the outlines of the emotional turmoil that rippled through sexually active young people. It does not take much imagination to sense how young dressmaker Jane

Forsyth felt when she joined friends for a Sunday picnic and then perceived that the man she fancied wished to sashay down the beach with another girl. "Oh, you two go on, you don't want me."[18] Harriet Parsons returned to her parents' home from the city after her boyfriend jilted her; she arrived during family planning for her sister's wedding.[19] Picnics and homecomings did not spread joy to all participants. We cannot presume to know exactly how emotionally charged occasions would engage self-reflection; however, the case files suggest that when young people socialized, there were heightened possibilities for dashed hopes. A good deal of writing on suicide, based on aggregate data, is by necessity devoid of clues about situations – picnics, dances, fairs, family gatherings – that could trigger adolescent crises.

We are not alone in being mystified by the desperate attraction evinced by young women to certain men, for parents were bewildered, panicky, and livid. The vulnerability and longing of lonely girls is undeniable, and so too are parental protectiveness and alarm. For insight into the totality of an infatuation, there is Nurse Katharine Smith's last letter to a man who was wedding another woman. "Believe me, sweetheart," she wrote. "I've always loved you with all my heart and soul and still do. That is why I can't go on living without you. I can't ever stop thinking about you and can't even sleep at night for thinking of you, and to know you love another girl is now more than I can bear."[20] Miriam Parker's mother disapproved of the way she dressed when stepping out with friends. The sixteen-year-old created a scene when told to change, and to punctuate her claims that her mother did not love her, she swallowed matches as a suicidal threat that unhappily went too far.[21] Her mother failed to realize the danger of her daughter's gesture. When she was fifteen and living with her parents on a Queensland cattle station, Mabel Johansen became intimate with a roving labourer passing through the region. When he left, she wrote letters, but he never replied; her father had warned her not to become attached because she was young. At the inquest, her mother explained that the boy's silence thrust Mabel into a terrible state of worry. There was no evidence of pregnancy but every indication that his sheer indifference had devastated her.[22]

Parting words could be cruel in their intended kindness. At the inquest into the suicide of Eliza McCaffrey, Thomas Bigwood stated, "I told her I did not intend to keep company with her any longer but we should part good friends."[23] Edward Duffy recalled what he said to Daphne Seiler just before she committed suicide: "I told her when she left that I thought it would be better if we just remained friends."[24] "We parted as friends," said Victor Nelmes when describing his last contact with Muriel Price. "I made no arrangements for any future meeting."[25]

Parents who tried to interfere walked a tightrope. If there were grounds to worry about the prospects and character of a young swain, inaction invited trouble, but a sharp response provoked rebellion. Thirteen-year-old Mary McKenzie turned insolent and cheeky when her mother disapproved of labourer Andrew Sands. Mary and Andrew subsequently tied themselves together and leapt into a stream.[26] Some parents lacked the diplomatic skill to negotiate the crisis. A few turned violent. When May Pursey's father suspected that she was having an affair with her employer, he beat her. "You know Mr Biddles," May wrote to the man in question; "he thrashed me something awful yesterday and he said he'll be the death of me before many days is over. So I am going to commit suicide by taking a dose of poison."[27]

Parents turned strong words on suitors or daughters. The father of nineteen-year-old Frances Fagan intimidated her boyfriend and told him to "cut it out." The boyfriend seemingly caved in: "I won't speak to her again." But the lovers carried out a suicide pact.[28] "They stopped us from seeing each other," wrote Harriet Newman. "I cannot live without you dearest. My Mother was cruel to try and part us." Harriet's mother wanted her to marry another man and had imposed herself so forcefully that the girl's lover fled the region.[29] Farmer and drover Jim Dorrie testified that the father of twenty-year-old Thelma White "knew that we were attached and told me he objected to me as a husband for Thelma. This he did on two occasions."[30] Determined to pry their daughter away from a young man they despised, Ada Ford's parents hounded her. "She generally resented what I said to her about this matter," declared her father, "and she did so on this evening [when she took rat poison]."[31] Parents who impeded a romance were common; parents who tried to move things along, though rare, could also fail. Alice Whiting explained at an inquest what had upset her daughter Frances. She had a boyfriend, and Alice asked him to come for a visit. Then, in front of her daughter, Alice asked him to marry her daughter to cheer her up. He replied that "your daughter is not in the same class as I am and I must keep away from her." "Deceased was terribly upset when Wilson [the boyfriend] left, and she told me life was not worth living." Alice sent her daughter away for a holiday to get over her depression, but to no avail.[32]

Instances of romantic misadventures are readily identified because they centred on dramatic confrontations. While the dreams of lonely, unpopular girls do not have the same documentary exposure, they too figure in the experiences of young women, and for a few girls, the dreams merged into critical self-evaluation. Twenty-one-year-old Irene Turner had goitre trouble, anemia, and an overwhelming feeling that "she was not making good in the world." Her parents noticed a gloomy turn. "She has been morbid and reading the Bible a lot. Owing to doctor's advice we have been keeping her on a strict look out." Her own assessment was that "life is not worth living. Not a soul in the world is to blame or can help me."[33]

The third of Greer's stages, defloration, is evident. It is hard to say how much sex adolescents engaged in, although Mary McMullen, who lived in a small Queensland town, alleged plenty. "I am like a lot more of the Mitchell girls. I have been led astray and cannot face it."[34] Domestic Margaret Kinsey went from chastity to pregnancy on the rebound from a man she truly liked. "Nobody knows how miserable I have been since I lost George," she confessed in her suicide note. "To make matters worse Jim has got me into trouble and I know he is as crooked as can be and the worst part is to think I went all this time without giving into boys and this is what I have got for it."[35] A pending pregnancy outside marriage massively complicated young lives.

Very young women from strict homes, such as fourteen-year-old Martha Fountain, lacked the coping skills needed to surmount their predicament. In tears Martha confided to her brother that her periods had stopped. Poison was her remedy because "she did not want to disgrace the family."[36] In addition to the anxieties of any pregnancy, single expectant mothers had to contend with pervasive disapproval. Isolation escalated as fast as the news spread. Each one of the scores of seduction and abandonment cases promises a book-length tragedy. In Ellen Crain's case, the tale was extraordinary because she was well-educated, clever, and determined to leave a record. She wrote to her lover's brother. Nineteen and from a respectable family that had nearly gone bankrupt during a drought, she attended a good private school. "I was healthy, popular, and admired," she wrote in her last communication. As it happened, the best lady tennis player in town had fallen for a shearer, and the family disapproved. "I trusted also that his sense of honour was as strong as mine and trusted too far. He wished for more than I could give him in accordance with honour. However, he and my love were too strong for me and my honour and self-respect fell." When she became pregnant, he came to marry her but backed out since he felt he could not support her. "I had to tell Mama of my disgrace and wickedness and it nearly broke her heart for I was her favourite." Her mother was a very strict woman who threatened to abandon Ellen; the daughter saw only one solution – poison.[37]

Ellen's isolation owed everything to her family, and in them she was unfortunate, but other young women had nothing like her social and educational advantages. For women living on their own, pregnancy jeopardized employment. A domestic servant who "showed" could expect prompt dismissal. The day after a doctor confirmed her pregnancy, domestic servant Mary Carroll consumed a bottle of Lysol.[38] Unable to hide her pregnancy, housemaid Ida Wells was discharged and had nowhere to go. "She said she had five married sisters but could not face going to them. They might turn her down. She had nothing else to do but jump in the river."[39] Expecting a child in a few months, forty-one-year-old domestic servant Evelyn Thompson wanted to be taken immediately into a private hospital, Alexandra Home. The matron remarked at the inquest that "at the time she was very worried and looked quite demented. I asked her if she couldn't take a situation and work for a time as it was rather early to come in. After a good deal of talk she seemed a little quieter in her mind and I got her this situation. She kept ringing me night after night after that saying she was worried in case the people would find out about her condition." As an older woman whose romance had ended without a husband, she was overwhelmed by fright, loss, and the passing of life.[40]

Few, if any, romantic misadventures encountered in either New Zealand or Queensland matched the assaults on the psyche experienced by fifteen-year-old Sarah Chalkly. Her want of love at home drew her into a perilous relationship. Her mother had remarried and then left that husband "to housekeep" for another man, and she wanted Sarah out of the way so she could hang onto him. Sarah went to live with grandparents and an aunt in a remote Queensland town. From her standpoint, her guardians abused her. "I am nothing but a slave for Grandma and Auntie Ada. I am full up of it. When I am sick I get no sympathy from any of them only called all sorts of names." She found solace in a young man's nocturnal visits to her bed. When her grandfather discovered them half-naked, he "nearly went off his head." At that point, the boyfriend admitted he had been "having connection" with deceased for three months and that Sarah had told him she was pregnant. She had asked him to "get her something" to get rid of the baby, but he refused, saying "it might injure her or take her life." Sarah's problems were compounded by her uncertainty about marriage. She hesitated when he offered. A dalliance was one thing, marriage another. Woken by the racket, her grandmother entered the room, called her "a dirty prostitute and a harlot," and threatened to kill her by poison. Crying throughout these confrontations, young Sarah saw suicide as the solution to an impossible situation. The police constable who investigated was profoundly affected by the tragedy; he reported that Sarah took poison "through fear of anger and abuse of her grand-parents."[41]

The most vulnerable – to suicidal thoughts and to multiple forms of exploitation – were possibly young women without protective parents, young women such as Sarah Chalkly. Another was Theresa Frazer, a ward of Queensland, who worked as a domestic servant. Pregnant and fearful of being sent back to an orphanage, she took strychnine. She wrote to her employer-cum-foster parent: "Mum it was a man came with pictures the day Dad and you were fishing that interfered with me. I did not mean it. He came in the house after me. I got too frightened to tell you. Mum I can't go back. You have all been kind to me. Don't worry Mum."[42] Family support was not altogether lacking in every instance, but it was very hard for families to work through the crisis of a pregnancy outside marriage.

Young women who lived at home with parents sometimes found that their mother or father wished to help them through pregnancy without a husband, but it was difficult for all parties to surmount prevailing morality. That was not the only complication; many young women wanted a trustworthy soulmate.[43] The night of her suicide, twenty-one-year-old domestic servant Emma Krabbeuholf had met with Jack Holloway, the father of the child she carried. As she went to meet him, she hoped that Jack would not throw her over. But he brushed her off with five pounds to help carry her through her confinement.[44] Fay Fischer died at her mother's grave. "Dad, it's the only way out. I am having Wally's baby and he doesn't want to marry me. I did not think I would end up like this but I don't want to be a burden to you. I gave him his ring back as he came tonight and tried to say I was seeing other boys which is untrue."[45] Impoverished twenty-year-old Mary Brown entered Te Oranga Home, one of many refuges for unwed mothers encountered in the files, and in return for privacy and the delivery of her son, the refuge placed her in domestic service and told her that she could not reclaim her child when she turned twenty because of poor conduct. She explained her grief – "she wanted to die" – to her employer's daughter after taking poison.[46] While conventional morality may have steeled some young women to retain their virginity until marriage, it created impossible problems for others, draining their self-esteem when they were in trouble and putting to the test a number of worthless but beloved boyfriends.

Revenge suicides by women were not as common as they were among men, who on balance were more inclined to direct violence at someone in order to assert pride and exercise a perverse control over "their goods." All the same, a few women took direct aim at a man when they ended their lives. Eveline McDonald jumped from a railway bridge because her boyfriend had broken off their relationship when he heard tales that Eveline, a domestic servant, had stolen from her employers. "Sometimes think of the girl you have ruined and drove to destruction but remember I am innocent of all those yarns so help me God."[47] In her short life of twenty-one years, Hilda Campbell believed that fate had dealt her only misery. She wrote to Jack, her boyfriend, "I am tired of the worry and toil of this life which it has been my luck to meet with ever since I can remember." Doubtless, whatever hardships she had experienced put her in a despondent frame of mind when Jack threw her over for another girl. So her suicide served a multiple purpose. It ended her run of bad luck and allowed her to strike back at Jack. "When he sees my dead body brought up from the river, he will be sorry for the way he treated me on Saturday."[48] She could relish the scene before the deed.

MODES OF ABUSE

Greer's seven metamorphoses did not include marriage, a change that has no biological status but is marked by a pronounced ceremonial sign and in many places and times ends a woman's legal independence. Older women suffering from nervous breakdowns, depression, nerves, and despondency occasionally had lived with an abusive spouse. Married women with children could rarely leave their husbands until they were able to move in with an adult child. That could help account for the mean age of almost fifty (46.7) for women experiencing nerves in New Zealand, although there also were age-related crises, including menopause, high blood pressure, heart trouble, and the compound stresses accumulated while raising a family. No one can really know someone else's marriage, and definitely not the historian decades later. It is impossible to discover what tainted relations between Flora Home and her husband. The rat poison she took did not kill her immediately, so she was asked by several people why she had done it. To her doctor, she replied she had been very depressed. To her husband, she responded "what do you think!"[49] There are better clues in some cases. Neighbours agreed that Gertrude Good's husband should be blamed for her death. An earlier pregnancy had not gone well, and since she was expecting again, the doctor ordered rest. Mr Good ruled otherwise and insisted that she work in his shop. His motives were plain; he had wanted her to take something "to get rid of the child." Quick- tempered, he would grab her by the hair, knock her about, and curse her.[50]

At inquests, husbands put their conduct in the best light, but their statements could betray the fact that wives had endured domestic toil, little peace, imposed isolation, and assorted forms of abuse.[51] Sarah Ann Bussey's husband recalled her saying on the fatal morning, "I would rather take poison than tackle that job" (milking the cows). "I cannot work."[52] Eva Archer had six children aged one to nine years and had warned husband, "I often feel inclined when the children are so crabby to jump down a well." She told her daughter, "If you don't stop crying I'll put myself in the tank of water."[53] Anastasia Smith's husband, a chronic drinker, denied responsibility for her suicide: "She didn't accuse me of drinking that day." "I only left her without money when I was out of work. It is not true that I left her starving in Sydney." A neighbour testified that she was often without money and that he had struck the child.[54] Under relentless questioning from a magistrate who knew something about him, Patrick McGinn admitted that "my drinking habits was the cause of most of the unhappiness in our home."[55] Martha Rowe set herself on fire. Her husband, a refinery worker, had taken her to a remote town, where she was "melancholy and had crying fits for no reason whatever." A neighbour said she was "despondent and had been hysterical"; this neighbour had known her "for about 30 years as a very respectable woman on good terms with everybody."[56] In an astonishing statement, John Kirby told the magistrate that his wife often complained about his absences. "You are always flying about the country having a good time," he reported her as saying, "while I am home doing all the work, with a pack of kiddies, and always in the family way." She was in a bad temper when she used these words.[57]

The testimony of a female friend or a suicide note occasionally exposed domestic strains that had precipitated or exacerbated nerves. Violence could be psychological. Amelia Smith, a selector's wife, married fifteen years and with children, took her life in her house while her husband was at work. Relying on a common exculpatory statement, her husband said that "we have always lived on friendly terms I have

never heard her say she would take her life." But Amelia's note sketched
a damning picture. Her husband dismissed it. "I don't know what it
means." Addressed to a neighbour, it said, "I may be ded [sic] before
Yabesy gets back. It is the same old story. I am pening [sic] this to let
you know I am taking my life with my own hand. I cannot stand to
be told to go to hell anymore. I might as well go so goodbye. Yours truly
A. Smith."[58]

Torrents of abuse destroyed Ivey Dean's will. She did not die immediately from the effects of poison, so Police Sergeant Michael Foley interviewed her. She told him, "I was sick of everything and wanted to die."
"Was there any domestic trouble in your home? She did not reply to this
question but said 'I want to sleep.'" Her de facto husband admitted
under questioning that he had been in jail two weeks earlier on a drunk
driving charge and she came to see him. "I do not remember throwing
the water over her when she called to see me that night in the cell."[59]
Eliza Rusk raised her sons, aged nine and twelve, while her husband,
Fred, carried on an affair. She left a note: "Fred Dear. I am cruel only to
be kind. I am making the children fools. You must put them where they
will be trained. I can't do it. They will be better without such a mother. I
am ruining them. Be happy with B. I am sure she is the one for you. I
have only been a misery to you. You are worth a dozen of me. Do all
you can for the children. Forgive me, I must atone for this in the next
world. I am a failure in this."[60] Eliza's alcoholism had contributed to
the disintegration of their marriage and her self-worth. When infidelity
was a motive, husbands were usually the wayward parties, but not
always. When Jack Mackenzie was with the army in France, his wife,
Agnes, fell in love with Otto. At first, she resisted his advances. "I tried
to keep you in your place and to keep myself straight. I wanted to keep
true to Jack who was away fighting for me, but you succeeded in your
motive." She hoped Otto would eventually marry her, but he refused,
and Agnes felt trapped and isolated. She wrote to Otto, "I dread the
lonely years ahead of me."[61]

REPRODUCTIVE TURNING POINTS

Childbirth and anxieties about child care were distressing, particularly
for women who had had their health, self-esteem, or stamina worn
down. Elizabeth Carson was living with her husband on their farm
when she drowned herself. She had had a child four weeks previously.
"She was depressed in spirits lately." A female friend said that "the

reason for her depression was I believe because she had lost her breast milk and was afraid for the child's future feeding."[62] What witnesses described as an unaccountable feeling of inadequacy gripped Mary Humphrey two weeks after her baby's birth. According to them and her husband, "she feared for the infant."[63] Fear and disappointment over-whelmed Margaret Christensen, who had hoped for the perfect baby. She asked her husband to take their new baby to town with him, requesting that he "take this little baby – if you leave it with me it will die." The doctor had told her that the baby would "always be delicate, he is weak in the bones." This prediction made her "so disappointed." She said, "I must now give up all hopes of my boy."[64]

The health of a child did not account for Lucia Macalister's depres-sion. Her husband was perplexed, for "she appeared to be in good health and the child is living." An acquaintance testified that "she was worrying about the responsibility of care of the child."[65] Dr William Baird gave an extended account of the symptoms of postpartum depres-sion at the inquest into the death of Ethel Hammond by Lysol poison-ing. He had delivered the baby and attended when her husband called to say that she had become despondent. "I had a talk with her and she expressed herself as unworthy and incapable of looking after her home and her child. Her condition amounted to delirium of melancholia. She had delirium of incapacity and unworthiness. She ceased to go out and I advised her husband to take her away." The holiday-rest prescription failed.[66] Dr Henry Thacker described Elizabeth Smithison's condition as "puerperal melancholia." He had visited her and usually discovered that "she had been crying, distressed about the baby."[67] Enduring a terrible inner conflict about her feelings of love and inadequacy respect-ing her sixteen-month-old son, thirty-year-old asthma sufferer Mary Pickup left an apologetic explanatory note. "I look at Harvey," she wrote, "and I know I can't look after him. It makes me sad. You have been a good and faithful husband and I thank you for your goodness towards me. I would like to give you a good bye kiss."[68] It is estimated that one in five new mothers suffer postpartum mood disorders, and little wonder, given erratic, unreasonable hours, anxiety, and fatigue.

Menstruation and premenstrual syndrome (PMS) were conspicuous by their near absence as alleged motives.[69] On the one occasion when a witness related menstruation to a suicide, she obviously had reached for it as a less traumatic explanation than what likely made the young vic-tim disconsolate. Esther Johnston's mother claimed that her daughter "was subject to excessive menstruation and that would have the effect of weakening her and making her subject to nervous trouble." A suicide note suggested more complicated circumstances. Esther had killed herself on her honeymoon. Deeply in love with a man who did not reciprocate, she had forced him to marry her, and she recognized her miscalculation too late.[70]

Witnesses often attributed nerves to the onset of menopause and described this motive in common, vague language without elaborating on symptoms. "She was suffering from the change of life. She was very depressed."[71] "She suffered from melancholic probably influenced by her time of life."[72] "She was affected by her change of life."[73] "Recently very poorly enduring change of life."[74] After the start of her change of life, forty-four-year-old Sarah Taylor began "to speak of being tired of life."[75] Margaret Cannon experienced a bad case of nerves during the change; she was under the observation of her daughter, who asked if she could go out. Her mother said yes because "she felt good that day." To assuage the daughter's likely sense of guilt at finding her mother dead, Margaret left note explaining that it was not the daughter's fault. Then she gave instructions: "Don't sing out Jean just go for Dad. I just can't put up with this head nerves any longer."[76] At numerous inquests, family doctors linked melancholy and the change of life. Treatment concentrated on rest and sedatives and could easily extend to five years.[77] John Moore explained at an inquest that during his wife's three-year-long crisis, she had "crying fits" which required a doctor's attention.[78] Thanks to Edith Johnston's frankness with her doctor, a glimpse is provided into the profound and puzzling anguish of depression connected with the start of menopause. Edith was fifty-two, was well cared for, and lived in relative luxury. Her fits came on suddenly; her outlook would change from cheery to gloomy within five minutes. During such periods she took no joy in anything. She told her doctor that, objectively speaking, she had nothing to worry her, but "in spite of that she could not shake off those fits of depression."[79]

For the sake of compression during the discussion of rates and motives in chapter 3, the onset of menopause was assigned to the general category of mental illness. For the women who committed suicide, the change of life contributed to serious mood swings; however, international studies show that most women do not experience an increase in dangerous psychological problems with perimenopause. Victor Bailey found that for women in Victorian Hull "one-half of the suicides who were ill were in the menopausal years of 45 to 50."[80] The New Zealand data, with its nearly complete age information, does not show this

result. Physical ailments and mental illnesses were not especially clus-
tered in any age cohorts, and significantly, only one in six women with
illnesses (16.4 per cent) were in the cohort that Bailey identifies
as menopausal.

The onset of menopause is certainly not a mental illness or a physical
illness, but, writes Dr Susan Love, "some women's brains are very sensitive to hormonal fluctuations."[81] Extreme sensitivity can convert manageable problems and annoyances into intolerable pain and emotional
devastation. In that sense, menopause – the other awkward age, as Jane
Page called it – contributed to the relatively large number of older married women whom close witnesses described as suffering some form of
mental illness.[82] The inquest files suggest that the manageable problems
could be daunting, even without the added sensitivity. Grace Bickford's
situation presents an extreme instance. The forty-nine-year-old had had
the strain of running the family farm alone while her husband was at war,
and there was constant worry about his survival. She had taken an overdose of sleeping pills two years earlier in an attempt to escape the stress
or to signal her need for help.[83] Fifty-three-year-old Honora Brooker,
attended by a doctor for five years for symptoms of menopause, had been
exhausted from raising thirteen children.[84] Although witnesses specified
triggering irritants in some cases, in most they did not but focused purely
on menopause as a motive, and by so doing, they may have avoided coming to terms publicly with their conduct toward the deceased.

The popular labelling of menopause as "the change" drew attention
to a passage in life. Like key birthdays or the start of another seasonal
labour trek, benchmark events in the lives of men, menopause possibly
triggered self-assessment. Single, unemployed housekeeper Grace Lamb
had what her doctor described as "great depression."[85] Her reproductive life had passed. It was in a similar state that Clare Moore, despite
consultations with doctors, "relapsed into a despondent state of mind
bringing to its brain morbid fancies one of which was to visit the scenes
of her childhood."[86] Elsie Osborn crossed a different but related life
and reproductive benchmark when she underwent surgery that prevented her from having children. One of her doctors told the inquest
that "she had been married seven years and had no family and was
anxious to have a family."[87] A similar plight overwhelmed twenty-
three-year-old domestic servant Nora Dixon, who had an operation for
ovarian trouble.[88] Childless and separated from her husband at age
forty, Victoria May had a nervous breakdown and entered a public
mental hospital as a voluntary patient.[89]

GENDER AND MENTAL ILLNESS

In New Zealand, mental illness appeared as a motive with much greater frequency for women than for men regardless of marital status (37.5 per cent for single women and 17.2 per cent for single men; 46.9 per cent for married women and 20.8 per cent for married men). In Queensland, it appeared with somewhat greater frequency for single women than for single men, but was mentioned with far greater frequently for married women than for married men (25.4 per cent for single women and 17.6 per cent for single men; 37.3 per cent for married women and 17.0 per cent for married men). Victor Bailey combined physical and mental illness when analyzing suicide in Victorian Hull,[90] but it is best to appraise them separately because witnesses certainly did. To a degree, the greater proportion of mental illness for women was affected by the doubtful inclusion of menopause. Witnesses seldom described the symptoms of mental illness or menopause at length but employed terms such as "melancholia" or "nervous breakdown" or "nerves" or "neurasthenia." The majority of mental illnesses mentioned at inquests were neuroses. Witnesses sometimes recounted medical histories and family histories of mental illness, and these rather common reports of long or intermittent treatments affirm the importance of mental illness in itself and as a stigma that burdened people who had quite a difficult time managing their days. Alice Allen, for example, went to England nine months before her death "to seek medical advice. She was suffering from great depression of mind and severe headaches." When she returned home, she "expressed great disappointment about going so far and obtaining no relief."[91]

The data on mental illness prompt three obvious questions. First, why was mental illness cited with relatively greater frequency as a motive for women? Second, was the difference a mere construction of gender stereotyping by male-dominated psychiatry that percolated into popular consciousness? Third, why did witnesses mention mental illness with relatively greater frequency in the suicides of married, rather than single, women? Was there something about marriages that could put women at risk? Sometimes, as mentioned in the discussion of marriage, witnesses attributed nerves to domestic violence, verbal abuse, the racking fatigue of farm and household work, and isolation. But there were instances, too, of family histories of mental illness. According to her father, Hannah Murdoch had become deranged when she had a child. She tried to shoot herself. After three months in a public

Table 5.1
Witnesses' reports of mental illness: New Zealand women, 1900–50

Description of motives	Number	per cent
Nerves or nervous breakdown mentioned	115	34.7
Depressed	100	30.3
Vague descriptions	43	13.1
Delusions mentioned	26	7.8
Melancholy mentioned	26	7.8
Despondency mentioned	17	5.1
Psychosis or schizophrenia mentioned	4	1.2
Total	331	100.0

Table 5.2
Witnesses' reports of mental illness: Queensland women, 1890–1940

Description of motives	Number	Per cent
Nerves or nervous breakdown mentioned	32	27.8
Delusions mentioned	22	19.1
Vague descriptions	16	13.9
Psychosis or schizophrenia mentioned	16	13.9
Depression mentioned	15	13.0
Melancholy mentioned	9	7.8
Despondency mentioned	5	4.3
Total	115	100.0

asylum, she went home. Her brother had committed suicide years before.[92] The fear of insanity in the family worried individuals, and in Hannah Murdoch's case an additional crisis of postpartum depression seems likely. Mary Simon had been born in an asylum in England where her mother was a patient. Mary stayed awake at nights, believing that someone planned to kill her.[93]

Statements about symptoms and rare clinical diagnoses suggest that psychoses played a part, though a very small one (see tables 5.1 and 5.2). When committed to a mental hospital, Thomasina Anderson had delusions that her house was affected by electricity.[94] Eliza Tafnell inquired about the voices she heard.[95] Jean Findlay killed herself and her infant son, Barrabas, by standing in front of a train at a level crossing. Both were naked. Her husband said that "she spoke to me of seeing visions occasionally" and that she had burnt their property deeds about two years before because she thought "they were not properly made out." Other witnesses thought she was "peculiar in her disposition and not right in her mind at times." A neighbour said she had once asked him to mind the children while she "went to burn Jones's store down because young Jones had crushed some of her pictures while framing them." "If the world didn't come to an end after the war," she once remarked, "she would do some desperate things."[96] Shortly after the start of World War I, Catherine Locking saw German flags on the hills around Napier. Apart from her conviction that the Germans had invaded, "she seemed fairly normal."[97]

In both jurisdictions, mental illnesses behind suicides were generally considered acute but not chronic, neuroses rather than psychoses (see tables 5.1 and 5.2). At one time, feminist critics of psychiatry – for example, English professor Elaine Showalter – would have proposed that the labelling of some women as mentally ill captured the biases of psychiatry, which perpetuated existing gender relations. Victorians who wrote about mental illness did remark that women would suffer breakdowns when they "attempted to compete with men instead of serving them."[98] However, much of the presumed mental trouble described at inquests expressed the anxieties of hard times, dashed hopes, and gruelling day-to-day routines; if there was a cultural construction of mental illness, there was also evidence of wounds to the psyche inflicted – unwittingly as well as deliberately – by assorted men in the lives of women.

Accounts of mental illness were boundlessly complex and varied in origins and expression. Two days before she was to enter a public mental hospital as a voluntary patient to recover from a nervous breakdown, forty-eight-year-old Martha Bradley took her life at home. The inquest collected extensive biographical information. Her father had died when she was three, and the family was broken up for adoption. Married at the age of seventeen, she gave birth to six children, one of whom died. That unhappy marriage ended when Martha was thirty- three.[99] The district nurse who visited Bertha Palmer noted that she had delusions, a buzzing in her head, and these symptoms had begun after a recent bout of rheumatic fever.[100] Mary Heenan had suffered from "attacks of despondency" since her marriage and had been under an unspecified form of treatment since her last child had been born. A month before her death, she suffered a "bad attack of melancholia." Her husband took her to the seaside for rest, but Mary did not improve. Two days before her death, her husband and a doctor discussed calling upon a specialist from the state mental hospital. She had "bad turns yearly," her husband reported. An aunt on her mother's side "became insane" and was now in an asylum.[101] Bridget Deere acted oddly. Her husband reported their final conversation. "'What are you going to do with me father, are you going to send me away?' I said 'no mother, just lay down and rest.' I then took her hand and drew her down onto my breast and kissed her and I said 'mother that is the kiss of peace. We won't send you away.'"[102] Whenever suggestions of stepped-up institutional treatment were mentioned at inquests, the remarks made it clear that the recommendation incited panic and could have precipitated the suicide.

Women's reproductive experiences and family-rearing tasks, as we have seen, affected mental states. Women with young children felt especially alone in relatively new communities or in places with a high population turnover, because here they lacked extended family networks or old friends. Fear of failing, losing control, or going mad was understandable in these circumstances, and it was a short step from these anxieties to fretting that treatment for mental illness had to follow. Agnes Fyfe was depressed; she had two older children and a baby and complained about raising them. Little things annoyed her. Her husband wanted her to see a doctor, but she refused.[103] Sarah Wessel had given birth; an older boy had an accident and lost a hand; then she had two operations. During her recuperation her husband found Sarah wandering on the beach. She said, "Oh my head, I think I will go and drown myself." He took her hand and escorted her home. "If you are not better tomorrow you will have to go to the Hospital."[104]

Family members were in a difficult position. How could they avoid mentioning a doctor and hospital care? Elizabeth Kenyon lived with her parents and siblings. "She had not been in good health for about the last nine months ... latterly got quiet and morose," recalled her father. "She used to get a little eccentric in the evenings and some nights she could not sleep. She seemed to be afraid lest we put her in an asylum and used to beg not to be put in one." Her father admitted that, during one fit, he said that "if you go on like this Lizzie we shall have to lock you up. This may have been a week or two before her death." Elizabeth had said about three or four weeks earlier that "she did not think she would live much longer because she had a fearful pain in her head. She often used to say this."[105] Just before she died on 25 October 1940, Ruby Yapp told a constable that if she survived her suicide attempt, she didn't "want to be sent to the General Hospital for there Dr Pye 'will only send me up the Line.'"[106]

Alcohol enabled men in the short run to handle stress, disappointment, and perhaps underlying mental illness. Whereas they could justify drinking as a reward, women could not. Female alcoholics rarely appeared in the files. Sister Elizabeth Bonning, a nurse at a remote hospital, poisoned herself. "I would say the deceased was addicted to liquor and very much so," declared another nurse. "The Kynuna Hospital is situated a good distance from the town, and the deceased told me that she was lonely and scared of living on her own. Some time before and after taking the black mixture [the poison she used] the deceased would call on God to take her, and say that she would be better dead."[107] Drinking could mask mental illness among men and became an obvious explanation for witnesses when much more was occurring. This masking effect was likely familiar to physicians. Queensland psychiatrist John Bostock lectured to medical students around 1940 that "alcoholism may be associated with any other mental disorder and then any one of them may be overlooked. Schizophrenics who at the same time are inebriates are generally taken for mere alcoholics. Paraphrenia and alcoholism are frequently associated, the former is probably the primary state, alcohol being taken as a mode of escape. In early dementia paralytics when inhibitions are failing there is often an over indulgence in drink."[108] The gendered division of labour, with its related reward of drink for men, probably skewed some witnesses' accounts so that they aligned men with drink and women with mental illness.

The stress of waged work overwhelmed a few women as it did men, and there were temptations for both. As a consequence of the pressures of her work as a secretary at a telephone company, Erica Dickinson had a nervous breakdown. Her doctor "repeatedly examined this patient with the object of discovering the cause of her depression and I have always failed to find any bodily cause for its existence. She was not concealing any pregnancy." He concluded: "I am forced to believe that the strain of five years telephone and telegraph work exhausted her nervous system."[109] Work upset nurse Rosabell Byron, who was interviewed as she lay dying from ingesting corrosive sublimate. Working with delicate babies in obstetrics had been a strain. Additionally, unmarried and living with her sister, she stated that she felt unwanted.[110] Mary Lingard's husband reported, "She was going around a bit on the quiet side. She gave me the impression she was not interested in anything. I took her from work and sent her away for a fortnight. She went to Wynnum. [It was common for people with nerves to rest at seaside communities such as Wynnum.] Then, when she came home, I took her to specialists, Drs. Youngman and Bostock. She was worse when she came from Wynnum. She went into their hospital Morooma. She was a month in the hospital and then was an outpatient. She said she would throw herself into the river. I did not believe she would do it. Customers used to get on her nerves." Her husband concluded: "She did not suffer with her men-stural [sic] changes. She used to come home and start to cry sometimes through worry over her work."[111] In these instances, the explanation that work brought about a breakdown came from men and not the women themselves. While the men possibly thought it unnatural for women to work outside the home, they evidently believed that work in itself could precipitate stress.

In comparison to some narratives of work and crisis, Barbara Weinholt's work-related problem was clear-cut. She committed suicide after the Queensland Country Women's Association, of which she was secretary, discovered malfeasance. To avoid a scandal, they would not bring charges. "The Financial Advisory Committee has decided that they must replace you with a more efficient Secretary."[112] Male suicides were more likely than women to have been in trouble with the law, but it happened to women too and often involved a motoring accident or shoplifting.[113]

While the entry of women into waged labour and business exposed them to workplace stress, some women in business and the workforce retained their hopes as women who expected to have caring husbands and children. Sales clerk Elizabeth Ratcliffe had a breakdown when she was single, forty-five, and felt alone. To shake the blues, she travelled to another city for a rest cure but became suicidal when faced with an ultimatum to return to work or lose her position.[114] Women in both New Zealand and Queensland ran boarding houses and hotels; these service enterprises related to the stereotype of domestic responsibilities, but they also entailed financial risk. Childless and separated from her husband, who had vanished in the Klondike gold rush, forty-year-old Augusta Jensen tried to run a boarding house, but the business failed. "She was only born for trouble" she told her brother.[115] The stress of managing an understaffed family hotel, plus the disappointment of ten years of marriage without children, contributed to Mary McRobie's drinking and bouts of crying. After swallowing Lysol, she told the hotel cook that she did it "because her husband did not want her."[116]

Nerve-racking situations at work were just a few of the troubles in the lives of women; working women had some things in common with men but often an additional assortment of woes they shared with other women. Despite slight rises in waged-work cases across the decades, the prevailing occupation for women who committed suicide was "housewife." Older married women worried no less than young single ones about their attractiveness and their ability to hold onto their husbands.

After several operations and goitre problems, Elizabeth Adamson felt her husband no longer wanted her. "You always been wanting to get rid of me so you got your freedom."[117]

A LOSS SO GREAT

Women affected by the death of someone close were described as withdrawn, despondent, melancholy, glum, depressed, and reserved. Instances of loss could be simple and powerful or complicated. In New Zealand, women who experienced a recent loss had a mean age of roughly fifty (48.7), although a few were in their twenties. For poignancy, Norma Smith's last walk has no rival. She was twenty-three. Her fiancée had died on 13 November 1918 during the influenza epidemic. To help Norma with her grief, Lily Vause took her for a walk along a river, but by and by they passed "the sacred little spot where she and Bob used to sit." Lily left Norma for ten minutes of solitary reflection. When she returned, she saw Norma's wedding hat and veil on the bank.[118] Straightforward grief induced Anna Schmidt to take strychnine. A friend told the inquest that Anna's "husband died in the hospital about six months ago. They had been only four months married." Anna had recently given birth to a child. She left the baby at the hospital, took poison in the public gardens, and caught a cab to her friend's place. Before she died, she said, "I want to see my baby once more before I die ... My husband is buried in 542 [cemetery plot number] and I want to be buried on top of him."[119]

War losses brought incredible heartache and financial strain. At the inquest into his wife's suicide, John Beardsley explained that "she seemed to miss very much her youngest son who was killed a little over a year ago at the Front."[120] World War I claimed husbands and fiancées but also beloved brothers. Sarah Freeman grew thin and weary. "She was most reserved. She seemed to have lost interest in everything. She would not read any books, although previously she had liked reading. She would glance through magazines without apparently any interest and was always sighing when she thought you were not looking. Her thoughts seemed so far away ... One of her brothers of whom she was fond was killed at the front."[121] Compound motives that included war loses built up until an individual could not carry on. At thirty-six, Mary Hawes had four children aged eleven to six and an infant under two, whose birth coincided with a deepening depression. However, her depression had begun "in 1917 when she received news of the death of her two brothers. She never seemed to get over that shock."[122] When her husband died of natural causes, Elizabeth Holdsworth found herself destitute because she could not depend on the support of her stepson, who was "at the Front." Following the sale of her house, she was hospitalized for a nervous breakdown.[123]

Mary Smith, a charwoman, poisoned herself shortly after her second husband, William Smith, drowned when working on the dredge *Platypus*. Her experience of loss was complicated and fused with domestic unhappiness and revenge. She had five children. "I can not live longer. I always said I would not live long after him." She had other problems. A stepsister had been burned to death two years earlier. A neighbour described Mary Smith as "a violent drunkard." To her fifteen-year-old daughter she wrote that "no one is to follow me to the grave as I am only too glad to die for my life with you all has been a hell and I will be better dead than living."[124] Her several suicide notes were instruments of retribution. Two events left Mary Howard without emotional support. Her husband had to work away and did not send a letter every week, and her mother's death upset her greatly.[125] Labour mobility left many labourers' wives coping alone with crises as well as demanding routines. A large family and a sick baby exhausted Mary Stevenson, and the oldest daughter testified that "my father is working away from home and only sees us occasionally."[126]

The loss of a child or the anticipated loss was a hard blow. A year after her infant daughter's death, Jemima Walsh "would sit and mope." Briefly, she entered a public mental hospital as a voluntary patient.[127] Only a few days passed between the death of Agnes Abbotson's three-week-old baby and her own suicide.[128] Mary Jackson had six children, and the youngest girl had been in hospital for ten months "suffering from a very serious complaint." "My wife was of the opinion that she [the girl] would never recover." Mary also had chest pains.[129] Isabella Swan, a married woman living at Gladstone, drowned herself; her only child had died three years earlier.[130] To shed the melancholy caused by her child's death, Martha Redshaw moved from England to New Zealand. But she remained in a depressive condition, "too miserable to do anything." As a telling reflection on contemporary male conduct, a friend testified with evident surprise that "her husband was very kind and never went out at night."[131] Catherine Waite had a stillborn child. "I feel so depressed. I will have to go. I will go to my dear one."[132] Ideas of an afterlife like that held by this young woman conceivably made suicide acceptable to a few. Organized religion is assumed to have exercised a moral check on suicide; however, adherents who contemplated suicide looked for forgiveness. As well as mothers who grieved, there were older spinsters who stayed at home to care for their parents until they died. For six years, Kate Lane had nursed her father; after he died, she told her brother that "she could not sleep and said she was thinking about her father all the time."[133]

Grief prostrated men too, although the death of a loved one was not as prominent a motive as it was for women. In New Zealand one in sixteen (6.1 per cent) women who committed suicide was believed to have done so because of a death in the family; only one in forty-five (2.2 per cent) male suicides was considered to have taken his life over a loss. In Queensland the proportions were one in ten (9.6 per cent) and one in thirty (3.5 per cent). The code of masculine conduct required men to bear blows in silence. Nevertheless, a few inquests show that men could display feelings without hesitation. To start a new life after a divorce, George Read moved from Australia to New Zealand. Influenza, an injury at work, poor eyesight, and a loss of wages upset him, but nothing compared with the news that his son had been killed at the front. His second wife testified that "at times he would cry and sob like a child." From that moment on, he began to say that "life is not worth living."[134] John Maher's son had died while playing on a construction project, and according to his wife, he was "very much attached to this boy."[135] Henry Edmonds asked his employer "to go for a walk with him round the street as he wanted to tell some of his troubles." He had just received a letter relating the death of his daughter-in-law. Over several years he had lost his wife and two daughters. He felt alone in the world.[136] "To whom it may concern," began Alexander Krause. "There is no doubt the sudden unexpected demise of my life partner has caused my intellect to receive a severe lasting strain."[137] Men, too, could make sentimental final gestures. Poor, old, and always complaining about his health, widower George Arundel opened a vein in his leg and bled to death at his wife's grave.[138]

IN DELICATE HEALTH FOR YEARS

Men and women led different lives. They affected one another, but these connections signify differences too. Their illnesses and representation of their illnesses by others amply demonstrate distinct as well as shared features in the lives of men and women. It is a shared fact that men and women experienced ailments which contributed to despon-

Graph 5.3
The increase in illnesses with age: New Zealand, 1900–50.

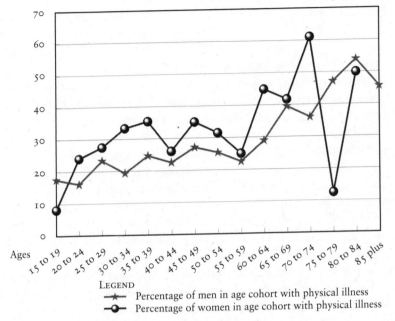

LEGEND
★ Percentage of men in age cohort with physical illness
○ Percentage of women in age cohort with physical illness

dency. Evidence from inquests suggests that illness formed a prominent motive for suicide. Roughly one in five suicides in New Zealand (22.1 per cent of male and 22.6 per cent of female suicides) and one in six in Queensland (14.6 per cent of male and 17.0 per cent of female suicides) were attributed to health problems. However, poor health showed in more instances than these figures suggest. In New Zealand a quarter of the men (25.8 per cent) and almost a third of the women (31.5 per cent) who committed suicide were having or had recently had treatment for a physical ailment. The proportions were comparable in Queensland (29.4 per cent for men; 25.2 per cent for women). It is important to note that these latter figures refer to treatment and not to illness as a motive; however, this distinction reactivates the warning, made in chapter 3, that classification has drawbacks. The physical medical conditions treated may not have been the primary factors leading to a suicide, but they likely contributed; moreover, the striking thing is that there was only a trivial difference in the distribution of physical aliments between men and women. If we accept that a person's health is the clearest indication of whether he or she is enjoying a happy life, then the presence of illness among a substantial number of suicides is understandable. Not surprisingly, moreover, the reports of illnesses rose with age for both men and women (see graph 5.3).

Medical conditions may not have been the primary factors leading to a suicide, but they contributed. Ailments were often gender-specific, represented by witnesses in a gendered manner, or described gender-related patterns of behaviour. This observation accords with the fact that "patterns of illness and health behaviour among adult women differ profoundly from those of adult men."[139] No women had cancer of the tongue from chewing tobacco, and relatively few had a dependency on alcohol; head injuries were mainly male, as were most other injuries.[140] Men fell and animals kicked. Men had prostate cancer, and women ovarian cancer. Before entering the hospital for an ovarian operation, Alice Forscutt had endured immense pain, and afterward she found that she could not eat and no medicine would cure her. For her family's sake, she waited until after Christmas to take her life.[141] Attending doctors and family members who mentioned heart and kidney problems and high blood pressure occasionally added that women worried that they could not complete their household chores.[142] That was the case with forty-eight-year-old Rose Stewart, who had seven children and on several occasions had said that "she wished that she were dead."[143] In her late fifties, Edith Hemery had very high blood pressure and heart weakness, according to the two doctors who attended her. Both agreed that this physical debility "would account for the neurasthenia." And as one doctor put it, "it used to worry her when she would not attend to her household duties."[144] Lung trouble kept Mary Russell from her housework.[145]

Men were disproportionately described as complaining about asthma, fevers, stomach problems, tuberculosis, blindness, and epilepsy. Women were disproportionately described as "being in delicate health for years"; men as "sick for years." Women who took their own lives at very advanced ages were quite rare, and thus there is an absence in the data sets of women eighty-five and older who had physical illnesses.

THE INTIMACY OF MURDER-SUICIDES

One subset of suicides deserves consideration apart from others because the acts were criminal and the suicides only a secondary event. They were also rare. Only about one in a hundred suicides (0.8 per cent) in New Zealand was associated with a murder, and about one in sixty (1.6 per cent) in Queensland. Murder-suicides almost always involved the relations of men and women, and therefore they are usefully considered at the end of a discussion of gender and suicide. Research has often used quantitative approaches that summarize and generalize, and in order to match the current study with the existing literature, a special investigation was undertaken in Queensland alone that searched in the odd numbered years as well as the even ones for murder-suicide files. What follows draws upon that intensive investigation.

A study by L. Danson and K. Soothill that collected one hundred years of reports of murder-suicides in the *London Times* provides an international comparison. It concluded that murder-suicides are mainly family affairs. Overwhelmingly, the women involved killed their children, while the men usually killed spouses or partners.[146] There are several Australian studies. In 1998 Carlos Carcach and Peter Grabosky, examining crime statistics in Australia, noted that "the most common situation surrounding a murder-suicide relates to disputes over the termination of a relationship."[147] They recommended a typology of murder-suicides based on relationships. Forty-three per cent of offenders in their 144 cases were partners or former partners of the victim. Most murder-suicides in Australia involved persons in intimate or parent-child relationships.

Jo Barnes revisited the topic in 2000 and argued that murder-suicide is both a familial and a gendered activity.[148] In her study of 405 incidents in Australia between 1973 and 1992, 90 per cent of offenders were male, and 70 per cent of victims were female. In Queensland eighty-three murder-suicides were subjected to inquests between 1890 and 1940: 82 per cent of perpetrators were male, and 85 per cent of their victims were female. Murder-suicide, Barnes claimed, was "essentially a domestic event." Mental or physical illness "did not appear to be prevalent in the majority of case." The dismissal of mental illness is problematic. In Queensland, when mental illness, alcohol abuse, violent tempers, and feelings of inadequacy are brought together, we have half the cases in which men were perpetrators; two-thirds of the women who killed their children had symptoms of a mental illness.

Barnes contended that "the patriarchal nature of our society provides a fertile context for an individual to kill a loved one and then commit suicide." The society is patriarchal and the majority of violent actors were male, but the Queensland cases from 1890 to 1940 indicate that patriarchy – fertile context though it was – fails to explain why a few possessive jealous males commit these terrible acts and countless do not. Moreover, the Queensland files indicate contributory factors besides patriarchy. Alcohol abuse, mental illness, and a history of criminal activity were often mentioned. An exceptional number of returned soldiers committed these acts, and an unusually large number of prostitutes were victims.

The suicide data for Queensland showed that a substantial proportion of women took their own lives on account of romantic disappointments. This motive was rare for murder-suicides, but it happened. Widow Annie Merchant drowned herself and her three-year-old son. She had been involved in a love triangle, but her lover returned to his wife. A final meeting was acrimonious. "Annie Marchant struck me with an umbrella. Mrs Marchant was in a passion. She might have said I was deceiving her. I said the best thing I can do is to clear out." The life of the poor widow was not easy, and Annie had been let down by a man who had trifled with her.[149]

Woman were failed by men in their lives, a fact noted throughout this chapter. Twenty-year-old Emily Sainsbury drowned her one-year-old son in the Brisbane River. Emily had lived at home until fifteen years of age, when she went into domestic service, and she continued in service up to the time she had a child. She received no support from the father. At the same time as she was trying to raise her son, she was giving her father money, and he could not abide her infant and wanted him out of the house. In these desperate circumstances, Emily went to the Salvation Army Home but soon left with her son, and the fatal events occurred shortly afterward.[150] Marion Spence was one month from giving birth when she poisoned her four children. The doctor who conducted the post-mortem claimed that "women will often take strange ideas into their head which cannot reasonably be accounted for." But there were concrete reasons for Marion's distress. Her husband had told her that he was going to quit work. Marion asked him to wait until the baby was born, but he would not answer. In the past, he said, she had threatened to kill herself when he got drunk and was locked up. "Since our marriage when talking generally she has said she would like to take all her youngsters with her when she was dead." The strain of raising four children, the prospect of a fifth, and dealing an irresponsible husband were hardly strange ideas in her head.[151]

Some women were mentally unbalanced. Margaret Finnan put a shotgun to her head after killing her only child; she had recently treated for "womb and ovary troubles." She left several notes that suggest that she suffered from a mental illness:

Mary was only seven weeks old when she said the words Jesus, Mary and Joseph. Oh! How soon I let them die away from her and wandered away from God, when she was only ten months old; now I can see it all too late. God expected me to look after myself, too, in order that I might be able to perform his will. Well! If I only had, my husband. I could have, for we should do that together, but now I have let my soul go to the devil; and poor man! I am not doing him justice to live with him although he is satisfied. If only I could have said Well! Let them do what they like. I will have no say, but I said all along and now I got no say.

Her daughter was not a normal healthy child. She blamed herself. "She is not right. I would like to kill her and then she would not live to be a scourge but I have not nerve. I was going to axe her yesterday. She cannot be any good, after what I gave her in my milk, and you are not the same man since I came back."[152] Men seldom killed their children, but in one rare instance the explanation was comparable to the Finnan case. Richard Croker shot himself in the head after killing his eight-year-old son.[153] He left a note:

The extreme step which I contemplate taking is the result of careful consideration. Enid [his nine-year-old daughter] has a chance in life, but Bob is so backward that I realise he has but a very poor chance. Indeed, rather than allow him to go through life with such a handicap, I will end it all. I realise that my action is going to be very hard on all those who are left behind, but Enid is young and will forget to a certain extent and I hope that all others will try to realise that I have tried to act in the interests of my backward child. If I am to be held responsible before any higher tribunal I am prepared to accept the responsibility.[154]

Mental illness, compounded by isolation, affected twenty-one-year-old Amy Tobler, who drowned her three children. Her husband said that "she appeared to be worried over not receiving letters from her mother. My wife was usually in good health but at times became depressed." Her mother-in-law testified: "She complained of a bad headache and refused to see a doctor. She seemed to recover from that, and a few days before her death in a conversation I had with her, I asked her to prepare my child for school during my absence. She said

she would if she was fit, as she had a bad head again."[155] Mental illness
was the verdict in the case of Bernice Sommers, who drowned her four-
year-old son and herself. The family was "always on the lookout every
night to see that she did not get away and kept the doors locked at
night." The police magistrate concluded that "the deceased had been
practically insane for a considerable time past and made several
attempts to put an end to her life." She had been treated by doctors
without success.[156] Vera McLaurin killed her four-year-old daughter,
Mary, and herself. Her husband, Douglas, testified that they had been
married for six years. His work took him away five days a week, and
they had often moved homes. "My wife was not of a very robust
nature, she often complained of pains in her back which necessitated
her having to go to bed at times. She was very high strung and of a very
nervous disposition and often complained to me of not being able to
sleep at night. She would not go to the Doctor for treatment. Recently
she complained of failing eyesight."[157]

MONSTROUS JEALOUSY

Patricia Easteal, who used Australian data from 1990, concluded that
"more than one-fifth of the offenders in homicides between adult sexual intimates took their own lives."[158] She identified two subgroups of
murder-suicide: namely, elderly partners facing deteriorating health
conditions and males estranged from female partners and pathologi-
cally possessive. Easteal further proposed that self-destruction "would
seem to be the principal object" in some cases, but in others "the principle motivator appeared to be the killing of the partner who either abandoned the offender or was perceived as unfaithful."[159] The Queensland
inquests disclosed no evidence of elderly partners but abundant variations on a theme of possession. Those variations are significant because
the challenge in this field of research is to seek what it is that differenti-
ates those who act violently when checked in their desires from those
who do not act violently after similar setbacks. It is insufficient to rely
simply on patriarchy as an explanation, although it was present.

Jealousy had real as well as imagined roots. Hugh Lawrence killed his
wife, May. Separated three weeks after they married, they had lived
apart. He accused her of "misconduct with other men." "I have heard
he was of a very jealous disposition and had a very passionate and
vindictive nature," said one witness.[160] Harry Lett killed his wife. He
claimed that she was planning to go away with another man. The man

in question said that May was tired of her husband and wanted to go to Sydney "to take up dancing on the stage."[161] Jealousy, poverty, and a sense of hopelessness destabilized Patrick McLoughlin, who shot his wife, Mary, at their home. Patrick was an older man and a hawker. They were poor and had "had periodical rows ever since they were married." A neighbour testified, "I think McLoughlin was jealous of his wife." Mary McLoughlin had left him to stay with a neighbour, to whom she "complained her husband was threatening to kill her and himself, and abusing her. She said she was frightened to live with him in the house. She asked me to go down and speak to him." The witness continued: "I said 'Paddy, what is up with the little woman?' He told me all about it. He got very excited and he said to me 'Has she been to you?' I told him I had met her casually. He said she was going about the town trying to ruin him. He said she had been unfaithful to him." He was told to see Father Lee but could not find him. "He said I am done for. I am ruined." Fifteen minutes later he shot his wife and himself.[162]

If a main motive in murder-suicides involving a murderous husband was jealousy, then it is worth striving to gain more insight and to investigate how precisely jealousy intermingled with male pride. Market gardener Charlie Wassell, a Melanesian, murdered his wife, Agnes, and their neighbour. Agnes and Charlie had been married for seventeen months. They were all drinking prior to the fatal incident; Charlie and Agnes were both seriously addicted to drink. "Wassell and his wife lived very unhappily. She was continually clearing out, she generally used to go to other kanaka boys and stay with them for some days." Charlie had been arrested the previous year for assaulting her. "He was a bad and violent tempered man," said a neighbour.[163] Some jealous men had volatile tempers. The bodies of estranged couple Florence and Fritz Skau were found at home by their son, who said they had separated about eighteen months earlier "on account of his threats to my mother. He was a very bad tempered man and often threatened to take my mother's life."[164]

Excessive drinking was occasionally mixed with jealousy, pride, and a quick temper. The murder-suicide of John and Maria Lewis was the fatal outcome of a drunken brawl. Addicted to drink, impoverished, and raising seven children, they had fought over two bottles of beer.[165] James Corday shot his estranged wife, Maria, who had fled from her husband and boarded with Mrs Mundey. Corday had invited his wife and Mrs Mundey to a concert. Afterward, they stopped for drinks at several hotels on their way home. "Corday and his wife were quarrelling all the time in the Theatre." The next morning he appeared outside the Mundey house and asked to see his wife. He said, "I will walk down with you as far as the Royal Hotel and bid her [his wife] goodbye. When near the Royal Hotel, he said 'Come in and have a parting drink.'" "We went into a parlour," reported Mrs Mundey. Corday shot his wife there. In a note he blamed her: "Dear friends, when you find me don't think it was cowardice that I have done but my life is wrecked through the wife I have had. I done it for revenge." Postscripts added "Revenge is sweet" and "Jealousy."[166] In this and in several other cases, the flight of the spouse to another house triggered outrage. The fact that the wife's new location was known and was unprotected put her at risk.

The themes of alcohol abuse, low self-esteem, and the flight of a spouse converged in the Trevethan case. Twenty-four-year-old William, a post- and telegraph master, shot his wife and then committed suicide.[167] He had been "addicted to drink for many months, but lately became worse, until he appeared to be thoroughly sodden with drink." Trevethan "had been recently suffering from perineuritis [nerve damage] causing paralysis of one arm." He could not work effectively and required his wife to help him sort mail. Feeling inadequate, he contemplated suicide. "My Dear Kate, I suppose this will be the last line you will receive through (or by me) as I have been determined to commit suicide and tonight will most probably be the last of me. I intended doing it before but it is up a tree now." William may not have intended to kill his wife, but when she fled to avoid his drinking, he raged and demanded she come home, make breakfast, and assist him with the mail.[168]

Jealousy could be mixed with a returned soldier's instability. Unemployed farm labourer George Moore, an orphan and returned soldier, committed suicide after shooting his three-year-old daughter while she slept. George and Elsie Moore had separated because of his violent fits of jealousy. He tried several times to take their three children away from her. Elsie recalled a conversation: "My late husband came in from his work and said to me I will finish you. I said Oh, what has gone wrong with you? He said I know all about you. Randall [his employer] has told me the lot. I said What has Randall told you? He said Randall told me that you have been out with all of the mob and that Farlow [a boarder with the family] and you were no good ... He caught me by the hair and threw me across the bed. He struck me several times and tried to choke me. I lost consciousness." George claimed he knew of "seven young men who had a do with her." "My late husband had a very violent temper and I am of the belief that his mind was deranged." His mother was supposed to have died in an asylum. His mother-in-law hoped the couple would reunite. She believed that the tragedy had been brought about through worry over unemployment and gossip concerning her daughter's sexual exploits·[169]

In what was another complicated, multi-factor case involving a returned soldier, wharf labourer William Griffiths killed his wife. Their daughter, Daphne, declared that her parents only argued "when Daddy was drunk. Then he used to hit and punch my mother." Alice and Daphne fled the family home. When Alice returned to get her sewing machine and announced that it was in her name, William erupted. He hit her with his closed fist and said to his daughter, "Don't touch her. Get out or I will cut your throat with a razor." A neighbour testified that "their home life was very unhappy with frequent quarrels." He provided details: "I would say at times he appeared to me to be mentally unbalanced, mostly when he was drinking. He would then seem to be always wanting to fight and he would come home at three or four in the morning and play his gramophone or lift his windows up to annoy people." William's daughter added that "sometimes we thought father was not right in the head. When Father was very drunk he would race up and down the verandah at home sometimes and knock his head on the wall. Father was a returned soldier, and in receipt of a pension. Father was getting the pension because of wounds he had received in the head. He used to complain of vile headaches."[170]

Attacks on a spouse might centrally be about intimate relationships, but wider family relationships could also be involved. Farmer Albert May shot his sleeping wife, Bertha, at their home.[171] Before he took his own life, he also killed their four children. Police noted that Albert appeared to sleep in a separate room, while Bertha slept with the children. In Albert's room they found a note: "Thank Mrs Labudda for it," a reference to his mother-in-law. The precipitating factor seems to have been a small debts court case. May had sued Mrs Labudda for defamation of character. The exact trajectory of the feud can never be known, but the conflict extended beyond husband and wife.[172]

Escape from economic distress and a perverse desire to take a spouse along formed a combination in several instances. The murder-suicide of Ferdinand and Phyllis Boie occurred in a hotel where they lived temporarily with their two sons. Ferdinand could not get regular work and appeared despondent. Witnesses said he was attentive and helped Phyllis on washdays, even when he was working.[173] William

Lum Wan, a storekeeper, fatally wounded himself after killing his wife. They had six children. Wan, a witness testified, was "worried over the depression.[174] Finances were part of James Crisp's problems. He shot his wife, Muriel, only two weeks after their marriage in Sydney.[175] James had lived at the hotel where Muriel worked and pursued her in July, when her mother took her in tow to Sydney. Muriel and James returned to Brisbane as a married couple. He was obsessed with her but also struggled with financial difficulties. He had drawn five cheques totalling over £500 from an account with a balance of £3. Criminal charges were pending.[176] A criminal aspect surfaced in another case. Richard Arnold fatally wounded his de facto wife, Maggie Zoeller, and then shot himself at a boarding house. Maggie and Richard had lived together but had separated. Somehow he persuaded her to return with him to a boarding house, where he shot her. He was no ordinary jealous male; this was no mere relationship. She had charged by him with theft, and he was out on bail on a cattle-stealing charge. Moreover, Richard was exceedingly jealous and had once followed Maggie and another man.[177]

UNWANTED ATTENTION

Possessiveness and jealousy affected men of all ages. Samuel Nelson, a tram conductor, shot Edith Willowdean.[178] Edith's husband had not returned to live with her at the end of the war. Samuel had moved in, and she needed his financial support. When he learned that she had another male friend, he left her. They were reconciled, but her association with the other man continued.[179] "My mother used to meet a man named Tom in Queen Street and in Edward Street. My mother told me that Tom was just a friend. My mother told Sam about him. I heard my mother say something about Tom at the table one night. I never heard Nelson say anything about Tom." Nelson was unhappy, said her son. "Since my mother told Sam about Tom he was sick. He said his nerves were bad and he could not sleep at night. After that he drank and smoked." Harold James was a young man who committed suicide after killing his girlfriend and her mother, who had tried to end the romance. He left a note: "I can't get a crack at the old woman so we will go the two of us.[180]

A number of men turned violent when women rejected a sexual pass. Some women were not girlfriends but acquaintances. There was nothing romantic in Vincenzo Oriti's association with Catena Guiffre, whom he killed near Ingham. He was friends with her husband, but he threatened her "because she refused to consent to his wishes to be intimate with her."[181] Asthma patient Charlie Fahl fatally wounded nurse Elsie Newton and killed himself. She had not encouraged him or given him her address, but he found her anyway. When she rejected his advances, he said, "You have got very uppish and beastly sarcastic." A suicide note indicated that he had become obsessed. He was married and deranged. Elsie was, Charlie wrote, his "only true love." "My wife thinks no more of me than medicine. God knows I have repeatedly tried to be a good husband but she was never satisfied with what I did. God forgive me for what I am about to do but I think it will be my only way to gain happiness and that is for Dear Elsie and I go to other worlds together. A better living girl I have never come in contact with."[182]

Farmhand Norman McDowell killed his former girlfriend, Bernice Skuse, after she ended their engagement. He left a note: "No doubt you will think what I have done is an awful thing, but there isn't anyone in this world who realizes what Bernice meant to me." It continued, "No one understands just what an orphan has to go through." "I just can't go on living this life and thinking of Bernice in someone else's arms." Although this was a relationship case, Norman's allusion to his hardships as an orphan perhaps intimates why he found lost affection so difficult.[183]

Albert Horne, a tanner, died at Brisbane. Widowed four years earlier, he was smitten with domestic servant Elizabeth Johnstone but cut her throat and his own. He left a note: "Goodbye to all from Elizabeth and Albert. We have had some trouble for some time which is better off not talked about. We have both decided to take our own lives, it is for the best. We wish to be buried together in Lutwyche cemetery." The police magistrate decided that they had quarrelled; Albert's note was a clumsy attempt to cover his culpability.[184] Charles Bayldon murdered his girlfriend when she broke off their engagement. A returned soldier, he had fought in Egypt and France. "He was suffering from shell shock," said one witness. Bayldon was told by the girl's mother that she did not want to marry him. She was sixteen; he was thirty-seven and "unattractive."[185]

A similar case involved Stanley Weight, a yardman and another returned soldier, who shot cook Elizabeth Zanetti. He entered her room and asked her whether she was "going to be different to me now?" She answered by telling him not to "be coming to the quarters." An acquaintance had talked with Stanley on the morning of his suicide. "He said 'I had a row with the girl last night. I said 'You do not want to take this to heart, forget all about it.' I said 'You will probably be with her again tonight.' He replied 'No, you will never see us in the street again.'" Another witness recalled a conversation: "He said to me 'Things do not look too bright for me. I have had a tiff with Liz.' I said 'Don't worry, let her go. You have your car – get out of the district – you will soon forget about it.' He said 'That is the trouble. I cannot seem to leave her. She is the only woman I have ever taken a fancy to and I seem mad over her.'"[186] The presence of seven returned soldiers among the eighty-three cases analyzed here is worth noting because it elaborates on the specific and recurrent theme of war's enduring dislocations and illustrates the general conclusion that historical events have to be taken into account in suicide studies.

Isabel Arnold and Clarence Walter Ney were found dead in her back-yard. Isabel's mother, Elizabeth, testified: "About twelve months ago Clarence Ney asked me if he could marry Isabel when she became eigh-teen years of age. I said, No. Not until she is twenty or twenty-one years of age. He said. I will wait until she is twenty-five if I can have her. He used to visit the house two or three times a day when he was in Nebo and came every night ... He seemed to be very fond of her. He was also very jealous of her." But Isobel tired of Clarence. His mother recalled: "On the 23rd March I said to him 'How is Bella?' He replied 'She is alright, she is down there for anybody. I have finished with her now.' I said 'Don't be silly boy.' He replied 'You will see.' I said 'Walter, always remember if there was good, there is always better.'"[187]

Not all murder-suicides that involved relationships were purely about those relationships. The next four cases capture further complexities. Robert Carey, a jockey, cab driver, and horse trainer, shot shopkeeper Lena Carter and then committed suicide. They had once been friendly, but Robert alleged that Lena had robbed him; so he went looking for her and demanded money. He told a witness he would get his money or shoot her. She refused.[188] Denniston Netterfield, a twenty-two-year-old clerk, committed suicide after shooting his nineteen-year-old girlfriend, Norah Campbell, in a car in the early hours. A letter to Denniston's mother read: "Most of my time is spent with a girl who I have been very friendly with in the last few months. She is a girl called Campbell, Norah Campbell, and she is down in Brisbane studying for pharmacy. She is an awfully nice girl and very good company to be with." Other letters revealed that Denniston owed money. His books at work were irregular. She may have rejected him because he had financial trou-bles; Norah was the daughter of a doctor. According to Denniston's employer, she had jilted him. He phoned her, asking her to go out "one last time as he was leaving for Sydney the next morning." His defalcations were a contributing problem that he sought to escape.[189]

The murder of twenty-five-year-old Amee Harris and the suicide of her forty-year-old brother-in-law, Robert McDowell, took place at a remote cattle station. Amee had been employed as his bookkeeper. The relationships were complicated. Alcohol abuse was involved. Robert's wife had fled the station and her husband's drinking on several occasions. She denied estrangement, but he and Amee had an odd relationship. He was very jealous of her, and she was protective of him. On a recent trip she threw a whiskey bottle from the car; on the day of the murder Robert pleaded with her for the key to the liquor cupboard. His wife insisted there was "nothing to notice between my husband and sister." She continued: "My husband was quick tempered; he often said we had hair trigger tempers."[190] Like many alcoholics, he was malnourished, and that condition may have affected his reasoning.

Returned soldier Ernest Rook committed suicide after killing his sister-in-law. He was receiving a war pension for head wound. Ernest's estranged wife lived in London; he had lived with his brother's wife off and on for about six months. Her daughter testified that "my mother told me on one occasion that she was afraid of my uncle as he had grabbed at her several times when passing her." She found her mother's attire unusual: "I have never known my mother to do her work about the house without having bloomers on." The examination of the body failed to show scientific evidence of intercourse, but everything pointed to it. A witness said Rook had told her he did not like his brother's wife because she had turned Roman Catholic. "I went to the War and I fought for the British, not for those Catholics." He added that "if Arthur's wife was mine I'd kill her." A mate of Rook said he had heard him, when under the influence of drink, speak about cutting his throat. Mental illness cannot be dismissed as a contributing factor. It would be easy and true, but also not illuminating, to portray these last four cases as involving a relationship.[191]

A broken romance or thwarted dalliance could affect a third party. Kathleen Bennett was fatally wounded by labourer William Haynes. The perpetrator and the victim knew each other only by sight.[192] William, who had been working out of town and "drinking pretty heavily," arrived at his brother's house asking for his brother-in-law. When Kathleen, a lodger, answered the door and said, "You know he does not live here," William fired at her. He likely suffered from mental illness;

he had been wounded three times at the front. A witness remarked that "when the deceased came back from the war he told me he had been wounded, gassed and had heart trouble. He said that he had a silver plate in his head." Another witnessed remarked that a girl had recently left him. That started him drinking. He was "a regular madman when he was drunk." Station hand Thomas Fitzgerald killed overseer Stanley Humble at Eddington station. Humble had warned Fitzgerald away from the jackeroos' quarters, where he had abused housekeeper Mrs Downey.[193] One witness recalled saying to Fitzgerald that "you can never have the woman," to which he replied that "as sure as the stars are shining, there are three bullets. One for Mrs Downey, one for Humble and putting his finger on his forehead said one for me straight up there and it won't miss."[194]

VIOLENT LIVES

Several men were either facing serious criminal sanctions or had been to prison and wanted to defend that secret. Reputation meant something even to the disreputable and unstable. Charles Young, a wood carter, shot himself in the head after fatally wounding his wife's brother, who had threatened to tell police that the deceased had repeatedly raped his daughter. The girl informed her aunt and uncle about the abuse. Young told his wife that "those bastards" would not "give him a second chance." Other witnesses said he was bad-tempered and had often threatened to kill his whole family.[195] Labourer Robert Donnelly fatally wounded cook Terence McDonald and then killed himself at a work camp. Donnelly came to breakfast with a rifle in his hands. "He said 'Teasdale, Henzel and Johnston, keep your seats. I won't molest you. I am going to shoot the rest of the bastards.'" McDonald told him not to "be a bloody fool, Bob." Donnelly turned toward him. "You are always pulling me to pieces. I will give it to you first." He left a note: "I here leave a few lines about the way my life has be slandered away by the low degraded people of Queensland." A pouch contained "A Notice to Offender upon his Discharge," showing that Donnelly, who had been sentenced to seven years in prison for manslaughter, had been placed on a seven-year good behaviour bond.[196] Alexander Bennett had been adopted at the age of two. At the age of sixteen, he shot his adoptive mother, Annie Bennett, and killed his adoptive father, William Bennett.[197] He then committed suicide. Alex had recently been fired from his job. His employer found him very hostile. A neighbour testified that "as a little chap the boy was very loveable. He altered after he left school. He got very wilful." In fact, Alex had been ejected as a problem child. Things worsened when he started keeping company with a fourteen-year-old girl. He ignored his mother's orders not to stay out at night, punched her, and left home on 1 May. According to Mrs Bennett, "he punched me on more than one occasion. He said to me 'If you throw your weight around I'll flatten you out.' I was always chastising him. I sometimes smacked him when he was a very naughty boy." She recalled speaking to him a fortnight before the tragedy. "He called me everything he could lay his tongue to. He said What the Hell do you want here?" "We did everything that was humanly possible for him. We purchased a piano for him and had him taught for six years. We also gave him a camera and a bicycle. There was nothing that the boy wished for that he did not get. He knew that if he had come and spoken kindly to us we would have given him anything willingly ... Often we thought there was just a bit of a kink in deceased's makeup. He often had fits of violent temper."[198]

Murder-suicides were and are predominately family affairs, and many occur at end of a relationship, but the suicide inquests in Queensland between 1890 and 1940 indicate additional factors such as mental illness, alcohol abuse, violent temper, and the impact of war. The victim is never a perpetrator; however, to explore murder-suicides it is necessary to consider relationships fully. Some relationships were dangerous. At least five of the women who died were prostitutes.

CONCLUSIONS

The course of life, an expression introduced in chapter 3, has defined the discussion of suicide motives for men and women. A further and concluding assessment of the term is essential because the course of life has a formal meaning, conceived by psychologists and psychiatrists. For specialists working in these fields, the life course conveys the idea of growing wisdom or adaptation. Moreover, the topics of wisdom and adaptation necessarily focus on the person and only secondarily consider the environment. This division into an inner and outer world, confessed Freudian Erik Erikson, "came as a puzzle to me in my early training [in psychoanalysis]."[199] In a bid to explain his bewilderment, Erikson proposed that the life course in clinical practice had departed from and actually progressed beyond entrenched theory. Theory remained fixed in nineteenth-century scientific concerns about the conservation of energy, he argued, while clinical work absorbed twentieth-century scientific interest in relativity and complementary relations, which, in reference to people's mental states, implied a role for society. In Erikson's hands, clinical flexibility led to psychosocial perceptions in which the life course was not tied exclusively to a rigid developmental logic. That logic of inner development remained, but society impinged, and that overlap required an adjustment in our thinking about the life course. There had to be room for biographical complexity.[200]

While reviewing the life course of men and women in relation to motives for suicide, I brought together society and developmental logic. The outcomes pointed to bleakness in certain suicidal life courses and extremely dark outcomes for a rare few men and women in prime adulthood who committed homicide-suicide. In a full psychosocial theory, unhappy life courses would be situated in relation to more pleasant outcomes that could result from adjustment. Erikson rendered his psychosocial perspective in a compact statement that accommodates tragic life courses as well as courses that epitomize cheerier adaptation. He did not want to reduce developmental logic to uncomplicated themes of wisdom, faith, hope, goodness, and charity. We are forced to consider, he wrote, "how emerging human strengths, step for step, are intrinsically beset not only with severe vulnerabilities that perpetually demand our healing insights, but also with basic evils which call for the redeeming values of universal belief systems or ideologies."[201] In choosing to speak of emerging strengths, Erikson still held onto developmental optimism; in his modified Freudian theory of the life course, he juxtaposed emotional traits that he felt epitomized people at particular stages, and he proposed how good outcomes might emerge from the conflicts inherent at each stage.

In the developmental logic of psychologists and psychiatrists, many stages are pre-adult; however, a life-course approach to suicide that uses historical evidence is limited to a few years prior to the act of self-destruction. Nothing was disclosed about childhood at an inquest unless the deceased was a child, and there were only a handful of child suicides. No life course was exposed in its totality during an inquest; however, motives for suicides can be aligned with stages in the life course, and that has been the scheme pursued in the preceding discussions of motives for suicides by men and women. Thus, instead of presenting lives longitudinally, they have to be grouped in life-course cross-sections. In other words, the inquest evidence is not perfectly matched to the type of life-course analysis that Erikson, Maris, and other social scientists have had in mind. Nevertheless, Erikson's suggestions resonate with the information at hand.

A few of his antithetical traits for stages in the life course relate to motives for suicide; they are also consistent with Germaine Greer's propositions about stages in the life course of women. For motives of suicide, the pertinent stages that Erikson remarked on were adolescence, young adulthood, adulthood, and old age. According to him, adolescents have a penchant for fidelity that is in the process of migrating from parents to other guides, and there is a period of sexual latency while the individual learns the rudiments for navigating society and acquiring a trade, but adolescent suicides were rare before the mid-twentieth century. To judge from the case files, adolescent suicides had poor role models, struggled with a vocation, and suffered abuse. They had trouble with parental rules, school work, entry-level jobs, and the law; they often lacked full parental guidance because they were living with grandparents, aunts, uncles, an overtaxed single parent, or adoptive parents. Child welfare departments supervised several.[202] Unfortunately for historians, authorities at inquests focused on immediate events, so that the upbringing experienced by adult suicides was not noted. It is estimated today that approximately a fifth of people who die by their own hand have been abused in childhood.[203]

For young adulthood, Erikson juxtaposed intimacy and affiliation with exclusivity and acts of rejection. As he saw it, young adults emerging from adolescence were willing and even eager to share intimacy with other individuals. In the suicide files young men and women had romantic misadventures and longings, and thus they sought intimacy but often could not make adjustments when the objects of their love rejected them.[204] The main antithesis for adulthood is procreativity and productivity, on the one hand, and self-absorption and stagnation, on the other.[205] Many mature men and women represented in the inquest files missed out on productivity; opportunities for satisfactory procreation at home and creation at work were truncated by the interjection of social forces and personal foibles. The last stage in the life course presents a fundamental antithesis of integrity and wisdom against disdain and despair. For integrity and wisdom to have a chance to function, for the elderly to stay really alive, according to Erikson, there must be a wilful act to keep things together mentally while bodily functions and memory weaken and generative interplay is lost. It is in this stage that "others who have become the main counterplayers in life's most significant contexts" have great importance.[206] Many of the older men

and women who committed suicide simply had painful, hopeless illnesses for which a psychosocial explanation is redundant; however, a
number of the elderly reached their last stage in the course of life without a companion, without a counterplayer.

Stages in the course of life, endowed with the physical changes
proposed by Germaine Greer or with the largely psychic traits recommended by Erik Erikson, hold prospects for considerable and identifiable forms of angst. But what considerations lead from life-course
crises – from motives – to attempts at self-destruction? To answer that
question, it is necessary to reconstruct the decision-making of suicidal people.

An elderly gold prospector on New Zealand's west coast. Poor elderly males living alone were at higher risk than other segments of the population. Roughly a quarter of all New Zealand men who committed suicide from 1900 to 1950 were fifty or older. Image MNZ–018656–F. Courtesy Alexander Turnbull Library, National Library of New Zealand, Te Puna Mātauranga o Aotearoa.

Collecting pension cheques at the post office, ca. 1943. New Zealand's early establishment of an old age pension relieved some of the financial stress for the elderly, but many proud individuals shunned it, dismissing it as no better than poor relief. Image number 1/4–000456–F. Courtesy Alexander Turnbull Library, National Library of New Zealand, Te Puna Mātauranga o Aotearoa.

Mustering inmates to the dining hall at the Dunwich Asylum, ca. 1920. Old destitute Queenslanders could apply to enter the asylum, but it was a feared destination, synonymous with life's end. One resident took his life in 1944 in a bid to publicize his claims of abuse; a few others committed suicide as a matter of self-euthanasia. Image 101339. Courtesy John Oxley Library, State Library of Queensland.

A hunting party near Christchurch, ca. 1915. Rifles and shotguns were commonplace in rural Queensland and New Zealand. Men favoured them as a method of self-destruction. Firearms accounted for over a third of their suicides in Queensland and a quarter in New Zealand. Image 1/1–023909–G. Courtesy Alexander Turnbull Library, National Library of New Zealand, Te Puna Mātauranga o Aotearoa.

Seacliff Hospital, ca. 1900. By World War 1, New Zealand's Department of Mental Health operated regional hospitals for mental illness. During the first half of the twentieth century, over 5 per cent of suicides had been patients in eight of these hospitals. Image PACOll–8769–02. Courtesy Alexander Turnbull Library, National Library of New Zealand, Te Puna Mātauranga o Aotearoa.

Rough on the Doctor.

DOTTYONE: (at Sunnyside, to other just up from Seacliff)—" Is Dr. Truby King still at Seacliff ?"

DOTTYTOO: " Oh yes, he'll never get better !"

A patient from Sunnyside asks a patient from Seacliff if Truby King is still at Seacliff. "Oh yes, he'll never get better." Truby King, the subject of this cartoon, was the immensely influential director of Seacliff Hospital, but he under-estimated the challenges of dealing with soldiers. Statements left by suicidal patients uniformly showed despondency or fear rather than facile humour. Image A–350–027. Courtesy Alexander Turnbull Library, National Library of New Zealand, Te Puna Mātauranga o Aotearoa.

A wartime building, ca. 1915. In response to public pressure, the New Zealand government established a hospital for "shell-shocked soldiers." The Queen Mary Hospital at remote Hanmer Springs was transformed in the 1920s into a centre for the treatment of nervous breakdowns, depression, and alcohol. It was mentioned in a number of medical summaries reported at suicide inquests. Image 1/2–000511–G. Courtesy Alexander Turnbull Library, National Library of New Zealand, Te Puna Mātauranga o Aotearoa.

Goodna Asylum, ca. 1938. Queensland's psychiatric hospitals were concentrated in the state's southeast. The treatment of the mentally ill followed trends in the United Kingdom and North America. For most of the first half of the twentieth century, gardens and outdoor work were considered therapeutic. Image 106376. Courtesy John Oxley Library, State Library of Queensland.

The Psychiatric Hospital at Porirua. In 1950 this hospital was New Zealand's third largest psychiatric facility. Well over one hundred patients and former patients of New Zealand's psychiatric hospitals committed suicide in the first half of the twentieth century. Image 57688 1/2. Courtesy Alexander Turnbull Library, National Library of New Zealand, Te Puna Mātauranga o Aotearoa.

PART THREE

Rationality, Psyche, and Treatment

6

What Becomes of the Broken-Hearted?
Intentions, Decisions, and Acts

Try as we may, it is impossible to access the conscious self – let alone the subconscious self – of other people. When someone says, "I feel your pain," we are skeptical. No real empathy – the power of projecting ourselves into another individual's situations and feelings – can be achieved, for we remain inside our own skin. Farmer Rob Roy Patterson puzzled about his own motives for suicide, and he knew others would too. "The Coroner will say insanity – who shall know whether he's right or wrong? Perhaps he will also say that drink has caused it – there may be a little in that." He condensed his motives into a situation: "I cannot rest. My mind is tortured."[1] "Seek not for a motive for there is but one, and that I carry with me," wrote Joseph Vercoe, who was being treated for depression.[2] Why some people endure hardships and others do not is mysterious. However, sympathy, distinct from empathy, can bring us close to comprehending decisions for suicide. With sympathy, there is an effort to be aware, from our imperfect vantage point, of problems and motives of others, to imagine the anguish of their trials and burdens. We will never feel someone else's pain, but by applying reason and evidence, we can move beyond motives, penetrate deeper than the predisposing causes or chronic causes, as they were called by some nineteenth-century writers.

The previous two chapters should have stirred sensitivity to what desperate people felt without pretending that we could feel their pain. The many voices should have awakened our awareness of distant and immediate motives, the chronic and acute causes mentioned by nineteenth-century writers. The burdens carried by individuals were recounted; the social, cultural, and economic background to problems was mentioned.

Having considered societal factors, I now want to reconstruct suicide decision-making. Doing so is tricky. The inquest depositions are not in-depth interviews, and even if they were, doubts would persist about candour. Still, some case files are startlingly suggestive. Obstacles to understanding are compounded by the impossibility of our achieving empathy; that impossibility cuts us off from firm knowledge. Even sympathy encounters an obstacle. In striving to imagine the torment of others and then squaring that with the finality of the act of suicide, we will still face instances when the person's frame of mind, insobriety, or immediate passions appear to inhibit rational thought. But if I exercise judgment about rationality, have I broken faith with the objective of sympathy by failing to imagine the totality of anguish and hence a decision to escape? Perhaps. Nevertheless, at least when viewed from outside the individual's conscious self, the observed rational states of people at or near the moment of suicide demonstrate differences, and we should be aware of them. With good cause, attempts to reconstruct suicidal reasoning are open to criticism, but accounts of existential crises in the case files are abundant and poignant enough to convey credibility. Later in this chapter's introduction, several examples will be given that can communicate the force of crises as they were taken in by individuals and allowed to overwhelm all else.

Along with the numerous motives mentioned in previous chapters, diversity in the capacity to reach a reasoned decision adds to the circumstances that make suicide many acts. There is dissent on the assertion about suicide amounting to a sum of diverse acts. Psychiatrists who focus on psychological pain, at one extreme of their thinking about suicide, maintain that it is fine to examine subpopulations for risk so long as there is a concurrent search for underlying commonalities. This classic stance came up in prior chapters; Maurice de Fleury drew upon the essentialness of anguish to dismiss the pertinence of sociology. There is a helpful strand of thought associated with the efforts of suicidologists to distill suicidal acts into a common introspective act with identifiable characteristics. Edwin Shneidman articulated this aim well when he wrote that "just as each suicidal event is exquisitely idiosyncratic, so also do all suicidal events, by virtue of their human quality, have a number of important psychological characteristics in common."[3] Shneidman begins with the assumption that suicide is never a pointless act but almost always "a way out of a problem, a dilemma, a bind, a challenge, difficulty, crisis, an unbearable situation."[4] Many cases encountered in New Zealand and Queensland conform to his observations.

The realization that suicide is a solution compels us to look for plausible common elements that would make it an acceptable escape. For guiding insights into those elements, it is worth citing what Shneidman dubbed his "ten commandments of suicide." First, the common purpose of suicide is to seek a solution. Second, the common goal is cessation of consciousness. Third, the common stimulus is intolerable psychological pain, or what he also called psychache.[5] Fourth, the common stressor is frustrated psychological need. Fifth, the common emotion is hopelessness-helplessness. Sixth, the common cognitive state is ambivalent. Seventh, the common perceptual state is constriction, or the narrowing of options. Eighth, the common action is egression. Ninth, the common interpersonal act is communication of intention. And tenth, the common consistency is lifelong coping patterns.[6] It is conceivable that Shneidman saw all of these points in most cases, but he never made that claim. In fact, in a recent reflection, he commented that he never presumed a single formula for suicide. "I believe," he remarked, "that each case of suicide has its own unique constellation of factors including, at its center, the vital role of idiosyncratically defined sociological need, which itself is pushed by a pattern of thwarted psychological needs that is special for that person."[7] Thus the ten concepts are ideal types, and perhaps only several appeared in a particular case. The third commandment, intolerable psychological pain, seems to me the key to Shneidman's theory of suicide. It is important to mention that his understanding of suicide originates in a psychotherapeutic tradition in which theory has been individual-centred and essentially uninvolved with crises in the individual's social environment. In the previous two chapters, the discussions of motives have shown the effects of economic, social, and even cultural circumstances. The focus now shifts to psychology.

Since this chapter probes psychological depths, as effectively as the sources allow, place and time are not as significant as when I reviewed rates and motives. The discussion will blend the New Zealand and Queensland cases because intolerable pain is indistinguishable from one jurisdiction to the other. The pain of feeling pain, a meta-pain of the human condition, is what robs life of joy and makes an escape desirable. As he lay dying from poison, Daniel Buisson told the doctor that the toxic concoction was "the most wonderful drink that he ever knew. It would put him out of his misery."[8] "Oh what a relief," sighed another.[9] "After a falling out with his girlfriend," Frederic Young shot himself. "What is life," he asked, "if you can not find happiness and love and suffer the pain of happiness? So goodbye to all."[10]

Many men and women could not hide their meta-pain. Their mental state, expressed by vacancy and detachment, is obvious in retrospect. They were on course for abnegation. Becoming more and more depressed after the death of his wife, Andrew McEwen suddenly ceased playing cribbage.[11] Shopkeeper James Baxter stayed in bed, would not open the shop, looked miserable, and did not eat.[12] Imagine the plight of farmer John Hills, who had had a bad case of shell shock and later lost his home to fire. He left an account of his mental ordeal: "I have been going through terrible worry and anxiety these last few days, but still praying and hoping to overcome the terrible depression of a nervous breakdown, such as only those who have suffered can understand." His last wish was that God would "preserve you from the terrible state of mind I am suffering." Hills concluded, "I am going off my head with nerves."[13] At the age of eighteen, farm lad Alfred Dewbery felt embarrassed about his appearance and saw no future. "I am sorry I had to leave you but I could not live any longer because I was unhappy all the time: do not think that anyone made me like that. It was because I was ashamed of myself and nothing in the whole world would make me happy."[14]

No one experiencing a breakdown, a failure in business or marriage, could experience enjoyment when in the depths of despair. When his business failed and his wife left him, Wilfred Smith had a bad case of nerves and entered a private hospital. He wrote to his parents, "It is dreadful, in fact hell on earth to suffer as I do – to see everyone going about in an ordinary way when everything is slipping away and I am powerless to stop it."[15] The state of total absorption in meta-pain, to the exclusion of being, is conveyed by the business partner of a financially strapped engineer. "He seemed unconscious as he put out his hand to shake hands with me as I sat in the car." In his suicide note the engineer wrote, "I can see no daylight of any kind. You can understand why I was so quiet at the weekend."[16] Ivan Hayward's wife left him when their infant twins died. "Every car going past the gate, every sound I hear, I think it may be you returning."[17] The delight in life shown by others became painful for one young man, who confessed to his parents that "seeing other people enjoying themselves is a hard thing to do."[18]

To accent the inner setting, the dates and places of events will be mentioned sparingly in this chapter, but age, occupation, and marital status appear often. It would be a mistake to look upon the thoughts revealed as universal and timeless. They belonged in part to a culture fading into history, a culture conditioned by manual labour, male work pride, serious drinking, recent land settlement, substantial rural sectors, extensive resource exploitation, public works, and enough medical knowledge to instill pessimism if not terror. Therefore the prominence of older, single males living in rural settings is a condition not merely of the aging process but of an era. As Ronald Maris wrote, the situation of older men derived from "the entire developmental history of white males and the meanings, habits, and adaptations they have acquired over a lifetime."[19] Indeed, this was the case. The seasonality of suicide discussed in chapter 3 lends support to the proposition that the motives for a number of male suicides were especially connected with the rural economy. An analysis of cases in the second half of the century might well lend credence to an argument about a cultural change if it showed, as part of a relative growth of youth suicides, a shift to urban locales and a decline in seasonality.

Drawing naturally upon the resources of their culture and education, men and women prepared rationalizations to counter what was for them the tenuous, weakening, but still vital pull of living. They had motives and meta-pain, but they needed self-reflection and arguments, or impulsiveness and clouded judgment, to ease them into a violent act that had perhaps shed moral censure but had recently acquired the stigma of cowardice. For justifications, men and women could turn to culturally rooted ideas such as self-sacrifice, a long rest, a journey to the other side, and God's intervention to save their souls.

MY LIFE IS A TERRIBLE WASTE

At various points, people take stock of their lives and estimate their remaining prospects. A crisis or a birthday initiates an evaluation.[20] The age cohorts for suicides in New Zealand and Queensland suggest that stock-taking usually started when people reached their forties and revived at subsequent milestone years. Looking at suicides in California from 1960 to 1985, David Phillips and Daniel Smith encountered age heaping at forty-five and sixty, and that discovery led them to hypothesize that some birthdays were more traumatic than others. The New Zealand data set, with its excellent age information, reveals that four ages (fifty, forty, forty-five, and sixty) accounted for one in eight (12.0 per cent) male suicides. No such pattern of heaping at particular ages appeared for women.

Men at certain ages were inclined to consider whether their lives had attained their expectations or met the expectations of people around them. Perhaps, like fifty-two-year-old Frederick Raine, they intended a change in their way of living, "but seeing nothing but an empty and lonely future ahead," decided on "a very unusual course to end matters."[21] Forty-one-year-old Leslie Baxter evaluated his situation in life and asked "what is there in it for me?"[22] At a prime stock-taking age of sixty, William Halliburton concluded that "my life I am sorry to say has not been one of success."[23] Unemployed and poor, mariner Alfred Stevens wrote his closest friend, "I am getting out. You know what I mean. I feel both mentally and physically unable to cope with a new scheme of things at 54."[24] Psychological, social, and biological factors converged around certain ages. Psychologically, men could look over their lives at symbolically important times; socially, they could face career- and life-changing phases at certain ages; biologically, the middle ages were synonymous with an accumulation of wear.

There will always be variation from a paradigm, and certainly, the New Zealand and Queensland suicide case files yielded instances of young people who concluded that their lives had neither a future nor a purpose. "Forgive me," wrote Alexander Kristoff, "but I don't like my life."[25] "I have made a bad start in life," supposed another young man.[26] From these firmly defeatist positions, the courses of actions were quite limited; however, it is one thing to think that "this is an accursed life I am leading" and another to end it.[27] How did men and women resolve upon a suicide solution? A suicidal man or woman could narrow his or her options by blocking out the very idea that to continue living amounted to a real life. In this formulation, a living death was no better than terminal death. Broken-hearted widower John Forsyth could see two options; both were death. "I prefer death to a living death as my health is done."[28] Single, unemployed clerk Horace Huddlestone, down on his luck, remarked that "his present life is a living death to him."[29] In a related vein, men and women asked "what have I got to live for?"[30] Abandoned by her lover and sure that her returned-soldier fiancé, "who was away fighting for me," would not understand her infidelity, Agnes Mackenzie wrote, "I dread the lonely years ahead of me."[31]

A few men and women began to think of self-destruction as a remedy when they heard of a suicide. A young woman with a hip disease that made her a shut-in told her father that she had heard of people gassing themselves and learned that "it was an easy death."[32] From time to time, the consideration of suicide as an option arose from an example close at hand. Suffering from a bad rupture and "some inward hurt," seventy-five-year-old William Short told his wife that "he would do like Ronald Miller who took his life at Brooklyn. They had been great friends. I kept the knives away from him but he got the razor without my knowledge."[33] Retired and depressed, Thomas Brown knew of a nearby and recent suicide case.[34] Bessie Blakeway had been depressed. "Two of her aunts had drowned themselves years ago," remarked her husband. "She knew of this."[35] Grace Alexander repeatedly mentioned that her brother had hanged himself, and "she felt as if she was becoming like him."[36] Waitress Elizabeth Gallop's uncle had committed suicide.[37] There were suicidal families: "The deceased's brother George committed suicide after the war on a troopship and his sister Jessie committed suicide by jumping off the Sydney Bridge, about two years ago."[38] Alice McMahon had been a witness at the inquest into her stepdaughter's suicide, and Elizabeth Watson's mother had recently committed suicide.[39] The executor for Randolph Miller's estate reported that Miller was "a brother of a man who about 23 years ago killed his parents and then committed suicide."[40] Models for suicide solutions were always available through rumour and did not require media accounts. A family history of suicide is widely accepted to increase the risk of suicide.[41]

The prospect that suicide was cowardly gave pause; propaganda during World War 1 had represented self-destruction as craven. It was not by chance that thirty-two-year-old labourer Lacey White, who shot himself in late 1918 and who had a brother at the front, wrote, "I will face death like a man."[42] Men whose suicide left widows and children without support were depicted as worthless as well as cowardly. Suicide was a coward's way, an unmanly way. Timothy Enright, a farmer and World War 1 veteran, left a letter lamenting his financial situation and apologizing to his family for his solution. "I take the coward's way out. Try to forgive me."[43] Single labourer Joseph Ward enjoyed good health but was out of work and indulged in drinking bouts; two weeks before he took his life, he told a friend that "a man who committed suicide was not a coward and instanced the case of German Charlie who had cut his throat."[44] Forty-eight-year-old Jesse Dorrington wanted his martial bravery known. "I went to India with the troops, served in the Punjab with troops and Rawalpindi. Took part in the action of Thelat, the time Kitchener took command as Commissioner in Chief. I have for some time been afflicted with a malady and partial blindness, which has caused me a lot of worry. I am only a burden to others and myself. I do not want the people and my friends to think that I am doing anything cowardly."[45] If men were following a script of masculinity, they had to present their suicide as fearless and decisive; this fulfillment of a role ordained that they had to complete the job and not merely attempt suicide, survive, and thus in a certain sense fail.

Suicidal men found distinct ways to represent their self-destruction as brave; for some, their resistance had been heroic. It was important to Andrew Carroll, sick and dependant on drugs for sleep, that his resistance to suicide be credited as bravery: "God how I fought against all temptation to end my suffering."[46] Much the same spirit was behind Alexander Krause's decision to leave a testament to his mental decline after "the sudden unexpected demise of my life partner." Krause recognized that he was having fewer and fewer lucid moments, and he contemplated suicide. "I fought against it."[47] To endure mental or physical anguish truly required bravery, but courage also was claimed by individuals who chose death. Worried about money matters at the outset of the Great Depression, farmer Henri Germane left a note for his wife and family: "Life being unbearable for me I find it courageous to put an end to it."[48] Charlie Benton took his own life rather than face a return to a mental hospital that he branded a "living hell" and "the home of lost souls." In a letter to his best friend, he represented his death as a sacrifice to expose the hospital. "Bill," he wrote, "don't think I am taking the coward's way out. It takes more guts than you think."[49] As a vaunted masculine trait, no more elevated than during and after wars, men claimed bravery for which ever way they handled their existential crisis.

Men could deflect an anticipated charge of cowardice by pointing to altruism or chivalry in their self-destruction. Sacrifice could be coupled with the ideal of the breadwinner. Bootmaker John Clark had a war wound that required his wife, in his estimation, to slave to keep him. She had enough to do "without a dud of a husband."[50] Forest ranger George Watson had a serious bladder ailment and took strychnine. He lived long enough for his nephew to ask, "what did you take that stuff for?" Watson replied, "I done it for her sake – my wife. She has been worked too hard and had enough worry."[51] The sudden death of his daughter plunged Gerald Matthews into depression. He felt that he encumbered his family. "I'll just be a burden on you all and an object of pity to men and just a wretched thing to my dear children and to you. I do it for the love of you all."[52]

Men and women debated within themselves as they dealt with their predicaments, their meta-pain, and their ambivalence. Dutch courage helped a few to reach a fatal decision. "Darling," wrote Robert Lockerbie, "I can't face the future. I know I am a coward. Have been the same all my life. I have just finished a flask of brandy and two bottles of beer which has given me the courage to take the step I have taken."[53] For three weeks Maori labourer Henare Maihi debated how to escape a family dispute.[54] Peter Collins, a heavy-drinking, single, fifty-one-year- old swagman without relatives in New Zealand, had run out of work and money. When a police constable examined the locale where Collins had jumped into the Wairu River, he "saw numerous footprints on the road. They resembled the deceased's. And he had been walking to and fro upon the road."[55] A stranger noticed that shortly before Alex Burgess blew himself up, "he walked to and fro."[56] For an unknown but significant number of suicides, a period of uncertainty of hours or weeks might have presented an opening for a rescuing hand that did not appear. Certainly, not all suicides were unexpected and unstoppable. During an inner debate, a mental walking to and fro, resistance weakened when men and women reviewed their situation from a vantage point of low self-worth. Suiciologists have speculated about whether there is an "internal debate that may exist in the mind of the suicidal person," and fragmentary evidence from the inquests intimates there is.[57]

By severing their ties with life, a few men and women were releasing something that they professed had little meaning; their choice of words was deliberate, economical, and devastating for those who read them. In many instances, rock-bottom self-worth was revealed indirectly, as when timber carter Charles Hickmott left instructions: "Bury me as you would a dog."[58] Ploughman Richard Ward, single and forty-five, put a note on his bunk in which he referred to himself as dirt and carrion.[59] Poor morale gripped accountant John Gordon when he lamented, "I am always down in the mud when things go wrong with me."[60] Single farm labourer John Lepper wrote to a women with whom he was infatuated: "I am a rotter, please don't worry over me." But of course entirely ambivalent, he did want her to worry and left her his war medals.[61] Men and women who maintained poor opinions of themselves might keep the exact reasons for this judgment private to the end. "I have tried to hang onto nothing," remarked unemployed salesman William Aston. Single and affected by shrapnel, he convinced himself that there was nothing to save.[62] In other instances, individuals explained their opinions of themselves. Sixty-year-old painter Robert Hurst arrived at a bleak assessment: "I just feel that I cannot give up the booze and rather than become a drunken hobo knocking about the streets, I prefer to end my life while I still have enough money to pay for funeral expenses."[63]

It is impossible to know how many men or women who committed suicide had managed to run down their self-worth by earnest reflection on their lives. Further, the case files suggest no handy rule of thumb about how self-criticism could escalate into an affliction. The roots of despair in personal history were dissimilar and even opposing, because for some individuals physical isolation contributed to feelings of defeat, but for others social interaction initiated gloomy comparisons.

One significant occupation was perfectly arranged to promote defeat on many fronts. Queensland miner-prospector Denis Downes concluded his had been "a wasted life. What's the use of me living to carry on like this."[64] His way of life contributed to feelings of futility because Queensland's mineral wealth attracted men following a rainbow, only to wind up poor, ill, and alone. One hundred and six Queensland miner-prospectors committed suicide in the years covered by this study, three-quarters of them (74.5 per cent) before 1910. Miner-prospectors comprised the third most common occupation of suicides, after labourers and farmers. Their ages suggest that many had been drawn to the far north during the gold rushes of the 1870s. Three-quarters of them (75.5 per cent) were either known to be unmarried or had no known marital status; most had problems associated with alcohol, mental illness, or physical aliments. Witnesses frequently mentioned that they did not believe the men had any relatives in Queensland, a statement that speaks as much to anonymity among the community of male transients as to an absence of family. Fantasy, hope, stoicism, loneliness, and indifference camped together, as did the men. Things were different in New Zealand. Miner-prospectors who committed suicide there numbered only thirty-two, and the occupation ranked tenth. The presence of miner-prospectors in significant numbers in Queensland likely contributed to the elevated suicide rate relative to New Zealand noted in chapter 3. The impact of historical contingencies, best discerned by case-by-case analysis, must guide interpretations of suicide rates if analysis is to be credible.

Many individuals who left testaments bearing on their feelings of inadequacy seemed absorbed in themselves. Like the miner-prospectors, some self-critical individuals were isolated, lacked social support, and at a crucial stage in their lives committed themselves to a gamble likely to fail. However, isolation was not a necessary condition for self- absorption. In fact, social interaction was a potent irritant, for it caused men and women to worry about sufficiency because in Western culture, in an age of capitalist consumption, many felt they had to validate themselves by individual attainment of property, marketable skills, and ideal-type spouses.[65] A few individuals elaborated on their sense of worth, and their estimations hinged on the company and perceptions of other people. It is impossible to imagine how anyone could have felt lower than James Mullins, whose poverty depressed him. "Many people hearing of my fate will no doubt say it was a jolly good job, it was the best thing he could ever have done; he wasn't much use anyway etc. etc. In this I quite agree with them, but I hope none of them will ever be as unfortunate as I am."[66] Such self-flagellation was matched from time to time. John Hewetson left a testament that stated at length how he was unfit to live, lacked even one redeeming feature, and made nothing but wrong decisions. "I feel that instead of being helpful that my future is nothing but a hindrance, my business is failing, I seem to quarrel. Every move that is made, my life is nothing but huge mistakes."[67] None of the case files contained remarks about what men and women saw in a mirror; however, New Zealand writer Janet Frame in her autobiography provided a description that could have been a shared experience: "I saw tiny triumphs of self-esteem fading as I angled the duchesse mirror, to contemplate the horror of my decayed teeth. There was no escape from them."[68]

There were uncompromising self-condemnations based on how men and women thought they had failed to succeed according to what contemporary culture projected as leading forms of self-validation. Twenty-year-old jackeroo Wallace Hudson was not earning enough to give a home to a certain Miss Beatty, of whom he was exceedingly fond. "Dear Mother. I am the greatest dope in the world with no brains or anything else. Everywhere I seem to go of late everyone seems to think me funny. So this is the best way for me to deal with myself."[69] Hotel porter Andrew O'Brien lived with his parents. When his girlfriend rejected his marriage proposal, he definitely evaluated his life and found it deficient on his own terms. "In every way," he confided to his parents, "I am a failure. Never could stick to a job. Always lived on you which was pretty poor of me."[70] O'Brien knew what he wanted from life: "I have always wanted three things in life. But did not get them. They were a good job, car, and girl."[71] Katherine Smith's boyfriend suddenly announced his marriage to another girl, and this convinced her of her inability to make good decisions. "I have made an awful lot of mistakes in my life in the past few months, and would like to end it now before I make more. It is a cowardly way out I know."[72]

Financial difficulties and work-related setbacks drove men into a state of mind where they thought of themselves as only out of step, ineffectual, and useless. Fifty-year-old New Zealand public servant William Lewis Robertson, who had laboured for a decade promoting consumer co-operatives and community medical services, felt betrayed, defeated, and adrift after key cabinet ministers denied funding for his projects. At the end of a 163-page testament recounting his activities, Robinson typed the following assessment of his place in a society that he assumed had no use for him: "So, now, this is it. I have done what I could. It seems that there is no place for my talents and services. So I must go."[73] More typical were terse notes that equated financial difficulties with impotence. Frank Beaumont's note conveyed how such troubles cratered men's confidence: "My affairs are so frightfully involved that I am about to terminate my useless life." He was middle-aged, single, and unemployed.[74]

Many people transformed into their own worst enemies and occasionally into a proficient prosecutor, judge, and jury. These individuals may not have worried so much about validating themselves, but they brooded over past misconduct and often took stock of the ravages of alcoholism. "I have passed sentence on myself. I have been absolutely rotten and am not fit to live" – philandering farmer Frederick Foster's verdict was extreme, but his exploits had jeopardized his finances and cost him the respect of his wife and daughters.[75] "From my boyhood," reflected Arthur Steele, "I have been beyond all reason bad."[76] What preyed on his mind, we will never know, but he had determined that past deeds made him loathsome. We will also never know exactly why returned soldier Walter Ford, whose "brains and nerves are all bung up," took his life. He was an alcoholic with a bad case of the horrors. His self-worth had collapsed but not his fundamental regard for his family. "Write mom," he told a friend, and "please tell her not to worry as I am not worth it."[77] Another alcoholic several times wasted money given to him by his family in England. With these remittances in his pocket, he stopped working to go on sprees until he finally decided, "I'm thoroughly disgusted with myself."[78] The social stigma and physical decay from alcoholism and venereal diseases left a number of men regretting that they had reached a "sad end to a life spoilt."[79]

Women, too, succumbed to low self-worth; their evaluations seldom involved work and money or critical reflections on past moral conduct, although there were such instances. Jean Hall, for example, had been involved in a dodgy financial scheme and solicitors were closing in when she used coal gas to end her life. "I'm a liar and a cheat and a thief and I can't live with myself any longer," she confessed to her husband.[80] More commonly, women expressed symptoms of depression and failure in the quest for a husband, in the discharge of domestic roles, or in procreation. Shop assistant Constance Smith was thirty-three when her fiancé broke off their engagement. A friend testified that Miss Smith "told me she was afraid of the future and of being left unmarried."[81] Awful depression besieged farmer's wife Isabella Symonds, but her downcast thoughts aggravated her condition. "I have done nothing but blunder along since coming here and for months have not understood this feeling of failure which has been stealing over me – and only very recently it has come home that all the fault is mine."[82]

Often the sense of failure centred on child-rearing, caring for a husband, or imposing an unreasonable burden on the family. Annie McGovern pined for her three stillborn children. Grief came out in her sensitivity to imagined rumours. "Everything is wrong. The people are saying that I am not doing justice to a good husband."[83] A hint of sacrifice occasionally accompanied testimonials of self-criticism. Evelyn Drewe explained to her husband, "I simply cannot manage anything lately, so this is why I am doing what I am doing. I pray God will send you another helpmate in time." Her twins had died at birth.[84] From the experiences of their prime years, older women knew what it meant to care for family, and as they became incapacitated, they considered self-sacrifice to spare others from what they had had to do. Sixty-seven- year-old Emily Cundall, an invalid for eight years, felt an obligation to release her family. "I feel the work and worry is too much for you. From four in the morning till bedtime is no joke."[85] In a note to her husband, Doris Cooper asked forgiveness for what "I am doing but I want to die. I am no good to you or the children."[86] Evidence of insecurity could be inserted outside the main communication, as it was in the case of Elsie Dimond: "My darling husband farewell and may God forgive me. I leave all my possessions to you. Your unworthy wife."[87] Critical self-evaluations were not motives for suicide but, rather, one means for getting over the hold on life. Men and women offered reasons for their low opinions of themselves or at any rate seemed convinced of their badness, but it is important to observe that guilt and low self-worth are symptoms of depression. That affliction conceivably supported a fatal resolve, not just through the motive of mental pain, but also by the exercise of self-condemnation and ideas of sacrifice that strengthened intent.

IMPAIRED JUDGMENT

Shneidman advanced his ten points without qualification and without allowing for variations in the reasoning capacity of individuals entering the suicide scenario. In fact, for sympathetic reasons, he insisted that suicide was a logical act that dealt with frustrated psychological need. The suicidal individuals that he knew best could enter a clinic or call a suicide helpline, and the logic that he referred to was their subjective logic. He made every effort to avoid a condescension that might preclude working effectively with suicidal individuals. Nevertheless, the concept of a suicidal logic and especially of a subjective suicidal logic should give us pause. Not every case in the New Zealand and Queensland inquest files involved individuals in a state of mind to seek help or to apply any logic that recognized suicide's finality. Subjective logic is a problematic term because psychiatrists who aspire to help individuals try to enlist or strengthen a reasoning capacity. Logic is a grey area even if we grant, as the pragmatism of suicide prevention and respect for dignity require, that people who have committed suicide had their own logic. It is a grey area because of evidence of five groupings of impaired judgment that have emerged from the suicide inquests. Four of these are delusional mental illnesses, senility, alcohol-related damage, and anger. As well, on rare occasions, witnesses felt that an individual had a low intelligence, a judgment with compound implications. (Anger will be discussed later in this chapter in connection with impulsiveness.)

Escape may have been desirable for most individuals, but did they all recognize suicide's quintessential nature? Could each have been reasoned with? One in a hundred suicides in New Zealand and Queensland took place at a mental hospital; many more individuals had been patients, were on parole, were awaiting committal, had been spared committal, or had been voluntary patients. Englishman John Grant had settled on remote Thursday Island, where he went mad, talked to imaginary people, and believed enemies wanted to try him for crimes. The magistrate ordered him aboard a vessel bound for Brisbane, where he was to be committed to the mental hospital. The warder secured him in a cabin and later took him for a walk on deck. Grant seized this moment of freedom to jump over the ship's side.[88] When Charles Tebutt was admitted to Auckland Mental Hospital, "he was acutely maniacal and actively suicidal."[89] There were men and women whose reality consisted of delusions. The lighthouse keeper at Cleveland Bay near Townsville had a brief stay at the Queensland mental hospital in

Brisbane. After his return home, he still imagined the lighthouse was falling down.[90] Elderly John Miller, a man without relatives in New Zealand, was a patient at the mental hospital at Porirua. His doctor described him as "suffering from delusional insanity and ... exalted."[91] John Cahill's wife testified that "voices speak to him at all times and mock him." He had been a patient at a mental hospital.[92]

Some irrational men and women had never spent any time in a mental hospital. Friends and relatives suspected they were deeply troubled, but respected their independence and took no steps for their committal so long as they seemed harmless.[93] Gustav Klepsch, a miner-prospector who regarded his rifle as his only friend, had assumed another man's name after his death and now could not sleep because the dead man was after him.[94] The publican at the Royal Hotel at Thargomindah, in outback Queensland, testified that a travelling watch repairman "appeared wrong in his mind. He told me he believed people were putting electric batteries on his head."[95] Laundry manager Gew Yew appeared very frightened and mentioned that someone intended to kill him. He also imagined that he was a character from a comic book.[96] Believing that somebody would soon shoot him, Leonard Bell would shout that "they're after me, they're after me." He feared the agents of a religious sect.[97] Phantoms threatened paranoid alcoholic Patrick Kellett, who told a constable they intended to beat him that night. "They're waiting for me in the shithouse with bottles."[98] Comparable cases were discussed in the chapter on men and their motives. In a few cases of paranoia, the hunters were shadowy detectives. John Miller claimed that pictures were being taken of his eyes and detectives intended to seize him.[99]

Albert Freeman would have agreed that his self-destruction was not the act of a reasonable man acting in a logical way. To assist the coroner, he left a letter alleging that because he was a spirit medium, an invisible force had taken him over. "Trance mediumship," he explained, "is an exceedingly dangerous business," and he was "not the first luckless medium to end in this sad tragic manner." According to the plainclothes constable who patrolled Wellington's botanic gardens, Freeman "had a habit of always talking to himself and driving away the spirits."[100] Friends thought miner-prospector Max Mehner was mad because he had four horses and "used to muster them during the night and talk to them as a mate would talk to his mates." He may just have been a good stockman, but when he chased the four at night with a rifle, doubts arose about his affection for them.[101] Thomas Christian complained for weeks that "he was not altogether master of his mind and that there was something inside him stronger than himself." He promised not to commit suicide "if he could help it."[102] The army had sent Charles Sheard home from Egypt on account of mad fits. Back in New Zealand he told people he was "subject to clairvoyant influences and required police protection."[103] On the morning of his death, Greek fishmonger John Dandes stood on his neighbour's chicken coop staring at the sky. A constable told him to come down. "I will Pat, when I see my brother passing away in the clouds."[104] Fletcher Hargreaves, a separated man who milked on shares, told co-workers that he had visions of his deceased father and brother. He explained that hell was better than heaven.[105] God spoke to Leslie Buckingham and "repeatedly told him to take his life."[106] Almost certainly, he and a few other individuals had schizophrenia.[107] The words of Len Bowers describe these acutely psychotic individuals. They were "plainly out of control and in such a state of suffering that it is clear they could not willingly endure it."[108]

There were also men and women whom witnesses believed had impaired mental functionality. Senility had overtaken them. Single and sixty-eight, farmer Edward Frost was judged "a simple man" by his son.[109] Widower and retired miner-prospector William O'Connell "lost his senses at times." He was seventy-six and lived with his son and daughter-in-law, who had taken him to a doctor for an assessment of his mental state.[110] Muddled was how William le Fleming described his seventy-three-year-old father. "It appeared to be the natural failings of a man getting up in years."[111] In the estimation of his daughter-in-law, sixty-five-year-old Daniel Kehely had been "strange in his manner. Somewhat childish of late."[112] Widower and pensioner Alfred Derbridge "was getting childish."[113] His boarding-house keeper described old Joseph Thompson – single, injured, and unemployed – as "a simple man."[114]

Senility was not the sole explanation for alleged simplicity. According to his foster parents, eighteen-year-old labourer Edward Hay "was not what you would call a bright boy." But no wonder. His father had committed suicide, and his life had been a misery.[115] Hotel porter George Fryer was single and thirty-six; a police constable told the magistrate, "I understand he was a simple man."[116] He had seemed "quite troubled" and wanted an escape, but was his mental state such that he appreciated the finality of suicide? We can dismiss the constable's comment merely as denigration, the type of characterization that during Fryer's lifetime added to his anguish, but it also may have been an accurate judgment. The possibility that one's actions would be judged fool-ish or insane caused many individuals to take steps to ensure that their motives would be understood and, they hoped, respected. "I have known the grief, the agony, the mental torture to a thousand fold," wrote twenty-one-year-old labourer Wilfred Burns. "People will look from the armchair and exclaim! Foolishness, weak mindedness, others will say mentally defective or perhaps love-mad or highly emotional." But he said that when he looked the future in the face, "I see noth-ing."[117] His foresight in writing a testament and his uniquely eloquent logic, an argument to pre-empt misunderstanding, put space between his action and the suicides of many others. Burns had calculated that his twenty-one years comprised a long span because, as he put it, "I have known no joys or pleasures which a normal being receives, but I have known the grief, the agony, and mental torture to a thousandfold."[118]

Remarks about mental capacity were provided at numerous inquests. An acquaintance of Edward Scholz said, "I came to the conclusion that he was not normal mentally."[119] Fifty-four-year-old cook Minnie Knott was described as "not quite normal just slightly mental."[120] George Lansdowne, forty-five and single, had worked on his father's orchard and garden at Havelock North his whole life, but one day when his father was gone, a land agent arrived to show the property to a buyer. They explained their business to him. The land was George's life, and not long afterward he cut his throat with a pruning knife. At the inquest he was described as "a simple man."[121] One man's life resembled that of an *enfant sauvage*. According to farmer Oliphant McKay, John Smith, if that was his name, was affected by the moon for about six days every month. McKay testified that "the deceased was mentally deficient. He was very eccentric, would not associate with adults and would run away and hide if any strangers came to the place. Due to his manner and dirty habits no person would employ him."[122]

Among the alcohol-abuse cases, there are several conditions in which it would be unwise to assume that the individuals committed suicide in a rational state. Men who fled toward peril when pursued by appari-tions were not rational. Alcoholic insanity caused dentist Robert Smith "many absurd delusions."[123] Sheer drunkenness impeded judgment. Alcoholic labourer William Cook "was in the habit of taking chloro-form."[124] Accountant Frank McNeil, fifty-three and married without children, had financial problems at the outset of the Great Depression. A creditor had taken him to court. Alcohol provided his immediate escape. While drunk, he consumed a bottle of Lysol. Swallowing Lysol often meant a lingering death with enough time for a police interview. In his statement to a constable, McNeil mentioned, "I suddenly conceived of the idea of committing suicide under the influence of alcohol."[125] Addicted to alcohol, shipwright John Northey had been drinking steadily for twelve months, and his son described him as "not blind drunk but muddled all the time."[126]

IMPULSIVE ACTS AND FITS OF PASSION

Planned suicides have been associated with depression and hopelessness, and psychiatrists and psychologists currently use a Suicide Intent Scale that includes questions about planning.[127] Sudden rash decisions complicate notions that logic applies to the act. The inquests examined for this study revealed a few extreme examples of rash behaviour. One minute Frederick Frampton was laughing and joking with friends aboard a ship, and the next he shouted "here she goes" and threw himself backwards between stern and the wharf.[128] While it is impossible to tell how many suicides were committed on the spur of the moment, the capriciousness of the act could be startling and baffling to onlookers, although the duration of an individual's anguish and reflection could have been of long standing. Joseph Hewitt loathed his situation as a publican in the outback and became despondent about bringing his family to such place. One day "he took a penny piece out of his pocket and tossed it up saying heads for life and tails for death, it came down tails."[129]

On a few occasions a dying man or woman spoke to a witness, or a witness could comment on a sudden change in mood and movement. At twenty-seven, Helen Deiderick was single and had had a romantic misadventure. When asked why she swallowed a solution of phosphorous made from match heads, "she said she took it in a passion."[130] Shortly after Helene Delabarca received an upsetting telephone call from her lover, William Marshall, she seemed to regain her composure but stole away to kill herself. She had secured a separation agreement from her husband, and Marshall had just called to tell her he planned to move away.[131]

It took George Flanagan about a day to die from rat poison, and during that time the unemployed labourer, a heavy drinker and a hospital outpatient, spoke to his wife. "He said God forgive me. I did it on the spur of the moment. He gave no other reason, but he seemed to be fretting over having done it."[132] Rheumatism and a bad heart made Ernest Timmins anxious and restless. At 2:45 one morning his wife heard him jump out of bed and run out of the house as fast as he could. "I was just in time to see him jumping the back fence." He drowned himself in a river.[133] Drinking and brooding ceaselessly, James Adam swallowed "Rough on Rats." He survived a few hours. His son lit a cigarette for him, and they talked. James said that "he had been worried a lot, took poison on the spur of the moment, and now regretted it."[134] Things had gone badly for twenty-two-year-old Frederick Cullen. He fled home at fifteen, entered into a carpentry business that failed, and had a bad case of the flu. Impulsively, he took poison in a hotel room. When he gained consciousness at the hospital, he told his former partner in the carpentry business that "he must have taken the spirit of salts in a moment of madness. He did not know why he did it, as he wanted to live."[135] He did live but only for fifteen days. Suicides and attempted suicides could be painful modes of escape with time enough for second thoughts and often no hope of going back.

Anger overwhelmed some men and women who seized upon a suicidal gesture from the repertoire of rage. The course of events diverged, because some carried out the threat immediately. Others waited and, after judging their tempers a terrible dangerous flaw that could cause the death of someone else, killed themselves instead. Lionel Barker was a man of action and habitually inebriated. When he came home with a friend and a quantity of beer, his wife needed his help to take one of their two children to the hospital. She ordered the friend to get out, and after he had gone, Charlie struck her twice and she hit him back. He told her that "you and I are finished. I'll show you what I can do. I'll cut my bloody throat."[136] He stormed out, slammed the door, and hanged himself with a child's swing. Young farmer Frederick Box, when questioned by his wife of five months about a girl and financial matters, refused any information. "He got in a very bad temper and got up and walked out." His wife found his body five minutes later on the veranda.[137] Judged unstable and excitable by his doctor, James O'Donoghue could not stand being rebuked by his wife for an evening of drinking at the billiard saloon. He threw crockery; she fled the house; he hanged himself.[138]

Alcoholic housewife Maria Millard did not die immediately from arsenic poisoning and thus had time to explain that she had acted rashly "while in a Scot." Witness said she "had a very hasty temper when she was put on and then became sorry for it."[139] Henry Weston habitually threatened his wife and children with violence. After one terrible outburst, his wife fled the house. The next day he called the children together and in a rage said, "I am going to die now," and went into a bedroom and shot himself.[140] Out of work for two years, frustrated, and drinking heavily, Alfred Fitchett so terrified his wife that she insisted on separate rooms. One night he threatened that "if you do not come to bed with me I will blow my brains out." She did not and he did. At the inquest she said he had often threatened to take his life and she had taken no notice.[141] Not only had he acted on an impulse, but his rash deed expressed frustrated psychological need and conveyed perverse revenge.

Although temper and impulsiveness ran together, there were cases in which temper was absent but headlong action was still part of the fatal equation. Farmer Duncan McDonald was so very depressed that he consulted a physician. When the magistrate at his inquest asked his wife why she thought her husband had killed himself with a shotgun, she had a simple answer: "He was usually a man of action."[142] That was much the description that William Thompson's wife offered: "He was of a daring disposition, impulsive by nature."[143] Witnesses adduced several motives for Joseph Breese to commit suicide: a girl rejected him, and his employer gave him notice that he would no longer be needed. "He was," said an acquaintance, "of an excitable nature."[144]

When a few men and women anticipated a visit from the police, they acted impulsively to avoid arrest. Or on the day of a court appearance, the accused escaped by suicide. Summoned to court to answer a charge of flogging his children, Frederick Nekal worried about humiliation and jail.[145] George Sanderson had already been convicted of theft when he hanged himself, but what wounded was the summons to appear at a meeting of the Oddfellows Lodge "to show cause why he should not be expelled."[146]

Sexual offences present a subset of crimes that truly shamed a few men into self-destruction. Nineteen-year-old Alfred Sylvester stalked Dorothy Hill and attempted to rape her. When she resisted, he struck her with a bottle. Arrested on her complaint, he stood accused of attempted murder. "I took the poison," he explained to his parents, "because of what I had done to the girl."[147] Detectives arrived at the home of butcher Thomas Bonham to question him concerning allegations of indecent assaults on girls. Soon afterward, he rode his bicycle down to the seashore and drowned himself.[148] Women were seldom charged with any serious offence, but there were minor scrapes. Brisbane prostitute Julia Hargreaves protested and consumed carbolic acid when the police served her with a summons to have a mandatory examination.

"The constable wants me to go to a doctor. I won't go to doctor. I won't go to gaol. I would rather poison myself."[149]

The prospect of being exposed for an indecent proposition or arrested for what was classified as an unnatural criminal sexual act drove some men to what they regarded as an honourable end, or at least one that spared them a shaming in open court followed by rough treatment in prison.[150] Station hand Douglas Lawson confessed he was "a wicked scoundrel" and tried to make amends with a bunkhouse mate by leaving him his watch. "If you won't accept the watch smash it. My own wickedness has brought me to this. I am no fit companion for you or anyone else."[151] At a remote post, Queensland police sub-inspector Hubert Durham had allegedly forced a young constable to have sex. The chief inspector was coming to investigate, and Durham used his "Boer War revolver" to end the business. The constable testified at the inquest that "something occurred – more than one thing occurred. These occurrences were of a vile nature. I was not a willing participator in these occurrences. I endeavoured to resist them."[152] Before he shot himself, Hugh Fiddes left a note for a friendly publican: "William Pearson has caused me to make up my mind to end my life. He accused me publicly of having asked him to allow me to commit an unnatural offence upon him and as he refused I had hunted him out of the harness room where he had lived so long. I need not tell you that this is an unqualified lie. However, sooner than face the horror of a public investigation of the charge, I have made up my mind to end my life."[153] Local men, suspicious of a New Zealand schoolmaster's conduct with a student, trapped him "buggering a boy." Together with a cooperative constable, they allowed him an honourable way out. Before poisoning himself, he wrote to the fourteen-year-old boy and told the constable, "I should like to be buried in my uniform."[154]

There were, of course, assorted common brushes with the law that destabilized men and women: arson, assault, forgery, and theft. Alexander Aitken, a heavy-drinking, separated farmer, threatened his son, who called the police. "I'm not going to meet the Police," shouted Aitken, who then shot himself.[155]

LIVING PAST DEATH AND TAKING THE LONG SLEEP

The first half of the twentieth century was a time of churchgoing and faith. The world wars, with their sermons and speeches of consolation, fortified popular belief in a heavenly reunion with loved ones and friends. Suicide notes and last words conveyed a strong faith in grace, a trust in divine power to help those left behind, a strong moral sense, and a personalization of a life hereafter. A few individuals, among them George Bagria, were overwhelmed by religious mania. He had been shown two paths, one to hell and one to paradise. What he learned now saved him: "I am going to Paradise, I am positively sure."[156] Poor Elizabeth Stevens was surrounded by loss and doubt. A young widow for six months, she had buried her father and younger sister. She had no doubts about an afterlife, although the idea that suicide ranked as a sin persisted. "God bless the children and take them to heaven to meet their father there some day, for I have gone to hell."[157]

Common everyday moral reality insisted on a justification by some general principles, and many suicidal individuals could construct that from their lives and faith better than Elizabeth Stevens had. Alice Burn, proud of how she had raised her children, was confident of her entry into paradise. "I am not afraid to meet God."[158] A mother of nine children, Elizabeth Maudsley suffered from depression and explained her feelings in a note to her pregnant daughter: "I went through it nine times. It is nothing to this dreadful affliction. Try all I can it will not go off. God knows how I try. Don't worry over me, think of your own and live for them. God knows I have tried hard and feel I can bear it no longer, may God forgive me. He knows what I go through day and night."[159] The important feature of this note and many more was the confidence that God would know all and forgive. A mother to the end, Mary Legood wrote with assurance or bravado to her son: "Where I am going to I'll watch over you and remember, dear, the straight and narrow path is the best."[160]

Quite a few suicidal individuals envisaged a heavenly reunion or had their fingers crossed when they prepared letters that mentioned a get-together in the beyond. A young Maori farm worker shot himself at his parents' graveside and addressed a note to his cousin explaining that "it is now all right Teri have gone to my father and my mother."[161] James Biggs survived for three weeks after he shot himself near his wife's grave. He told police that, although he had many reasons for suicide, "the ultimate reason was he wanted to join his wife."[162] Fearing that in a mad rage he would kill a man whom he detested and thus make two widows, coach painter John Geddes decided to take his own life. His death would leave his wife in a terrible way. For this, he apologized and instructed his wife and children to "kiss each other for me and comfort each other until me meet again."[163] "Good-bye for a little while" was Ivan Newdick's message to his friends and relatives.[164] In a note intended for his pal, an out-of-work salesman wrote, "I hope to meet you again Mac, in the great beyond."[165] Reginald Robinson's mother died in October, and he took his own life the following January. The forty-year-old bachelor had spoken to his sister before his death. He told her that "mother was better off and he would be with her."[166]

Insurance agent Cyril Swift promised his mistress "we will meet again."[167] When some men and women prepared to leave this life, they were expectant about a better one. For his children, pensioner Robert Wilson left a message of hope: "May we all meet in a better world."[168] Estranged from his wife and lonely, war veteran Alfred Ward thought of death as a new start: "I will be in new surroundings and I feel I am going to be much more contented and happier than I have been for a long time."[169] The sources for a trust in life after death were not all Christian. Margaret Armstrong "was a theosophist and believed in the spirits of the dead."[170] To find life's answers and cope with loneliness, widow Rubina Livingstone corresponded with Melbourne astrology professor Henri Astro. Without a sign of new romance from the stars, she returned to her late husband. "I am Mrs. Livingstone first and last. I shall meet my Husband."[171]

Men and women in a suicidal frame of mind took what they wanted from organized religion and ignored the rest. In his suicide note, thirty-year-old farm labourer John Kenneally, who suffered from tuberculosis and had tried several cures "all without success," left instructions that suggest he was unaware suicide would preclude a Roman Catholic funeral. "I might mention I am a Roman Catholic and I do not want a protestant minister of religion praying over my body."[172] Religious belief drew upon literal interpretations of the scriptural promise of eternal life. Injury prevented teamster George McKeown from doing heavy work. Not only would his problems end with his demise, but there was a bonus: "I am going to meet Jim Tobias."[173] Returned soldier and labourer Charles Carter, a single man, wrote that his nerves were so bad he was living in hell. "I am taking this means of uniting body and soul."[174] Seduced and abandoned, Ida Wells was dismissed as a housemaid at a hotel. As she walked with a friend along a road by the Maori church, she asked if there was a life hereafter. "I said yes, and after that she was very glad."[175]

Many who deliberated paused to consider the fact that suicide was considered a sin. "Forgive me," wrote Eliza Ruska. "I must atone for this in the next world. I am a failure in this."[176] Sixty-year-old Alice Hill left a one-sentence note: "God forgive me for what I have done."[177] Some individuals offered a prayer an instant before the fatal act. "May the God of infinite mercy grant me a final pardon and grant the great consolation of his presence to sustain my wife & children," wrote Henry Wood, who could not face selling his farm.[178] On a fence board above his body, fifty-four-year-old single farmer Joseph Coombs had scratched "God forgive me. Joe."[179] The plea "may God have mercy on my soul" or something like it ended many suicide notes.[180] A poor bookkeeper who owed rent and had written bad cheques cut his wrists with a razor and left a note that simply said, "God have mercy on me."[181] Ivan Lulich began his note with a comparable prayer: "First I ask God's forgiveness."[182]

People may have felt respectful of the Scriptures to the point of literal interpretations and visions of heaven, but they were concurrently subversive toward organized religion and supposed that an omniscient God would forgive them or that prayer would save their souls even if their church proclaimed suicide a sin.[183] "God will have mercy upon my soul," proclaimed bookkeeper Charles Wentzel, who imagined he deserved a heavenly reward because he had endured low pay, overwork, and a sick wife and child.[184] "If there is a God," wrote Annie Trevor to her daughter, "He will know all that I have suffered and forgive me."[185] When her daughter left her alone for the day, widow Eliza Austin took strychnine but first chided her daughter for treating her disrespectfully and not conversing. "I hope I shall be in heaven for the Lord did not mean us to live the life I have done for a long time past."[186] In a final letter which described her depression, Margaret Dann tried to reassure her parents: "I am going to Heaven. I have been praying and I know God will take me."[187] Annie Law expressed exactly these feelings when she wrote to console her husband and children: "Don't worry about me for God will forgive me. Hope to meet in heaven soon."[188]

Heaven did not figure in the imagination of every person preparing to commit suicide. Alfred Mulligan, a fifty-year-old single farmer, had financial problems and a convenient shotgun. Despite uncertainty as to whether God would take his soul, he wrote, "I cannot live on earth any longer."[189] Religiosity and suicide may have been affected by world events, because the suicide notes for New Zealand and Queensland prior to World War 1 rarely mentioned heaven, God, or prayer; afterward, however, the idea of a heavenly reunion appeared in assorted ways. A neighbour and friend told a magistrate in 1920 that Mary Henley spoke often of her husband, who had died in the war, "saying she would like to be with him."[190] Women more than men trusted in a busy God's justice and in prayer, although, curiously, not in prayer's power to lift their anguish. Men often seemed less worried about damnation than whether their action would be construed as a cowardly failure to stand up to troubles. Frank Tyler was understandably concerned about cowardice, because he was a soldier. "Dear comrades, Forgive me. I must die tho a coward. I hope to be forgiven by one and all."[191]

Some individuals had only tentative trust in a heavenly destination but retained the trip or crossing-over metaphors. Not sure of a heavenly abode, Eric Wylie simply wrote, "I hope I will be better off where I am going."[192] William Hallinson rolled the dice. "For myself I gladly exchange the certain misery of this world, for the uncertainty of the world to come."[193] Naval drill instructor Arthur Steele left a long explanation that began, "I am on the point of entering that unknown land, that unknown land from whence no traveller returns."[194] As if moving livestock down the trail to another town, cattle drover William Graham left a note for his boarding-house keeper with his forwarding address. "I am leaving here tonight for another world, I am very sorry to say." He had been robbed of a great deal of money and complained of pain.[195] Another stockman tired of a life that alternated between the outback and Brisbane hotels; additionally, he feared losing his mind on account of a recent bout of dengue fever. "I can't bear the thought of going west again," he wrote his wife, "and I think when I leave here it will be for my last long trip of all."[196] Compositor James Shanks told his son he was "going on the long long trail."[197] War veteran William Smith, one of the many unfortunate men who had been gassed and later committed suicide, wrote his boss to apologize. "I am very sorry for 'crossing the border.'"[198] Unemployed labourer Harry Alfred left a note for a friend. "Dear Harry," he wrote, "I have made up my mind to go over the fence tonight."[199] In some fashion or another, these people had minimized death's sting by conceiving of it as a saunter across a line they tried to trivialize.

For the more secular individuals before and after the war, suicide could beckon as a rest. Troubled by his wife's decision to take him to court over maintenance for her and their two children, Henry Savage decided he would escape his responsibilities through suicide. "By the time you receive this," he wrote to his wife, "I will be having my long sleep and my trouble will be over."[200] In a similar situation, Thomas Jackson wrote a revenge note to his wife and denounced his "blockhead" father-in-law. But he also remarked, "I am so tired and I feel as if I must go to sleep for ever."[201] Farmer Francis Fay left a simple message: "I'm tired of life and only wish to sleep for ever."[202] Taking revenge on his wife – giving up his friends and happy life rather than "support such as yourself" – middle-aged stockman James Kearnan mentioned that "by the time you read this I will be in the land of rest."[203] He knew that he was putting his wife in the land of turmoil, and for him this outcome doubled his gain. In cases like these, we need to be reminded that suicide may have a meaning for the person committing it, but the underlying reasoning may not accord with our way of thinking.

To the hope of the faithful and the practicality of would-be sleepers, it is possible to add one more consolation, namely, the fatalism that focused on life's limited years. The governing attitude here was that no one survives life. Even sixteen-year-old Leslie Franklin dismissed life as transitory and called suicide "this short cut."[204] Twenty-eight-year-old William Anderson knew that life was fleeting, but rather than seizing every moment, he reasoned that brevity removed a barrier to self-destruction.. "What is a few years any-way? It is only a matter of time and we all will be dead and gone."[205] Mary Legood made a calculation: "I am 63 years old. My deformity makes me 73, 70 years is the allotted span so you see I will be 3 years over my time."[206] When William Butt's fiancée broke off their engagement, he penned a letter to his father to rationalize his extreme action. "Remember the soldiers, they were shot. I very likely would have been too, if I had been a little older, so it is nothing strange, only there is no wars, so will have to do it myself."[207] One lesson from these validations for fatal action might be, as Shneidman insisted, that there was and is for the person about to commit suicide a real logic to the act. For some people, the need for logic meant that they enlisted argumentation and religion. Using reason and revelation, they picked their way over barriers that deterred others.

GOODBYE TO ALL KIND FRIENDS: THE PRE-EMPTIVE DEATH

In one type of suicide, the deceased most likely acted with full knowledge of the consequences of the act, and the suffering involved was not psychological meta-pain but sheer physical distress. Many resolved to commit suicide rather than bear pain during a terminal illness; however, in some instances individuals merely presumed they were incurable or soon to die. Folkways made many fearful of medical attention and inclined to think the worst. In New Zealand, witnesses in one in five suicides (22.2 per cent) gave priority to illness as a motive, and the validity of their belief is supported by a mean age of fifty-two, which was the oldest for any motive. Not as many Queensland suicides were attributed to illnesses (14.9 per cent). Leading ailments in both jurisdictions included the debilities of old age, incurable cancer, tuberculosis, sciatica, and liver, kidney, and heart problems. Influenza was prominent in New Zealand alone. A stroke left Henry Johnstone partly paralyzed. A former soldier who had landed in New Zealand with the British army in 1858, he became a self-reliant settler. To expedite his own inquest, Johnstone addressed a letter to the coroner: "Unable through paralysis of performing the slightest offices for myself [bodily functions], and treated as I am in close proximity to the lowest wretches, I should desire to end an existence that is a burden to me."[208] Spitting blood from tuberculosis, a rural labourer who was only thirty-one simply told a mate, "I am buggered."[209] Another farm labourer with pulmonary tuberculosis knew that "the disease was progressing."[210] It was not psychological pain that made William Heare cry out, "I wish I could die and get out of this misery." He had been gassed during the war, could not work, and had no money at all. A post-mortem revealed deeply congested lungs and an empty stomach.[211]

Frail seventy-seven-year-old James Richardson resided at the Victoria Home for the Elderly in Oamaru. Going blind and unwilling to endure this burden, he selected his last day. He asked a friend to walk him to the top of a hill, and there he lay down on the grass to eat an orange before he cut his throat.[212] No one prepared for suicide quite like John Bell, a hospitalized invalid. He made his own gun. "I did take my life. No blame. I made the Gun. I got the parts from Marshalls four years ago. I made preparation. The Climax. Senility. Senility and senile decay at 82 years. Born 30th Nov. 1840 Island of Granada. Insomnia. Catarrh. Dysentery of Bowels and urinary problem." His doctor stated he had no bowel or urinary problems but suffered from delusions.[213]

Seldom does an emotional portrait with accompanying sounds emerge from the depositions. Occasionally the spontaneous honesty of a witness renders a shattering account of a person's fears, humanity, and dignity. Facing an operation for a tumour, Steven Burgess spoke to a friend about his condition and his likely intention to take his fate in his own hands. He put his hands on his stomach and said, "you see Joe I am swelled." "'God bless you,' I said. He started to cry bitterly. He said you won't see me again."[214] A schoolboy passed James Graham as the elderly labourer walked toward Freeman's Bay in Auckland. They exchanged greetings. The boy reported that "he looked sad and tears were in his eyes."[215]

Serious illnesses, common as a motive among older men, had multiple attributes that readily account for suicides. The more terrible illnesses had a poor prognosis, inflicted a diminished quality of life, and assaulted self-esteem. Cancer terrified men, and it is likely that many had facial cancer. The outdoor life ensured exposure to excessive sunshine. As well, tobacco use produced jaw and tongue cancer. A recurrence of painful face cancer precipitated William Burton's decision to end his life.[216] Residents of Croydon in Queensland knew Thomas Rea as "Cancer Tom" because of the running sore on his face.[217] Sixty-year-old prospector-miner Peter Cant, who had cancer of the mouth, used his rifle to end the torment. "I do not want to live in pain night and day," he wrote to his mate Charlie. "If there was any hop[e] of me getting right I would like to live as long as I could but there is no hop[e]. You can tell all the popel that it was hard for me that I could not go anny whar."[218] Sidney Grant "was suffering from the loss of his nose and was complaining of a pain in his nasal organs." An acquaintance staying at the same hotel deposed that the deceased "told him his disfigurement prayed on his mind very much indeed and he thought people shunned him."[219] Peter Spaulding's face and neck lesions would not heal, and his doctor told him there was nothing further that he could do.[220]

Of course, there were other forms of cancer, and they too brought suffering and indignities. Sixty-five and single, miner-prospector James Lythgar had been operated on for cancer of the testicles. Facing more treatment, he decided, "I can't stand no more."[221] A brain tumour caused Robert Jamieson lapses of memory, and he decided to use a revolver while he still could.[222] Nothing could be done for Charles Charman's advanced stomach cancer; he was in pain and could no longer eat.[223] Prostate cancer upset older men terribly. To urinate, sixty-five-year-old labourer James Glover "had to use an instrument."[224] As a consequence of George Stevenson's refusal to go into a hospital, his doctor "drew his water off" and left a tube so he could do it himself.[225] With inoperable growths in the lymph glands, fifty-year-old labourer Charles Edwards was on morphine and could swallow only liquids. His doctor estimated that he could live only ten to twenty days and judged that when Edwards cut his throat, he had done so "with his full faculties."[226] Occasionally, men and women who diagnosed themselves as cancer victims avoided doctors or refused to listen to them. In a panic about a presumed tumour, they pre-empted the disease with a sudden death. When she detected a lump in her throat, Ethel Bird went completely to pieces. "I am not getting any better," she told her family. "I suppose it is cancer and I would rather be dead than ill and helpless." She did not stop with self-diagnosis but went on to advise her children: "Tell, Barry to get his tonsils out and Pat to get her throat seen to."[227]

Several diseases challenged cancer's frightful standing. Heavy drinking could result in cirrhosis of the liver. Alcohol had destroyed Thomas Heaney's stomach, and his liver was largely finished. "He was under the impression he would not get better," stated his doctor. "He might have lived another 12 months."[228] Miner's phthisis, or pulmonary tuberculosis, inflicted excruciating symptoms of racking coughs and laboured breathing. The work-related disease caused Harry Webber "terrible agony," and he pleaded with the doctor to give him something to put him out.[229] Isaac Cole's brother had seen him so "convulsed with coughing that he would require for a time to support his weight by holding onto a post."[230] Angina pectoris and asthma made life miserable for forty-year-old Joshua Machlin, who ended his life at a lake resort. "My God," he had exclaimed to his doctor, "how can I bear this?"[231] Advanced diabetes and an associated loss of use of her limbs contributed to Violet Grace's periodic breakdowns. Eczema and an abusive husband added to her woes, until, even though she wanted to live, "it had been made impossible."[232] Failing eyesight and heart trouble convinced a few men and women that their remaining years were not worth living.[233]

One disease frightened men of most age groups. Until the general introduction of penicillin as a treatment in the late 1940s, men believed syphilis incurable. Nevertheless, a few had numerous casual sexual encounters, and the wars probably increased unprotected contact.[234] A few swagmen, moreover, did more than spend on drink during a spree. Young Peter Cornford Lovell-Smith tramped the countryside north of Auckland in 1935–36, looking for work, seeking adventure, and seducing women. He recorded liaisons with kitchen maids and Maori girls. In one hectic month, he "dipped old Archie a few score times."[235] A diagnosis of syphilis was equivalent to testing positive for HIV today. In its later stages, syphilis led to insanity and committal to a mental hospital. It may have taken twenty-five years before Richard Harvey had a proper diagnosis. "All the time," he wrote his wife, "I was doomed." He feared going mad.[236] A few younger men also could not face a decline, leg pains, and a final mental collapse. Nineteen-year-old John

Sherman, an illegitimate child without work or prospects, skipped Christmas dinner with his aunt and left his false teeth behind. He told his stepfather that he had an incurable disease, "a venereal disease."[237] One young man lost a girlfriend as a result of his condition. "I was rotten with it," he regretted in his suicide note.[238] Forty-five and single, Henry Smith had advanced syphilis when he finally visited a doctor. "Shocked at the state he got into," he became very depressed during the examination.[239] Travelling salesman Walter Bibbing had no work, no money, and a substantial "shanker" (chancre) on his penis that "indicated a very bad form of syphilis."[240] Unemployed sailor Peter Murphy alleged that "this is all over the dirty Prostute [sic] of a woman that I was living with and She gave me the Pox."[241] "A married woman is the cause of this," wrote William Martin. "Oh God, what have I done. I thought I had a cold. The doctor laughed at me."[242] Hospitalized for alcoholism, William Quick's complete examination turned up something unexpected. "I never knew until this week I had developed the dreaded disease. In 1928 I had a blood test in Los Angeles and there were no signs of any disease."[243] Stevedore George Smith could no longer work on the wharfs and tried to secure injury compensation, but a medical examination disclosed his real trouble. "I made a mistake when I was a boy but I always thought I was cured of that until I saw Dr Grey and I have been very much worried since."[244] Station hand William Dale had been treated by a number of Sydney specialists; when they could not cure him, he took strychnine.[245]

There is no telling how many men committed suicide after a diagnosis of syphilis, because shame kept them silent and symptoms could be passed off as rheumatism, sciatica, headaches, and senility. A few women also had contracted the disease, and in Queensland, if suspected of prostitution, they were subjected to an obligatory examination under the health act. Beatrice Brosnan, a heavy drinker, took her own life rather than suffer a mandatory return to the hospital. She told a friend "the treatment was too severe."[246]

The last entry in John Peter's diary forecast that it would be his last day. He did not specify his ailment but was sure there was no cure. "I don't see why I should linger."[247] He summed up the feelings of many people.

FAREWELL JIM: COMMUNICATING INTENT

Shneidman's sixth and ninth points together relate to advanced warnings. The ambivalent cognitive state means that an individual in a suicidal state wants to cease living, but concurrently wishes to be prevented and may communicate intent. Shneidman proposed that 80 per cent of suicidal individuals will give a warning. He could be right, although the inquests only produced evidence of a warning in about a quarter of the cases (25.3 per cent in New Zealand; 27.3 per cent in Queensland). Clear warnings had occurred in one in ten cases (10.8 and 9.5 per cent respectively), vague warnings in about the same proportion (8.4 and 13.1 per cent), and prior attempts at a lower frequency (3.9 and 4.2 per cent). John Miller's conversation with his doctor was representative of a clear warning. He had asked his physician for "something to make him sleep for a long time."[248] It is possible that for a few men and women, writing a note was part of the process of making a decision, a metaphorical walking to and fro.

The figures on warnings in New Zealand and Queensland underestimate the probable number because witnesses held back, particularly since testifying to a knowledge of intent could have been painful or a source of shame. Threats were frequently ignored by family, friends, and employers. In an offhand manner, Ernest Knight testified that his employee Harry Edmonds "has not threatened to commit suicide for twelve months."[249] Admission about shunned threats could have put witnesses in a bad light at an inquest. When George Mansell, a heavy drinker, consumed a bottle of hydrochloric acid, his wife telephoned the doctor to say calmly, "I think George has done it this time."[250] She and others in comparable situations had heard multiple threats, had not taken them seriously, and had been reticent before the inquest to admit anything that would feed gossip. It is conceivable that many spectators simply did not take warnings seriously and discounted them as a psychological tactic by the deceased or as an exaggeration. George Waugh's wife heard him say often that he would do away with himself if he did not get work: "I did not take him seriously."[251] Witnesses also ignored a warning on account of the context. William Tracey jumped overboard not long after a witness heard him saying, "I think I will do myself in." People who listened to his threats thought he was "recovering from a heavy drunk."[252]

The fact that witnesses missed a warning was not necessarily their fault, because a number were garbled by a confused mind or originated as subtle private airings of intent appreciated by others only in retrospect. A young labourer on a remote sheep station withdrew his money from the bank and gave it all to a friend; as he did so, he seemed melancholy and "looked down while talking."[253] The warnings could embody the ambivalence of wanting to be stopped but seeking release.

"The deceased shook hands with me," reported one witness, "and I thought it rather strange as it was not his custom to do so."[254] Barman Patrick McCarthy had said, "Goodbye, not goodnight to his mates."[255] Camped near a Queensland pastoral station and on the tramp for work, labourer William Campbell told a dingo hunter that "if I don't soon get right I've got the recipe."[256] Jackeroo Richard Horrobin walked around with two horseshoes in his belt and said that when he found the third, he would have to do something.[257] An old man with sciatica confided to the daughter of his boarding-house keeper, "I have not a friend in the world." On the morning of his death he was seen burning papers and letters.[258] "This might be the last time you'll drink with me," Samuel Knight told a mate, "as I'm going away." The friend replied, "what, are you going back to Boulia?" The deceased answered, "no I'm going a bloody sight further than that this time."[259] These conflicted men and others like them put out indistinct distress calls to recipients who were not able to understand the coded message or chose to let it pass in disbelief.

Insights about ambivalence or firm intent are represented powerfully by words. Even though the quantitative evidence suggests a modest proportion of warnings in suicide cases, the qualitative evidence vividly evokes the social interactions and mindsets of the deceased. In a few rare instances, the deceased had debated the pros and cons of suicide with a close friend, doctor, or family member. The representations of these arguments support Shneidman's insistence on the prevailing subjective logic of suicide. Eighty-year-old George Harrow, a single, retired prospector-miner, said that "when a man is old, in trouble, and indigent, the best thing is to commit suicide."[260] Grocer's assistant Alfred Drive had not worked in two years and had a debilitating mental illness. He asked his boarding-house keeper "whether it would not be better for him to end his life quietly. I argued with him. He expressed the view that he ought to have a voice in the matter as to whether he should live or die. He said he was useless and could not get employment and that he would be better out of the world."[261] Contractor Edwin Low had long suffered from eczema and told a friend, "I would cut my throat because of the pain I suffer if it was not for the disgrace to my family." Frightened of what he might do to himself, he asked his wife to remove his revolver and all the knives several days before death.[262] Unemployed long-time drug addict Richard Clunn had been threatened by his wife with a legal proceeding to send him to the Inebriates' Institution at Dunwich if he didn't give up drugs, but he said, "I would shoot myself first before I would go to an Institution"; he also told his wife he would shoot himself if he lost his land, which he had recently.[263]

LETHALITY

The historical context for suicide and the individual's decision to cease consciousness intersect in the choice of methods, because some methods are more likely to be selected at a particular time and place than others. Opportunity is important for suicide. If a rash decision was made, then the choice of instruments was opportunistic. Men and women who took poison had a better chance of surviving than if they had used a firearm, and in many poison cases there was deliberation to secure the chemical and, especially among young women with romantic troubles, a likely calculation that they would be saved. Parallels and differences are apparent between New Zealand and Queensland (see table 6.1). Among men, shooting led the way in both jurisdictions, but it was more common in Queensland. That pattern may capture the greater number of firearms in a part of the world that had more natural threats and rivals to livestock than were found in New Zealand. The latter's islands had neither large indigenous animals nor venomous snakes. The presence of dingo and kangaroo hunters among the occupations of men who committed suicide in Queensland bears on the topic of access to lethal methods. As well, in the mid and late nineteenth century, outback Queensland still had connotations of a wild and dangerous place where prospectors and graziers had once been attacked by Aboriginals in retaliation for encroachment. The New Zealand wars between colonizers and Maori were confined to the North Island and on the whole involved organized military operations, in contrast to the independent murderous actions carried out by prospectors and graziers in Queensland. There are good reasons to presume that firearms were more prevalent in Queensland. When there was no firearm in the house, men had no problem borrowing one from neighbours on the pretext of wanting to shoot rabbits, stray dogs, cats, birds, or flying foxes.[264] If some men intended to take their own lives and demonstrate male decisiveness, action, and bravery, then firearms were effective and accessible as a largely male tool. A study of gender, adolescents, and methods of suicide in thirty-four countries concluded that "the male gender role ... prevents males from 'cry-for-help' parasuicides." That outcome accords with cases from New Zealand and even more so with those from Queensland.[265]

A common article in the male kit was the straight razor. Cutting was far more evident among men than among women, and the straight razor, with its especially sharp blade, was the instrument of choice for one in ten of all male suicides (11.0 per cent in New Zealand; 11.3 per cent in Queensland). Among deaths by cutting, it was the instrument in about eight out of ten instances (79.7 per cent in New Zealand; 71.8 per cent in Queensland). The safety razor, with small disposable blades and protective clasp, was not manufactured until 1903 and only achieved widespread popularity after World War 1 in the United States, where it was invented. It is safe to say that most men in the high-risk older age groups would have had immediate access to a lethal razor until mid-century. Even when men were watched on account of suicidal tendencies, a razor was readily obtained. Only a slight lapse in attention could have fatal consequences. Normally, suicidal patients in a hospital were kept away from razors, but Lawrence Wyatt simply asked another patient for one. "About a fortnight ago he said his razor had been taken and asked me to bring one so that he could shave himself."[266] An orderly at a private mental hospital described precautions and how readily they could be circumvented: "I was not aware that the patient Paterson had obtained possession of a blade razor. I usually shaved Paterson myself with a safety razor. A few times he may have shaved himself with a safety razor, but I always stood by while he was doing so. The patient Paterson has been occasionally sent to my room with messages. He must have opened a drawer in my room and taken the razor."[267]

Cutting was not always a sure and swift means of suicide since it was easy to miss the carotid arteries.[268] Sheep shearer Charles Ashcroft told a doctor that he wished he had made a better job of cutting his throat. He lived long enough to say that "he was too old now to work and obtain employment and that he was no further use to any person and would be pleased to be dead."[269] A man was hired to sit at Alexander Beadie's hospital bedside and take a statement because Beadie had not cut well enough to bring a quick death. His only words were "I wish to Christ I had done a better job of it."[270] If men and women hoped for a quick end, they often erred. Eric Rodley, who threw himself from a hotel window, was found in the courtyard "struggling for breath."[271]

Despite the regulated sale of highly toxic poisons, households in New Zealand and Queensland were surprisingly well-stocked because farms in both jurisdictions suffered plagues of rabbits, rats, and other pests. "We had strychnine about the place for rabbits," testified the father of

Table 6.1
Methods of suicide: men and women in New Zealand and Queensland, 1890–1950

Method	Number and per cent for New Zealand men	Number and per cent for New Zealand women	Number and per cent for Queensland men	Number and per cent for Queensland women
Shooting	865 (25.9)**	51 (5.8)	669 (34.2)**	24 (6.3)
Poisoning	778 (19.7)	327 (37.2)**	366 (18.7)	173 (45.1)**
Drowning	604 (18.1)	262 (29.8)**	299 (15.3)	113 (29.4)**
Hanging and strangulation	597 (17.9)	121 (13.8)	229 (11.7)	41 (10.7)
Cutting	459 (13.8)*	70 (8.0)	312 (16.0)*	19 (4.9)
Jumping from heights	65 (1.9)	27 (3.1)	26 (1.3)	9 (2.3)
Jumping in front of vehicle	38 (1.1)	8 (0.9)	23 (1.2)	0
Explosives	42 (1.3)	1 (0.1)	29 (1.5)	0
Other	10 (0.3)	12 (1.4)	2 (0.1)	5 (1.1)
Total	3,337 (79.1)	879 (20.8)	1,955 (83.6)	384 (16.4)

* Over-represented.
** Significantly over-represented.

twenty-six-year-old New Zealand farmer Edward Huddleston, who swallowed some when deeply depressed.[272] A sixty-six-year-old farm labourer took strychnine that he fed to fowls for the purpose of killing weasels.[273] Domestic servant Hazel Osbourne took arsenic purchased for killing weeds.[274] It is likely that poisons were more commonplace in Queensland, where farmers and graziers set about eliminating kangaroos and dingoes as far as possible and where a "cyanider" was an occupation. In Queensland about one in fifteen suicides involved strychnine (6.9 per cent), and cyanide accounted for roughly one in thirty (3.6 per cent), whereas in New Zealand these poisons were less prominent (2.6 and 0.8 per cent respectively). Suicidal men and women on farms, a population at high risk, had a choice of poisons beyond strychnine, cyanide, and arsenic. A tablet of chloride of mercury was a fatal dose, and New Zealand dairy farms kept it on hand. "They were a douche for cows."[275]

Chemists whose shops carried strychnine, cyanide, and arsenic had to maintain a poison register. For much of the twentieth century, laws stipulated that clients had to sign for their purchases, and a witness had to vouch for them unless the chemist knew the buyer by sight. Time and again chemists would appear at an inquest and recount how the deceased had duped them by cheerfully asking for poison to do away with rats, cats, or stray dogs. "He came and asked for something to poison a dog quickly. I suggested that he should shoot the dog. He said he could not do anything so violent to the dog. It had been a long time in the family and he did not want to see it mutilated. I then suggested that he should chloroform it. He agreed to that, and I sold him one ounce of chloroform."[276] In 1936 a Brisbane journalist went from chemist shop to chemist shop using a comparable dog story, and when he tired of that, he claimed he wanted to put his cat down. Only one chemist insisted on a witness, and when the journalist did not provide one, he left the shop under a cloud of suspicion.[277] In both jurisdictions, two popular brand-name poisons, Rough on Rats (arsenic) and Black Leaf (nicotine sulphate), were occasionally used, as were various opiates and, in the late 1940s, barbiturates. Had they know that death would be slow and painful, some suicidal individuals would have had second thoughts. Carpenter John Dunlop, experiencing distressful memory lapses at work, consumed spirits of salts (hydrochloric acid) and white ant poison. He did not die immediately, and he told his brother "that spirits of salts was terrible. I thought it would have finished me in a couple of minutes."[278] After swallowing Chlorodyne, Rudolph Ens choked on mucus for fourteen hours.[279] When the police found the body of mental patient Robert Cross, they saw a scene of a great struggle with grass around the body torn up. He had taken strychnine.[280]

In both jurisdictions, among women who committed suicide and were younger than thirty and with romantic problems, more than one in three took poison (41.8 per cent in New Zealand; 37.6 per cent in Queensland). Some young women expected to survive the attempt and foster sympathy, a finding which contributes to the idea that suicide and suicide data encompass many acts, motives, and intentions. Through incremental doses of rat poison, Margaret O'Toole sought attention by making herself ill. A friend testified, "I got the impression that the girl was trying to upset somebody." A co-worker stated that "we became great pals," and Margaret confided that "her parents treated her like a little child." To retaliate, "she said she would like to give her mother a fright."[281] Sometimes the audience for dangerous performances did not follow the drama until the curtain came down. Elizabeth Mattars's de facto husband testified that he paid no heed, although he "occasionally heard her suffer and groan."[282] A neighbour dismissed Elizabeth Bell's cries for help because she felt the woman was "addicted to drink and lately appeared insane."[283]

Lysol was commonly used and accounted for around one in thirty suicides (3.1 per cent in New Zealand; 3.3 per cent in Queensland).[284] It was favoured by women; about half of the Lysol deaths were committed by them, a far greater proportion than their share of all suicides. Taking Lysol could have been an awful gamble if only an attempt was intended. A few hoped to be rushed to hospital and saved; however, rescue was not a sure thing, and death could be slow and painful. Cora Lancaster, a drug addict who believed her husband was unfaithful, wrote that she was getting out of his life. "I am now just going as I took the poison about 2 minutes ago and I feel awful."[285] It was not uncommon to live as long an hour or more, enough for a police interview.[286] It took one woman thirteen days to die from Lysol poisoning.[287] Hanging was not a sure thing either, and a few men and women died later of bronchopneumonia, the result of asphyxia.[288]

New Zealand's abundant rivers, as well as the short distances to the nearest ocean beach, meant that drowning was convenient. However, it often was more complicated than a jump into the water, because men and women took steps to prevent involuntary struggling for survival. Their precautions help establish that a number of open verdicts were truly deaths by suicide and not accidents. Arthur Gowing told a friend that "the best cure for melancholy was to put a stone around the neck and throw oneself into the creek," which is what he did.[289] Individuals also tied tools around their necks, put rocks in pockets, and tied their hands and feet.[290] Farmer William Goodwin fastened a stumping jack to his neck.[291] It was very difficult to disguise a suicide as an accident, and there was no shortage of lethal methods close at hand.

CONCLUSIONS

Edwin Shneidman's ten points frequently agree with what witnesses said or what people wrote in their suicide notes in the cases examined for this study, but commonalities sacrifice specificity, and Shneidman's ten points border on abstraction. Nevertheless, it was not his intention to lose contact with individual motives but, rather, to add a layer of understanding, and in that respect his analysis has much to recommend it.

Suicide is a solution. Meta-pain is a useful concept, and logic often connects the pain to the solution. The common stimulus to pain is psychological need – the need for achievement, avoidance of shame, understanding, love, work and fulfillment, and avoidance of harm. These needs were apparent in the discussions of motives. The cessation of consciousness is a strong urge, and many suicide notes mentioned sleep and rest. By definition, feelings of hopelessness had to have overwhelmed suicidal people; however, their words made clear their sense that they could do nothing other than commit suicide to alleviate their pain. At the same time, some were ambivalent and communicated intent with a possible wish to be stopped. The verbal and behavioural clues found in the inquest files conform to those listed by Shneidman; suicidal people said farewell, mentioned long trips, and told friends they would never see them again.

The action of suicide, as Shneidman explained, is an escape or egression that conforms to patterns in people's prior conduct. They may have left a spouse, quit a job, deserted the army, fled to the sociability of the bar, or taken off work to go to the racetrack. Compared to suicide, these are trivial escapes, but they demonstrate egress as a general coping mechanism. Quite a few individuals in the case files fled someone or something.[292] There is insufficient biographical material to discern if the suicidal individuals studied conformed to Shneidman's tenth supposition that such individuals would have shown a shown a partiality for dichotomous thinking.[293]

The ten points are stimulating and often on the mark. Still, caveats are necessary. Shneidman emphasized that, as a solution, suicide was directed toward meta-pain. That admittedly useful concept has limitations. All-encompassing psychological pain is palpable in numerous cases files, but another form of pain, physical pain, drove a fair percentage of suicides. It is impossible to say what proportion of suicides amounted to euthanasia, because quite a few individuals with serious illnesses had additional motives. However, instances of euthanasia seem to have been far fewer than cases involving psychological meta-pain. As soon as commonalities are tested against cases, exceptions and intricacies tug at the fabric of the argument. Without doubt, suicide is a solution to a problem, and often there is logic behind the act, although the notion of logic is not without difficulties because of the irrational states that sometimes clouded witnesses' understanding.

Shneidman's commonalities applied equally to men and women. Yet men and women thought somewhat differently, and this divergence was evident not just with regard to motives but also in the mental processes for dealing with the finality of suicide. Men and women came to positions of low self-worth by distinct routes because they were in and of a society with gendered roles. Men and women also subscribed to different ideas of what might occur after the fatal act, and thus their framing of the solution generally had distinct features. Women seem to have invoked faith in God more than men. Commonalities, insisted Shneidman, are the bedrock of suicide studies because if suicides were essentially alike, then there would be "*a* way to prevent suicide." His ten-point model could effectively guide prevention, he promised, because "it is tailor-made – without regard to race, sex, or age – to the contours of a viable suicide model."[294] At a certain degree of distillation, he was prescient in looking beyond motives for psychache; however, assistance for suicidal individuals surely must benefit from knowledge about the life course, gendered expectations, and culture. Shneidman's notion of psychache neatly expresses the symptoms of someone in an existential crisis. Yet therapy is directed to the individual, not the symptoms. Despite the assertions of social scientists and medical specialists, suicide is an individual act, carried out for individual motives, and deemed a solution for individual reasons according to reasoning processes that are often personal even when they have a cultural overlay.

The treatment of suicidal people and the idea of prophylaxis enlisted new techniques during the twentieth century, and the suicide-prevention initiatives of psychiatrists and voluntary agencies matured and gained broad public recognition in the latter half of the century. Perhaps more striking than any innovation during the twentieth century was the desperation with which people sought help for themselves, family members, and friends. Although the prevention of suicide occupied a good amount of energy from general physicians, psychiatrists, state mental hospital doctors, clerics, and social service personnel, the families, friends, and acquaintances of suicidal individuals were usually in the front lines. The medical treatment of suicidal people, as the next chapter elaborates, became a collision point for modernity, the protection of liberty in the common law, and dynamics within the family. The outcomes and how we should assess them are as vexed and individualized as the acts of suicides. For example, the fact that suicidal feelings would readily be categorized as treatable, as symptomatic of mental illness, raises a problem because of the variety of motives and reasoning processes, seen in this chapter, which could appear understandable and rational. Nevertheless, for the best of intentions, family members and physicians acted to put loved ones in an expanding and diversifying mental health system.

Managing Mental Crises: Psychiatry and Suicidal Patients

A historical account of mental illness grounded in the experiences of hundreds of people treated at home, in private hospitals, and in public mental hospitals can depict ties between society and psyche. It may do so, first, by personalizing connections between social circumstances and emotional trauma. Second, it can associate social norms to people's critical self-evaluation; stock-taking can adversely affect mental health, especially among individuals already experiencing symptoms of mental illness. There is no reflection without the mirror of society. Third, a historical account can disclose how men and women looked down upon mental illnesses and their treatment and can describe, in the words of the people affected, how the stigma of therapy impinged upon their lives. Time and again a scheduled return to a mental hospital after a parole, a doctor's recommendation for treatment, or a pending committal precipitated a fatal panic. Fourth, a history of mental illness that relies on case histories can trace the rise of particular therapies and society's credulity with respect to touted cures. Fifth, individual reports show extensive private facilities accessible on the basis of an ability to pay. There were private as well as public mental hospitals. The quality of care had a lot to do with class and family resources, and in that sense, society and psyche were again fused. Finally, the medical treatment of individuals inclined toward self-harm is revealed as an extremely difficult subject.

In the previous chapter, where I recounted the reasoning of individuals who took their own lives, I remarked on the subjective rationality of a number who reasoned that self-destruction was a solution. Additionally, some individuals adopted beliefs or constructed rationales to surmount the fear of death. They deliberated. In these instances, rationality of a sort fits poorly with the representation of self-harm as a mark of mental illness. In chapter 3 I proposed, "Mental illness remains today determined by the social conduct and expression of feelings by the sufferer." That assessment stirs up the ambiguous relationship between mental illness and suicide that has featured in treatises on suicide from at least the early nineteenth century. This ambiguity is compounded when threats of suicide are considered, because the intention with threats and even certain types of failed attempts is unclear. Imprecision in the diagnosis and treatment of suicidal men and women placed them and their families under the stress of choosing, deferring, or rejecting medical intervention. No discussion in this chapter will dispel the ambiguous relationship between suicide and mental illness. Rather, the narrative will unwind this core uncertainty as it entered households, posing impossible dilemmas for families to work through, aided by only sketchy medical advice. The decisions that befell families were agonizing and disruptive to all concerned.

Any patient-based history of health and health care covering the first half of the twentieth century is bound to be uncommon because of the confidentiality of patients' medical records. A thorough case-based history of mental health practices covering the expression of symptoms, doctors' diagnoses, committal processes, prescribed treatment, effectiveness of treatment, and release is impossible without patient records; however, inquests open a back door. Doctors gave testimony at inquests, and family members reported illnesses and treatment. By far the largest class of medical problems reported at suicide inquests consisted of mental illnesses, broadly defined to include nervous breakdowns. Hundreds of files yield information about the symptoms, diagnosis, and treatment of neuroses and psychoses. The effectiveness of their treatment is elusive because suicide records capture only unsuccessful outcomes, however.

Inquests are an exceptional source of information on mental illness, but there are other resources. The inquest files indicate how general practitioners dealt with mental illnesses, and they also unearth a number of private psychiatric hospitals and small clinics that primarily catered to the middle class. The inquests carry medical history beyond public institutions and into private practice, beyond histories of therapies and into lives. New Zealand and Queensland also hold documentary material relating directly to mental illness. The two jurisdictions do not have identical records but, rather, complementary holdings that have been tapped for this chapter. New Zealand repositories possess information on mental hospitals starting in the late nineteenth century; there are also military records demonstrating how shell shock had a formative impact on postwar civilian psychiatry. The private papers of a leading Queensland psychiatrist and medical educator disclose mental health trends in private practice and public policy from roughly 1930 to 1950. Historians in both jurisdictions and the British Empire more widely have written about mental health institutions and have been prominent in "an academic industry [that] has blossomed around writing about lunatic asylums."[1]

There are several circumstances in which suicide inquests depicted aspects of mental illness. It appeared as a motive for suicide, and in that sense it has been discussed in several preceding chapters. In quite a few cases, however, an individual received treatment for a mental illness, but the motive for suicide, while related, was something different. For example, men had breakdowns because of business failures or war trauma; women experienced breakdowns following the death of children. A further complication enters the picture because some suicidal individuals with symptoms of mental illness were not treated for such illness at all. On the basis of a person's conduct prior to the suicide, there were attributions of mental illness as a motive after the fatal act; there may have been instances of deceit when mental illness was alleged by a family member to make events more palatable than, say, cruel treatment. For the most part, however, the lay descriptions of symptoms and the individual's situation accord with the idea of an untreated mental illness.

Some people, even in remote rural areas, sought medical attention for themselves or others. A number did not because of their fear of mental hospitals, and many families avoided committing a spouse or parent because they needed that person's labour. As a crucial element in the history of society's management of mental illness, family deliberations have attracted more and more attention. They certainly emerged at inquests.[2]

THE MENTAL HEALTH ARCHIPELAGO, 1890–1950

From the turn of the nineteenth century to the middle of the twentieth, treatment of mental illness proceeded out of the public eye, although government-run mental hospitals exercised a foreboding presence all the same. The scale of their main buildings, spacious grounds, and fearful reputation shaped mental health's public face. Recalling her first period as a psychiatric patient, New Zealand writer Janet Frame articulated a dark characterization: "Seacliff, up the main trunk line, the hospital of grey stone, built like a castle. Seacliff, where the loonies went."[3] Her experiences up that main trunk line upended her life. For her, the world was henceforth divided "into the 'ordinary' people of the street, and these 'secret' people whom few had seen or talked to but whom many spoke of with derision, laughter, fear."[4] There was little comprehension about what went on inside. In truth, more was happening in mental health than the activities at institutions such as Seacliff; there was more range in public responses to mental illness than Frame's portrayal allows, more dispersal of authority than what she experienced, and sometimes more resistance to committal of relatives than her family exhibited.[5]

Before the rush toward deinstitutionalization that started in the late 1960s, mental hospitals dominated the imagery connected with mental illness. Frame's novel *Faces in the Water* and her *Autobiography* were shots in a devastating fusillade aimed at mental health institutions around the Western world.[6] The depiction of patients imprisoned without past or future, residents isolated and regimented on an eternal island, has proven durable even among revisionists who have demonstrated "that patient life was much more diverse and rich than has often been assumed."[7] Confinement in wards without prospect of release is a common popular image of the treatment of the mentally ill, and for many that was the case. The full picture is more complicated, although it is not in basic conflict with Frame's poignant sketches or at odds with her biographer's depiction of her spells in mental hospitals from 1945 to 1954. Frame's suicidal behaviour, wrote her biographer Michael King, resulted in "other people making decisions about how much control she would be allowed over her own life."[8]

In New Zealand about one in eight male suicides (13.5 per cent) and one in four female suicides (29.2 per cent) had received some treatment for mental illness. Altogether, there were 348 case files with evidence of treatment; half of them (49.0 per cent) involved a doctor and no institutional arrangement. Very few doctors were specialists; general practitioners had the front-line task of helping men and women through emotional crisis that attended stock-taking periods in their lives, defeats, and the main phases of biological changes which contributed to disturbing psychological episodes. Over two hundred doctors who treated mental illnesses were named in the New Zealand inquest data set; quite a few individuals consulted several. David Clyde, who suffered from depression, told a constable friend in late 1918 that "he had visited all the doctors in Christchurch pretty well and got no relief."[9] Rural doctors commonly dealt with depression, delusions, and senile dementia. In 1900 Dr Edward Palmer of Featherston, New Zealand, took into his home a young man with melancholia at the father's request. This case captures a rural doctor's compassion. Other instances cropped up at inquests. Dr John Reekie knew that retired farmer George Mackinder had senile delusions, insomnia, loss of appetite, and suicidal tendencies; so he "visited him often and at short intervals."[10] On rare occasions, doctors employed by public mental hospitals examined patients who were not institutionalized.[11]

Institutional care occurred principally in New Zealand's regionally based mental hospitals and a special government-run facility at Hanmer Springs established initially for soldiers who had suffered shell shock. After shell shock cases diminished, doctors there turned to light cases of nerves among civilians. In 1922, when farmer William Wardell had a nervous breakdown due to financial troubles, his doctor advised him "to obtain specific treatment at Hanmer."[12]

Additionally, a major private facility in Dunedin, New Zealand – Ashburn Hall – treated suicidal patients. Tragically, a former superintendent of this hospital, treated for depression, committed suicide in 1916. His doctor gave ironic testimony that articulated the stigma associated with mental illness. Frederick Hay characterized Edward Alexander as an eminent hospital superintendent prone to anxiety; Hay further remarked that he was "very loath to send him to a mental hospital considering the position he had held but I stated that that might ultimately have to take place."[13] There were many smaller private hospitals that took patients with moderate mental illnesses.[14] However, Ashburn Hall was not only unique in its capacity to sort patients and provide graduated treatment but unusual in the fact that it received public funding through the health provisions of New Zealand's National Security Act 1938.[15]

Early in the twentieth century and surely prior to that, there were so-called hospitals that took in men and women for a rest. A doctor who treated a postmaster for a nervous breakdown in 1906 "arranged for him to go to a private hospital [in another community] as he thought quietness might do him good." He was told to go to that hospital or face committal to the mental hospital. The proprietoress of the hospital remarked at the inquest that "he came in for a rest treatment."[16] Dr Ruth Huntley, who ran Laburnum House in Wellington, New Zealand, during World War 1, provided more than rest. Women who had had breakdowns received hydrotherapy, special diets, and massages.[17] Often, convalescent homes were operated by women, business-minded nurses who developed working relationships with particular doctors.[18] Women entering menopause who "might do harm to themselves" understandably preferred to enter a convalescent home rather than a public mental hospital.[19] Despite the growth in government institutions in the late nineteenth century, the public favoured home care or care in the home-like setting of a private hospital.

Doctors as well as nurses owned these establishments. After treating returned soldier Walter Woodward for depression and sleeplessness for six years, Dr Maurice Greville removed him to his private hospital at Dargaville.[20] The Hayes family tried many things to help daughter Margaret, who was subject to nervous breakdowns. "My wife and I kept a special watch on her," remarked her father. They also had her "removed to a private hospital and attended by Dr. Clay, where she remained some time."[21] For families with the means to pay, the convalescent homes might cushion the blow of a doctor's grim prognosis. Dr Kenneth Ross warned Cornelius Moss that his wife could do harm to herself and she would be better in a mental hospital. "He was opposed to the idea and she was placed in a Convalescent Home at Wellington where she did no good."[22] The decorum and discretion offered by the homes meant that they usually lacked the burly male attendants trained to handle obstreperous patients. The public mental hospitals specialized in patient control. An Auckland nursing home in 1930 could not keep Lester Gardiner after his breakdown because he was disruptive; his doctor telephoned around the city to find a hospital that would take him, but failed on account of Gardiner's unmanageable conduct. In the end, the YMCA hostel took him in and retained an unemployed man to keep a suicide watch.[23]

In Queensland, treatment for mental illness was less common than in New Zealand. Merely one in thirteen male suicides (7.6 per cent) in Queensland was reported as having received medical attention for mental illness, and one in five female suicides (20.0 per cent). Most likely, the relatively modest scale of treatment for mental illness captured the state's dispersed population and the concentration of facilities near Brisbane. Doctors alone, without the involvement of an institution, had treated slightly more than a third (39.5 per cent) of the men and women who received medical help for mental illnesses.

At the beginning of the twentieth century, people with mental illnesses in Queensland, like their counterparts in New Zealand and most Western societies, turned first to a local doctor. The inquest files named approximately one hundred who treated men and women for nerves, depression, and assorted psychoses. The capital city had more to offer by way of specialization. Commencing in 1891, Dr Lillian Cooper focused on children's and women's diseases, and treated women for nervous disorders. As early as 1903, she used the expression "decidedly neurotic."[24] Cooper was an anomalous pioneer because specialists who treated mental illness outside the mental hospitals made an enduring appearance in Brisbane only after World War I, and they all were men. A few desperate individuals left the state to consult a specialist, sought treatment at an out-of-state private hospital, or entered Broughton Hall, a public mental hospital in New South Wales established exclusively for voluntary patients.[25] Edward Campbell's brother-in-law took him to see three doctors in Mackay in late 1936, and when they could do nothing except agree on a diagnosis of neurasthenia, he intended to take Campbell to Sydney to consult a specialist."[26] The southern metropolis was well ahead of Brisbane in terms of mental health facilities.

Statistics on the treatment of suicidal people in New Zealand and Queensland outline a contrast in the proportion of the population receiving treatment. In so far as the suicide case files may be representative of mental health care, New Zealand provided a greater distribution of public facilities, and, not surprisingly, doctors and family members made use of them because of the challenge of handing mental illness cases on their own. Family members were a crucial factor in committals and, subsequently, in taking patients back into the home.[27] Family consultations with doctors often led to an individual having an examination preparatory to a committal.[28] The deracinated character of a substantial number of Queenslanders may thus help explain the relatively small number of cases of suicide with a history of treatment for mental illnesses. In many instances, there were no family members around to press for an evaluation, treatment, or committal.

Despite the greater attention to mental health issues in New Zealand, patients moved in similar grooves in the two jurisdictions, with some evidence of accompanying thoughtfulness but also signs of the toll exacted by a terror of institutions, medical high-handedness, and ineffectual practices. Men and women experiencing nervous breakdowns, melancholia, neurasthenia, and depression were usually treated solely by a local physician, who prescribed a sleeping draught to deal with insomnia. By the mid-1920s in Queensland, as in New Zealand, three types of doctors treated mental illnesses: general practitioners, the doctors employed at public mental hospitals, and a tiny knot of private specialists, who likely had had wartime training in neurology or had studied at a hospital that developed a mental health emphasis during the war.

It was not unusual for men and women with "nerve trouble" to consult several doctors in their community and then beyond. Widow May Hayes testified in 1937 that her husband "was under treatment from different doctors for nervous trouble prior to his death."[29] Queensland dairy farmer James Evans complained of indifferent health for much of 1934–36; in late 1936 he consulted a practitioner at Dalby, who diagnosed a nervous breakdown and prescribed a sedative. Evans consulted another doctor in Toowoomba, who ordered him to Wairoa Private Hospital, where he underwent an unspecified treatment lasting two weeks. He took sedatives on his return home.[30]

The prevalence of nervous conditions among returned soldiers after World War I helped somewhat to legitimize mental illness and promote specialist training; these developments in turn inclined more people to seek help for themselves or family members. Country doctors by the late 1930s routinely advised patients with persistent nervous disorders to travel to see a city specialist.[31] Family physicians continued to administer sedatives, offer friendly advice, recommend a change of work, and write holiday prescriptions.[32] A few employers in the early twentieth century accepted a doctor's certificate prescribing a nerve rest for a valued employee.[33] "A change and a rest" was what Dr Ernest Hendley recommended in 1908 for Martha Milgrew's nerves and delusions.[34] To try to alleviate Norman Kirkaldie's neurasthenia, his doctor made frequent house calls, admitted the affluent young man to private hospitals, and "recommended him to change his occupation and go to the country."[35] During the early 1930s Josephine Fuller's family doctor treated her for nerves and melancholy; she went to Sydney on a recommended rest. "Her nerves appeared to be more steady on her return."[36] Queenslanders who had suffered a nervous breakdown also went to the seaside or south to the Blue Mountains near Sydney to recuperate.[37]

For at least the first half of the twentieth century, conventional medical opinion insisted that "a person with a mental breakdown is never altogether safe" and had to be watched.[38] In such instances, the family might be advised to hire a nurse. Kate Feilder's brother was a barrister, and so the family afforded a nurse to "to keep and eye on her."[39] Susan Smith's working-class husband could not afford to take that precaution, but thinking that his wife was suicidal, he told shopkeepers not to sell her Lysol.[40] Middle-class families could disguise an attendant or nurse as a companion or domestic.[41] "For three years Patrick Heslop had been attending Kate Feilder for depression and had recently advised her husband to hire a nurse "to keep an eye on her."[42] Four doctors examined Janet Brown; she then went to Seacliff for six weeks. Discharged as of a sound mind, she returned home, and there her husband stayed with her. "I left the railway service much earlier than I intended to be company for my wife," he deposed.[43] No doctor's suggestion was needed for Martin Moir to act after his brother's breakdown and threat of suicide. "We had an attendant in charge of him. He must have avoided his attendant."[44] At the inquest in March 1920 into the death of farmer Walter Wilkes, his wife Elizabeth stated, "I have always kept a guard over him as the doctor informed me to do so."[45] The theme of love and support continues in the case of Lillian Beaumont, whose husband of nineteen years stayed as close as possible to her for two weeks, but she pried open a window, slipped out, and drowned herself while he slept.[46]

If problems persisted or the general practitioner diagnosed a more serious problem, the patient would be referred to one of the small cadre of specialists. Reginald Houghton, a veteran with a war-related case of nerves, took up farming in Queensland following his discharge in 1919. After a mental breakdown, he was taken to Brisbane in 1927 for medical attention and placed under a specialist's care for nine months.[47] The scarcity of specialists and the absence of public information about mental illness meant that some patients looked to unconventional treatment. For his neurasthenia and migraine attacks, New Zealand farmer Paul Cressy turned in 1918 to James Martin, who described himself as "a suggestive therapist."[48] In Brisbane in the 1930s a number of men and women with depression sought relief from an herbalist.[49]

City-based specialists adjusted treatment to the severity of symptoms and the patient's ability to pay. Assorted fads came and went during the years in question. More will be said later in this chapter about the succession of therapeutic approaches; however, it is worth noting now where these treatments occurred, since choices depended on local doctors, who functioned as the system's gatekeepers. For some patients with seemingly minor problems, general practitioners prescribed a sedative. Until the introduction of barbiturates in the late 1940s, doctors normally prescribed a bromide to help the patient sleep, but morphine was occasionally employed.[50]

With a doctor's recommendation, men and women could apply to enter a public mental hospital as voluntary patients or, if able to afford it, board at a private hospital. Voluntary patients were accepted at public mental hospitals earlier in New Zealand (1912) than in Queensland (1938).[51] Patients signed a consent form that placed them under the discipline of the superintendent, although in Queensland voluntary patients could have their own nurses and specialists. In New Zealand arrangements could be quite liberal. Periods of depression put David Gillies in Sunnyside as "a voluntary border." His wife could visit any time, and he was free to go to the shops.[52] There were cases of multiple admissions over many years. After the birth of her son in 1915, Claire Hammond went into a public mental hospital voluntarily for three months. In 1941, at age fifty, she entered again as a voluntary patient for another three months, and in 1942 she was admitted twice more.[53] More commonly, patients were committed to public mental hospitals by order.

COMMITTAL AND PAROLE

Language and law surrounding entry into and departure from mental health hospitals reflected the system's criminal justice ties. Patients had been called inmates, though that term faded from common use early in the twentieth century; a judicial process committed patients; they might earn parole; if showing improvement, they might be sent home on probation. A few patients cogently maintained they were prisoners in "a gaol miscalled a mental hospital," but the processes for committal included safeguards that produced an assortment of outcomes, including non-committals and prompt releases.[54] Committals resulted from a discussion among several parties about what was a mental illness, and there were negotiations over the risks of non-intervention.

If family doctors sensed that poorer patients were a danger to themselves or others, they would mention and likely urge admission to a public mental hospital. Non-voluntary admission to public mental hospitals proceeded by strict rules, although Stephen Garton and Catharine Coleborne, historians of psychiatry in Australia and New Zealand, note that the homeless, eccentrics, and poorly understood racial minorities were more likely than other individuals to be detained by police for observation.[55] Persons deemed a danger to themselves or others could be committed to one of the public institutions; processes similar to those that served New Zealand and Queensland existed with variations in common-law jurisdictions around the world. The first step could be taken by either family members or a police officer or on rare occasions an employer; it required filling out forms to initiate a hearing.[56] If the police detained someone, constables were instructed to watch carefully to prevent suicide attempts. Some police stations in the larger towns of New Zealand and Queensland maintained a padded cell.[57] Until the provision of special psychiatric beds in larger public hospitals in the 1920s, major Queensland towns also had reception houses with a handful of beds for committal cases or for certified patients awaiting transport to a public mental hospital. Soon after taking someone into custody for possible committal, the police contacted a stipendiary police magistrate or, if none was available, two justices of the peace. These officials conducted the all-important hearing.[58] Two justices of the peace rather than one police magistrate heard evidence that sent James Broughton to the Porirua Mental Hospital; the magistrates made the committal "on the medical certificate of Drs Hay and Sinclair."[59]

The party initiating a committal could line up two doctors to testify to insanity, or the magistrate could prevail upon two for their opinions. Catherine Vincent suspected that her husband suffered from mental illness and prepared to take steps, but he hanged himself first. "I fully intended to send him to the Asylum," she testified at his inquest, "and asked Dr. Marchesni to come and see him."[60] Constable John Murphy arrested retired farmer William McNeill as "being a lunatic at large, but the medical evidence went to show he suffered from drink."[61] Authorities detained Toowoomba contractor John Cahill for an assessment. After his suicide, his wife deposed that "for some months back he has had bad health: was in very low spirits, did not seem right in his head." She stated he was attended by two doctors and ordered to the hospital for the insane. "But he was not sent out at my wish. As I thought I could look after him. He was very quiet and easily managed." She was unduly hopeful and worried about how to support her family without him. Cahill had a serious affliction. A doctor who signed the man's committal papers testified that he diagnosed melancholia with suicidal tendencies. The medical certificate noted that Cahill "states that ever since he took a contract that voices have told him to 'give up – you won't succeed.' Feels at times as if he is under a cloud. These voices speak to him at all times and mock him. Has twice tried to poison himself and once tried to cut his throat at the instigation of these voices."[62]

Time and again, husbands and wives rejected a doctor's recommendation to initiate a committal. Evelyn Thomson's doctor testified that he had done all that he could. "I have known deceased since she was married and I was called on the evening of July 3rd. Her conduct was not normal and she had delusions. I had discussed her going away to Seacliff for her benefit. At the time I did consider her certifiable and thought she would be in the next week to have it attended to. I told the husband. He recognized it was the right thing to do, but thought he could stay at home and watch her."[63] Thomas Cuddihy's doctor advised his family to send him to a public mental hospital, but his wife refused. The family needed his income.[64] For a related reason, Mary Bearpark neglected to report to police that her husband had attempted suicide several times. "Had I done so," she told an Auckland magistrate, "my husband would have been charged with the offence and I should have suffered."[65] A farmer with five children, John McDonald worried greatly in 1914 when his wife became peculiar in her manner. If she were committed, he asked, what would happen to the children?[66]

The departure of a husband or wife to a mental hospital upset the domestic economy, but there were instances when a parent or spouse initiated a committal proceeding or threatened to have a family member committed because of disruptions to the household. During a hysterical fit, Elizabeth Kenyon's father said that "if you go on like this Lizzie we shall have to lock you up."[67] The process for committals endured unchanged and widely known. Labourer Sidney Gibson told a hotel manager to "have me arrested George. I think I am going mad."[68] The process was simple; however, love, fear, pride, and poverty complicated cases.[69] Medical historian Edward Shorter proposed that "one component of the rise in asylum admissions was lessened family willingness to tolerate mental illness."[70] This conjecture can be neither proven nor rejected because routinely generated sources on family decisions against committal do not exist. However, Victor Bailey concluded that in Victorian Hull "families did not readily dump difficult members in the new asylums, as historians of these institutions suggest." Rather, they coped with "deranged and suicidal relatives."[71] It would be wrong to extrapolate from Shorter's supposition that families, when looking into committal, considered only the disruption caused by mental illness. They had that and more to worry over. At the same time, not every decision to retain a family member at home was based on tenderness.

The legal framework for committal remained constant over the decades. Queenslander Joseph McCarragher took his life in 1908 while on remand charged with attempted suicide. Asylum conveyance orders had been issued. McCarragher had been in the Beaudesert reception house several years before his suicide, and his mother was in Wolston Park mental hospital.[72] Decades later later, in 1944, the committal

Table 7.1
Annual admissions to New Zealand mental hospitals, 1900–50

Year	Official admissions	Approximate population	Ratio of patients to people
1900	598	772,000	1:1290
1910	1010	1,008,000	1:998
1920	1270	1,218,000	1:959
1930	969	1,345,000	1:1388
1940	1053	1,500,000	1:1429
1950	1778	1,930,000	1:1085

SOURCES: Reports on Asylums or Mental Hospitals, *Appendix to the Journals of the House of Representatives of New Zealand.*

Table 7.2
Annual admissions to Queensland mental hospitals, 1900–50

Year	Reception house beds	Official admissions	Approximate population	Ratio of patients to people
1890 (1892)	62	291	410,000	1:1408
1900	62	347	498,000	1:1435
1910	47	305	599,000	1:1963
1920	26	531	738,000	1:1389
1930	12	513	747,000	1:1456
1940	0	578	1,000,400	1:1730
1950	0	781	1,205,000	1:1542

SOURCES: *Queensland Statistical Yearbooks.*

process had not fundamentally changed. Police at Cairns received a telephone call from Mossman Hospital about Alfio Sorbello, who had a fantasy that he was flying to America the next day. He was arrested and conveyed to the Mossman police station, where a doctor examined him. Sorbello was put in cell, watched, and examined again. The doctor certified him "mentally sick." The arresting constable testified at Sorbello's inquest that "the deceased was examined by two Justices of the Peace and later I gave evidence before two Justices of the Peace at Mossman Court of Petty Sessions." Sorbello was remanded to Cairns and conveyed by ambulance. Once there he was searched, put in a padded cell, and held for transportation to the state mental hospital.[73]

The numbers of patients who entered public mental hospitals annually by committal and voluntary admission were substantial. However, throughout the first half of the twentieth century, until the decades of deinstitutionalization, New Zealand committed more people relative to its population than Queensland (see graph 3.9 and tables 7.1 and 7.2).

Some of the difference derived from New Zealand's early establishment of regional mental hospitals. Contrasts in public health policy, settlement history, and geography meant that New Zealanders with mental illnesses were likely to be noticed and, once they were, waylaid for assessment. In both jurisdictions, elderly men and women characterized as senile comprised 10 to 20 per cent of the mental hospital population. The private hospitals took them as well. According to Dr Edward King of Ashburn Hall, sixty-year-old John Bulleid "was suffering from a form of insanity associated with degenerative arteries." At his wife's insistence, he was reassessed and moved from the main building to a cottage.[74] Again, it is notable that family members could and did take an active part in the management of the mentally ill and maintained a vigorous, compassionate stance.

Older patients with deteriorating mental functions and a few others with irreversible brain damage were unlikely to leave the institutions. Senile men and women and patients admitted with dementia paralytica – "general paralysis of the insane" – caused by syphilis likely spent their remaining years after committal in a mental hospital.[75] Syphilitic patients accounted for approximately 10 per cent of males in public mental hospitals during the first half of the twentieth century.[76] The father of former New Zealand prime minister Robert Muldoon, admitted to a mental hospital in 1928 with a probable nervous breakdown, remained there for twenty years with syphilis he had contracted as a soldier in World War I.[77]

Many patients with light syndromes – problems other than senility, syphilis, or psychoses – were released soon. Those who remained for more than a year, Mark Finnane notes in reference to Queensland, "had a high likelihood of staying many years." But this pattern means that "a reality of the asylum was not the long-term incarceration of the insane but the high turnover of its population."[78] Recently discharged from Wolston Park, William Scott cut his throat with a razor. An acquaintance deposed that "he told me he was afraid to be by himself. He said he was afraid that his madness was coming on again and that he might do away with himself.[79]" William Webb was confined in 1898 for a period of three weeks for attempting suicide and subsequently suffered from fits of despondency.[80] William Gordon had been released from Wolston Park – prematurely, thought his wife.[81] According to his sister's 1918 deposition, John Winkel had been in a mental hospital briefly twenty-one years earlier.[82] Theresa Loeffler, who died in 1922, had been in a mental hospital for twelve months in 1911.[83] Sarah Martin spent four weeks in Wolston Park in 1922 and wrote, "If I am to die I will die at home." A few individuals moved between institutions.[84] Labourer James Maloney had been admitted to Wolston Park from the asylum for inebriates at Dunwich in 1908 suffering from melancholia.[85] Some patients, like Janet Frame, were eventually declared cured, but not until they had been in and out of several institutions over many years.

By 1900 or earlier, patients with a good prognosis could leave for extended periods on parole, to see if they could be released. After six weeks during her first period in mental hospitals, doctors granted Frame a six-month parole.[86] Doctors at mental hospitals paroled or released patients who made suitable progress, those who had entered as voluntary borders and felt well enough to go home, and those who had a caring family who pressed for release and were prepared to supervise. If there were family members, the hospitals sent them progress reports; family members took an interest and could negotiate paroles.[87] For all its isolation, the mental hospital was connected with the outside world.[88] In 1896 Catherine Gillick's husband deposed that "she was a patient at Goodna Lunatic Asylum [Wolston Park] for about two months and I took her out on the 15th January last. For some weeks after she came out of the asylum she seemed to be much better and I did not think it necessary to keep any constraint on her. Until lately she had a delusion that everyone about the place wanted to get rid of her."[89] In the late nineteenth century, mental hospitals had graded patients and assigned them to facilities with greater or lesser control over their movements. Cottage residents were in line for paroles.[90] At the Porirua mental hospital by the 1920s some cottages were known as parole villas.[91] It was not unusual for men and women to come and go, to be released and readmitted with years between.[92] Annie Fleming, diagnosed a melancholic, set herself on fire while on leave from Wolston Park in 1906.[93] The superintendent of Seacliff, Truby King, discharged Isabella Hitchcock after two years, believing she was taking a hopeful view of her future. King told her brother that "she had been a bad case but when such cases do recover they are generally permanent."[94]

At the age of forty-five and subject to fits since childhood, Agnes O'Brien lived with her parents her entire life. She entered Willowburn, a small public mental hospital in Queensland, for a year around 1911, was discharged, returned to the hospital two years later, was discharged, and re-entered. Her suicide note suggests she went with family urging but also with her consent. "God bless father and mother for what they have done for me."[95] Anna Potrezeba's mother testified in 1918 that her daughter "was always strong and healthy until last March when her baby was born." During the month of April she had to be removed to Wolston Park, and she remained there until September, when she left on probation. "Since she came home from the asylum she always had to be watched closely for fear she might do harm to herself. She always had the opinion since she came home that people looked down on her through her having been an inmate of the asylum. Her husband took her different places to try and restore her."[96]

A stay at a public mental hospital further depressed the sagging self-esteem of men and women. Janet Frame's intense prose takes readers into the normal world she had left but which judged her when she tried to re-enter. "Inwardly I kept describing myself in the words that I knew relatives and friends now used, 'She's been in Seacliff. They had to take her to Seacliff.'"[97] The return to the hospital at the end of a parole put patients under incredible stress and elevated their foreboding. "I was fearful always," recalled Frame, "like a condemned person returning to the executioner."[98] She described from experience what others feared from conjecture. Farmer John Lawson's financial woes led him to remark that "the way things were going on it would drive him to the asylum." Rather than allow that, he shot himself.[99]

Some committals were pro forma, and a few people doubtless were misdiagnosed. Janet Frame felt that she had been wrongly labelled schizophrenic. However, attending doctors could be very cautious about a diagnosis of mental illness. Elizabeth Knox "thought her head was going wrong," and in the past she had had "some mental trouble," but Dr Stanley Bull reassured her that she was perfectly sane and gave her a sedative.[100] Divided opinions at committal hearings produced dismissals, and these states of affair put families and doctors in a quandary. Four doctors acting under the directions of a concerned brother treated farmer George Barnes for a breakdown, but only one thought he should be certified insane. Something had to be done, however, because he lived alone and threatened suicide. As a compromise, he was placed in the local hospital.[101] Farmer Joseph Henry's wife made an application to commit him. While two local doctors certified him, the superintendent of Avondale Mental Hospital refused to admit him. Two Auckland doctors then re-examined and discharged him. He killed himself on his trip home.[102] When Alexander McWilliam's wife, Mary, suffered a severe nervous breakdown in early 1930, he applied for "a reception order to a mental hospital." Her doctor agreed, but a second one did not. "So, she did not go." Two doctors and a chiropractor attended her at home, and she went away for a rest.[103] Attempts by John O'Brien's family members to commit him stalled with his physician, who told them that, despite delusions and erratic conduct, he was not sufficiently bad to warrant committal.[104] The two doctors who examined Mary Shanks "could see nothing wrong with her" and rejected her husband's application for committal. She had attempted suicide by firearm and knife and eventually hanged herself with a clothesline.[105]

Constables acted cautiously in domestic situations; they preferred family members to persuade a suicidal individual to undergo assessment. A constable told Edward Smyth that his wife, Sarah, suffering from delusions and postpartum depression, should go to the hospital, but "he did not want to have to force her."[106] If there were no family members, police officers screened individuals before they held someone for a committal hearing. When the matron of the Auckland People's Palace, a hostel run by the Salvation Army, called police about a shell-shocked veteran from Australia who was behaving erratically, Senior Sergeant of Police John McNamara "put him through an examination," which lasted about twenty minutes. It touched on many subjects, "including the war, labour troubles, and the last Commonwealth elections. He answered intelligently and was not a subject for detention mentally. Being quite rational, I let him go."[107] Police attention to the mentally ill could be considerate. During her detention awaiting recommittal to Avondale Mental Hospital, Jessie Smith was cared for by Constable Frederick Wild's daughter.[108] In the course of detaining labourer William Pinkerton for a committal hearing, Constable James Henry thought he was suicidal and took away his razor, but missed a concealed knife.[109] Arbitrary or erroneous detention without compassion, therefore, was only part of the story. If there were wrongful committals, there were also poor medical judgments in the other direction. Witnesses in a few suicide cases regretted that men and women had not been detained earlier, that doctors had disagreed about committal, or that a patient had been granted parole or release.[110]

SHELL SHOCK AND THE RISE OF PSYCHIATRY: THE NEW ZEALAND CASE

In New Zealand and Australia the return of shell-shocked soldiers after World War I forced governments to intervene in mental health more than they would have liked. Suicides among returned men comprised a national problem. The demand for treatment created by war trauma promoted the training of specialists from around the empire in England during and immediately after the war. Within the history of psychiatry, researchers have identified war neurosis as significant in the history of medico-psychological thought, illustrating the extent to which external trauma, rather than internal biological or neurological lesions, could cause certain forms of mental illness.[111] It thus opened a century-long formal concern about neurotic disorders and highlighted the need for strong psychotherapeutic outpatient, as well as in-patient, treatments. As a consequence, shell shock has been often been identified as the precursor to post-traumatic stress disorder (PTSD) and an archetype for understanding war-related physical ailments generally.[112]

Responses to shell shock differed sharply among national political and medical cultures. In Britain shell shock was conceived as effeminate in terms of contemporary notions of masculinity. Thus psychological treatment focused on restoring men to their true aggressive dispositions and, ultimately, on making them fit for the battle.[113] In other contexts, shell shock encapsulated a generalized form of social deviance for those apparently not coping with the readjustment to civilian life, regardless of whether or not those so labelled suffered from a recognized mental disorder.[114] By contrast, the central powers, influenced by Freudian psychodynamics, proved more supportive of soldiers suffering from war neuroses.[115] German political leaders supported psychoanalytically oriented medical treatment of soldiers.[116]

Within the context of demobilization, the presence of shell shock among discharged soldiers posed social problems for families, communities, and political leaders. Within the context of the shortcomings of demobilization, the provision of psychological therapies and pensions for mentally troubled former soldiers was limited. Despite bouts of guilt, governments adopted narrow definitions of disability that made pensions difficult to access for suffering ex-servicemen.[117] However, soldiers and the veterans' associations were not helpless. Organizations such as the American Legion lobbied hard to prevent the stigmatizing label of mentally ill from being assigned to men returning from the battlefield. They were instrumental in influencing the application of new psychiatric classifications to veterans suffering from neuro-psychiatric problems and the founding of new medical institutions divorced from the state mental hospitals, such as the psychopathic hospital.[118] New Zealand eventually pursued the latter solution, and in peacetime the innovation broadened the array of treatments for suicidal men and women.

The impact of shell shock on New Zealand health care was part of an immense crisis. Just over 100,000 men had embarked for overseas, or 42 per cent of the male population of military age; New Zealanders had a high casualty rate.[119] At the front senior medical officers followed British army guidelines on shell shock. At home the military and civilian authorities manoeuvred to mislead the public about how profoundly the conflict had affected some soldiers' mental health. Press censorship was imposed on military suicides. But despite army and government predilections to manage mental health issues, struggles over the neurological and psychological damage of war could not be avoided.

By war's end, public pressure had forced the New Zealand army to graft a dedicated hospital for shell shock and neurasthenia onto the older system of mental hospitals and to add psychotherapy to more traditional national mental health practices. By no means were the government's seemingly progressive steps what they purported to be. Army officials misrepresented the scope and quality of facilities awaiting shell-shocked soldiers at home. Yet real changes transpired because shell shock posed political troubles for a government in an intimate, socially innovative democracy where many people, having sacrificed much, questioned British direction of the war from Gallipoli in early 1915 through to the country's darkest days after Passchendaele in late 1917.[120] Regional patriotic and returned soldiers' associations pressed for compassion and generosity in mental health policy. They alerted authorities to episodes of mental illness among returned men. The government paid attention but shuddered at the financial burden of recognizing war as a cause of mental illness, and it therefore attempted to blame pre-war alcoholism and mental illness for the problems that men experienced.

The Federation of New Zealand Patriotic War Relief Societies lobbied in mid-1917 for special treatment for "light mental disorders or neurasthenia and shell shock," suggesting that men with such conditions "require more care and attention than they can expect to receive in a boarding house." "Is it right that these men should be discharged to roam aimlessly? Surely they are the care of the State."[121] The associations did not want former soldiers trundled off to mental hospitals.[122] They would have preferred that shell-shocked men be "placed in homes where they could receive special attention, and their lives be made bright as possible."[123] An officer responsible for contacting next of kin complained in December 1917 that the terse designation "mental" which he put into telegraphs gave no sense of prospects for recovery. "Omitting deaths, these messages probably cause more distress to the next of kin than any other."[124] Families and friends did not seek a general reorganization of mental health services, just special treatment and perhaps thereby a validation of sanity for their boys. The shell shock or neurasthenia labels satisfied community emotional needs, even if, in particular cases, they fulfilled no medical purpose.[125]

Wartime and postwar governments also heard from public health administrators and army medical officers. Discussions involving these parties were not uncontested briefings. Junior and senior medical personnel clashed over explanations for neurological problems and the extent of the army's responsibility for the mental health of returned soldiers. Junior medical officers were attuned to civilian medical ethics and recent medical practices. The official history of the medical services points out that "the definition [of shell shock] of the New Zealand ADMS [acting director of the Medical Service] did not please neurologists."[126] This admission attests to professional tensions over the causes of neurological war cases. Medical controversies and rising political needs during the conflict meant wartime transitions in the government's understanding of mental illness. But the greatest chronological divide concerns how the army approached shell shock and neurasthenia during the immediate postwar years compared to wartime conduct. During the war the medical services collected more and more information about mental illness as the war progressed and briefed the minister of defence.[127] But once the war was over, attitudes changed, and different debates arose.

Field control over the number of traumatized soldiers ceased, replaced by looser evaluation processes at home and a greater willingness to accept the legitimacy of neurasthenia as a service illness. The military dam controlling the flow of shell shock and neurasthenia cases home was about to burst, and the army knew it. It would be difficult to deny demobilized soldiers medical help for trauma if and when they requested it. Free from maintaining combat strength, the army more earnestly addressed appropriate treatments for shell shock and now, too, neurasthenia. This shift in military attitudes translated into a clear policy for a new initiative in national health, but it appeared also as a more pervasive form of postwar compassion. Thus following the suicide of a returned soldier in January 1921, his colonel instructed officers to act tactfully: "There was a large number of such cases, some may still be in the Regiment." The colonel remarked that the deceased was not thought "mentally deranged," only "somewhat depressed and nervous."[128] Suicides and public committal hearings of soldiers to mental hospitals remained political nightmares.

The army's handling of shell shock and neurasthenia began in 1915 when the narrow official definition of shell shock – the somatic definition, which accented organic damage – served to push back into combat men who had no signs of shell- or blast-related injury. Men without somatic causes of mental illness, but who exhibited symptoms of mental illness, were designated as fatigued and requiring brief rest or classified as malingerers. Men whose mental illnesses could be attributed to somatic causes were to be evacuated to England. The senior medical officer aboard the New Zealand hospital ship *Maheno*, which cleared casualties to England, reported on a trip after the Somme offensive in 1916. There were 568 cot cases, and "12 of the patients were insane."[129] By at least August 1917, the medical service had in place a special neurological section at Number 1 New Zealand General Hospital, Brockenhurst. "The urgent demand for expert advice and special treatment for the wide group of functional disorders, eg. neurasthenia, shell shock, etc." was met here. Captain Marshall MacDonald, who had had experience with neurological cases in France early in the war and had returned to New Zealand, was sent to England to supervise the unit.[130] The inclusion of neurasthenia – classified as a non-somatic illness – for treatment at Brockenhurst is important because it implies that some army doctors had accepted emotional trauma as a legitimate source of mental incapacity.

Shell shock could not be ignored; some men were incapable of functioning as soldiers. Immediately after the disastrous offensive at Passchendaele in October 1917, an Australian doctor who saw New Zealand as well as Australian casualties reported that he gave medical discharges to men who had suffered a mental illness which had psychological origins, and that he could not always explain cases in terms of what was physical and what was psychological.[131] So-called nerves made men unfit for further service, and the army wanted them off the payroll. Before the end of the war, then, men ordered home with mental illness likely included not just those with presumed somatic mental illness but some with non-somatic neuroses.[132] Even without the addition of these emotionally traumatized men, somatic shell shock cases were sufficiently visible at home in early 1916 to send the army and government scrambling to appear responsive to the medical needs of heroes and respectful of their dignity.

The early returned soldiers made an impression. Trooper John Petersen qualified as an early victim of shell shock. He had been "blown up and shot" at Gallipoli, and his injuries possibly made him a "homicidal epileptic." It took half a dozen men to restrain him during raging attacks, which he later could not recall.[133] From early 1916 until at least 1922, returned soldiers stood before magistrates, facing committals to mental hospitals for serious mental illnesses. The army tried to avoid public committal proceedings, but it nevertheless pursued hospitalization. With or without court appearances, it is likely that mental illness of all classes led to the institutional confinement of roughly 1,500 returned soldiers.[134] How many traumatized men suffered without encountering a police magistrate, either for committal to an mental hospital or for conviction as drunk and disorderly? We can never know.

Trouble for the government started when the hospital ships *Maheno* and *Marama* reached Auckland. *Marama* had special quarters and attendants for two violent mentally ill cases. Mild cases had the freedom of the ship. On some of the eighteen trips from England, these ships carried ten to twenty "mentals" each.[135] When a hospital ship reached Auckland in early 1916, the army requested that a doctor from the nearby Avondale mental hospital examine patients thought to have mental illness and, if absolutely necessary, prepare paperwork to initiate a court committal to a mental hospital. The director general of the Medical Service reminded camp medical officers that they had to report men with mental illness to magistrates through the police.[136] Recourse to proper legal channels prompted an internal caveat. On 21 April the director of military hospitals cautioned the DGMS that it was unwise to commit soldiers to mental hospitals, a step that required a hearing in open court. "The public would no doubt much resent any soldier with mental symptoms being committed to the ordinary Mental Hospitals if such could be avoided."[137] If returned soldiers were committed to mental hospitals, "a great howl will be raised."[138]

The army risked a political uproar if it transformed heroes into asylum inmates. It would affront patriotic associations, which insisted that New Zealand's heroes deserved better than committal with "any old loon."[139] The army's expedient solution to its image problems was to retain returned soldiers – even discharged soldiers – under army authority and illegally order them to an institution. The director general of military hospitals negotiated this course with the minister of health and the inspector general of mental hospitals. The latter helpfully advised the army to avoid committing even violent cases. These, he suggested, could be placed in a mental hospital under remand for observation.[140] Less violent cases could be placed directly, without committal, in cottage annexes associated at mental hospitals. In April 1916 the director of military hospitals finalized an arrangement with the minister of health establishing that returned soldiers with mild mania should be sent without committal to the regional mental hospital Seacliff and placed under the care of its director, Dr Truby King, at that time one of the country's few specialists in mental illness.[141]

King maintained a cottage facility at Karitane near Seacliff. By this time many larger mental hospitals in New Zealand and Australia that had kept pace with the latest innovations provided annexes or cottages for light or improving cases. Mental health experts by the early twentieth century laboured to classify patients, and improving ones progressed to these facilities and to paroles. New Zealand's mental hospitals arranged patients in eight classes, each with special staff and facilities. King worried from the start about his staff's ability to develop appropriate classifications, associated facilities, and trained orderlies.[142] The army's avoidance of committal hearings at first misled him into a belief that soldier patients coming his way had mild problems. But only a few weeks after he opened Karitane to soldiers, he discovered that as they recovered strength, these men became difficult to manage and firm in their delusions. "We have come to the crossroads as to the destiny of neuropath troopers who cannot be managed in outside quarters."[143] During the war, abroad and in New Zealand, mental health professions included therapeutic pessimists and those who experimented with new treatments. "Regarding the prospects of *recovery*," King wrote to the director of army hospitals, "I am sorry to say that there is going to be a larger proportion of hopeless chronics than we hoped."[144]

King's facility allowed the army to bypass public committals. It posed – in ministerial announcements and in replies to queries from associations – as a separate, gentler, restorative place. King's participation enhanced the legitimacy of the army's ad hoc and devious arrangement, for he had a reputation as a mental health sage.[145] The army kept sending quite serious cases, masking them as mild or describing them as under remand for assessment. The deception included illegal placement in mental hospitals. From early 1916 to early 1920, the army medical service ordered a number of soldiers with mental illnesses directly to Seacliff without a committal order. A staff doctor tried to determine if the men had functional or light mental illness by inquiring about the soldiers' "life in France" and, in a nod to the growing influence of psychoanalysis in English-speaking psychiatric circles, questioned them about their mothers. Appropriate emotional reactions to "mother" provided a hopeful sign; King felt that men with moral and emotional reactions had material with which his staff could work.[146] This attitude was by 1900 long established in more enlightened mental hospitals in the English-speaking world; mental illness was seen as a deficiency of the will, curable in light cases by re-education and encouragement.

Light mania soldiers who passed the classification process went to King's special facility, where staff encouraged them to play games, take walks, and garden. Another light-supervision annex, Wolfe's Home, operated from 1916 to 1918 near Auckland's Avondale hospital. The facilities at Seacliff and Wolfe's Home could each take a dozen patients at a time; the treatment time is unknown but was swift. Patients who failed an initial interview entered mainstream institutions without lingering in the showcase recuperative homes. The army's practice of sending men to special facilities, rather than having its personnel initiate committals, continued beyond the end of the war.[147]

BORDERLAND CASES, 1918–1922

Significantly for the development of mental health in New Zealand, the army transformed a mountain spa into a psychotherapy institute. Early in the twentieth century, the New Zealand government's tourism department established two health spas, one at Hanmer Springs on the South Island and the other at Rotorua on the North Island. Through good fortune, the government had two facilities with hospital potential. By at least late 1916 the army was sending some functional mental illness cases to Hanmer (the official name was Queen Mary Hospital, Hanmer Springs), even as it sent other men, presumably with more severe problems, without committal papers to special facilities. Isolation played a role in the selection of Hanmer, because the army worried about disorderly conduct by returned men and refused to place them in private convalescent homes where their presence could demoralize the war effort.[148]

By 1918 the army was streaming men into, through, within, and among institutions. Serious cases went to mental hospitals. Some were processed by formal committal, but others proceeded without a committal order. The army by now called presumed light cases of shell shock or neurasthenia borderland cases. Exceptionally light cases proceeded directly from hospital ships and demobilization camps to Hanmer. Patients at district mental hospitals, as well as from Karitane and Wolfe's Home, also went to Hanmer if they showed progress. Respecting serious alcoholics, the army arranged for committals by family members or the men themselves to the Salvation Army's inebriates camp on Rotoroa Island at Auckland. Men moved among institutions, and families occasionally appealed for transfers of their boys to the closest facility. There was a mental health network and a managing bureaucracy.

In planning for demobilization, the army prepared for a deluge of shell shock cases and hoped to avoid committing many men to mental hospitals because patriotic and returned soldiers' associations kept attacking the mixing of shell shock cases with "the worst lunatics."[149] The army's senior medical officers worried, too, about having former troopers, who often still wore uniforms, committed as insane or inebriate in open court. There were going to be thousands of discharged men in uniform milling about the country for awhile, and the army was under no illusions about the mental state of some. Senior officers sought to minimize government involvement in committals by convincing returned soldiers to go voluntarily to a hospital or to have a relative initiate a committal.[150]

At a Defence Department medical conference in Wellington on 18–21 March 1919, it was decided to concentrate shell shock and neurasthenia rehabilitation efforts at Hanmer. Thanks to the medical service's demobilization anxieties, a modest revolution occurred in the treatment of mental illness. At war's start the standard approach for helping treatable patients had consisted of encouragement, sunshine, music, walks, gardening, simple vocational instruction in carpentry, mat-making, and activities generally calculated to keep men busy. By late 1918 the medical service was edging beyond these practices; it accepted the legitimacy of more recent ideas from European military psychiatry to the extent of sponsoring the training of personnel in neurology and psychotherapy in London and bringing them home to treat returned soldiers. The minister of defence was briefed in November 1918 on "the neuroses of war."[151] In February 1919 the army decided that two or more medical officers should stay in London for training in "psychotherapy for treating functional nerve cases."[152] The DGMS, Brigadier-General D.J. McGavin, minuted this cable: "I consider this is a [useful] suggestion and that two medical officers should be trained in psychotherapy on modern lines – a science which has developed much during the war."[153]

New practices made their way to New Zealand, by way of these army-sponsored initiatives, but at Hanmer the old therapies were still going strong in 1919; men were exposed to "bracing climate, the quiet games and baths, and last, but not the least, work."[154] Whatever the course of treatment at Hanmer, the facility remained distinct from the mental hospitals and was soon made available to the public. Beginning in January 1921, it started to accept "civilians suffering from neurasthenia, psychasthenia, etc." Civilian health authorities notified doctors throughout the country that they could now recommend patients for specialist treatment by applying though medical health officers situated in cities and major towns.[155] Hanmer's superintendent thought that women were "the biggest field" for expansion.[156] It became a busy postwar centre for the treatment of neurasthenic and some suicidal men and women.[157]

If professionalization and compassion for returned soldiers constituted progress, then a glimmer of progress attended mental illness during and, above all, immediately after the war. However, greater trauma existed than any government could hope to heal. Men could not find or hold jobs; families could not understand their sons, brothers, husbands, or fathers. Shortly after demobilization, amidst critical episodes of personal adjustments for former soldiers, senior officers pondered the cost of healing the shell-shocked and tried to deflect some responsibility, but again popular forces intervened. Medical boards established to process demobilized soldiers designated an unexpectedly large number of men as eligible for Hanmer. The numbers alarmed the army.[158] When men sought disability pensions, pension boards might accept their claims for shell shock or shattered nerves and assign them places at the facility.

Senior officers were reeling under the weight of postwar numbers. An unknown number of neurasthenia cases had to be treated as outpatients at major civilian hospitals.[159] If not recovering quickly, local cases were supposed to be sent to Hanmer. Doctors sometimes could not determine if returned soldiers needed hospitalization, but they were conscious of community opinion. "I could not treat him as a malingerer seeking a bed," wrote one hospital supervisor, because "he has received considerable local sympathy on account of being a poor soldier suffering from shell shock."[160] Another class of patients arrived at Hanmer in unanticipated numbers. Local hospitals dispatched troublesome chronic alcoholics there, expediently classifying them as neurasthenics.[161] A committee looking in July 1920 at a scheme to cure alcoholic returned soldiers estimated that 70 per cent had been heavy drinkers before the war.[162] Psychiatrist Marshall MacDonald believed otherwise: "With regard to alcoholism I think in some cases at least it is one indication of a loss of balance caused by war service in individuals not necessarily neuropathic and I do not see how the Defence Department can refuse responsibility but of course each case would have to be decided on its merits."[163] Several years after the end of the war, patients kept arriving at Hanmer. Caught off guard, senior army officers proposed that mental illnesses were due to neither pre-war nor war circumstances but to "increased strain and anxiety causing a relapse of functional nervous condition, and to the lack of employment which encourages individuals to make a lodging house of Hospitals wherever possible to do so."[164] Economic dislocations, the disabilities of returned men, and mental illness were combined in individual lives, as the suicide inquests showed.

The great world war insanity helped to professionalize the treatment of less harmful forms of madness. With the flood of male patients expected to subside in the mid-1920s, specialists trained to deal with war trauma looked ahead to women as their next patients. These developments affected public consciousness. Witnesses at inquests began to use terms such as depression, neurasthenia, nerves, and nervous breakdown with greater frequency. Popular classifications of mental illness expanded, and soldiers traumatized by war assisted in that change of opinion, if only by their presence in the community. So common had references to shell shock become that when civilian Wilfred Smith attempted to explain his nervous breakdown in 1920, he wrote, "I am so bad with nerves like Shell Shock."[165] Mental illness remained misunderstood by many, but less so than before the war, and there was evidence of progressive thinking among urban elites. Traditional and advanced methods of managing a suicidal patient were evident in the extraordinary case of Ena Gee, who went to Hanmer for her nerves. The twenty-four-year-old single woman had had formal training for self-analysis. "Her mind had been disturbed," claimed her disapproving doctor, "by analyzing herself by the methods of psychoanalysis for which she had been taught some years previously." His remedy was a sleeping draught.[166]

PROLOGUE TO THE ASYLUM'S ECLIPSE: QUEENSLAND, 1920–1950

Queensland did not establish a special hospital to treat shell shock and neurasthenia as New Zealand had; however, the Commonwealth of Australia set up a special facility on the grounds of Callan Park mental hospital in New South Wales.[167] More generally, the war introduced new trends in treatment without effacing older practices and institutions. Prominent Queensland psychiatrist John Bostock recalled that "the most vivid period was in the years immediately after the first world war. Initial spade work had taken place, stress in armed combat revealed the vulnerability of the psyche to stress. The basis of Psychiatry was in a state of upheaval, one might term it a battleground of ideas."[168] Psychiatrists emerged from the asylum or mental hospital's planned isolation, and by the 1930s they frequented special wards at public hospitals in the cities and treated patients in consulting rooms or private hospitals. By 1950 the state was promoting outreach into general hospitals as a "new outlook on mental health."[169]

A handful of psychiatrists maintained private practices in Brisbane in the 1920s. As early as 1924, when Gertrude Ashley committed suicide, consultations were possible for those who could afford them. Twelve months before she died, Gertrude's "nerves gave out due to the illness of her youngest son." Her husband described the medical attention she received: "I had her attended by Dr Davidson of Sandgate, but her health grew worse. About six months prior to her death, I had her attended by Professor Lawson of Wickham Terrace, Brisbane; also previous to that I had her attended by Mr Morrison of the Medical Institute, Queen Street. Latterly, I had her under treatment by Dr Christian Rivett of Wickham Terrace. None of them did her any good." Just prior to her death Gertrude was under the care of Nurse Griffith. Her husband had stayed home from work to help.[170] None of her doctors were registered specialists, although it is clear from other inquest files that several handled nerve cases. The Queensland Medical Board did not yet have the statutory authority to license psychiatrists, so the specialists were in limbo.[171]

The Queensland board's limited authority was a liability to doctors with appropriate training and experience who wanted to advertise and charge appropriately for extra services. In April 1925 Dr Norman W. Markwell applied to the board for registration as a specialist in psychological medicine. Markwell had graduated from the University of Sydney in 1910.[172] After the war he secured a diploma in psychological medicine issued by the Royal College of Physicians of London and by the Royal College of Surgeons of England. The medical board deferred his application pending further inquiry.[173] Private care for patients with mental illnesses operated with minimal scrutiny because the medical board lacked the statutory power to define specialist qualifications. The

Medical Act of 1939–40 finally empowered the board to register specializations.[174] Control was necessary, explained the undersecretary for the minister of health and home affairs, because the prospect of higher fees enticed doctors to claim specialization and it was feared that "they learn their specialities in the train."[175] The board registered three specialists in psychiatry in 1941: Markwell, John Bostock, and Basil Stafford.[176]

Stafford, a graduate of the University of Melbourne Medical School, had been appointed director of a small public mental hospital at Ipswich in 1927 and became director of the main mental hospital at Wolston Park at Goodna, near Brisbane, in 1937. In that year he visited medical schools, mental hospitals, and clinics in the United States, the United Kingdom, and Europe.[177] Markwell and Bostock had been operating private psychiatric practices without specialist registration for many years already, Markwell probably since 1925 and Bostock since his arrival in Brisbane in 1927. In subsequent years Bostock became highly visible as a founding member of the Royal Australian and New Zealand College of Psychiatry. In the 1930s and 1940s he practised as a doctors' doctor, treating practitioners with alcohol or drug addiction problems.[178] Well positioned to know about foibles, he warned medical students that "the morphine habit is to a large extent a professional risk, for we find that medical men and nurses constitute a large proportion of addicts."[179]

Born in 1892 in Glasgow, Bostock had attended the London Hospital and London University. During World War 1 he served as a temporary surgeon in the Royal Navy. After his discharge, he studied at the Maudsley Neurological Hospital in London and then emigrated to Western Australia and worked in that state's mental health department at Claremont Mental Hospital. Prior to coming to Queensland in 1927, he had been assistant superintendent at Callan Park mental hospital in New South Wales, that state's centre for returned soldiers.[180] The Queensland medical board approved his registration as a general practitioner in 1927, and he immediately sought a part-time hospital appointment.[181] Doctors with overlapping private-public activities increased in Australian metropolitan areas between 1925 and 1950.[182] In 1930 Bostock co-founded the Brisbane Clinic as a group practice composed of specialists. By the late 1930s, as an active consultant at the Brisbane General Hospital, he had developed separate psychiatric wards for men and women.[183] Specialized treatment of mental illness was breaking free of the mental hospital. In 1940, after the retirement of a teaching doctor who specialized in shell shock cases, the University of Queensland appointed Bostock Research Professor of Psychological Medicine, a position created in 1920 with a Red Cross endowment for the study and treatment of psychoneuroses among returned soldiers.[184] He remained in private practice until 1953 and continued as chair of medical psychology at the university until 1962.

The Medical Act of 1939–40 precipitated a burst of registrations in psychiatry. Seven doctors, all of whom had already been practising in a public or private capacity, received specialist standing in 1942. This was the largest cohort in the 1940s and 1950s.[185] The medical board registered two more in 1943, including Norman Youngman, who was sponsored by Bostock.[186] By 1950 there were sixteen registered psychiatrists. Just over half worked as state health department employees, most at state mental hospitals, but the state initiated psychiatric services at regional hospitals in the late 1940s.[187] Psychiatry was migrating out of the public mental hospitals even as these facilities expanded. Its reputation was never higher, and more than ever people sought clinical help.

Specialists placed some patients who could meet the expenses in private hospitals. At the forefront of this trend were Bostock and Youngman, who treated patients at Marooma, a private hospital in operation by at least 1939.[188] Two sisters owned it, but Bostock placed a number of middle-class patients there in the late 1930s. He and Youngman applied the latest therapies, ahead of the public mental hospitals: in the early 1930s they tried narcotherapy (insulin coma treatment) and then Cardiazol-induced convulsion treatment; around 1940 they were using electroconvulsive (shock) therapy.[189] Several other small private hospitals where psychiatrists treated patients were reported in 1939. In 1953 one of them, Nundah, had twenty-two beds; another, Tarrawan, forty-six beds. A fourth, Rosslara, appeared on the government list in 1939. A fifth hospital for nerves was unnamed.[190] Brisbane in the late 1930s and into the 1940s likely had one hundred beds in private facilities that dealt in part with psychiatric patients, a good number of whom were considered suicidal. Private specialists had no trouble finding patients. A few Queenslanders pursuing secrecy went into private hospitals in New South Wales: Mount St. Margaret's at Ryde, which was exclusively for women, and Bay View House at Tempe, for men and women.[191] A 1938 advertisement for the latter stated, "Nervous Disorders and Mental Alienations of all grades have been successfully treated. Medical men may visit their own patients. Terms arranged according to the requirements of the patients."[192]

The appearance in the 1930s of private facilities in Queensland, the departure of residents to out-of-state facilities, and the state's ongoing efforts to recover costs for treatment at the public mental hospitals resulted in a provision in the Mental Hygiene Act of 1939–40 that enabled voluntary patients to make private arrangements for care at state mental hospitals.[193] In under a half-century, and spurred on by the discovery of war trauma, the treatment of mental illnesses had moved from sedatives and asylums to any array of allegedly scientific treatments in an assortment of public and private facilities. Since a substantial proportion of suicides involved men and women believed to be mentally ill, suicide had become decisively medicalized.

SOCIAL CLASS AND THE CONSULTING SPECIALISTS

It is possible to discuss the types of people who went to public mental hospitals, private practices, and clinics because of the suicide inquests and police reports on suicides. The inquest files have limitations, but they provide glimpses into the workings of public and private psychiatry.

Five Brisbane specialists emerge from the Queensland inquest files, including Bostock, who either was the busiest or had the most unfortunate cases because his name was mentioned most often at inquests. This experience with suicide coloured his lectures to medical students. He cautioned that anxiety neuroses among women could evolve into "acute depression or confusional psychosis" with a "grave risk of infanticide or suicide." He continued, "The physician must always bear in mind the risk of suicide in anxiety cases. It is probably greater than in any other psychoneurosis or psychosis."[194] In his lecture on alcoholism, he remarked that chronic alcoholics were susceptible to depressive states with intense anxiety, and "in them the alcoholic is likely to commit suicide."[195] Bostock's name first appeared in the suicide inquest records in 1932, and subsequently it was often connected with other doctors. In 1938 Florence Reithmuller, who jumped into the Brisbane River, was described as menopausal; the inquest into her death noted that she went to Dr Bostock, but he was too busy, so she went to Dr Foote.[196] From 1942 to 1950 the suicide investigations conducted by the police in Brisbane mentioned thirty-four doctors; at least six were specialists. Bostock again appeared prominently as the attending specialist.

Brisbane statistics indicate the importance of private as well as outpatient care at mid-century. In even numbered years from 1942 to 1950, forty-nine suicide cases (19.2 per cent of all cases in the Brisbane data set for those years) received private care or outpatient treatment; thirteen cases (5.1 per cent) had treatment at the state asylum; another ten cases (3.9 per cent) were patients at Brisbane General Hospital's ward 16 or Mater Misericordiae Hospital. Military hospitals attended to three cases (1.2 per cent). The shift to facilities other than public mental hospitals occurred partly as a result of new forms of treatment which will be discussed shortly. Public mental hospitals had been built in park-like settings, because at the time of their formation and expansion, treatment depended on rest, scenery, rural occupational therapy, and the classification and separation of patients by presumed prospect of recovery. Architecture and patient management were united. Psychotherapy as well as the even newer physical modes of treatment could be handled at private clinics and hospital wards; there could be follow-up therapy in a specialist's consulting room or at an outpatient clinic. These new and more labour-intensive therapies had a class dimension.

Brisbane's affluent citizens, starting around 1925, could pursue help from a tiny group of private psychiatrists, while public mental hospitals dealt with the state's poor. Individuals who took their own lives and who had been patients at public hospitals consisted disproportionately of labourers, farmers, and domestic servants. Among those who committed suicide and had a history of treatment at public mental hospitals, there were no business executives. However, men who committed suicide after care in a private hospital or clinic predominantly had elite or at least middle-class occupations. Bostock, in a 1940 article on therapeutic judgment, cautioned that the patient's financial state should be carefully reviewed prior to any discussion of treatment, because if an expensive hospital stay or a long period of psychotherapy proved economically impossible, that circumstance could slam the door of recovery shut in the patient's mind.[197]

Cheaper treatment was available, according to the omni-present Bostock: "In psychiatry there are usually many lines of treatment as alternative routes to health."[198] The Brisbane Clinic published a quick aid brochure titled *Nerves and Worry*: face every problem; do not brood; never repress; practise muscular and mental relaxation; the past is past; occupation brings happiness; sleep; avoid alcohol and cigarettes.[199] In 1958 and likely earlier, Australian and New Zealand psychiatrists attempted to set a schedule of fees that covered initial consultation, succeeding consultations, electroconvulsive therapy, insulin coma treatment, legal work, workmen's compensation cases, jail visits, conferences with legal counsel, and reception house visits to certify for committal. Most of these activities had existed in the late 1930s; so the list summarizes work done by private psychiatrists as they gained clients and affirmed their professional niche.[200]

From suicide inquests, it is impossible to establish the social standing of married women, and that is unfortunate since almost 70 per cent of married women who had been treated for mental illnesses and who subsequently committed suicide had had therapy outside a mental hospital. A substantial number likely came from middle-class households. When Bostock summarized the etiology of two hundred cases for an article, he mentioned the social background of a few, and while not all were affluent, the middle class predominated, and women were notable.[201] Class alone did not determine the course of treatment, because the inquest files suggest that severe mental illnesses were more likely to be treated at an asylum and lighter ones by private arrangements.[202] This proposition cannot be treated as watertight because of vaguely described cases. In his lecture on manic-depressive psychosis, Bostock told medical students that "milder forms can often be cared for at home or in private hospitals."[203]

"WHAT YOU NEED IS ..."

A suicide inquest case from 1940 suggests the range of contemporary treatment options. Witnesses who knew Edna Watson described a postpartum crisis. A specialist told her husband that she was "suffering from melancholia, childbirth melancholia. He advised me to put her in a private hospital for what he called shock treatment. He told me that this treatment put the patient into a convulsion." One alternative was to put her on medication for a week. Other options were the special ward at the General Hospital or confinement at the state mental hospital. "She pleaded with me not to send her to the mental hospital."[204] The Watson case exposes how class, severity of symptoms, and the diversity of institutional arrangements came together. In this case, a specialist provided choices. The situation of well-to-do urban women in 1940 differed from that of their rural counterparts in 1900, who would have been given a lecture and a sedative.

The treatments that patients experienced in the public mental hospitals, hospital wards, consultation rooms, and private hospitals can be reconstructed by describing the practices of John Bostock, who lectured and wrote about diagnosis and treatment. For medical students, he provided extended and sophisticated lectures; for psychiatric nurses, he generalized and wanted them to accentuate the positive; for the public, he radiated optimism; for government officials during wartime, he simplified. Basically, Bostock subscribed to a theory of internal conflict that had evolved from Freudian psychiatry but was altered by William Halse Rivers for the treatment of British officers who had mental breakdowns during World War I. For Bostock, a classic wartime mental conflict provided a starting point for explaining the origin of syndromes. Men in combat had a natural survival instinct that was portrayed as a crude urge, but it was in tension with a herd instinct that called upon men to act for the betterment of the collective. War accented these contrary emotions, and their unresolved clash engendered assorted syndromes. Peacetime problems raised more subtle conflicts.[205] Bostock insisted that each patient was unique and clinicians had to devote a considerable amount of time applying psychoanalysis to discern the roots of conflict: "There must be intense attention to detail. Every word, every test, every prescription must be regarded as part of a general plan."[206] His lectures and publications frequently attributed conflict to over-possessive parents.[207]

Ideally, he thought, psychiatrists should build up a case history from psychoanalysis with the patient on the examining couch; additional details should be collected from interviews with friends and relatives. However, with his eye on the cost of treatment, Bostock proposed short cuts. For nervous breakdowns, he informed radio listeners in a 1948 broadcast, "a word and an appropriate sedative may speedily change your whole outlook."[208] Sedatives remained hugely popular, although Bostock lectured that "bromides are prescribed so freely in the treatment of nervous disorders that it is not surprising that patients occasionally become addicts."[209] Nevertheless, he recommended a pharmacopoeia – Luminal, Dial, Amytal, Bromidia, Somnos, Trional, Medinal, Sulphinal, Allonal, Somnifen, Benzedrine – and thought it best not to tell patients about possible addiction for fear of compounding their anxieties.[210] While psychiatrists at private clinics could prescribe proprietary drugs, public hospitals in the mid-1940s continued to order paraldehyde and phenobarbital in bulk.[211] Despite the older practices at the public institutions, psychiatry was turning toward pharmacology in a major way. In one sense, this approach was not new. Doctors had been sedating patients for decades, but now there alternative means with suitably mystifying names that would eventually acquire cultural currency.

At the same time, psychoanalysis thrived. Bostock recognized several modes of psychoanalysis. First, there was a common form for which no training is needed and everyone engages in when dealing with other people. Second, there was a type practised by experts and dependant on knowledge of character formation and psychological mechanics. It was used to determine the exact type of mental disorder. Third, there was the expert type that more intensely probed the subconscious; the Freudian type, he proposed, was the best known, but there were others based on the works of Adler and Jung. Fourth, Bostock identified free association, in which the analyst was careful not to suggest an answer but observed in order to become aware of the patient's mental trends and subconscious. Fifth, he was aware of the Jungian technique of association with a set of words. Hesitation, he remarked, could be revealing. Finally, he knew about the analysis of dreams and analysis under hypnosis. In his practice, Bostock favoured the second and third forms of psychoanalysis and the building up of a case history that included observing conation, cognition, and affect. Psychoanalysis sessions of an hour several times a week and repeated for weeks or months, Bostock felt, were critical to a sound diagnosis. The pace should not be rushed. Analysts had to be prepared to abandon seemingly promising avenues of analysis about a basic conflict because, as trust developed between the psychiatrist and the patient, the latter could divulge something that altered prior assumptions. Wise analysts prepared for a retreat.

During World War II, when he wrote *The Nervous Soldier*, a guide book for army doctors, Bostock put military expediency ahead of slow-paced analysis. A quick diagnosis could distinguish nervous soldiers who were ineligible for pensions from those with serious syndromes who might be eligible. He condemned pensions as a source of neurosis, alleging that people worried too much about entitlements and needed to immerse themselves in work. Except for his reference to an inexpensive course of treatment for people with limited funds and his wartime concession to haste, which, among other things, demonstrated continuing ties between psychiatry and war, Bostock promoted the idea that diagnosis required patience in the psychoanalysis phase. Psychiatrists possessed several advantages over family physicians. Experience was one, but another was a psychiatrist's lack of connections with the family which permitted a bond of trust. He accepted Freud's theory of transference, whereby the patient came to identify the doctor with a person of affectionate attachment.[212] After analysis to establish diagnosis and prognosis, psychiatrists could begin the treatment campaign.

Bostock's pragmatic approach had menacing, condescending, and manipulative airs. "It is not what we think which is important but what the patient can be made to think."[213] For some syndromes, he preferred psychotherapy sessions that extended his psychoanalysis sessions. Other patients, he claimed, responded to gentle but firm persuasion. The psychiatrist should take notes and elaborate on any improvements, however slight. He cited the example of a woman approaching menopause who sighed deeply. The essential idea in her psychotherapy sessions was to let her draw the conclusion that her sighs were influenced by something deep within, a romantic disappointment that she had to face. To persuade her to continue to open herself, Bostock told her that her sighs had already diminished. Sidetracking was another tactic he recommended. He suggested that the mind could only hold a limited number of thoughts, and thus it was good to divert it in healthy directions. Find a decent passion: "cultivate rare tulips, collect autographs, breed rabbits, hunt butterflies."[214] "The mind glides into saner things."[215] This idea that unhealthy ideas could be displaced by sound ones may have been widespread by the late 1930s. For example, at the inquest into her husband's suicide, May Hayes deposed that her husband "was under treatment from different Doctors for nervous trouble prior to his death." "Acting under Doctor's orders I kept him working."[216]

Bostock's university lectures dating from about 1940 considered the symptoms, etiology, diagnosis, prognosis, and treatments for sets of neuroses and psychoses. Among neuroses he included hysteria, anxiety states such as frigidity and an inferiority complex, neurasthenia, hypochondria, and compulsions; among psychoses he listed reactive depression, reactive excitement, stupor, confusion, manic-depressive psychosis, schizophrenia, paraphrenia, paranoia, and alcohol psychosis.[217] In lectures to medical and nursing students, Bostock employed patient pseudonyms as mnemonics for syndromes. The hypochondriac was Mona Winge; the obsessional type, Jerry Doodle; the hysterical patient, Miss Hissy Fit; the anxiety type, Job Sadman; the nervous male, Mr Willy Willies; neurasthenia patient, Mr Ifeales Low; and the sexual deviant, François Mouton.[218] His preferred treatments were typical for the period. For hysteria, he recommended the Weir Mitchell method. The patient was kept in a single room and given an over-liberal dose of milk. No visitors were allowed. The patient received no sympathy. "Brilliant results," Bostock stated, "have been achieved by shock treatment."[219] For anxiety states, he recommended barbiturates and psychotherapy; for neurasthenia, shock treatment; for manic-depressive psychosis, Cordiazol-induced convulsions; for schizophrenia, insulin coma and electroconvulsive therapy, but he noted the prognosis was very poor. For confusional psychosis, he suggested rest and a powerful sedative.[220]

Psychotherapy remained important; however, from the late 1920s through the 1930s. therapies expanded to include physical intervention, which figured in Bostock's lectures and his work at Marooma. Psychiatry and neurology had been strongly connected through the observation and treatment of soldiers in World War I, and they continued to be associated through the interwar period; that connection helps explain the pursuit of physical interventions and the proposed link between influenza and mental illness. Bostock, who called himself a neurologist at times in the late 1920s, discerned a cycle of intellectual reactions in psychiatry's history. A somatic tradition in the early nineteenth century responded to demonic conceptions of mental disorders and the concept of suicide as a sin; in the late nineteenth and early twentieth centuries, psychoanalysis challenged this somatic tendency. Nevertheless, up to and during World War I, there were instances in Australian and New Zealand where the family of a suicide victim asked for a post-mortem with an examination of the brain in the hope of finding lesions to suggest an organic cause of a life-ending act.[221] Psychoanalysis was not dominant until after the war.

Psychoanalysis faced a rejoinder when physical treatment came into vogue. That phase had its foundation in 1917 with the discovery that advanced syphilis, and thus dementia paralytica, could be arrested by injecting patients with malaria and inducing fevers that heat-damaged the spirochetes. This breakthrough inspired hope for greater cures. In 1928 European specialists observed that controlled comas induced through insulin injections improved the condition of patients with some mental illnesses. In 1933 experiments with intramuscular injections of camphor showed that attendant convulsions effaced some syndromes. These clearing exercises purportedly allowed psychotherapy sessions to address root problems.[222] The means of inducing convulsions almost immediately became more refined with the replacement of camphor by the drug Cardiazol, which left patients with distressing memories of the treatment and some with fractured jaws and limbs caused by the convulsions.

Electroconvulsive therapy (ECT) originated in 1937 and was credited with erasing memories of the unpleasantness of the treatment. It was likely first practised in Queensland in 1940 and in New Zealand in 1942.[223] Janet Frame recalled her two hundred applications of ECT in New Zealand hospitals between 1945 and 1954. Each application, she wrote, was "the equivalent in fear, to an execution, and in the process having my memory shredded."[224] For budgetary reasons, Queensland's public mental hospitals were slow to replace Cardiazol with electroconvulsive treatment, but Bostock pioneered its use at Marooma around 1940. He set out in 1945 to research which syndromes 'it would benefit.[225] With co-author Bertram J. Phillips, Bostock published findings in 1948 which indicated effectiveness for depressives and anxiety-state patients. The authors deemed it not useful for manias or paranoid states, and they claimed that insulin coma therapy was better for schizophrenia. The good results, they suggested, were not necessarily lasting. They proposed that "more success is obtained by the time-honoured but still modern method of explanation, suggestion, and firm handling."[226] Dr Basil Stafford, of the state mental health department, urged the government to purchase an Ediswan Shock Therapy Apparatus in 1942.[227] Electroconvulsive therapy was commonplace in psychiatric circles by 1950. In that year, for example, a family doctor attended Richard Pomeroy for six months for "a Mental Disorder." Pomeroy then underwent a course of shock treatment at the Brisbane General Hospital but refused further sessions and later took his own life.[228] In Frame's experience, patients were processed one after another on treatment day; they witnessed prior patients being wheeled out.[229] She may have been misdiagnosed, and ECT could have been inappropriate for her condition. It would be a mistake to generalize from her moving descriptions of a traumatic experience. A New Zealand contemporary, painter Rita Angus, received the same treatment in late 1949 and regarded her hospitalization as helpful.[230]

In the 1940s, if not earlier, the public mental hospitals were no longer alone as places of treatment and training. As the refuge of the poor and the holding facility for difficult cases, the public mental hospitals persisted and expanded after World War II, until pharmacological developments completed a process of deinstitutionalization in the 1970s. The groundwork for that monumental shift had been prepared with the growth of psychoanalysis after World War I, a rush toward physical treatment in the late 1930s, and the expansion of barbiturates in the 1940s.

The 1950s were a boom time for psychiatry and psychology. Practitioners, researchers, and writers promoted the concept that many social ills stemmed from mental problems. Alcoholism, crime, and delinquency were not just social issues but phenomena for psychiatric treatment and psychological investigation. Attuned to trends, John Bostock in 1940 counted sociology among his hobbies. Convinced that cures for mental illnesses were possible but costly and time-consuming, he felt that "the best solution is social prophylaxis.[231]Psychiatry in this period has been called "one of the instruments of soft coercion which liberal societies use to keep their citizens in line."[232] Bostock had moved toward soft coercion during World War II when he wrote morale-boosting pamphlets for the army. Not only did this psychiatrist participate in a designation of social problems as problems of the mind, but he inflated the mental illness crisis. Society and psyche were to be unified, with psychiatry taking the lead. In 1951 Bostock wrote in the introduction to *The Dawn of Australian Psychiatry* that "we are manufacturing neurotics, psycho-neurotics, and psychotics on a large scale. The amount of mental illness is staggering."[233] Across the prosperous Western world, psychiatry in the 1950s had left its intramural public mental hospitals era behind and embarked on an extramural period of outpatients and pontificating about human organization. That these trends surfaced so clearly in a lightly populated and, from a North Atlantic perspective, distant place denotes a global diffusion.

CONCLUSIONS

The management of others is offensive to liberal sensibilities. One risk of an exercise of medical-legal power over others is that a wrong diagnosis and treatment can be painful, debilitating, fear-inducing, and conducive to suicide. Cases from the inquest files support these worries. Panic over losing control and facing further treatments was palpable in many suicide cases. Another risk of our accepting the management of others without cavil is that a government can acquire the habit of acting in the best interests of citizens in other situations. Who would set that agenda for improvement? If we were to judge the quality of prescriptions for life set by a number of moral statisticians and social scientists, based on their suicide investigations, the verdict should be that we would not entrust society to their good intentions. Psychiatry, meanwhile, has switched directions so often to tackle anguish that it is sensible to remain agnostic about its achievements and potential. Critical commentary is a service that historical inquiry provides. After historians stand back and scrutinize past enthusiasms and claims of success, they feel justified in asking whether this time anything will be different.

But critical senses can and should reach in several directions. An unstinting critique of the management of others is itself open to warnings. The evidence assembled for this chapter's narratives on the shifting operations of mental health authorities includes confirmations of, but also exceptions to, the master tale of arrogant authorities telling people what they need. In several respects, the historical record challenges a critical orthodoxy that directs a spotlight only at the mental hospital's failings. To be sure, mental illness had stigmatizing and terrifying connotations; however, numerous statements by suicidal individuals affirm mental anguish, and the treatment of what is still unfortunately labelled mental illness "creates specific benefits as well as handicaps."[234]

It has long been fashionable to follow Michel Foucault when analyzing the treatment of mental illness or writing about suicide from the perspectives of religious and civil authorities. The ideologies and agencies for managing the person ("inscribing" politics and ideas on the body) have now been exposed by a generation of scholars. Their insights are supported by the published literary sources common to intellectual and cultural history and by archival gleanings. However, the critical generation has not had access to abundant accounts of men and women caught up in the shifting modes of treatment and the interplay of law, medicine, individual, and family. The inquest documents used in this study furnish that access, and it seems to me that they modify and massively complicate but do not erase the literary-critical trends in scholarship.

Here are some suggested adjustments or addenda. First, public mental hospitals responded to the diversity of illnesses by making case-based judgments about the duration of treatment and used paroles to test the patient's restoration to health and adjustment to life outside. Many patients were not locked up for long periods, if their syndromes showed promise of alleviation. Second, some who were close to committal were saved by the rules of a legal process, but a few of these individuals ended badly. Third, public mental hospitals took in voluntary patients with mild mental illnesses; some men and women put themselves into these facilities. Fourth, the public mental hospital was not the only institution in town; even in rural areas, there was awareness by 1930 of urban-based private alternatives to public mental hospitals. Admission to the private hospitals was voluntary, and the difference in health care based on affluence raises an issue separate from the usual condemnation of public mental hospitals. The relative poverty of the patients and budgetary constraints at public mental hospitals encouraged regimentation and experiments with quick-fix remedies. The fifth finding is that there was also a separation of treatment by the severity of cases in public hospitals; this fact is not a novel discovery, but the inquest cases confirm it. Finally, there is abundant evidence of family involvement: attentive families who pursued several avenues of care for their loved ones or who favoured home care; other families who weighed labour loss against committal; still others who moved too eagerly to commit someone or who threatened committal. When families were present, the treatment of mental illness required that they deliberate, and they were not always passive in relations with medical authorities.

Rather than end here, we must double back into a critical mode and conclude with an observation by Janet Frame. The family's role in the management of someone with mental illness must be considered from a patient's position. In a time and place when the general public considered the mentally ill as outcasts, a family's decision to commit was hurtful. No child of mine, Frame's mother had once said, would go to the mental hospital. "But I was a child of hers, wasn't I? Wasn't I? And she signed the papers to send me. I felt uneasy, trying to divide out the portions of family love to discover how much was mine."[235] Family management of mental illness could heap new troubles on old. Families, too, were sites of power and negotiation, as well as compassion and confusion.

Conclusion

Historians, psychoanalysts, and psychotherapists deliberate over people's words. Words are significant in fields that strive to comprehend the human condition. Suicide studies gain from seeing in abundance the words and circumstances of individuals caught in life's troubles; social history gains because suicide inquests let us glimpse tragedy, hear people, and sense emotions from shivers of defeat to surges of rage. Social historians would do well to invigorate the past with a feel for emotions.

Whether the purpose is to comprehend suicide or detect a pulse in social history, there are challenges to working with the inquest files, even though they offer tremendous opportunities for documenting emotions. In the first place, the lives on view are seen purely in episodes of distress; there is so much more to life than tragedy. Second, the population under scrutiny is a special one. However, the crisis episodes likely have analogues throughout the society. In other words, motives for suicide describe crises and stresses that may not be unusual. A third problem with inquests is that they were not extended inquisitions carried out for the benefit of historians or suicidologists, but were relatively short meetings to discover or confirm a cause of death. Furthermore, it is possible that some statements were fabrications by witnesses with ulterior motives. However, trust in the contents of depositions is advanced by the fact that, out of curiosity, police constables and magistrates probed and that witnesses seeking catharsis unburdened themselves. Plain facts speak volumes. Protracted unemployment, financial collapse, alcoholism, marital breakup, and deep grieving were not matters of opinion or diversionary explanations from circumspect witnesses with ulterior motives. They were matters of fact. Moreover, some men and women wanted their actions understood. Parties seeking vengeance, intending to impose a burden of guilt, made their motives known. Medical records or witnesses' concurrence about a person's medical condition established likely euthanasia decisions. Abusive husbands may have attempted to obscure their role in driving a spouse to self-destruction, but other witnesses, police inquiries, suicide notes, and even a husband's unwitting comments exposed crucial background.

In the well-chosen words of Susan Morrissey, people who wrote suicide notes "claimed authorship over the meaning of their deaths."[1] They authored messages in assorted mediums: long typed letters, short notes in pencil, and words scratched on whatever was handy – a laundry bill, the cover of a school scribbler, a scrap of newspaper, a rifle butt, a fence board. The medium was not the whole message, but occasionally it did convey something about the person's life. A few men and women authored thought-provoking gestures, memorably the returned amputee who left his folded uniform on the bank of Brisbane River and jumped in wearing a new civilian suit paid for as an aid to adjustment by the Commonwealth of Australia or the elderly Kiwi who walked to a hill top to feel the wind and sun and eat his last orange.

Another challenge with inquests is that the bounty of information requires organization, and the unavoidable prospect of such tampering recommended that I search for concepts in the abundant literature on suicide. Unfortunately, as I established in chapters 1 and 2, many studies disclosed more about the political and intellectual milieu of their authors than about suicide. The title of this book, A Sadly Troubled History, is an apt description for much suicide research. All the same, some writers had known suicidal individuals or had worked with judicial or medical case files; these facts do not mean they escaped bias, but it does mean they considered the lives of individuals, rather than the bloodless relations of published data, and occasionally they did more than just parrot the politics of their age. On account of their working with case files, some researchers throughout the decades encountered and remarked upon epistemological problems. They wondered how best to sort and assemble surviving fragments of personal feelings. How can we respect the suffering of individuals while applying analytical perspective? they asked. How can we balance sympathy and analysis, anecdotes and patterns? To get around mere narration and to order their inquiries, suicide specialists during the previous hundred and fifty years commonly arrayed their discussion in two phases.

INTEGRATING THE LIFE COURSE AND SUICIDE RATES

Nineteenth-century commentators regularly divided their material and arguments into background motives, or chronic causes, and proximate motives, or acute causes; or they found alleged predisposing causes, such as hereditary mental weakness, and determining causes, such as a financial catastrophe or a loss of honour. Background motives for those who looked at social and cultural factors effloresced into condemnations of secularism, liberalism, and urban deracination. For those who came at the subject from medicine, the background or preconditioning that made people vulnerable was mental illness or mental fragility. Proximate motives or triggering episodes included recent rejection, a death, or unemployment. The essential point is that a two-step analysis has been commonplace for a long time. In a late twentieth-century book about the ethics and politics of suicide, Thomas Szasz also separated explanations into background motives (circumstances) and the more immediate pains (reasons). "We should," he wrote, "distinguish among the great variety of circumstances in which people kill themselves and the many reasons why they do so."[2] Some recent discussions have divided the comprehension of suicide into motives and intentions. Bifurcation makes tactical sense, although it fails to respect the coherence or unity in a suicide decision. *A Sadly Troubled History* has dealt first with motives for suicide and then shifted to the proximate reasoning processes through which people progressed from pain to compelling reasoning – as well as impaired reasoning – to a fatal solution.

Insights from a few modern studies were helpful in coaxing meaning from the cases. Ronald Maris's theory of pathways to suicide, which essentially indicates that suicidal people become that way over a long time, was useful. Admittedly, this thesis, along with the related proposition that suicide rates increase with age, clashes with an inconvenient fact, namely, the advent of rising adolescent suicide rates. However, the long-term perspective remains important for social historians, social scientists, medical practitioners, and health policy analysts because middle-aged men have recently been identified in some Western societies as the group most at risk. It remains imperative to retain a dynamic understanding of life and not just to approach suicide from statistical or diagnostic snapshots. Western societies are experiencing aging populations, and that shift recommends keeping gerontology in mind when we assess age cohorts and suicides. *A Sadly Troubled History* adopted a life-course approach which Victor Bailey had introduced in *This Rash Act*. As well, the current book incorporates a few leads from the developmental theories of psychologists and psychiatrists. Inquests, regrettably for historians or suicide specialists, did not reach far back into individual lives. The life-course approach to the case files cannot produce anything remotely like full histories, but from fragments left in the files, it can assemble rough composites of the lives of men and women at particular life-course stages. While the puzzles remain, as they invariable do in history, science, and medicine, we can venture tentative conclusions based on reasonable evidence.

The life-course discussions highlighted motives for suicide emerging from eternal human concerns as well as from specific events. The twofold analysis re-enters the picture. Motives, which are easier to document than intention or reasoning, deserve attention first. Later in these concluding remarks, I will resurrect the subject of suicidal reasoning. But first, let us re-examine motives. The central point about them can be quickly made. Both eternal deep concerns and specific events have the capacity to alter people; the insults to the mind may, as physiological reports suggest, have harmful consequences for neural cells and can affect their capacity to recover.[3] The eternal concerns and specific events also have consequences for memories that affect self-esteem. Events on the life course are momentous for the psychological and neural-physiological development of individuals. These events also fall within the scope of social history.

The eternal human concerns include sexual drives, the desire for a purpose in life, the need for respect, and anxiety about physical decline. The intensity of these concerns varies with age, gender, the degree of support from others, and the nature of particular cultures; evidence from the inquest files has personalized these variables. The inquests showed how world economic developments, not only the familiar cyclical depressions, impacted on lives in a myriad of unexpected ways, sometimes with debilitating consequences realized only decades later. Gold rushes left behind alluvial tailings and washed-up lives. Commodity production drew young men to manual labour, and sooner than they expected, it made them elderly, isolated men without prospects or family, close perhaps only to a few work mates and chums around the bar. Scores of lonely old men died by their own hands in tents, boarding houses, and hotel rooms. Pastoral industries in both jurisdictions pulled in gangs of labourers who lacked security, followed a seasonal rhythm, accumulated injuries, and sometimes succumbed to alcohol. War not only resulted in broken bodies but inflicted trauma that left men miserable for years. Depressions and booms affected people's outlooks. The 1918 influenza epidemic, which struck New Zealand far harder than Queensland, was a global event that pushed up suicide rates. Then, too, there were historical events with a narrowly regional character, such as Queensland's severe droughts. When eternal human concerns, their age-related intensity of impact, and specific disastrous events mixed in individual lives, they produced the life-restricting circumstances encountered in this book's discussion of motives and glimpsed again in the profiles of men and women gripped by meta-pain and deciding to finish their lives. The fact that at inquests witnesses presented truncated versions of lives should not deter us from sketching tentative patterns of motives, intentions, and reasoning. I believe (others can take exception, but they should first examine the records) that when making their statements at inquests, most family members, friends, co-workers, and doctors strained sincerely to understand events, and they occasionally had the benefit of intimacy and the trust of the person who had contemplated self-destruction.

Life-restricting circumstances can be portrayed in a rough sequence that covers gendered life courses. Lovelorn young men and women entered a rite of passage through the trials of competition for partners. Rejection wounded. For many girls and a few boys, parental involvement in their mating activities challenged their incipient autonomy and barred them from an object of love. Older itinerate manual workers had the multiple challenges of working past their prime, competing with younger men, coping with injuries and illness, and sometimes succumbing to alcohol addiction. Farmers faced many of the same physical hazards, labour strains, seasonal stresses, and alcohol-abuse issues; moreover, they fretted over weather, expenses, crop-sowing or stock-selection decisions, debts, and market prices. Some labourers and farmers had never married or had separated and found it difficult in later years to get on alone. Middle-class men were not always secure in their employment or investments, and a few lived large and encountered an unhappy reckoning when luck and money ran out. Old age for men who had lived by brawn or manual skill brought poverty, dependency, and ever more severe ailments. The wives of working men coped with shortages of money, childbirth and child-rearing in difficult surroundings, domestic labour, and the absences of husbands or disruptive family moves as a result of male quests for waged employment. Drudgery punctuated with bursts of unwanted excitement wore many married

women down, and so among them there was a slight bunching of suicides at middle age. Various forms of mental illness, but mostly nerves,
nervous breakdowns, and depression, appeared often among the files
dealing with the suicides of women, as did accounts of their treatment.
Disclosures about mental collapse deepen social history by connecting
major events with personal wellness, with the quest for healing by troubled men and women, and with considerable groping in the dark by
medical science. If some of the alcoholism prominent as a motive for
men was symptomatic of depression, then the relative prominence of
mental illness among women should be seen as a gendered construction
that affected men in a way too. Many men coped, not by admitting
mental illness, but by means of an acceptably masculine and convivial,
but ultimately harmful, measure. They self-medicated with alcohol.

In the process of looking sequentially at rates, motives, and illustrative examples, I plotted a course through the book's chapters from the
detachment of the social sciences to an emotional plane. The life course
involves deeply emotional moments. When the consequences of economic depressions, wars, and droughts become manifest in people's
words, searches for help, and tragic deeds, these great events of conventional history are not only understood intellectually but are now
felt by us. The sociological approach to suicide, so insistently pioneered
by Durkheim, neglected the personal and emotional dimensions
of knowing.

The complexity of the life course and missing elements in the documentation add to the difficulty of explaining suicide rates in different
jurisdictions with anything other than vague generalities. Suicide rates
continue to fascinate a number of academics as well as international
and national health agencies, despite a chain of problems with aggregate data. In the first place, little is known about the variability in
reporting on violent deaths in different countries. A rigorous nation-by-
nation investigation of reporting practices and reporting cultures is
overdue. Even in Australia and New Zealand, where the administration
of justice and the bureaucratic collection of data were reasonably good
in the early twentieth century, suicides were undercounted, at least from
the perspective of academic inquiry. However, from a strictly legal point
of view, some of the sudden deaths that I have counted as suicides
would not have been so determined by coroners. Jurisdictions around
the world differ over the standard of proof. Some have required that
for a determination of suicide, the proof must be beyond a shadow of
doubt, while others accept a preponderance of evidence. Currently,

New Zealand coroners take a middle position.[4] Unless there is the added motivation of a suspicion of foul play, not many countries today have the commitment necessary or the resources at hand to inquire openly into violent and sudden deaths in the manner of Australia and New Zealand, and some that do have resources apply distinct standards of proof.

However, it is likely that not all the variation in suicide rates among the world's countries results from errors, cover-ups, and indifference. If reliable rates existed or ever could exist, their explanation would have to take into account the factors introduced in chapter 3, where I showed how social policy and general economic well-being affected rates at the margins. Wars, natural disasters, and epidemics can intervene too. Short-term factors arising from political and economic events influence suicide rates. As we just saw, that was not the end of the story on rates. The life course threw up challenges. There seems to be a basic or "natural suicide rate" that, I suggested, is connected to the life course. The term "natural suicide rate," introduced by Bijou Yang Lester, is an unfortunate one for an important concept, because it may give an impression of something driven by nature.[5] It is a natural rate, I propose, only because it is related to people's life course, a natural affair. A fairly steady portion of a country's suicide rate originates in self-inflicted deaths where the motives derive from how individuals cope with taxing episodes punctuating the biological life course. The idea that this component of the rate is "natural" breaks down when it is realized that life-course stages are accommodated differently from culture to culture. Courtship, rejection, marriage, infidelity, childbirth, child-rearing, work, aging, and terminal illnesses are subject to cultural norms and practices. Psychache originating in these trials and strains can be mitigated or intensified by norms and practices which, unlike the short-term factors of political and economic circumstances, have a deep presence. The study of suicide rates can benefit from a major rethinking that pays attention to clues from case-based studies from different cultures. It is hoped that this book may promote a quest for significant runs of case files that will lead to an evidence-based consideration of suicide and culture.

This book has been roundly critical of Durkheim. His disciples could now rally to his defence by suggesting my claim that culture may adjust a natural rate of suicide appears to be close to his notion that social institutions and norms could modulate a suicidogenic current. Three differences separate what I have proposed from what Durkheim argued. First, he invested vague concepts with assertive authority, but when his leading ideas, such as social integration, are scrutinized, they say very little. Something that can include anything becomes nothing. Moreover, his specific instruments of integration, such as marriage, are undercut by realistic assessments of them. For example, there are good and bad marriages. I, too, may not have avoided a priori reasoning, but I have repeatedly remarked on the limits to what we can know about others. Second, Durkheim dismissed both individuals and case files. It strikes me, as it has others before, that case files in abundance are essential for any sociological or anthropological studies that seek to know if, or to understand how, cultural practices and values might cushion the impact of particular sources of stress on individuals. A few case studies or the manipulation of separate sets of aggregate data cannot lead far enough. Finally, Durkheim's entire project was hostile to working with the emotions of individuals. *A Sadly Troubled History* has taken a contrary position. Emotions are part of life. They are integral to the social sciences and history.

SUICIDE, SCIENCE, AND HISTORY

More than just the men and women who committed suicide were exposed to the assorted life-restricting circumstances spread across these pages; I have often conjectured in this book that the motives for suicide are widespread and have surely weighed down the lives of the non-suicidal as well as the suicidal. Therefore the means are at hand to slip commentaries on trauma and emotion into the social historians' imaginative reconstructions. Conversely, the claim that the sorrows described at the inquests were familiar creates a problem for suicide studies, because if the motives of people who commit suicide are shared with a good portion of the general populace, then that admission leads into the classic problem of explaining why some suffering individuals take their own lives but most do not. The ideas of Jack Douglas and Edwin Shneidman help explain the leap from motives to suicide. Douglas dismissed aggregate data as remote from the act and simply unhelpful; he advocated constructing a social meaning for suicide from real-life instances. *A Sadly Troubled History* has followed up on his call for more real-life situations, and it has shown what can be achieved with case-based information. Conjoined with his accent on the individual, Douglas claimed that for the suicidal person, the act was rational. Long-time suicidologist Shneidman also insisted that suicide makes sense to the person committing it. Many individuals encountered in the research for *A Sadly Troubled History* disclosed a subjective rationality. Clinical psychologists and psychiatrists can recount cases of suicidal individuals whose deep existential crisis was so well worked out, so logically argued, that they could nearly convince their therapists that self-destruction offered the only remedy.[6] However, instances of profound mental illness, rage, and impulsiveness suggest exceptions to the prevailing pattern of rationality that emerges from the inquests.

To reconstruct the thought processes of suicidal individuals in order to appraise rationality, I organized and recounted the words of justification that helped men and women abandon their struggle for life. Historical circumstances affected people's thoughts about their life-restricting circumstances and remedies. An embrace of religion during and after World War I, for example, conditioned some men and women to think of death as a transition to a better life. To cite another example of historical contingencies influencing the manner in which people reflected on their lives, itinerant labour provided a few men with metaphors about "moving on." More generally, the masculine ideal, shot through with images of heroism, toughness, and sacrifice, assisted with eroding the common countervailing fear of death. "Finishing the job" – to take another male metaphor – played a part. "Doing the job right" with the unforgiving and all-too-handy male instruments, razors and rifles, introduced fatal certainty into many male suicide attempts. Plenty of people debated within to convince themselves that suicide was not an end to life but a solution. The reaching out for a rationale that would make it easier to slip the bonds of earthly existence is distinct from actually deciding on self-destruction, but it contributed to the vital reasoning process, which could be long and deliberate, short and reasoned, impulsive and irrational.

Euthanasia decisions are different from other suicide decisions, for they stand at the near end of a continuum of comprehensibility, where the pain is such that everyone understands it and the natural course of life remaining is truly short. As for non-euthanasia suicides, which were the great majority, what Shneidman called meta-pain or psychache presents a vital feature in the reasoning processes of a suicidal individual. The merit of his summary concept is that it allows for many individual experiences; there are many sources of meta-pain. Individuals who took their own lives had narrowed their remedies for meta-pain on account of one or more of the following considerations and circumstances: the habits of binary thinking (either I suffer more or I escape by death; either I suffer more or I exact revenge), the sheer overwhelming and immobilizing intensity of the meta-pain, the recognition of an opportunity for self-destruction, the absence of someone to break the binary thinking, and impaired reasoning.

The foregoing propositions rely on what we have seen in the words of the deceased, their words as reported by witnesses, and observations on behaviour that the witnesses put into words. Language has well-known shortcomings. There are difficulties with evidence and analysis. Yet perceptive witnesses – numerous in a large study – reported on someone else's troubles with sensitivity. Doctors occasionally presented their perceptions. But the testimony of all witnesses at inquests should be read critically, for many parties could have ulterior reasons for what they said and less than full knowledge of what disturbed someone else. The epistemological barrier mentioned throughout this study remains in place, although Victor Bailey expressed well the mitigating case when he wrote that the witnesses' words were "informed by the experiences and knowledge of the pressures of everyday life."[7] As for objections that inquests did not probe as deeply as one would like and that even with deeper probing we might never truly understand a suicide, Bailey quoted Jean Baechler: "It is not necessary to be able to explain everything to try to explain something."[8]

Text strung across a flat page is an imperfect device for melding motives with rationales, intentions, and reasoning. In life all things are united, but existential unity eludes appropriate articulation, and anyone who studies suicide is likely to have to resort to compressing the statements of witnesses and the words of the deceased into the imperfect categories of motives. It is essential to attempt to reconstruct the inner dialogues leading to intention and from intention to action; yet it is equally fundamental to point out again and again the distance between us and the mental processes of the deceased. Furthermore, some precision regarding motives was sacrificed by compression during research or simply was impossible to effect because complete information is never available. However, the quantitative and qualitative information offered plausible motives through the life course and revealed intentions such as curing meta-pain and taking revenge. Individuals turned over in their minds background motives as they considered solutions to the anguish that motives caused. A few suicidal individuals put their motives as well as their attendant meta-pain into heart-rending words.

A Sadly Troubled History has commented on assorted investigative tools, including statistics, formulaic questionnaires, diagnostic manuals, and biochemistry. Social scientists and medical specialists have jockeyed for prominence in rendering suicide knowable. They have never eliminated the necessity of taking an interest in the life history of individuals because suicide is the act of an individual, although advocates of some techniques have promised economical and effective alternatives to protracted listening and intensive talk therapy. After we have read the words of people in torment, mechanistic tools of investigation and biochemical research seem, in the words of Gary Greenburg, "essential but forever dumb."[9] He was expressly criticizing the super-streamlined medical responses to depression that rely on diagnostic checklists and pharmaceuticals, but his arresting comment could equally apply to any studies of suicide that omitted or slighted coming to terms with individual trajectories on the life course.

It may be that there are levels of particular hormones such as cortisol, mentioned with respect to seasonality in chapter 3, which could serve as a suicide-prediction tool, although one suspects that a thorough study would disclose such a high percentage of false positives that the test would be an absurdity. In other words, plenty of people would be shown to have high cortisol readings without suicide ideation, suicide attempts, or death by suicide. Quite apart from the implausibility of it serving as a true predictor, this so-called tool would reveal nothing about the mix of genetic and stress factors that contributed to the elevated level of the hormone in the first place. Stress, it seems, may have a role in another biochemical process now being related to suicide, because stress switches off a gene that codes for ribosomal RNA, which in turn governs the production of proteins. A study of a small number of brains of people who had died by suicide and who had also suffered childhood abuse showed that in the hippocampus more of the gene of interest had been switched off (methylated) than in a set of brains from individuals who had died in accidents. The reduction in protein synthesis could have affected neural connections in a part of the brain that is influential with regard to mood. So far, the biochemical and neurological mechanisms leading from stress through to mood are conjectural.[10] Moreover, even if altered methylation patterns could be determined from a blood sample, it would be a poor predictor of suicide unless it could be shown that a high proportion of individuals with the condition committed suicide. A determination of risk would require an enormous long-term study of people and their patterns of methylation until their demise. One of the essential problems in suicide studies, noted throughout this book, now re-enters the picture. Not everyone who experienced stress or who had elevated levels of cortisol or who exhibited inhibited protein synthesis in the hippocampus will have died by his or her own hand. What, then, separates those who did from those who did not? That nagging question persists.

This book has likely failed the individuals whose lives it has covered because a practical research decision led to a compression of motives into a mere ten categories. To recover diversity, the words and intentions of individuals were emphasized in chapters 4 to 6; the individuality of the pathway and the meaning of the act were kept in the forefront in these chapters. Still, the categorization of motives produces a vital, if shaky, platform; categorization might have been a problem if statistical inferences were made to test a theory, but precisely because of the diversity of individual motives, no theory has been statistically tested. However, there was shape to the argument and the argument was historical.[11] Men and women in different stages of the life course encountered age- and gender-related crises; exogenous events intervened and complicated their lives. How they endured or shed their troubles were individual matters over which many deliberated. This book's position favouring the individual meanings of suicide has been developed throughout and now is restated as a caution about the promises of social and biomedical sciences to discover predictive truths about self-destruction.

New Zealand schizophrenia patient Dorothy Walker presumed a limit to medical science when she wrote in her diary in 1977 that "scientists cannot say, let not your heart be troubled, cannot give help in the face of the baffling mystery of human anguish."[12] It is likely that in recent years scientists have helped alleviate the suffering, although human anguish remains mysterious. We can consider the pre-eminent example of antidepressants, which are currently hailed as either a cost-effective means for preventing suicides or not much better than placebos.[13] Even though it is most probable that they are therapeutically effective, their prescription cannot help us fathom anguish. The conclusion that antidepressants or any other medication for a mental illness could lead to a decline in suicides would be cheery news, but it would not make medication or the science behind it any more insightful, any less dumb.

Dorothy Walker realized intuitively that medical science takes mental illnesses' subjective first-person experiences, recasts them as objective third-person experiences, and thus veers away from experience. Historical inquiry can represent anguish and despair as subjective experiences but likewise not in the first person. I admit that it is their pain, and I cannot feel it. However, I can try and I should have an awareness of the pain's outward forms and consequences, for they communicate the human condition, which must interest all social historians. The inquest evidence on life-restricting circumstances, meta-pain, intentions, rationales, and degrees of rationality documented the spectral shapes of mental crises and thrust emotions into social history's recovery of the lived past. Historical inquiry is no less useful to suicide studies than biochemistry or psychiatry, and history is just as reliant on remarkable and imperfect information. But historians can at least endeavour to communicate "the baffling mystery of human anguish" in words that touch the heart.

Notes

ABBREVIATIONS USED
IN THE NOTES

AD   Army Department, Archives New Zealand
ADMS   acting director, Medical Services, New Zealand
DGMS   director general, Medical Service, New Zealand
J 46   Justice Department, Coroners' Inquests, Archives New Zealand
JU   Justice Department, Archives New Zealand
JUS/N   Justice Department, Inquest Files, Queensland State Archives
NZEF   New Zealand Expeditionary Force
QSA   Queensland State Archives

PREFACE

1 Sean Gouglas and John Weaver, "A Post-colonial Understanding of Law and Society: Exploring Criminal Trials in Colonial Queensland," *Australian Journal of Legal History.*7, no. 2 (2003): 231–53.
2 Jonathan Richards, *The Secret War: A True History of the Queensland Native Police* (St Lucia: University of Queensland Press, 2008).
3 One of the chapters to Doug Munro's forthcoming book is "Richard Gilson – The Perfectionist Historian of Samoa," *Pacific Studies* 29, nos 3/4 (Sept–Dec 2006): 33–73.
4 John Weaver and David Wright, "Shell Shock and the Politics of Asylum Committal in New Zealand, 1916-1922," *Health and History* 7, no. 1 (Fall 2005):.17–40.

INTRODUCTION

1 Among historians, the pioneer of integrating social history and emotions is Peter N. Stearns. See Stearns, *Jealousy: The Evolution of an Emotion in American History* (New York: New York University Press, 1989). Also see Carol Zislowitz and Stearns, *Anger: The Struggle for Emotional Control in America's History* (Chicago: University of Chicago Press, 1986).

2 All Queensland cases come from the Justice Department, Inquest Files (hereafter JUS/N), Queensland State Archives. The specific record designation is by bundle number followed by the file number within the year. Thus the case cited is JUS/N1143/230, Ella Krimmer. All subsequent Queensland cases will be cited in this abbreviated form.

3 Ibid.

4 Karl Andriessen, "On 'Intention' in the Definition of Suicide," *Suicide and Life-Threatening Behavior* 36 (October 2006): 533–7.

5 Karl A. Menninger, *Man against Himself* (New York: Harcourt, Brace and Company, 1938), 18. For a restatement and its significance for clinical work, see M.M. Linehan et al., "Reasons for Staying Alive When You Are Thinking of Killing Yourself: The Reasons for Living Inventory," *Journal of Consulting and Practicing Clinical Psychology* 51 (April 1983): 276–86. Also see David A. Jobes and Rachael E. Mann, "Reasons for Living versus Reasons for Dying: Examining the Internal Debate of Suicide," *Suicide and Life-Threatening Behavior* 29 (Summer 1999): 1023.

6 Edwin S. Shneidman, "The Commonalities of Suicide across the Life Span," in *Life Span Perspectives of Suicide: Time-lines in the Suicide Process*, ed. Antoon A. Leenaars (New York: Plenum Press, 1991), 40.

7 A recent comparison of suicide rates in France and Spain by class shows little consistency and suggests that explanations must be sought "in the changing economic and social conditions affecting workers in France and Spain during the 1980s." See Lourdes Lastao et al., "Social Inequality in Suicide Mortality: Spain and France: 1980–1982 and 1988–1990," *Suicide and Life-Threatening Behavior* 36 (February 2006): 117.

8 Jack P. Gibbs and Walter T. Martin, *Status Integration and Suicide: A Sociological Study* (Eugene: University of Oregon Books, 1964), 159.

9 Susan K. Morrissey, *Suicide and the Body Politic in Imperial Russia* (Cambridge: Cambridge University Press, 2006), 149. Morrissey believes that the conventionality of suicide notes still makes them interesting for historians, but in Russia most peasants did not leave written records, and thus she depended on notes written by affluent individuals and notes depicted in fiction.

CHAPTER ONE

1 Thomas Szasz, *Fatal Freedom: The Ethics and Politics of Suicide* (Westport, Conn.: Praeger, 1999), 17.
2 Ty Geltmaker, *Tired of Living: Suicide in Italy from National Unification to World War I, 1860–1915* (New York: Peter Lang, 2002), 27.
3 Karl Gustav Dahlgren, *On Suicide and Attempted Suicide* (Lund: Hakan Ohlssons Boktryckeri, 1945), 1.
4 Ronald W. Maris, in association with Bernard Lazerwitz, *Pathways to Suicide: A Survey of Self-Destructive Behaviors* (Baltimore: Johns Hopkins University Press, 1981), 1.
5 "Auf keinem Gebiete der Moralstatistik giebt es viele und so gründliche Vorarbeiten, wie auf der Selbstmordstatistik." See Alexander von Oettingen, *Die Moralstatistik: Inductiver Nachweis der Gesetzmässigkeit sittlicher Lebensbewegung im Organismus der Menschheit* (Erlangen: Verlag von Andreas Deichert, 1868), 907–8.
6 Anthony Giddens, "The Suicide Problems in French Sociology," *British Journal of Sociology* 16, no. 1 (March 1965): 3.
7 Émile Durkheim, *Suicide: A Study in Sociology*, trans. John A. Saulding and George Simpson, with an introd. by George Simpson (New York: Free Press, 1951), 45.
8 Ibid., 46.
9 Jack D. Douglas, *The Social Meanings of Suicide* (Princeton: Princeton University Press, 1967), 350–83. Douglas provides a brilliant discussion of the troubles with definitions, but he does not take readers by the hand through a subtle, complex argument.
10 A.S.K. Strahan, *Suicide and Insanity: A Physiological and Sociological Study* (London: Swan Sonnenschein and Co., 1893), 63.
11 Gabriel Tarde, *Penal Philosophy*, trans. Rapelje Howell (Boston: Little, Brown, and Co., 1912), 353–4.
12 Jean-Pierre Falret, *De l'hypochondrie et du suicide* (Paris: Crouillebois, 1822), 1–2. For a profile, see Gregory Zilboorg, in collaboration with George W. Henry, *A History of Medical Psychology* (New York: W.W. Norton, 1969; 1st ed., 1941), 395–6.
13 Douglas, *The Social Meanings of Suicide*, 97. Douglas points out a moral taint in the Chicago ecological school of social sciences. The Chicago approach and other American studies are considered in chapter 2 below.
14 Pierre-Egiste Lisle, *Du suicide: Statistique, médecine, histoire et législation* (Paris: J.-B. Baillière, 1856), 11–14, 25.
15 Ibid., 25.

16 Ibid., 482.

17 Henry (Enrico) Morselli, *Suicide: An Essay on Comparative Moral Statistics* (New York: D. Appleton and Co., 1882), 16–35.

18 The relationship of suicide to a criticism of urban and industrial society is explored in Howard I. Kushner, "Suicide, Gender, and the Fear of Modernity in Nineteenth-Century Medical and Social Thought," *Journal of Social History* 26 (Spring 1993): 461–90. A revised and updated version appears as "Suicide, Gender, and the Fear of Modernity," in *Histories of Suicide: International Perspectives on Self-Destruction in the Modern World*, ed. John Weaver and David Wright (Toronto: University of Toronto Press, 2008).

19 Morselli, *Suicide*, 35, 375.

20 Strahan, *Suicide and Insanity*, 66.

21 Stereotyping continued into the twentieth century. See Julie Parle, "'This Painful Subject': Citizens, Subjects and Suicide in Colonial Natal and Zululand," and Andrew M. Fearnley, "Race and the Intellectualizing of Suicide in the American Human Sciences, c. 1950–1975," both in Weaver and Wright, eds., *Histories of Suicide*.

22 Thomas (Tomáš) Masaryk, *Suicide and the Meaning of Civilization*, trans. William B. Weist and Robert B. Batson, with an introd. by Anthony Giddens (Chicago: University of Chicago Press, 1970; first published as *Der Sebstmord als sociale Massenerscheinung der modernen Civilisation* in 1881),.53–8; Durkheim, *Suicide*, 228–39.

23 Adolph Wagner, *Statistik willkührlicher Handlungen: Vergleichende Selbstmordstatistik Europas, nebst einem Abriss der Statistik der Trauungen* (Hamburg: Boyes & Geisler, 1864), xvi.

24 Louis Proal, *Le crime et le suicide passionnels* (Paris: F. Alcan, 1900), passim.

25 Gustave-François Étoc-Demazy, *Recherches statistiques sur le suicide, appliquées à l'hygiène publique et à la medecine légale* (Paris: Germer-Baillière, 1844), 7.

26 Forbes Winslow, *The Anatomy of Suicide* (London: Henrey Benshaw, 1840), vi.

27 Ibid., vi, 265–80.

28 See, for example, Ferdinand Tönnies, *Der Selbstmord in Schleswig-Holstein: Eine Statistisch-Sociologische Studie* (Breslau: Ferdinand Hart, 1927), 30.

29 Geltmaker, *Tired of Living*, 27.

30 Von Oettingen, *Die Moralstatistik*, 908.

31 Susan K. Morrissey, *Suicide and the Body Politic in Imperial Russia* (Cambridge: Cambridge University Press, 2006), 183.

32 Falret, *De l'hypochondrie et du suicide*, 98–104.

33 Ian Hacking, *The Taming of Chance* (Cambridge: Cambridge University Press, 1991), 2.

34 Stephen M. Stigler, "Quételet, Lambert Adolphe Jacques," in *Leading Personalities in Statistical Sciences from the Seventeenth Century to the Present* (New York: John Wiley & Sons, 1997), 64.

35 Hacking, *The Taming of Chance*, 69; Gerd Gigerenzer et al., *The Empire of Chance: How Probability Changed Science and Everyday Life* (Cambridge: Cambridge University Press, 1989), 38–45.

36 Quételet (1835) quoted in Stephen Stigler, *The History of Statistics: The Measurement of Uncertainty before 1900* (Cambridge, Mass.: Belknap Press of Harvard University, 1986), 172.

37 Stigler, *The History of Statistics*, 173.

38 Hacking, *The Taming of Chance*, 130–1.

39 Ibid., 131.

40 Ibid.

41 Adolph Wagner to — Shwanger, 13 October 1869, in *Adolph Wagner: Briefe, Documente, Augenzeugenberichte, 1851–1917*, ed. Heinrich Rubner (Berlin: Duncker & Humbolt, 1978), 75.

42 Wagner, *Statistik willkührlicher Handlungen* , xii–xvii.

43 Gigerenzer et al., *The Empire of Chance*, 50.

44 Von Oettingen, *Die Moralstatistik*, 940.

45 Henry Thomas Buckle, *History of Civilization in England*, vol. 1 (New York: D. Appleton and Co., 1880; first published, 1857), 20.

46 Hacking, *The Taming of Chance*, 125_6; Stigler, *The History of Statistics*, 227.

47 G.H. Knibbs, "Mortality," in Australia, Bureau of Census and Statistics, *Census of the Commonwealth of Australia ... 1911*, vol. 1, *Statistician's Report* (Melbourne: McCarron, Bird, and Co., 1917), 427.

48 Falret, *De l'hypochondrie et du suicide*, 171–2.

49 Lisle, *Du suicide*, 11–12.

50 The best example was an inquiry into suicide written as if it were the edited notes of a scholar contemplating his own suicide and studying the question. It may have been written this way to pass censorship as fiction. It was critical of Brierre de Boismont for collecting data but not discerning the oppressive political life that could drive people to despair. See Edmond Douay, *Le suicide ou la mort voluntaire* (Paris: Décembre-Alonnier, 1870).

51 Jan Goldsmith, *Console and Classify: The French Psychiatric Profession in the Nineteenth Century* (Cambridge: Cambridge University Press, 1987), 158.

52 Ibid., 156.

53 Jean-Étienne-Dominique Esquirol, *Mental Maladies: A Treatise on Insanity*, trans. Raymond de Saussure (New York: Hafner Publishing Co., 1965; reprint of 1845 ed.).

54 Winslow, *The Anatomy of Suicide*, 337.

55 Ibid., 253–69.

56 Claude-Étienne Bourdin, *Du suicide considéré comme maladie* (Batignolles: Imprimerie de Hennuyer et Turpin, 1845), 7–21.

57 Ibid., 53–66.

58 Ian R. Dowbiggin, *Inheriting Madness: Professionalization and Psychiatric Knowledge in Nineteenth-Century France* (Berkeley: University of California Press, 1991), 32.

59 Ibid., 5.

60 Goldstein, *Console and Classify*, 189–90.

61 Falret, *De l'hypochondrie et du suicide*, 139–54.

62 Anthony Giddens, "Introduction," in Masaryk, *Suicide and the Meaning of Civilization*, xxxiii.

63 Falret, *De l'hypochondrie et du suicide*, 5–89.

64 Jean-Baptiste Cazauvieilh, *Du suicide de l'alienation mentale et des crimes contre les personnes, compares dans leurs rapports réciproques* (Paris: J.B. Baillière, 1840), 15–28.

65 Étoc-Demazy, *Recherches statistiques sur le suicide*, 163–92.

66 Proal, *Le crime et le suicide passionnels*, 671.

67 Ibid., 95–7.

68 Lisle, *Du suicide*, 11.

69 A. Brierre de Boismont, *Du suicide et de la folie suicide* (Paris: Librairie Germer Baillière, 1865), iii.

70 Ibid., xiii.

71 Ibid., 539–41.

72 Goldstein, *Console and Classify*, 387.

73 Brierre, *Du suicide et de la folie suicide*, iii–ix.

74 Lisle, *Du suicide*, 205.

75 Brierre, *Du suicide et de la folie suicide*, xv–xvii.

76 Ibid., 244–92.

77 Falret, *De l'hypochondrie et du suicide*, 226–33.

78 Alfred Legoyt reviewed publications from 1839 to 1879 and used their arguments to support his own list of preventive measures, which stressed moral education and censorship of the press and literature. See Legoyt, *Le suicide ancien et moderne: étude historique philosophique, morale et statistique* (Paris: A. Drouin, 1881), 409–29.

79 Cazauvieilh, *Du suicide*, 8, 26.

80 Étoc-Demazy, *Recherches statistiques sur le suicide*, 201–2.

81 Proal, *Le crime et le suicide passionnels*, 672.

82 Winslow, *The Anatomy of Suicide*, 336–7.

83 Wagner, *Statistik willkührlicher Handlungen*, xviii.

84 Masaryk, *Suicide and the Meaning of Civilization*, 86.

85 Ibid. For Masaryk's claim to have advanced a sociological inquiry, see 4–5. His thesis on irreligiosity is repeated often; see 223.

86 Ibid., 113.

87 Ibid., 222–4.

88 Alexander von Oettingen, *Ueber akuten und chronischen Selbstmord: Ein Zeitbild* (Dorpat and Tellin: E.F. Karow's Universitätsbuchhandlung, 1881), 1.

89 Ibid., 7.

90 Ibid., 38.

91 Ibid., 8.

92 Ibid., 52–61.

93 Roger Price, *The French Second Empire* (Cambridge: Cambridge University Press, 2001), 171–209. These pages cover a chapter on "constructing the moral order." See also Sudhir Hazareesingh, *From Subject to Citizen: The Second Empire and the Emergence of French Democracy* (Princeton: Princeton University Press, 1998), 96–161, 306–21.

94 Koenraad W. Swart, *The Sense of Decadence in Nineteenth-Century France* (The Hague: Martinus Nijhoff, 1964), 254.

95 Karl Marx, "Peuchet on Suicide," trans. Eric Plaut, Gabrielle Edgcomb, and Kevin Anderson, in *Marx on Suicide*, ed. Eric A. Plaut and Kevin Anderson (Evanston, Ill.: Northwestern University Press, 1999), 49, 63.

96 August Bebel, *Women in the Past, Present and Future* (London: Zwan Publications, 1988; first published, 1879), 47.

97 Masaryk, *Suicide and the Meaning of Civilization*, 3.

98 The phrase *le courant suicidogène* is from Émile Durkheim, *Le suicide: étude de sociologie* (Paris: Librairie Félix Alcan, 1930, 132. The English translation by Spaulding Simpson is "suicidal current" (Durkheim, *Suicide*, 138), but "suicidogenic current" seems closer to what Durkheim intended. He later bestows upon it the quality of electricity and light: "L'intensité de courants électriques ou de foyers lumineux" (*Le suicide*, 349).

99 On Freud and literature, see Peter Gay, *Freud: A Life for Our Time* (New York: W.W. Norton & Co., 1988), 127–30.

100 Steven Lukes, *Émile Durkheim: His Life and Work: A Historical and Critical Study* (New York: Harper & Row, 1972), 189; Durkheim, *Suicide*, 66.

101 Hugh P. Witt, "Durkheim's Precedence in the Use of the Terms *Altruistic and Egoistic* Suicide: An Addendum," *Suicide and Life-Threatening Behavior* 36 (February 2006): 125–6.

102 Durkheim, *Suicide,* 66–7.

103 Ibid., 59.

104 Ibid., 67–72.

105 Ibid., 145.

106 Ibid., 306.

107 Ibid.,151.

108 Masaryk, *Suicide and the Meaning of Civilization,* 140–1.

109 For a different articulation of the same argument, see Theodore Porter, *The Rise of Statistical Thinking, 1820–1900* (Princeton: Princeton University Press, 1986), 69.

110 Durkheim, *Suicide,* 297–306. The importance of this modification of Quételet has not received the attention it deserves. Although he was no statistician, Durkheim appreciated the importance for his sociology of a shift in interest from the predictability of the mean to the predictability of the outlying cases in a normal distribution.

111 Ibid., 151.

112 Émile Durkheim, *The Rules of the Sociological Method,* trans. Sarah A. Solovay and John H. Mueller; ed. George E.G. Catlin (New York: Free Press, 1964), 7.

113 Durkheim, *Suicide,* 38.

114 Ibid., 299.

115 Ibid., 305.

116 Ibid., 50–1.

117 Giddens, "The Suicide Problem in French Sociology," 5.

118 Jack D. Douglas, a critic, claimed that Durkheim "obviously considered 'society' (or 'the social,' or 'social reality,' etc.) to be the fundamental cause of suicide." See *The Social Meanings of Suicide,* 41. Douglas was "obviously" wrong.

119 Durkheim, *Suicide,* 321.

120 Ibid, 258.

121 Ibid., 234.

122 Ibid., 276.

123 Ibid., 36.

124 Durkheim, *The Rules of the Sociological Method,* 142.

125 Lukes, *Émile Durkheim,* 200; Durkheim, *Suicide,* 277.

126 Durkheim, *Suicide,*151.

127 Ibid., 289–92.

128 Douglas, *The Social Meanings of Suicide*, 73–4.

129 Durkheim, *Suicide*, 51.

130 Ibid., 169–70.

131 Morrissey, *Suicide and the Body Politic in Imperial Russia*, 205.

132 Étoc-Demazy, *Recherches statistiques sur le suicide*, 33–4.

133 Strahan, *Suicide and Insanity*, 50.

134 Maurice Halbwachs, *The Causes of Suicide*, trans. Harold Goldblatt (London: Routledge & Kegan Paul, 1978), 15–25.

135 Buckle, *History of Civilization in England*, 20.

136 Wagner was skeptical about the reported suicides by drowning from Russia. See his *Statistik willkührlicher Handlungen*, 246–8.

137 Falret, *De l'hypochondrie et du suicide*, 16; Étoc-Demazy, *Recherches statistiques sur le suicide*, 63.

138 Lukes, *Émile Durkheim*, 205.

139 Ibid., 81.

140 Ibid., 12.

141 Halbwachs, *The Causes of Suicide*, 329.

142 Howard I. Kushner, *Self-Destruction in the Promised Land: A Psychocultural Biology of American Suicide* (New Brunswick, NJ: Rutgers University Press, 1989), 144.

143 Ibid., 330.

144 Morselli, *Suicide*, 361–2.

145 Ibid., 374.

146 Strahan, *Suicide and Insanity*, 32.

147 Ibid., 65.

148 Ibid., 222.

149 Ibid., vi.

150 Durkheim, *Suicide*, 368.

151 See, for example, Paulo Drinot, "Medico-legal and Popular Interpretations of Suicide in Early Twentieth-Century Lima," in Weaver and Wright, eds., *Histories of Suicide*.

152 Durkheim, *Suicide*, 44.

CHAPTER TWO

1 Andrew F. Henry and James F. Short, *Suicide and Homicide: Some Economic, Sociological and Psychological Aspects of Aggression* (Glencoe, Ill.: Free Press, 1954); Martin Gold, "Suicide, Homicide, and the Socialization of Aggression," *American Journal of Sociology* 63 (May 1958): 651–61; David Lester, "Regional Variations in Suicide and Homicide," *Suicide and*

Life-Threatening Behavior 15 (Summer 1985): 110–15; Antoon A. Leenaars, "Suicide and Homicide Rates in Canada and the United States," *Suicide and Life-Threatening Behavior* 24 (Summer 1994): 184–91.

2 Alvin F. Poussaint and Amy Alexander, *Lay My Burden Down: Unraveling Suicide and the Mental Health Crisis among African-Americans* (Boston: Beacon Press, 2000). Also see Committee on Cultural Psychiatry, Group for the Advancement of Psychiatry, *Suicide and Ethnicity in the United States* (New York: Brunner/Mazel, 1989).

3 World Health Organization, *Suicide and Attempted Suicide,* Public Health Papers, no. 58 (Geneva, 1974).

4 Notable suicidologists from the 1960s to the 1990s include, in alphabetical order, Norman L. Farberow, Jack P. Gibbs, Herbert Hendin, Antoon A. Leenaars, David Lester, John T. Maltsberger, Ronald W. Maris, and Edwin S. Shneidman.

5 Sanford Labovitz, "Variation in Suicide Rates," in *Suicide,* ed. Jack P. Gibbs (New York: Harper & Row, 1968), 65.

6 André Haim, *Adolescent Suicide,* trans. A.M. Sheridan Smith (New York: International Universities Press, 1970), 78–88. This conclusion challenges a major finding in one of the most sophisticated of the modern studies of suicide. See Ronald W. Maris, in association with Bernard Lazerwitz, *Pathways to Suicide: A Survey of Self-Destructive Behaviors* (Baltimore: Johns Hopkins University Press, 1981), 297.

7 See, for example, Leon Yochelson, ed., *Symposium on Suicide* (Washington, DC: George Washington University School of Medicine, 1967). The symposium was sponsored by Wallace Laboratories, which marketed Miltown, the first specific anti-anxiety drug developed in the United States. Its president, F.M Berger, delivered an address on "The Role of Drugs in Suicide," which included a section on drugs that reduced suicidal tendencies.

8 For example, Jack Gibbs cites Henry Garrett, *Statistics in Psychology and Education,* 3rd ed. (New York: Longmans, Green and Co., 1950); Ronald Fisher, *Statistical Methods for Research Workers,* 12th ed. (London: Oliver and Boyd, 1954); Quinn McNemar, *Psychological Statistics* (New York: John Wiley and Sons, 1949). See also Jack Porter Gibbs, "A Sociological Study of Suicide" (PhD thesis, University of Oregon, 1957), 118–50.

9 The trends in research are mirrored in the contents of *Suicide and Life-Threatening Behavior,* which by the 1990s had a heavy representation of statistical studies from authors from various disciplinary backgrounds.

10 Howard I. Kushner, *Self-Destruction in the Promised Land: A Psychocultural Biology of American Suicide* ((New Brunswick, NJ: Rutgers University Press, 1989), 74. For a hostile interpretation of Freudian psychoanalysis in the

United States and a survey history of its rise and fall, see Edward Shorter, *A History of Psychiatry: From the Age of the Asylum to the Age of Prosac* (New York: John Wiley & Sons, 1997), 170–89.

11 David Shaffer cited in feature article on suicide by Robert Mannion in the *Dominion Sunday Times*, 19 February 1989, ABQZ, 16363, YA 1/9/1//2/2, Ministry of Youth Affairs, Archives New Zealand.

12 François Achille-Delmas, *Psychologie pathologique du suicide* (Paris: Librairie Félix Alcan, 1932), 152.

13 Maurice de Fleury, *L'angoisse humaine* (Paris: Les Éditions de France, 1926), 118. On suicide among French soldiers in World War I, see Patricia Prestwich, "Suicide and French Soldiers of the First World War: Differing Perspectives, 1914–1939," in *Histories of Suicide: International Perspectives on Self-Destruction in the Modern World,* ed. John Weaver and David Wright (Toronto: University of Toronto Press, 2008).

14 De Fleury, *L'angoisse humaine,* 115.

15 Ibid., 105.

16 Ibid., 126.

17 Ibid., 136.

18 Achille-Delmas, *Psychologie pathologique du suicide,* 217.

19 De Fleury, *L'angoisse humaine.,* 100–58.

20 Maurice Halbwachs, *The Causes of Suicide,* trans. Harold Goldblatt (London: Routledge & Kegan Paul, 1978), 262.

21 Milton Rosenbaum, chair of the Department of Psychiatry, Albert Einstein Medical College, and director of Psychiatric Services at Bronx Municipal Hospital Center, remarked that "almost all persons who attempt or commit suicide are ill (94 percent psychiatrically ill and 4 percent physically ill, according to one survey)." See Rosenbaum, "Recognition of the Suicidal Individual," quoted in Stanley Yolles, "The Tragedy of Suicide in the United States," in Yochelson, ed., *Symposium on Suicide,* 77. On the defence of de Fleury, see Achille-Delmas, *Psychologie pathologique du suicide,* 217.

22 Edwin Shneidman, *Definition of Suicide* (New York: John Wiley & Sons, 1985), 29.

23 Kushner, *Self-Destruction in the Promised Land,* 74.

24 Martin Bulmer, *The Chicago School of Sociology: Institutionalization, Diversity, and the Rise of Sociological Research* (Chicago: University of Chicago Press, 1984), 1–7, 89–94, 155–63.

25 Ruth Shonle Cavan, *Suicide* (New York: Russell & Russell, 1965; first published, 1928). Out of fifty-five cases that Cavan discusses, twenty-eight involved women who committed suicide. Also see her comments about the family on 323–4.

26 Ibid., 218.

27 Ibid., 333.

28 Jack D. Douglas, *The Social Meanings of Suicide* (Princeton: Princeton University Press, 1967), 96–100; Kushner, *Self-Destruction in the Promised Land*, 65.

29 Cavan, *Suicide*, 77–105.

30 Ibid., 331.

31 Ibid., 330.

32 Ibid., 81.

33 Ibid., Preface, n.p.

34 Ibid.

35 Ibid.

36 Ibid., 179.

37 Ibid., 196.

38 Howard Kushner proposes that Cavan was tripped up by attempting "to employ social statistics to uncover social meaning." See Kushner, *Self-Destruction in the Promised Land*, 66. I think she was aware of the difficulty and tried to resolve it with the case studies. Like Brierre de Boismont, she lacked the computing power to manipulate case studies.

39 Cavan, *Suicide*, 289.

40 Douglas, *The Social Meanings of Suicide*, 99–100.

41 On psychology, see Kurt Danziger, *Constructing the Subject: Historical Origins of Psychological Research* (Cambridge: Cambridge University Press, 1990), 24–48. On psychiatry, see Karen Kaplan-Solms and Mark Solms, *Clinical Studies in Neuro-psychoanalysis: Introduction to a Depth Neuropsychology* (London and New York: Karnac Books, 2000), 3–42.

42 Kushner, *Self-Destruction in the Promised Land*, 79.

43 Cavan, *Suicide*, 33.

44 Kushner, *Self-Destruction in the Promised Land*, 162–3.

45 William Cronon, *Nature's Metropolis: Chicago and the Great West* (New York: W.W. Norton & Co., 1991). All chapters convey this theme, but see especially chapter 5.

46 Some of Cavan's case histories recount histories of migration. See Cavan, *Suicide,* cases I, II, III, IV, V, VI, VIII, IX, X, XXX, XXXII, XL, XLII, XLIV, and LII.

47 Calvin F. Schmid, "Suicides in Seattle, 1914–1925: An Ecological and Behavioristic Study," *University of Washington, Publications in the Social Sciences* 5, no. 1 (October 1928): 1–93; the quotation is from Schmid, *Social Saga of Two Cities: An Ecological and Statistical Study of Social Trends in Minneapolis and St. Paul* (Minneapolis: Bureau of Social Research, Minneapolis Council of Social Agencies, 1937), 380.

48 Calvin F. Schmid et al., *Social Trends in Seattle* (Seattle: University of Washington Press, 1944; reprint, Greenwood Press, 1969), 215.

49 Ibid., 378.

50 Calvin F. Schmid, *Suicide in Seattle, 1914 to 1925: An Ecological and Behavioristic Study* (Seattle: University of Washington Press, 1928), 1, 25–65.

51 Rev. Kenneth B. Murphy, "Community Action in the Prevention of Suicide: Rescue, Inc., Boston, Massachusetts," in Yochelson, ed., *Symposium on Suicide*, 139.

52 Ronald Maris wrote, "I hesitate to call Ruth S. Cavan's *Suicide* representative of the sociological approach ... because her study is more descriptive than analytical." See Ronald William Maris, "Suicide in Chicago: An Examination of Emile Durkheim's Theory of Suicide" (PhD thesis, University of Illinois, 1965), 51.

53 Cavan, *Suicide*, 148.

54 Jack Douglas was likewise amazed and remarked that Cavan was rare in that she saw that individuals within the same socio-cultural system imputed "different normative meanings to suicidal actions." See Douglas, *The Social Meanings of Suicide*, 107.

55 Halbwachs, *The Causes of Suicide*, 264.

56 Ibid., 265.

57 Peter Sainsbury, *Suicide in London: An Ecological Study* (London: Institute of Psychiatry, 1955), 26.

58 Ibid., 24.

59 Ibid., 89–92.

60 Gibbs, "A Sociological Study of Suicide," 13–99.

61 Ibid., 118–59.

62 Ibid., 200.

63 Ibid., 168.

64 Gibbs discussed various types of integration theory and studies. Ibid., 161–9.

65 Jack P. Gibbs and Walter T. Martin, *Status Integration and Suicide: A Sociological Study* (Eugene: University of Oregon Books, 1964), 25–6.

66 Gibbs, "A Sociological Study of Suicide," 174.

67 Ibid., 422.

68 Gibbs and Martin, *Status Integration and Suicide*, 197.

69 Ibid., 213–35 238–54.

70 William A. Rushing, "Individual Behaviour and Suicide," in Gibbs, ed., *Suicide*, 96–121; Herbert Hendin, "The Psychodynamics of Suicide," ibid., 133–50.

71 Stephen Senn, *Dicing with Death: Chance, Risk and Health* (Cambridge: Cambridge University Press, 2003), 26–90.

72 Maris, "Suicide in Chicago," 221.

73 Warren Breed, "Occupational Mobility and Suicide among White Males," *American Sociological Review* 28 (April 1963): 179–188; T.L. Dorpat and H.S. Ripley, "Study of Suicide in the Seattle Area," *Comparative Psychiatry* 1 (1960): 349-59.

74 Gibbs, "Introduction," in Gibbs, ed., *Suicide*, 28.

75 Douglas, *The Social Meanings of Suicide*, 86–91.

76 Kushner, *Self-Destruction in the Promise Land*, 74–5.

77 Ibid., 75.

78 Karl Menninger, *Man against Himself* (New York: Harcourt, Brace and Co., 1938), 16.

79 Karl Menninger, "Psychoanalytic Aspects of Suicide," in *A Psychiatrist's World: The Selected Papers of Karl Menninger, M.D.*, ed. Bernard M. Hall (New York: Viking Press, 1959), 330–1.

80 Ibid., 332.

81 Howard J, Faulkner and Virginia D. Pruitt, eds, *The Selected Correspondence of Karl A. Menninger, 1919–1945* (New Haven: Yale University Press, 1988), 11; Menninger, "The Amelioration of Mental Disease by Influenza," in Hall, ed., *A Psychiatrist's World*, 156–66.

82 Faulkner and Pruitt, eds., *The Selected Correspondence of Karl A. Menninger*, 6.

83 See the definitions in Jean Laplanche and J.-B. Pontalis, *The Language of Psychoanalysis*, trans. Daniel Lagache (New York: W.W. Norton & Co., 1973).

84 Faulkner and Pruitt, eds., *The Selected Correspondence of Karl A. Menninger*,, 345. Freud approved of Menninger's interest in the death instinct, which he felt had become unpopular among analysts. See Freud to Menninger, 14 February 1938, in Faulkner and Pruitt, ed., *The Selected Correspondence of Karl A. Menninger*, 258.

85 Sigmund Freud, "Mourning and Melancholia," in *The Standard Edition of the Complete Works of Sigmund Freud*, vol. 14, *On the History of the Psycho-analytic Movement and Other Works*, trans. under the general editorship of James Strachey (London: Hogarth Press and the Institute of Psychoanalysis, 1975; 1st ed., 1957), 243–58. Also see Peter Gay, *Freud: A Life for Our Time* (New York: W.W. Norton & Co., 1988), 372–3.

86 Faulkner and Pruitt, eds., *The Selected Correspondence of Karl A. Menninger*, 333.

87 Ibid., 334–5; Menninger, *Man against Himself*, 17–83.

88 Faulkner and Pruitt, eds., *The Selected Correspondence of Karl A. Menninger*, 337-40.

89 Joel Paris, *The Fall of an Icon: Psychoanalysis and Academic Psychiatry* (Toronto: University of Toronto Press, 2005), 185.

90 Menninger, *Man against Himself*, 124 and 126.

91 Ibid., 57.

92 Ibid., 70 and 75, for example.

93 Elizabeth Kirkpatrick, "A Psychoanalytic Understanding of Suicide," in Gibbs, ed., *Suicide*, 154.

94 Ibid.

95 Menninger, *Man against Himself*, 87–350.

96 Ibid., 357.

97 Ibid., 361.

98 Peter D. Kramer, *Against Depression* (New York: Penguin Books, 2005), 60–1.

99 Quoted in Stanley Yolles, "The Tragedy of Suicide in the United States," in Yochelson, ed. *Symposium on Suicide*, 17–18.

100 Thomas Szasz, *The Myth of Mental Illness: Foundations of a Theory of Personal Conduct* (New York: Harper & Row, 1974; 1st ed., 1961), 39–41. The quotation appears on 40.

101 Kramer, *Against Depression*, 49.

102 Norman L. Farberow, Edwin S. Shneidman, and Charles Neuringer, "Case History and Hospitalization Factors in Suicides of Neuropsychiatirc Hospital Patients," in Gibbs, ed., *Suicide*, 177–8.

103 Kurt Danziger, *Constructing the Subject: Historical Origins of Psychological Research* (Cambridge: Cambridge University Press, 1990), 73–87.

104 Farberow et al., "Case History and Hospitalization Factors," 194.

105 Emma Evans, "The Prevelence of Suicidal Phenomena in Adolescents: A Systematic Review of Population-Based Studies," *Suicide and Life-Threatening Behavior* 35 (June 2005): 23–48. For an example of a population study of suicide ideation, see Ted Miller, "Adolescent Suicidality: Who Will Ideate, Who Will Act?" *Suicide and Life-Threatening Behavior* 35 (August 2005): 425–33.

106 William Rushing, "Individual Behaviour and Suicide," in Gibbs, ed., *Suicide*, 99–100.

107 Douglas put these comments in his doctoral thesis: Jack Daniel Douglas, "The Sociological Study of Suicide: Suicidal Actions as Socially Meaningful Actions" (PhD thesis, Princeton University, 1965), 543.

108 Douglas, *The Social Meanings of Suicide*, 338.

109 Ibid., 339–40.

110 Ibid., 340.

111 Ibid., 273.

112 Ibid., 286–7. See Douglas's discussion of the difficulty with definitions of suicide, ibid., 350–83.

113 Ibid., 288–300.

114 Ibid., 302–19.

115 Kushner, *Self-Destruction in the Promised Land*, 69.

116 Ibid., 72.

117 Antoon A. Leenaars, *Suicide Notes: Predictive Clues and Patterns* ((New York: Human Sciences Press, 1988), 211. To gain some insights, David Lester assembled and discussed a set of suicides and attempted suicides by literary figures. See Lester, *Understanding Suicide: A Case Study Approach* (Cormac, NY: Nova Science Publishers, 1993).

118 Maris, *Pathways to Suicide*, xviii.

119 Ibid., 2.

120 Ronald W. Maris, *Social Forces in Urban Suicide* (Homewood, Ill.: Dorsey Press, 1969), 188.

121 Ibid., 177–82.

122 Ibid., 183–9.

123 Ibid., 293.

124 Ibid., 291.

125 Ibid., 290.

126 Ibid., 67.

127 Ibid., 11-15.

128 Ibid., 16-22.

129 For Kushner's assessment, see *Self-Destruction in the Promised Land*, 70–2.

130 Ibid., 313.

131 Herbert Hendin, *Suicide in America: New and Expanded Edition* (New York: W.W. Norton, 1995), 86.

132 Ibid., 87.

133 Roger Blashfield, *The Classification of Psychopathology: Neo-Kraepelinian and Quantitative Approaches* (New York: Plenum Press, 1984), 1–20. Also see Emil Kraeplin, *Memoirs*, ed. H. Hippus et al., trans. Cheryl Wooding-Deane (Berlin: Springer-Verlag, 1987), 43–4, 156–9.

134 Kushner, *Self-Destruction in the Promised Land*, 166.

135 Ibid.

136 For a review of the third edition that discusses the challenges of classification and of adding new syndromes, see Gary L. Tischler, ed., *Diagnosis and Classification in Psychiatry: A Critical Appraisal of DSM-III* (Cambridge: Cambridge University Press, 1987). Also see Blashfield, *The Classification of Psychopathology*, 263–6.

137 Blashfield, *The Classification of Psychopathology*, 19–22; Peter McGuffin and Anne E. Farmer, "Are There Phenotype Problems?" in *Psychopathology in the Genome and Neurosciences Era*, ed. Charles F. Zorumski and Eugene H. Rubin (Washington, D C: American Psychiatric Publishing, 2005), 66–8.

138 Samuel H. Barondes, *Mood Genes: Hunting for Origins of Mania and Depression* (New York: W. H. Freeman and Co., 1998), 61.

139 McGuffin and Farmer, "Are There Phenotype Problems?" 69.

140 John T. Maltsberger, *Suicide Risk: The Formulation of Clinical Judgment* (New York: New York University Press, 1986), Appendix B.

141 Elyn R. Saks, *The Centre Cannot Hold: My Journey through Madness* (New York: Hyperion, 2007), 304.

142 Edwin E. Shneidman, *Essays in Self-Destruction* (New York: Science House, Inc., 1967), 35–6. Also see his discussion of dichotomous thinking, 139–42, and on prevention, 225–35.

143 Kramer, *Against Depression*, 168.

144 Ibid., 207.

145 Kushner, *Self-Destruction in the Promised Land*, 177.

146 Dean Hamer and Peter Copeland, *Living with Our Genes: Why They Matter More than You Think* (New York: Doubleday, 1998), 121.

147 Kramer, *Against Depression*, 133.

148 Ari Kiev, "Suicide Prevention," in *Identifying Suicide Potential*, ed. Dorothy B. Anderson and Lenora J. McLean (New York: Behavioral Publications, 1971), 4–5; Shneidman, "Preface," in *Essays in Self-Destruction*, ix–x.

149 See the essays in Norman L. Farberow, ed., *The Many Faces of Suicide: Indirect Self-Destructive Behavior* (New York: McGraw-Hill Book Co., 1980). For short summaries of studies of suicide in a variety of disciplines, see David Lester, *Thinking about Suicide: Perspectives on Suicide* (New York: Nova Science Publications, 2004). Lester also has co-edited a collection of lucid studies on a variety of screening, assessment, and therapy practices: Robert I. Yufit and David Lester, eds., *Assessment, Treatment, and Prevention of Suicidal Behavior* (Hoboken, NJ: John Wiley & Sons, 2005).

150 To review the content patterns of hundreds of suicide books, I used EndNote software to collect all titles on the subject of suicide published in New York, Chicago, Boston, and Los Angeles. Next I organized them by date of publication and read the brief notes on content when these were available. The method is imprecise and impressionistic, but I would stand by the results. For an example of scholarly research in the vein, see Brian Mishra, "Conceptions of Death and Suicide in Children Ages 6–12 and their Implications for Suicide Prevention," *Suicide and Life-Threatening Behavior* 29 (Summer 1999): 105–18.

151 Roger Lane, *Violent Death in the City: Suicide, Accident, and Murder in Nineteenth-Century Philadelphia* (Cambridge, Mass.: Harvard University Press, 1975).

152 Kenneth M. Pinnow, "Violence against the Collective Self: Suicide and the Problem of Social Integration in Early Bolshevik Russia," in Weaver and Wright, eds., *Histories of Suicide.*

153 Andrew M. Fearney, "Race and the Intellectualizing of Suicide in the American Human Sciences, circa 1950–1975," ibid.; Junko Kitanaka, "Questioning the Suicide of Resolve: Medico-legal Disputes Regarding 'Overwork Suicide' in Twentieth-Century Japan," ibid.. On ethno-methodology, see Maxwell Atkinson, "Some Cultural Aspects of Suicide in Britain," in *Suicide in Different Cultures,* ed. Norman L. Farberow (Baltimore: University Park Press, 1975), 156–8.

154 Douglas, *The Social Meanings of Suicide,* 168–283.

155 Georges Minois, *History of Suicide: Voluntary Death in Western Culture,* trans. Lydia G. Cochrane (Baltimore: Johns Hopkins University Press, 1999), 313.

156 Éric Volant et al., *Adeiu, la vie: Étude des derniers messages laissés par des suicides* (Montréal: Éditions Bellarmin, 1990), 305.

157 Leenaars, *Suicide Notes,* 181–2.

158 Olive Anderson, *Suicide in Victorian and Edwardian England* (Oxford: Clarendon Press, 1987), 13.

159 Ibid., 418–19.

160 Simon John Cooke, "Secret Sorrows: A Social History of Suicide in Victoria, 1841–1921" (PhD dissertation, University of Melbourne, 1998), 415–16.

161 Kevin Siena, "Suicide as an Illness Strategy in the Long Eighteenth Century," in Weaver and Wright, eds., *Histories of Suicide.*

162 Victor Bailey, *This Rash Act: Suicide across the Life Cycle in the Victorian City* (Stanford, Calif.: Stanford University Press, 1998), 31.

163 Ibid., 32.

164 Ibid., 234–5.

165 Myrna Dawson, "Intimate Femicide Followed by Suicide: Examining the Role of Premeditation," *Suicide and Life-Threatening Behavior* 35 (February 2005): 76–89; Laura E. Lund and Svetlana Smorodinsky, "Violent Death among Intimate Partners: A Comparison of Homicide and Homicide Followed by Suicide in California," *Suicide and Life-Threatening Behavior* 31 (Winter 2001): 451–8; Rosemary Gartner and Bill McCarthy, "Twentieth-Century Trends in Homicide Followed by Suicide in Four North American Cities," in Weaver and Wright, eds., *Histories of Suicide.*

166 Kushner, *Self-Destruction in the Promised Land*, xiv.

167 James Gilbert, *Another Chance: Postwar America, 1945–1968* (New York: Alfred A. Knopf, 1981), 8.

168 "Eisenhower Is Firm for Middle of Road," *New York Times*, 28 July 1960, 1. For follow-up on the controversy begun by President Eisenhower's remarks, see *New York Times*, 6 August 1960, 18; Werner Wiskari, "Rejoiner to Sweden's Critics," *New York Times*, 23 October 1960, SM61–6.

169 According to one recent study, the suicide risk in major depression is estimated to be twenty times greater than expected in the general population, and suicide ideation is widespread in psychiatric patients. See Marko Sorvaniemi, "Recorded Suicidality among Patients with Major Depression in Psychiatric Outpatient Care in Finland (1989–2001)," *Suicide and Life-Threatening Behavior* 35 (December 2005): 605.

170 Maris, *Pathways to Suicide*, 297–303.

171 Douglas, *The Social Meanings of Suicide*, 251–4.

172 Ibid., 340.

173 Bailey, *This Rash Act*, 29.

CHAPTER THREE

1 The comparison of national rates has long been acknowledged as notoriously unreliable. See the remarks of Edwin Stengel in "National Cultural Aspects of Suicide and Attempted Suicide," in *Symposium on Suicide*, ed. Leon Yochelson (Washington, DC: George Washington University School of Medicine, 1967), 39–41, and the remarks of Sanford Labovitz in "Variation in Suicide Rates," in *Suicide*, ed. Jack P. Gibbs (New York: Harper & Row, 1968), 58–9. For longer assessments, see Jack D. Douglas, *The Social Meanings of Suicide* (Princeton: Princeton University Press, 1967), 163–231.

2 Jack P. Gibbs, "A Sociological Study of Suicide" (PhD thesis, University of Oregon, 1957), 23.

3 Frederick Cooper, with Rogers Brubaker, "Identity," in Cooper, *Colonialism in Question: Theory, Knowledge, History* (Berkeley: University of California Press, 2005), 59–90.

4 Jack P. Gibbs undertook an early exploration of age and martial status to test Durkheim's theory of integration. See Gibbs, "A Sociological Study of Suicide," 273–342.

5 Margaret Soper, *Coroners* (Wellington: Butterworths, 1996), 3–54. For a first-hand account, see Edwin Arnold, "Inquests," in "Unpublished Autobiography," 97, MS-Papers-7237-26, Alexander Turnbull Library, National Library of New Zealand.

6 For a discussion of problems with this method, and by extension problems with inquests, see Alian D. Lesgae et al., "Suicide and Mental Disorders: A Case-Control Study of Young Men," *American Journal of Psychology* 151 (July 1994): 1066; and Louise Pouliot et al., "Critical Issues in Psychological Autopsy Studies," *Suicide and Life-Threatening Behavior* 35 (October 2006): 491–504. Both mention the passage of time and the emotional state of the informants. The latter applies to inquest witnesses.

7 Jerome Kagan, *An Argument for Mind* (New Haven: Yale University Press, 2006), 46.

8 Walter Morgenthaler quoted in Udo Grashoff, *Let Me Finish* (New York: Thunder's Mouth Press, 2004), 8.

9 Olive Bennewith et al., "The Usefulness of Coroners' Data on Suicides for Providing Information Relevant to Prevention," *Suicide and Life-Threatening Behavior* 35 (December 2005): 607–13.

10 Jack P. Gibbs and Walter T. Martin, *Status Integration and Suicide: A Sociological Study* (Eugene: University of Oregon Books, 1964), 160.

11 Sub-inspector A.E. Shersby, "Coroners' Inquests," *Police Educational Series*, no. 42, file A/44822, Department of Justice, Queensland State Archives (QSA).

12 For the Dulcie Barclay affair, see *The Truth*, 1 September 1929, 15; 20 October 1929, 17; "The Office of Coroner," *Brisbane Courier*, 2 January 1930, 9; Queensland, *Official Record of the Debates of the Legislative Assembly during the Twenty-fifth Parliament [21 George V]*, vol. 155 (Brisbane: Government Printer, 1930), 578; vol. 156, 1317–18; *Official Record of the Debates of the Legislative Assembly during the Twenty-ninth Parliament [6 and 7 George VI* (Brisbane: Government Printer, 1943), vol. 180, 1763–5, 1809–11; An Act to Amend the Coroners Act of 1930 in Certain Particulars [22 April 1943], 7 Geo. VI, no. 8, in Queensland, *Acts of the Parliament of Queensland, 6 and 7 George VI, 1942–1943* (Brisbane: Government Printer, 1943), section 2A.

13 P.L. Carlew and Simpson, Solicitors, to the Under Secretary, Department of Justice, 9 October 1941; Sergeant Pilkington, Roma Street Station, to the Inspector of Police, 27 October 194; Memorandum, Commissioner of Police, to District Officers in Charge of Stations in the City of Brisbane, 27 September 1943, A/44823, Department of Justice, 1940-1956, Coroners' Inquests, QSA.

14 "Coroners," in *The Public Acts of New Zealand (Reprint), 1908–1931*, H. Alleyn Palmer, managing editor (Wellington: Government Printer, 1932), vol. 2: 31–44; Coroners Act 1951, *The Statutes of New Zealand, 1951* (Wellington: Government Printer, 1952, vol. 1 (1951), no. 73, 466–78.

15 See An Act to Abolish Coroners' Juries and to Empower Justices of the Peace to Hold Inquests of Death [17 July 1866], 30 Vic., no. 3, *Acts of the Parliament of Queensland, 30 Victoriae, 1866* (Brisbane: Government Printer, 1866).

16 The record designation is by file number followed by the year in which that file was created. Thus Justice Department, Coroners' Inquests (hereafter J 46), file 693, in 1924 is 693/1924, followed by the name of the deceased. All J 46 files are held in the Wellington repository of Archives New Zealand. For the quotation, see J 46, 693/1924, Philip Pentecost.

17 Jack Gibbs reported on the same circumstances. See Gibbs and Martin, *Status Integration and Suicide*, 160. For a study of official and actual numbers in another jurisdiction, see the examination of coroners' files for Dublin: Traolac Brugha and Dermot Walsh, "Suicide Past and Present – The Temporal Constancy of Under-reporting," *British Journal of Psychiatry* 132 (1978): 177–9.

18 Ian Hacking, *The Taming of Chance* (Cambridge, New York: Cambridge University Press, 1990), 66; Roger Lane, *Violent Death in the City: Suicide, Accident, and Murder in Nineteenth-Century Philadelphia* (Cambridge, Mass.: Harvard University Press, 1979), 19. For an early discussion, see Gustave-François Étoc-Demazy, *Recherches statistiques sur le suicide, appliquées à l'hygiène publique et à la medicine légale* (Paris: Germer-Baillière, 1844), 150.

19 Douglas, *The Social Meanings of Suicide*, 182–190.

20 World Health Organization, Regional Office of Europe, *Changing Patterns of Suicide Behaviour* (Copenhagen: WHO Regional Office for Europe, 1982), 15–19.

21 Frances Krsinich, "Statistical Institutions: Early Official Statistics in New Zealand," in *A History of Statistics in New Zealand*, ed. H.S. Roberts (Wellington: New Zealand Statistical Association, 2000), 9–15.

22 "Industry: Explanatory Introduction," in Australia, *Census of the Commonwealth of Australia, 30th June, 1933: Statistician's Report* (Canberra: F. Johnston, Commonwealth Government Printer, 1938), 214.

23 Erik Olssen and Maureen Hickey, *Class and Occupation: The New Zealand Reality* (Dunedin: University of Otago Press, 2005), 29–114. Also see Appendix 2 in Miles Fairburn and Erik Olssen, eds, *Class, Gender and the Vote: Historical Perspectives from New Zealand* (Dunedin: University of Otago, 2005), 235–8.

24 Paul Baker, *King and Country: New Zealanders, Conscription and the Great War* (Auckland: Auckland University Press, 1988), Appendix 3, 242.

25 "Ex-Soldiers Rehabilitation Commission," *Appendix to the Journals of the House of Representatives*, vol. 3, H-35 (Wellington: Government Printer,

1936), 6. Information was collected on war pensions but not on actual need. See New Zealand, *Population Census, 1936, Appendix B, War Service* (Wellington: Government Printer, 1938), 9.

26 JUS/N777/212, Olof Pearson.

27 Gibbs, "A Sociological Study of Suicide," 67. The entire thesis is predicated on the need for a general theory of variability in suicide rates among different populations. Nowhere does Gibbs suggest that variation may be wholly or partly due to an array of historical circumstances, including demography, economic structure, social policies, religions, and cultural differences.

28 For the diversity of tables, C.J.L. Murray et al., "WHO System of Model Life Tables," GPE Discussion Paper Series, no. 8, EIP/GPE/EBD (World Health Organization, 2003), 1-33; and Mitsuo Segi, *Cancer Mortality Statistics in Japan, 1990-1954* (Nagoyo: Segi Institute of Cancer Epidemiology, 1954), 40. For the value but also the arbitrariness of normalization tables, see "Comparison between Registries: Age Standardized Rates," in John Waterhouse et al., *Cancer Incidence in Five Continents* (Lyons: International Agency for Research on Cancer, 1976), 453-9.

29 After cases with missing ages were assigned, normalization proceeded. Both gender-specific and overall rates were calculated. The former was established by calculating the percentages of population for standard age cohorts for men and women separately. These percentages were divided into the Segi percentage for the same cohort. The resulting adjustment figure for each cohort was multiplied by the number of suicides in that cohort to compute the number of suicides that would have occurred had the population been distributed according to the Segi table. The normalized rate of suicide was then calculated for each cohort using population figures for cohorts. That produced age-cohort and gender rates. To establish an overall normalized rate, the same process was employed but without separation into men and women. To avoid small numbers in some cohorts, rates were calculated for a decade with the population figure taken as the mean of the two census figures closest to the start and end of the decade.

30 For graph 3.5, the crude rates by gender for Queensland used data reported in the *Queensland Yearbook*. No data was available from that source for 1932 to 1942. The data permit a comparison of Queensland and New Zealand for the war and postwar years. For graph 3.6, the Queensland data used for normalization had to come from the case files. Because there were gaps in the 1920s and files were not reliable after 1942, the line has breaks.

31 An Australian study reported that when both the federal government and the New South Wales state government were conservative, the relative risk of suicide for men in the state was 1.17 (p<0.001) and for women 1.40

(p<o.oo1), compared with under Labor (1.00). The authors related social democratic polices to Durkheim's theory of integration. See A. Page, S. Morrell, and R. Taylor, "Suicide and Political Regime in New South Wales and Australia during the 20th Century," *Journal of Epidemiology and Community Health* 56 (2002): 766–72. Case files might have provided a better understanding of the relationship of despair, economics, and politics.

32 Michael Bassett, *The State in New Zealand, 1840–1984* (Auckland: Auckland University Press, 1998), 85–90.

33 J 46, 399/1906, Patrick McCormack.

34 JUS/N1086/864, John Ryan.

35 Jean Giles-Sims and Charles Lockhart, "Explaining Cross-State Differences in Elderly Suicide Rates and Identifying State-Level Public Policy Responses that Reduce Rates," *Suicide and Life-Threatening Behavior* 36 (December 2006): 704. Also see David Lester and Bijou Yang, "Social and Economic Correlates of the Elderly Suicide Rate," *Suicide and Life-Threatening Behavior* 22 (Spring 1992): 45.

36 Bassett, *The State in New Zealand*, 93.

37 David Hamer, *The New Zealand Liberals: The Years of Power, 1891–1912* (Auckland: Auckland University Press, 1988), 60–1.

38 Peter J. Coleman, *Progressivism and the World of Reform: New Zealand and the Origins of the American Welfare State* (Lawrence: University of Kansas Press, 1987), 31.

39 JUS/N1012/359, James King.

40 JUS/N783/529, Robert Lynn.

41 JUS/N747/712, Charles Phillips.

42 For an account of sheep-shearing, see Stuart Svenson, *The Shearers' War: The Story of the 1891 Shearers' Strike* (St Lucia: University of Queensland Press, 1989), 41–7. Also see Denis J. Murphy, ed., *The Big Strikes: Queensland, 1889–1965* (St Lucia: University of Queensland Press, 1983), 80–98, 144–59, 202–15.

43 D.J. Murphy, "Thomas Joseph Ryan; Big and Broad-minded," in *The Premiers of Queensland*, ed. Denis Murphy, Roger Joyce, Margaret Cribb, and Rae Wear (St Lucia: University of Queensland, 2003), 81–92; Murphy, "Edward Granville Theodore," ibid., 117–23; Brian Carroll, "William Forgan Smith,: Dictator or Democrat," ibid., 218–43.

44 JUS/N1144/274, Adam Morrow; clipping from *Telegraph*, 7/7/44. Also see the police investigation, which notes that Morrow had often been arrested for drunk and disorderly conduct: Justice Department, Police Investigations into violent deaths, JUS/Y10, Adam Morrow.

45 The process for application, the police review of the character of the appli-
    cants, and asylum conditions are described in letters held in A/45339, Police
    Commissioner's Correspondence, Benevolent Asylum (Dunwich) and Even-
    tide Home Sandgate, 1931–1959, QSA.

46 J 46, 1784/1900, Edward Thomas.

47 J 46, 919/1900, John Chorley.

48 The casual labourers, who carried a bedroll or swag when they tramped the
    countryside for employment.

49 Edwin Arnold, "People Nobody Wants," 1–28, and "No Friends, No
    Home," 1–7, in "Unpublished Autobiography," MS-Papers-7237-25,
    Turnbull Library.

50 J 46, 200/1916, James McKay.

51 JUS/N782/465, Unknown.

52 Michael King, "Between Two Worlds," in *The Oxford History of New Zea-
    land*, ed. Geoffrey W. Rice, 2nd ed. (Auckland: Oxford University Press,
    1992), 312.

53 Ross Fitzgerald, *A History of Queensland from 1915 to the 1980s* (St Lucia:
    University of Queensland Press, 1982), 204.

54 Sheridan Gundry, *Making a Killing: A History of the Gisborne-East Coast
    Freezing Works Industry* (Gisborne: Tairawhiti Museum, 2004).

55 M. Murphy, "Agriculture in New Zealand," in *The New Zealand Year-Book,
    1902* (Wellington: Government Printer, 1902), 539.

56 George A. Duncan, *The New Zealand Dairy Industry* (Palmerston North,
    New Zealand: H.L. Young Publishers, 1933), 3; Ossie Collinson, *Dairy Fac-
    tories of the South* (Bluff, New Zealand: Craig Publishing, 2000), 5–140.

57 Gerald T. Bloomfield, *New Zealand: A Handbook of Historical Statistics*
    (Boston: G.K. Hall & Co., 1984), tables V.3, V.4, V.8 and figure VII-1;
    Duncan, *The New Zealand Dairy Industry*, 240; W.M. Hamilton, *The Dairy
    Industry in New Zealand* (Wellington: Government Printer, 1944), 107.

58 Hamilton, *The Dairy Industry in New Zealand*, 101.

59 Tom Brooking, "Economic Transformation," in Rice, ed., *The Oxford
    History of New Zealand*, 230.

60 S.H. Franklin, "The Village and the Bush: The Evolution of Village Commu-
    nities," in *Social Process in New Zealand: Readings in Sociology*, ed. John
    Forster (Auckland: Longman Paul, 1969), 109–20.

61 Hamilton, *The Dairy Industry in New Zealand*, 5–9.

62 For a first-hand account, see Jim Gasteen, *Under the Mulga: A Bush Memoir*
    (St Lucia: University of Queensland Press, 2005), 117–22.

63 Commonwealth of Australia, *Labour Report, 1951* (Canberra: Common-
    wealth Statistician, 1952), 118.

64 Raymond Evans, *A History of Queensland* (Melbourne: Cambridge University Press, 2007), 180–3.

65 Ibid., 183.

66 Bassett, *The State in New Zealand*, 102.

67 Erik Olssen, "Towards a New Society," in Rice, ed., *The Oxford History of New Zealand*, 255–9.

68 Charlotte Macdonald, "Too Many Men and Too Few Women: Gender's 'Fatal Impact' in Nineteenth-Century Colonies," in *The Gendered Kiwi*, ed. Caroline Daley and Deborah Montgomerie (Auckland: Auckland University Press, 1999), 32.

69 Robert Chapman, "From Labour to National," in Rice, ed., *The Oxford History of New Zealand*, 357.

70 H.C.D. Somerset, *Littledene: Patterns of Social Change* (Wellington: New Zealand Council for Edicational Research, 1974), 19–20.

71 Tim Frank, "Bread Queues and Breadwinners: Gender in the 1930s," in Daley and Montgomerie, eds., *The Gendered Kiwi*, 132.

72 There were 60,000 Australians killed in World War I and 45,000 in World War II. See Wray Vamplew, ed., *Australians Historical Statistics* (Collingwood, Victoria: Fairfax, Syme, and Weldon Associates, 1987), 441.

73 Melanie Nolan, *Breadwinning: New Zealand Women and the State* (Christchurch: University of Canterbury Press, 2000), 206–29.

74 Miles Fairburn and S.J. Haslett, "Stability and Egalitarianism: New Zealand, 1911–1951," in Fairburn and Olssen, eds., *Class, Gender and the Vote*, 30.

75 *Labour 1951*, 51 and 118.

76 Male rates may generally be more volatile than female rates. See W. Clifford and J. Marjoram, *Suicide in South Australia* (Canberra: Australian Institute of Criminology, 1979), 26.

77 "Lunatic Asylums of the Colony," *Appendix to the Journals of the House of Representatives of New Zealand, 1901*, vol. 4, H-7 (Wellington: Government Printer, 1901), 1–21. On Ashburn Hall, see Alan Somerville, "Ashburn Hall, 1882–1904"; Caroline Hubbard, "Seacliff and Ashburn Hall Compared"; and Judith Clare Medlicott, "Ashburn Hall, 1905–1947"; in *"Unfortunate Folk": Essays on Mental Health Treatment, 1863–1992*, ed. Barbara Brookes and Jane Thomson (Dunedin: University of Otago Press, 2001), 83–122; and Wendy Hunter Williams, *Out of Sight Out of Mind: The Story of Porirua Hospital* (Porirua Hospital, 1987), 5–139.

78 "Report of the Director, Division of Mental Health," in "Annual Report of the Director-General of Health," in *Appendix to the Journals of the House of Representatives of New Zealand, Session of 1951*, vol. 3, H-31 (Wellington: Government Printer, 1952), 19.

79 Bassett, *The State in New Zealand*, 204.

80 Jock Phillips, *A Man's Country: The Images of the Pakeha Male – A History*, rev. ed. (Auckland: Penguin Books, 1996), 71–9, 225–6.

81 W.H. Oliver, "The Origins and Growth of the Welfare State," in *Social Welfare and New Zealand Society*, ed. A.D. Trlin (Wellington: Methuen, 1977), 13.

82 Bijou Yang Lester, "Learning from Durkheim and Beyond: The Economy and Suicide," *Suicide and Life-Threatening Behavior* 31 (Spring 2001): 19–27.

83 James Bennett, *"Rats and Revolutionaries": The Labour Movement in Australia and New Zealand, 1890–1940* (Dunedin: University of Otago Press, 2004), 153.

84 Ronald W. Maris, *Pathways to Suicide: A Survey of Self-Destructive Behaviors* (Baltimore: Johns Hopkins University Press, 1981), 67.

85 Louis I. Dublin, *Suicide: A Sociological and Statistical Study* ((New York: Ronald Press Co., 1963), 56–60; David Lester and Michael Frank, "Seasonal Variation in Suicide Rates in the United States," *Journal of Clinical Psychiatry* 49 (September 1988): 371; Udo Grashoff, *Let Me Finish*, 22; Bailey, *This Rash Act*, 138-40.

86 Karl Menninger, *Man against Himself* (New York: Harcourt, Brace and Company, 1938), 15. As late as 1914, a writer for *The Times* of London proposed that the explanation for the suicide season was hotter blood and aroused emotions; see *The Times*, 25 April 1914, 5.

87 Robert R.M. Dent et al., "Diurnal Rhythms of Plasma Cortisol, Beta-Endorphin and Prolactin, and Cerebrospinal Fluid Amine Metabolite Levels before Suicide Case Report," *Neuropsychobiology* 16 (1986): 64–7; Joan Arehart-Treichel, "Long-Term Study Confirms DST as Suicide Diagnositc Tool," *Psychiatric News* 36 (4 May 2001): 40.

88 D.B. Copland, *Wheat Production in New Zealand* (Auckland: Whitcombe and Tombs, 1918), 28.

89 Duncan, *The New Zealand Dairy Industry*, 284.

90 Miles Fairburn, *Nearly Out of Heart and Hope: The Puzzle of a Colonial Labourer's Diary* (Auckland: Auckland University Press, 1995), 83–5.

91 Calvin F. Schmid, *Suicides in Seattle, 1914 to 1925: An Ecological and Behavoiristic Study* (Seattle: University of Washington, 1928), 46.

92 Fairburn, *Nearly Out of Heart and Hope*, 137.

93 New Zealand, *Population Census, 1936*, vol.11, *Unemployment* (Wellington: Government Printer, 1945), 21.

94 See chapter 4.

95 Boarding houses included a parlour and a dining area for common meals. They may have provided more social interaction.

96 Entry for 30 October 1935, Diary of Peter Carter Lovell-Smith, MSX-5461, Alexander Turnbull Library, National Library of New Zealand.

97 Entries for 18 and 25 October, 24 November, 14 December 1935, ibid.

98 J 46, 665/1922, Fred Williams.

99 John E. Martin, *The Forgotten Worker: The Rural Wage Earner in Nineteenth-Century New Zealand* (Wellington: Allen & Unwin/Trade Union History Project, 1990), 35.

100 Schmid, *Suicide in Seattle, 1914 to 1925*, 42–3.

101 Hamilton, *The Dairy Industry in New Zealand*, 106.

102 Ronald Maris, "The Adolescent Suicide Problem," *Suicide and Life-Threatening Behavior* 15 (Summer 1985): 91. Recalling trends in research, Robert Litman remarked on the wave of reports on youth suicide that appeared in the 1980s. See Robert E. Litman, "Suicidology: A Look Backward and Ahead," *Suicide and Life-Threatening Behavior* 26 (Spring 1996): 5.

103 Clipping files maintained by the Ministry of Youth Affairs tracked the issue. See ABQZ, 16363, YA 1/9/1/2/2, Youth Suicide, November 1987 to June 1989, Ministry of Youth Affairs, Archives New Zealand.

104 David Lester, "Suicide across the Life Span: A Look at International Trends," in *Life Span Perspectives of Suicide: Time Lines in the Suicide Process*, ed. Antoon A. Leenaars (New York: Plenum Press, 1991), 71–80.

105 Diego De Leo, "Century of Suicide in Italy: A Comparison between the Young and the Old," *Suicide and Life-Threatening Behavior* 27 (Fall 1997): 247.

106 World Health Organization, *Changing Patterns of Suicide Behaviour*, 7; World Health Organization, *Suicide and Attempted Suicide in Young People* (Copenhagen: World Health Organization, 1974), 7. Also see André Haim, *Adolescent Suicide*, trans. A.M. Sheridan Smith (New York: International Universities Press, 1970), 63–96; Herbert Hendlin, *Suicide in America*, new and expanded ed. (New York: W.W. Norton, 1995), 51–80; Ministry of Health, *Suicide Trends in New Zealand, 1974–1994* (Wellington: New Zealand Health Information Service, 1997), 21.

107 Wilhelmina Drummond, *Suicide New Zealand: Adolescents at Risk* (Nagare & BCU Press, 1996), 3–5.

108 Maris, *Pathways to Suicide*, 43 and 297.

109 Jaggedness in the Queensland graph for men is attributable to the small number of cases in some cohorts in a given year; this problem was dealt with for New Zealand by taking sums for a decade and averaging. The existence of nearly complete age data for New Zealand facilitated that process.

110 This pattern had been foreseen. See John L. McIntosh, "Older Adults: The Next Suicide Epidemic," *Suicide and Life-Threatening Behavior* 22 (Fall 1992): 322–31.

111 *Herald on Sunday*, 22 October 2006.

112 "Midlife Suicide Rises, Puzzling Researchers," *New York Times*, 19 February 2008, 1.

113 JUS/709/410, Richard Swift.

114 For a firm criticism of assigning motives, see A.S.K. Strahan, *Suicide and Insanity: A Physiological and Sociological Study* (London: Swan Sonnenschein and Co., 1893), 63. Strahan believed it was impossible to rank motives. My position is that it is not impossible for the great majority of cases, although errors are unavoidable.

115 I worked for several months of each year of research (2002–06) alongside my New Zealand and Queensland research assistants, Douglas Munro and Jonathan Richards respectively. We often discussed coding decisions and shared files in an effort to get to the bottom of a case. I checked several hundred cases that each coded and found only slight variations between their coding of cases and how I would have coded them. I let their coding stand.

116 Ira Wasswerman, "The Effects of War and Alcohol Consumption Patterns on Suicide: United States, 1910-1933," *Social Forces* 68 (December 1989): 527.

117 Kate Hunter, "Anything but a Roll in the Hay: Romance in Rural Communities in Federation Australia," in *Communities of Women: Historical Perspectives*, ed. Barbara Brookes and Dorothy Page (Dunedin: University of Otago Press, 2002), 109.

118 Sally Parker, "A Golden Decade? Farm Women in the 1950s," in *Women in History 2*, ed. Barbara Brookes, Charlotte Macdonald, and Margaret Tennant (Wellington: Bridget Williams Books, 1992), 221.

119 In what Oliver Sacks hails as "the most lucid and hopeful living memoir of living with schizophrenia," Elyn R. Saks has written about her own denial until a relatively successful treatment by medication revealed to her the contrast between illness and management of the illness. Her memoir is interspersed with reconstructed descriptions of her episodes. See Saks, *The Centre Cannot Hold: My Journey through Madness* (New York: Hyperion, 2007), 35, 40, 68, 83–4, 91, 97–9, 110–11, 125–6, 132–4, 141–2, 155, 199–200, 215–16, 302–4.

120 For a philosophical investigation of the issues, see Len Bowers, *The Social Nature of Mental Illness* (London: Routledge, 1998).

121 Ibid., 142–65.

CHAPTER FOUR

1 JUS/N601/61, William Tretheway.

2 J 46, 150/1912, Charles Morse.

3 JUS/Y17, Police Investigations into Sudden and Violent Deaths, Brisbane, file 121, George Hurkett.

4 J 46, 33/1912, James Crombie.

5 J 46, 573/1920, Anthony Paterson.

6 J 46, 813/1900, Ernest Villens.

7 J 46, 435/1936, Francis O'Connell.

8 JUS/N567/14/590, William Walsh.

9 JUS/N182/527, Robert Lewis.

10 JUS/N507/546,George McIntyre..

11 JUS/N753/1, Charles Whalen.

12 JUS/N1157/94 William Cobb.

13 JUS/N1086/856, Leslie Palmer.

14 Ernest Hunter et al., *An Analysis of Suicide in Indigenous Communities of North Queensland: The Historical, Cultural, and Symbolic Landscape* (Canberra: Commonwealth Department of Health and Aged Care, 1999), 8. Studies of North American native peoples indicate variation by tribe and region. See T. Kue Young, *The Health of Native Americans: Toward a Biocultural Epidemiology* (New York: Oxford University Press, 1994), 189–95.

15 J 46, 87/1908, Tangata Te Kupa; J 46, 59/1910, Harry Roberts; J 46, 314/1924, Reta Rawera; J 46, 350/1924, Edward Hohoia; J 46, 165/1926, Ruru Kahukuru; 1464/1936, Tata Maui; J 46, 1528/1936, Nohi Wateno.

16 J 46, 109/1926, Rimi Raunui.

17 J 46, 434/1914, Rauwene Turu.

18 "Tragedy at Thursday Island," *Queenslander*, 2 November 1895, 893.

19 JUS/N237/360, Fugita Tatsu.

20 JUS/N401/336, Tomosabro Shintani.

21 JUS/N584/345, Hayashi.

22 "Murder and Suicide," *Brisbane Courier*, 22 January 1914, 7.

23 JUS/N548/150, Iwamatsu Kohara.

24 Edwin Arnold, "Chinamen in New Zealand," in "Unpublished Autobiography," n.p., Ms. Papers 7237-26, Alexander Turnbull Library, National Library of New Zealand.

25 J 46 73/1904, Ah Lie.

26 J 46, 829/1908, Ah Man.

27 JUS/ N246/429, Tommy Lew.

28 On the cultural and social standing of suicide, see Junko Kitanaka, "Questioning the Suicide of Resolve: Medico-legal Disputes Regarding 'Overwork Suicide' in Twentieth-Century Japan," in *Histories of Suicide: International Perspectives on Self-Destruction in the Modern World,* ed. John Weaver and

David Wright (Toronto: University of Toronto Press, 2008). For a contrast between the status of suicide in Chinese and Japanese culture, see Committee on Cultural Psychiatry, Group for the Advancement of Psychiatry, *Suicide and Ethnicity in the United States* (New York: Brunner/Mazel, 1989), 68. The suicide of the rural elderly in China has been reported as notably high. See Paul S.F. Yip, "An Epidemiological Profile of Suicides in Beijing, China," *Suicide and Life-Threatening Behavior* 31 (Spring 2001): 69.

29 Further evidence of the importance of culture is found in the study of suicides in Fiji, a bicultural society. Indo-Fijians appear to have a much higher rate of suicide than other Fijians. See Mensah Adinkrah and Andand Chand, *Suicide in Fiji: Report of a National Survey* (Suva: Department of Sociology, University of the South Pacific, 1996), 2–90. Also see "Death Be Not Proud: A Rash of Suicides Horrifies Japan," *Economist*, 3 May 2008, 52.

30 For a brief statement on a coefficient of marital protection, see David Lester, "Benefits of Marriage for Reducing Risk of Violent Death from Suicide and Homicide for White and Nonwhite Persons," *Psychological Reports* 61 (1987): 198.

31 J 46, 234/1914, George Taylor.

32 The rates for single and married men over eighty-five have been removed because they were based on small numbers in the cohort and small numbers of suicides.

33 Ronald Maris, in association with Bernard Lazerwitz, *Pathways to Suicide: A Survey of Self-Destructive Behaviors* (Baltimore: Johns Hopkins University Press, 1981), 12.

34 Thor Norström, "The Impact of Alcohol, Divorce, and Unemployment on Suicide: A Multilevel Analysis," *Social Forces* 74 (September 1995): 310. For a study that uses aggregate data and argues along Durkheimian lines that divorce indicates poor social integration and thus helps explain variations in suicide rates, see Frank Trovato, "The Relationship between Marital Dissolution and Suicide: The Canadian Case," *Journal of Marriage and the Family* 48 (May 1986): 341-8; and Trovato, "A Durkheimian Analysis of Youth Suicide: Canada, 1971 and 1981," *Suicide and Life-Threatening Behavior* 22 (Winter 1992): 413–25. Steven Stack was a pioneer in showing close associations between the incidence of divorce and the rate of suicide. See Stack, "The Effect of Marital Dissolution on Suicide," *Journal of Marriage and the Family* 42 (February 1980): 83–90. He has also written on divorce and suicide in Norway and Denmark.

35 Kenneth R. Connor, "Violence, Alcohol, and Completed Suicide: A Case- Control Study," *American Journal of Psychiatry* 158 (October 2001): 1703–4.

36 JUS/N712/573, John King.

37 J 46, 1252/1942, John Tasker.
38 J 46, 1029/1930, Henry Millen.
39 J 46, 119/1904, Robert Hanna; J 46, 1442/1926, William Murray.
40 J 46, 352/1936, Cecil Fowler.
41 J 46, 190/1912, Alexander Stewart.
42 J 46, 1028/1906, Walter Flemingham.
43 J 46, 849/1936, Ronald McMaster.
44 J 46, 600/1904, William Race.
45 J 46, 1950/1313, Pat Johns.
46 J 46, 1187/1918, George Rackley.
47 JUS/N248/20, George Blythe.
48 JUS/N265/331, George Fairbrother.
49 JUS/N613/457, Harry Martin.
50 JUS/N245/385, Albert Darwen.
51 JUS/N705/213, Lance Tindall.
52 JUS/N782/468, Robert Taylor.
53 JUS/N621/6, William Brown.
54 JUS/N1144/279, George Fildes.
55 Roderick Phillips, *Divorce in New Zealand: A Social History* (Auckland: University of Auckland Press, 1981), 57–60.
56 JUS/Y13/125, David Hayes.
57 JUS/N1148/455, Leslie Love.
58 Alec Roy and Markku Linnoila, "Alcoholism and Suicide," in *Biology of Suicide,* ed. Ronald Maris (New York: Guilford Press, 1986), 162–6.
59 Ross Fitzgerald, *From the Dreaming to 1915: A History of Queensland* (St Lucia: University of Queensland Press, 1982), 305. Alcohol was noted as a leading motive in suicides among the police in Queensland. See Christopher Henry Cantor, Ruth Tyman, and Penelope Joy Slater, "A Historical Survey of Police Suicide in Queensland, " *Suicide and Life-Threatening Behavior* 25 (winter 1995): 499–508.
60 JUS/N612/301, Joseph Scholl.
61 JUS/N394/159, George Hampson.
62 JUS/N1059/69, Eugene Guilliard.
63 Peter N. Stearns, *Be a Man! Males in Modern Society* (New York: Holmes & Meier, 1990), 48–107.
64 JUS/N716/5, Frederik Gollan.
65 Silvia S. Canetto, "Gender Roles, Suicide Attempts, and Substance Abuse," *Journal of Psychology* 125 (1991): 611.
66 Entry for 13 December 1935, Diary of Peter Carter Lovell-Smith, MSX-5461, Alexander Turnbull Library, National Library of New Zealand.

67 JUS/N680/773, Thomas Fox.

68 JUS/N266/367, John Brennan.

69 JUS/N546/87, Jack Sala.

70 JUS/N776/194, Francis Rudolph.

71 JUS/N712/565, Richard Evett.

72 For an explanation that relies on neurochemistry, see Heather Ashton, "Delirium and Hallucinations," in *Neurochmistry of Consciousness: Neurotransmitters in Mind*, ed. Elaine Perry, Heather Ashton, and Allan Young (Amsterdam/Philadelphia: John Benjamins Publishing Co., 2002), 185–6.

73 JUS/N676/610, John Blizzard.

74 Dean Hamer and Peter Copeland, *Living with Our Genes: Why They Matter More than You Think* (New York: Doubleday, 1998), 133–4.

75 John Bostock, Lecture on Alcoholism for Medical Students [c.1940], box 13, John Bostock Papers, Fryer Library, University of Queensland.

76 Ibid.

77 JUS/N206/1914, Andrew Lawson.

78 Louise Brådvik and Mats Berglund, "A Suicide Peak after Weekends and Holidays in Patients with Alcohol Dependence," *Suicide and Life-Threatening Behavior* 33 (Summer 2003): 189–90.

79 JUS/N546/1912, Patrick O'Connell.

80 JUS/N630/1916, Charles Schultz.

81 J 46, 122/1922, Austin Bergan.

82 J 46, 443/1914, James Alexander.

83 J 46, 116/1914, Anthony Gratz.

84 J 46, 1245/1914, Alexander Rae.

85 J 46, 628/1916, Charles Chandler.

86 J 46, 843/1916, Richard Lynch.

87 J 46, 689/1910, William Thompson.

88 J 46, 504/1912, Thomas O'Neill.

89 J 46, 968/1914, Walter Scott.

90 J 46, 358/1914, Robert Carter.

91 J 46, 1001/1914, Thomas Manley.

92 J 46, 1215/1914, Hugo Retowski.

93 J 46, 302/1916, Nelson Colenso.

94 J 46, 734/1916, Richard Fulton.

95 J 46, 1388/1916, Daniel O'Brien.

96 J 46, 58/1917, Matene Kingi.

97 J 46, 1058/1914, Edward Vince.

98 J 46, 36/1914, Daniel Doolan.

99 J 46, 843/1914, Richard Lynch.

100 J 46, 183/1914, James Ford.

101 J 46, 206/1914, Andrew Lawson.

102 J 46, 210/1916, Robert Irwin.

103 J 46, 1148/1916, James Whittaker.

104 J 46, 127/1922, Janet Scott.

105 J 46, 19/1922, Andrew McKendry.

106 J 46, 437/1912, Thomas Davidson.

107 J 46, 1393/1938, Charles Edwardson.

108 J 46, 341/1942, John Clow.

109 J 46, 80/1950, Lawrence Blakie.

110 J 46, 274/1918, George Ironside.

111 J 46, 174/1914, Stephen Guiton.

112 J 46, 1290/1912, Ernest Butler.

113 J 46, 59/1916, Robert Walker.

114 J 46, 1175/1914, Frederick Jellyman.

115 J 46, 914/1926, James Cullen.

116 J 46, 295/1910, Arthur Joy.

117 J 46, 955/1914, William Lane.

118 J 46, 186/1910, William Anderson.

119 J 46, 1474/1940, Ernest Teague.

120 J 46, 728/1916, Frank Humphrey.

121 J 46, 138/1942, Albert Ballard.

122 Hamer and Copeland, *Living with Our Genes*, 131–9.

123 J 46, 404/1916, John Downing.

124 J 46, 1087/1906, George Nicholson.

125 J 46, 30/1922, Daniel Murphy.

126 J 46, 684/1912, William Prior.

127 J 46, 372/1914, Alfred Ransley.

128 J 46, 469/1914, John Finn.

129 J 46, 183/1914, James Ford.

130 J 46, 1076/1914, George Manson.

131 J 46, 1347/1914, August Pederson.

132 J 46, 36/1915, Daniel Doolan.

133 J 46, 1001/1914, Thomas Manley.

134 J 46, 61/1922, William Hunter.

135 J 46, 811/1922, Henry McEwen.

136 J 46, 327/1916, Richard Hiatt.

137 J 46, 425/1912, Frederick Pollock.

138 J 46, 501/1914, Henry Johnson.

139 J 46, 879/1914, John Roberts.

140 For a brief discussion of a recent study that found a high rate of suicides among hotel occupants, see Paul Zarkowski and David Avery, "Hotel Room Suicide," *Suicide and Life-Threatening Behavior* 36 (October 2006): 580.

141 Stephen Garton, *Medicine and Madness: A Social History of Insanity in New South Wales, 1880–1940* (Kensington, Australia: New South Wales University Press, 1988), 119.

142 The New Zealand data set consisting of inquest files for even numbered years includes nearly three hundred returned soldiers between 1918 and 1938. The corresponding number for Queensland was almost one hundred and fifty.

143 J 46, 526/1930, William Ayre.

144 J 46, 529/1936, Robert Davie.

145 Ira M. Wasserman, "The Impact of Epidemic, War, Prohibition and Media on Suicide: United States, 1910–1920," *Suicide and Life-Threatening Behavior* 22 (Summer 1992): 249.

146 J 46, 1307/1920, Robert Gillespie.

147 J 46, 29/1922, Thomas Hanna.

148 J 46, 1000/1918, George Faulkner.

149 J 46, 296/1920, Joseph Murphy; J 46, 755/1920, John McLeod; J 46, 366/1920, Alexander Haugh.

150 J 46, 1242/1930, Thomas Adamson.

151 JUS/N711/530, Vladimir Valicha.

152 J 46, 873/1920, James Mill.

153 J 46, 4/1921, Philip Connell.

154 J 46, 1231/1920, George Tyler.

155 J 46, 550/1924, Herbert Wittner.

156 J 46, 1281/1920, Arthur Best.

157 J 46, 959/1922, William Fox.

158 J 46, 70/1920, Thomas Corcoran.

159 J 46, 532/1924, George Murray.

160 J 46, 1101/1922, George Hoare.

161 J 46, 265/1920, Archibald Gilchrist; J 46, 292/1922, Alfred Donald.

162 J 46, 402/1918, Sidney Martin.

163 J 46, 707/1918, Isaac Taylor.

164 J 46, 578/1930, Frederick Tarmery.

165 J 46, 61/1930, William Keast.

166 J 46, 1265/1930, Harold Leslie.

167 J 46, 610/1918, Charles Hunter.

168 J 46, 83/1920, William Fawcett.

169 J 46, 167/1918, David Sutherland.

170 J 46, 346/1924, Francis Johnson.
171 JUS/N601/64, John Reeves.
172 Australia, *Census of the Commonwealth of Australia, 30th June 1933* (Canberra: L.F. Johnston, Commonwealth Government Printer, 1938), vol. 2: Table on War Service, 1080. It is difficult to estimate veterans living in Queensland in 1920. Altogether, 57,705 Queenslanders enlisted; however, only 80 per cent served outside Australia, and deaths amounted to 15 per cent of the contingent. As well, some men did not return to Queensland. See Table WR 2-8 in Wray Vamplew, ed., *Australian Historical Statistics* (Collingwood, Victoria: Fairfax, Syme, and Weldon Associates, 1987), 445.
173 JUS/N750/851, Joseph Conlon.
174 JUS/N671/495, John Halligan.
175 JUS/N745/649, Frederick Marshall.
176 JUS/N705/210, Herbert Taylor.
177 JUS/N715/712, William Keller.
178 JUS/N739/314, Leonard Jarvis.
179 JUS/N706/264, David Molloy.
180 JUS/N782/493, John Reardon.
181 JUS/N738/253, Ivan de Grouchy.
182 JUS/N716/163, Francis Ryan.
183 JUS/N703/115, John Hitchcock.
184 JUS/N713/615, Patrick Ryan.
185 J 46, 127/1918, George Flanagan.
186 J 46, 1253/1918, Harry Barlow.
187 J 46, 1372/1918, George Hill.
188 J 46, 759/1922, William Brennan.
189 J 46, 11/1902, Robert Keys.
190 J 46, 47/1904, Herbert Bolwell.
191 J 46, 375/1904, Alexander Dunn.
192 J 46, 1141/1910, Robert Bennett.
193 J 46, 839/1910, John Hunter.
194 J 46, 518/1900, John Amodeo.
195 J 46, 459/1904, John Northey.
196 J 46, 699/1908, Gilbert Oswald.
197 J 46, 1233/1910, George Halloran.
198 Karl Menninger, "The Schizophrenic Syndrome as a Product of Acute Infectious Disease," in *A Psychiatrist's World: The Selected Papers of Karl Menninger, M.D.*, ed. Bernard Hall (New York: Viking Press, 1965; 1st ed., 1959), 153. Also see Menninger, "The Amelioration of Mental Disease by Influenza," ibid., 158.

199 William Osler, *The Principles and Practices of Medicine* (New York: Appleton, 1912), 118.

200 Menninger, "The Schizophrenic Syndrome as a Product of Acute Infectious Disease," 138–41.

201 Menninger, "Psychosis Associated with Influenza," in *A Psychiatrist's World*, 112.

202 Menninger, "The Schizophrenic Syndrome as a Product of Acute Infectious Disease," 155.

203 J 46, 570/1928, Hamilton Miles.

204 J 46, 1031/1928, Arthur Drayton.

205 J 46, 986/1926, Frank Muir.

206 J 46 779/1928, Victor Macken.

207 J 46, 1259/1940, Gerald Dempsey.

208 J 46, 1207/1938, James Telfer. On Queensland, see "Six 'Pennorth' of Strychnine, Please!" *Brisbane Sunday Mail*, 27 September 1936.

209 Entry on "Chronic Fatigue Syndrome," in Centers for Disease Control and Prevention, www.cdc.gov/cfs/cfscauses.htm; accessed 16 June 2007.

210 Louis Dublin, *Suicide: A Sociological and Statistical Study* (New York: Ronald Press Co., 1963), 66.

211 A. Leenaars, Bijou Yang, and David Lester, "The Effects of Economic Stress on Suicide Rates in Canada and the United Sates," *Journal of Clinical Psychology* 49 (November 1993): 918–21. Lower rates for white American men in the 1990s may have been connected with the decade's prosperity. See Bijou Yang Lester, "Learnings from Durkheim and Beyond: The Economy and Suicide," *Suicide and Life-Threatening Behavior* 31 (Spring 2001): 22. On the lag effect, see Ira M. Wasserman, "The Influence of Economic Business Cycles on United States Suicide Rates," *Suicide and Life-Threatening Behavior* 14 (Fall 1984): 153.

212 JUS/N702/63, Farrow Jarvis.

213 J 46, 1000/1914, James Brown.

214 J 46, 947/1912, John Harvey.

215 It is impossible to be precise about the percentages, because the suicide files show that many men who died in towns and cities worked in the countryside, and that phenomenon makes it difficult to match the suicide data with the breakdown of urban occupations provided by Eric Olssen.

216 H.C.D. Somerset, *Littledene: Patterns of Change* (Wellington: New Zealand Council for Educational Research, 1974), 14–15.

217 In graph 4.4 the two estimates on the numbers of men employed or self-employed in agriculture in New Zealand and who committed suicide were made in the following way. All men listed with a rural occupation were

included, even if death occurred in a town or city. Also, men with unknown occupations were deemed rural if they died in the country; there were very few. The difference between the estimates results from two ways of allocating labourers. In one estimate, labourers were included as rural workers only if they died in the country; in the larger estimate, they were included if they died in the country or in small towns in rural districts. The latter might overestimate the number of men in the rural economy, but the numbers were small. In neither estimate were any pensioners assigned to the rural sector. Thus the rate could have been higher. Graph 4.5 is based on a firmer idea of who had been a rural worker; thus there is only one estimate. Both sets of rates relied on a linear interpolation to estimate the rural male population between censuses; New Zealand had more census points to work with in that respect.

218 Raymond Evans, *A History of Queensland* (Melbourne: Cambridge University Press, 2007), 179–80.

219 Steven Stack and Ira Wasserman, "Research Note: Economic Strain and Suicide Risk: A Qualitative Analysis," *Suicide and Life Threatening-Behavior* 37 (February 2007): 110.

220 J 46, 1047/1922, Herbert Cooper.

221 J 46, 825/1900, William Hubble.

222 J 46, 759/1922, William Brennan.

223 J 46. 1309/1922, Tasman Henderson.

224 J 46, 486/1930, Tui Nicholson.

225 J 46, 685/1926, Charles Gimlett.

226 J 46, 935/1928, Solomon Rowe.

227 J 46, 1226/1934, Alexander Shaw.

228 J 46, 859/1906, Fred Brown.

229 J 46, 677/1908, John Walsh.

230 J 46, 471/1914, John Moyan.

231 J 46, 1336/1920, James Scott.

232 J 46 125/1924, John Crawford.

233 J 46, 718/1928, John Hill.

234 J 46, 803/1928, Edmund Bennett.

235 J 46, 278, William Beehre.

236 J 46, 1499/1926, John Rowntree.

237 J 46, 1051/1928, Andrew Bennie.

238 J 46, 1050/1924, Henry Forsyth.

239 J 46, 529/1928, Hector Cole.

240 J 46, 12/1912, William Johnston.

241 J 46, 821/1916, Frederick Wybrott.

242 J 46, 830/1916, Thomas Glaister.

243 J 46, 974/1936, William Todd.

244 J 46, 1362/1936, Ralph Heald.

245 J 46, 1409, Ernest Lilly.

246 J 46, 1937/193, George Henry.

247 J 46, 297/1930, David Brown.

248 J 46, 1110/1906, Johann Gloy.

249 JUS/N265/350, Carl Harden.

250 JUS/N310/366, Arthur Garlich.

251 M.J. Crawford and M. Prince, "Increasing Rates of Suicide among Young
     Men in England during the 1980s: The Importance of Social Context," *Social
     Science & Medicine* 49 (1999): 1422.

252 JUS/N705/245, Albert Poulsen; JUS/N742/454, Matthew Brennan.

253 JUS/N514/19, Thomas Rumney.

254 JUS/N206/490, William Hallinson.

255 JUS/N242/224, Thomas Williamson.

256 J 46, 1409/1934, Albert Maurice.

257 JUS/N704/164, Clarence Orange.

258 JUS/N1096/126, William Brown.

259 J 46, 135/1900, Charles Deane.

260 J 46, 404/1916, John Downing.

261 J 46, 543/1908, Thomas Craig.

262 J 46, 626/1908, Lawrence Laurenson.

263 J 46, 625/1924, Percy Coffey.

264 J 46, 648/1924, James Nevin.

265 J 46, 214/1924, Thomas Johnson.

266 J 46, 9/1929, James Christmas.

267 J 46, 370/1930, Frederick Peters.

268 J 46, 1193/1930, Angus Macgregor.

269 J 46, 646/1908, Lindsey Staples.

270 J 46, 23/1912, Nelson Bunting.

271 J 46, 117/1904, Hector Parkman.

272 J 46, 506/1930, William Tough.

273 J 46, 548/1930, William McKernan.

274 On Chlorodyne, see the entry for 10 April 1901, George Welch Diaries,
     MSX-6129, Alexander Turnbull Library, National Library of New Zealand.

275 J 46, 579/1924, Clifford Hood.

276 J 46, 1227/1936, Ngatai Wanoa.

277 J 46, 676/1950, James McAuliffe.

278 JUS/N552/231, Thomas Cross.

279 JUS/N262/200, Georges Robert.

280 JUS/N678/696, Jules Lareher.

281 JUS/N267/404, William Palmer.

282 JUS/N569/14/645, William McClosky.

283 JUS/N955/836, Andreas Arntzern.

284 JUS/N948/481, Hugh Sim.

285 JUS/N950/559, Michael Harrigan.

286 JUS/N950/565, William Carvasso.

287 JUS/N1091/27, John Kachel.

288 Somerset, *Littledene: Patterns of Change*, 199.

289 Stearns, *Be a Man! 108–53.*

290 JUS/N448/330, Robert Catt.

291 JUS/N401/334, William James.

292 JUS/N1059/69, Eugene Gilliard.

293 JUS/N/1087/589, James Rhodes.

294 JUS/N392/124, Daniel Smith.

295 JUS/N562/468, Frederick Bunce.

296 JUS/N668/393, Daniel Gillespie.

297 J 46, 92/1922, William Todd.

298 J 46, 1046/1920, George Parker.

299 J 46, 197/1914, Charles Johnson.

300 J 46, 638/1916, Patrick Herald.

301 J 46, 665/1902, George Main.

302 JUS/N701/48, William George.

303 Edwin Arnold, "Visiting Justice," in "Unpublished Autobiography," 123.

304 J 46, 60/1900, Richard Reid.

305 J 46, 1095/1924, Leonard Hindley.

306 J 46, 69/1902, Thomas McKenzie.

307 J 46, 692/1922, Peter Maskrey.

308 J 46, 243/1902, John Crimmons.

309 J 46, 814/1906, Samuel Bullivant.

310 J 46, 1191/1914, William Hale.

311 J 46, 1028/1930, George Moorcroft.

312 J 46, 635/1930, John McDonald.

313 JUS/Y9/118, Phillip Denham.

314 JUS/N326/345, George H. Sweet.

315 JUS/N241/183, John Norton.

316 JUS/N678/670, George Grayton.

317 JUS/ N705/221, Johann Struckmeir.

318 JUS/N946/384, Walter Palmer.

319 JUS/N978/216, Jesse Dorrington.

320 JUS/N1145/324 James Barrett.
321 JUS/N943/249, Robert McSporran.
322 JUS/N1150/78, Neville Rice.
323 J 46, 892/1914, Robert Davis.

CHAPTER FIVE

1 See the discussion of Durkheim and women in Howard I. Kushner, "Suicide, Gender, and the Fear of Modernity," in *Histories of Self-Destruction: International Perspectives on Suicide in the Modern World,* ed. John Weaver and David Wright (Toronto: University of Toronto Press, forthcoming).
2 See the claim that males are under greater pressure in Charles Neuringer and Dan J. Lettieri, *Suicidal Women: Their Thinking and Feeling Patterns* (New York: Gardner Press, 1982), 22, 94.
3 J 46, 445/1908, Alfred Penny.
4 J 46, 1451/1930, Linda Page.
5 Ministry of Health, *Suicide Trends in New Zealand, 1974–1994* (Wellington: New Zealand Health Information Service, 1997), 17. This pattern is consistent with international findings that, roughly speaking, the gender ratios of suicide and parasuicide are reciprocal. In most countries, three times as men as women commit suicide, and three times as many women as men commit parasuicide. See R.F.W. Diekstra and W. Gulbinat, "The Epidemiology of Suicidal Behavior: A Review of Three Continents," *World Health Statistics Quarterly* 46 (1993): 66.
6 See the thorough discussion of several explanatory theories and a strong case for a cultural explanation in Silvia Sara Canetto and Isaac Sakinofsky, "The Gender Paradox in Suicide," *Suicide and Life-Threatening Behavior* 28 (Spring 1998): 1–20.
7 J 46, 1055/1906, Mary Gough.
8 Canetto and Sakinofsky, "The Gender Paradox in Suicide," 17–19.
9 Quoted in Germaine Greer, *The Change: Women, Ageing, and the Menopause* (London: Hamish Hamilton, 1991), 53.
10 Ibid., 55.
11 Ibid., 56.
12 David Lester, "Benefits of Marriage for Reducing Risk of Violent Death from Suicide and Homicide for White and Nonwhite Persons: Generalizing from Gove's Findings," *Psychological Reports* 61 (1987): 198.
13 Victor Bailey, *This Rash Act: Suicide across the Life-Cycle in a Victorian City* (Stanford: Stanford University Press, 1998), 179.

14 Janet Zollinger Giele, *Women in the Middle Years: Current Knowledge and Directions for Research and Policy* (New York: John Wiley & Sons, 1982), 21.

15 J 46, 325/1910, Ivy Pomare.

16 J 46, 912/1910, Bessie Bunny.

17 J 46, 915/1918, Alicia Hintz.

18 J 46, 1026/1902, Jane Forsyth.

19 J 46, 190/1916, Harriet Parsons.

20 J 46, 1366/1940, Katharine Smith.

21 J 46, 1176/1910, Miriam Parker.

22 JUS/N561/432, Mabel Anne Johansen.

23 J 46, 58/1912, Eliza McCaffrey.

24 JUS/N1091/19, Daphne Seiler.

25 JUS/N775/178, Muriel Price.

26 J 46, 38/ 1925, Mary McKenzie.

27 JUS/N302/23, May Pursey.

28 JUS/N617/562, Frances Fagan.

29 JUS/N391/84, Harriet Newman.

30 J 46, 496/1926, Thelma White.

31 J 46, 658/1904, Ada Ford.

32 JUS/N1078/115, Frances Whiting.

33 J 46, 805/1930, Irene Turner.

34 JUS/N452/436, Mary McMullen.

35 JUS/N1046/369, Margaret Kinsey.

36 JUS/N269/514, Martha Fountain.

37 JUS/N744/556, Ellen Crain.

38 J 46, 384/1912, Mary Carroll.

39 J 46, 195/1922, Ida Wells.

40 J 46, 624/1924, Evelyn Thompson.

41 JUS/N403/376, Sarah Chalkly.

42 JUS/N882, Theresa Frazer.

43 J 46, 1410/1916, Mary Curry.

44 JUS/N272/115, Emma Krabbeuholf.

45 JUS/N1178/11, Fay Fischer.

46 J 46, 467/1910, Mary Brown.

47 JUS/N204/362, Eveline McDonald.

48 J 46, 272/1902, Hilda Campbell.

49 J 46, 677/1930, Flora Home.

50 J 46, 3/1909, Gertrude Good.

51 See references to studies on satisfaction and the demands of numerous children in Giele, *Women in the Middle Years*, 21.

52 JUS/N200/175, Sarah Ann Bussey.

53 JUS/N602/87, Eva Archer.

54 JUS/N791/29, Anastasia Smith.

55 J 46, 1264/1926, Bridget McGinn.

56 JUS/N611/288, Martha Rowe.

57 JUS/N753/51, Frances Kirby.

58 JUS/N259/40, Amelia Smith.

59 JUS/N1097/178, Ivey Dean.

60 JUS/N288/381, Eliza Rusk.

61 JUSN711/50, Agnes Mackenzie.

62 JUS/N260/68, Elizabeth Carson.

63 J 46, 821/1906, Mary Humphrey.

64 JUS/N283, 116, Margaret Christensen.

65 J 46, 413/1914, Lucia Macalister.

66 J 46, 402/1914, Ethel Hammond.

67 J 46, 683/1902, Elizabeth Smithison.

68 J 46, 1148/1922, Mary Pickup.

69 On the controversy over whether PMS is a mental illness, see Anne E. Figert, *Women and the Ownership of PMS: The Structuring of a Psychiatric Disorder* (New York: Aldine De Gruyter, 1996).

70 JUS/N786/683, Esther Johnston.

71 J 46, 17/1914, Susan Dowdle.

72 J 46, 1258/1930, Kathleen Haggith.

73 J 46, 1940/1300, Alice Trezise.

74 J 46, 1413/1920, Jane Bassett.

75 J 46, 650/1918, Sarah Taylor.

76 JUS/N1079/196, Margaret Cannon.

77 J 46, 191/1900, Elizabeth Brizley; J 46, 340/1914, Honora Brooker.

78 J 46, 872/1916, Jessie Moore.

79 J 46, 338/1914, Edith Johnston.

80 Bailey, *This Rash Act*, 233.

81 Susan M. Love with Karen Lindsey, *Dr. Susan Love's Menopause and Hormone Book* (New York: Three Rivers Press, 2003), 59.

82 Jane Page, *The Other Awkward Age: Menopause* (Berkeley: Ten Speed Press, 1977).

83 J 46, 609/1920, Grace Bickford.

84 J 340/1914, Honora Brooker.

85 J 46, 925/1904, Grace Lamb.

86 J 46, 866/1918, Clare Moore.

87 J 46, 818/1914, Elsie Osborn.

88 J 46, 27/1916, Nora Dixon.

89 J 46, 961/1930, Victoria May.

90 Bailey, *This Rash Act,* 170, 184, 205, 221.

91 JUS/N611/288, Alice Allen.

92 JUS/N304/149, Hannah Murdoch.

93 JUS/N555/288, Mary Simon.

94 J 46, 814/1916, Thomasina Anderson.

95 J 46, 120/1908, Eiza Tafnell.

96 JUS/N614/49, Jean Findlay.

97 J 46, 1173/1914, Catherine Locking.

98 Elaine Showalter, *The Female Malady: Women, Madness and English Culture, 1830–1980* (London: Virago Press, 1987), 123.

99 J 46, 600/1930, Martha Bradley.

100 J 46, 877/1930, Bertha Palmer.

101 JUS/N513/691, Mary Heenan.

102 JUS/N755/139, Bridget Deere.

103 JUS/N657, Agnes Fyfe.

104 JUS/N790/855, Sarah Wessel.

105 JUS/N238/25, Elizabeth Kenyon.

106 JUS/N1090/727, Ruby Yapp.

107 JUS/N1090/734, Elizabeth Bonning.

108 John Bostock, Lecture on Alcoholism for Medical Students [c.1940], box 13, John Bostock Papers, Fryer Library, University of Queensland.

109 J 46, 493/1916, Erica Dickinson.

110 J 46, 751/1908, Rosabell Byron.

111 JUS/N1095/69, Mary Lingard.

112 JUS/N1082/329, Barbara Weinholt.

113 J 46, 284/1922, Emily Agnew.

114 J 46, 523/1916, Elizabeth Ratcliffe.

115 J 46, 806/1900, Augusta Jensen.

116 J 46, 961/1916, Mary McRobie.

117 J 46, 312/1914, Elizabeth Adamson.

118 J 46, 77/1918, Norma Smith.

119 JUS/N244/327, Anna Schmidt.

120 J 981/1916, Matilda Beardsley.

121 JUS/N740/351, Sarah Freeman.

122 JUS/N702/55, Mary Hawes.

123 JUS/N663/254, Elizabeth Holdsworth.

124 JUS/N281/19, Mary Smith.

125 J 46, 725/1912, Mary Howard.

126 J 46, 1031/1906, Mary Stevenson.

127 J 46, 471/1916, Jemima Walsh.

128 J 46, 1148/1912, Agnes Abbotson.

129 JUS/N682/37, Mary Jackson.

130 JUS/N322/205, Isabella Swan.

131 J 46, 193/1906, Martha Redshaw.

132 JUS/N866/302, Catherine Waite.

133 J 46, 882/1922, Kate Lane.

134 J 46, 987/1918, George Read.

135 J 46, 7/1912, John Maher.

136 J 46, 961/1912, Henry Edmonds.

137 J 46, 95/1910, Alexander Krause.

138 J 46, 875/1900, George Arundel.

139 Constance A. Nathanson and Gerda Lornz, "Women and Health: The Social Dimensions of Biomedical Data," in Giele, ed., *Women in the Middle Years*, 47.

140 J 46, 856/1922, Charles O'Neil.

141 J 46, 154/1930, Alice Forscutt.

142 J 46, 1537/1930, Pearl Fletcher; J 46, 788/1922, Beatrice Kidd.

143 J 46, 788/1930, Rose Stewart.

144 J 46, 836/1930, Edith Hemery.

145 J 46, 614/1916, Mary Russell.

146 L. Danson and K. Soothill, "Murder Followed by Suicide: A Study of the Reporting of Murder Followed by Suicide in *The Times*, 1887–1990," *Journal of Forensic Psychiatry* 7 (1996): 310–22.

147 Carlos Carcach and P.N. Grabosky, *Murder-Suicide in Australia* (Canberra: Australian Institute of Criminology, 1998), 3.

148 Jo Barnes, "Murder Followed by Suicide in Australia, 1973–1992: A Research Note," *Journal of Sociology* 36 (2000): 3.

149 "A Mysterious Affair," *Queenslander*, 28 March 1901, 592; JUS/N188/120, Annie Marchant.

150 JUS/N357, Emily Sainsbury.

151 JUS/N224, Marion Spence.

152 JUS/N327/351, Margaret Finnan.

153 "City Tragedy," *Brisbane Courier*, 4 November 1932, 14.

154 JUS/N956/895, Richard Croker.

155 JUS/N710/455, Amy Tobler.

156 JUS/N738/277, Bernice Sommers.

157 JUS/N858/1139, Vera McLaurin.

158 Patricia Weiser Easteal, *Killing the Beloved: Homicide between Adult Sexual Intimates* (Canberra: Australian Institute of Criminology, 1993), 94.

159 Ibid., 108.

160 JUS/N702/57, Hugh Lawrence.

161 JUS/N744/558, Harry Lett.

162 JUS/N293/66, Patrick McLoughlin.

163 JUS/N543/4, Charlie Wassell.

164 JUS/N905/184, Fritz Skau.

165 JUS/N756/161, John Lewis.

166 JUS/N297/261, James Corday.

167 "A Deplorable Tragedy," *Queenslander*, 4 March 1893, 426.

168 JUS/N211/160, William Trevethan.

169 JUS/N930/490, George Moore.

170 JUS/N1006/71, William Griffiths.

171 "Tragedy at Wooroolin," *Queenslander*, 30 August 1902, 503.

172 JUS/N307/262, Albert May.

173 JUS/N706/269, Ferdinand Boie.

174 JUS/N915/687, William Lum Wan.

175 "A City Tragedy," *Brisbane Courier*, 4 August 1927, 17.

176 JUS/N859/1160, James Crisp.

177 JUS/N897/794, Richard Arnold.

178 "Tragedy at East Brisbane," *Brisbane Courier*, 30 September 1918, 8.

179 JUS/N684/107, Samuel Nelson.

180 JUS/N983/460, Harold James.

181 JUS/N869/454,Vincenzo Oriti.

182 JUS/N781/334,Charlie Fahl.

183 JUS/N1055/810, Norman McDowell.

184 JUS/N545/71, Albert Horne; "Sensation at Lutwyche," *Brisbane Courier*, 21 January 1914, 5.

185 JUS\N788/775, Charles Bayldon.

186 JUS/N819/438, Stanley Weight.

187 JUS/N1063/252, Clarence Walter Ney.

188 JUS/N527/329, Robert Carey.

189 "Two Dead: New Farm Park Tragedy," *Brisbane Courier*, 17 May 1929, 15; JUS/N896/24, Denniston Netterfield.

190 JUS/N897/755, Robert McDowell.

191 JUS/N926/298, Ernest Rook.

192 JUS/N729/651, William Haynes.

193 JUS/N774/55, Stanley Humble.

194 JUS/N774/56, Thomas Fitzgerald.

195 JUS/N400/301, Charles Young.

196 JUS/N418/176, Robert Donnelly.

197 "Triple Shooting: Two Dead," *Courier Mail,* 1 July 1937, 13.

198 JUS/N1032/492, Alexander Bennett.

199 Erik H. Erikson, *The Life Cycle Completed: A Review* (New York: W.W. Norton, 1982), 19.

200 Ibid., 21.

201 Ibid., 60.

202 J 46, 624/1900, Bertram Taylor; J 46, 167/1910, Allen French; J 46, 150/1912, Charles Morse; J 46, 731/1936, Barton Harneiss Bradshaw; J 46, 767/1936, Mervyn Bishop; J 46, 1147/1936, Fred Hall; J 46, 1605/1938, Tame Wi Paraone; J 46, 1987/1938; Ina Roger; JUS/N713/618, Frederick Baillie; JUS/N403/376, Sarah Chalkly; JUS/N716\22, Lily Wilkins; JUS/N1058/45, Ivan Malcolm Dow.

203 "Silencing of the Lambs," *Economist,* 10 May 2008, 90.

204 Erikson, *The Life Cycle Completed,* 71–2.

205 Ibid., 69–72.

206 Ibid., 61–5.

CHAPTER SIX

The title of this chapter was inspired by New Zealand author Alan Duff's *What Becomes of the Broken Hearted* (Auckland: Vintage, 1996). It is also the title of a Motown song with appropriate lyrics written by William Weatherspoon, Paul Riser, and James Dean and first performed by Jimmy Ruffin in 1966.

1 JUS/N984/529, Rob Roy Patterson.

2 J 46, 1444/1934, Joseph Vercoe.

3 Edwin S. Shneidman, "The Commonalities of Suicide across the Life Span," in *Life Span Perspectives of Suicide: Time-lines in the Suicide Process,* ed. Antoon A. Leenaars (New York: Plenum Press, 1991), 40.

4 Ibid.

5 Edwin S. Shneidman, "The Psychological Pain Assessment Scale," *Suicide and Life-Threatening Behavior* 29 (Winter 1999): 287.

6 Shneidman, "The Commonalities of Suicide across the Life Span," 43.

7 Edwin Shneidman, "Prediction of Suicide Revisited: A Brief Methodological Note," *Suicide and Life-Threatening Behavior* 35 (February 2005): 2.

8 J 46, 121/1910, Daniel Buisson.

9 J 46 1290/1948, William Halliburton.

10 JUS/N510/619, FredericYoung.

11 J 46, 730/1908, Andrew McEwen.

12 J 46, 374/1908, James Baxter.

13 J 46, 1440/1930, John Hills.

14 J 46, 1388/1934, Alfred Dewbery.

15 JUS/N706/258, Wilfred Smith.

16 J 46, 492/1950, Andrew Fletcher.

17 J 46, 1518/1950, Ivan Hayward.

18 J 46, 1364/1946, Andrew Henry O'Brien.

19 Ronald W. Maris, in association with Bernard Lazerwitz, *Pathways to Suicide: A Survey of Self-Destructive Behavior* (Baltimore: Johns Hopkins University Press, 1981), 45.

20 David P. Phillips and Daniel G. Smith, "Suicide at Symbolic Ages: Death on Stocktaking Occasions," in *Life Span Perspectives of Suicide,* ed. Leenaars, 81–7.

21 JUS/N986/648, Frederick Raine.

22 JUS/N1047/437, Leslie Baxter.

23 J 46 1290/1948, William Halliburton.

24 J 46, 318/1914, Alfred Stevens.

25 J 46, 471/1930, Alexander Kristoff.

26 J 46, 605/1930, Henare Maihi.

27 JUS/N263/206, Richard Gardiner.

28 J 46, 968/1902, John Forsyth.

29 J 46, 546/1910, Horace Huddlestone.

30 JUS/N714/696, Edith Armistead.

31 JUS/N711/504, Agnes Mackenzie.

32 J 46, 534/1940, Nola Sophia Fafeita.

33 J 46, 462/1906, William Short.

34 J 46, 544/1908, Thomas Brown.

35 J 46, 498/1908, Bessie Blakeway.

36 J 46, 919/1916, Grace Alexander.

37 J 46, 927/1922, Elizabeth Gallop.

38 J 46, 649/1936, William McNicholl.

39 JUS/N989/14, Alice McMahon; J 46, 978/1904, Elizabeth Watson.

40 J 46, 689/1902, Randolph Miller.

41 P. Qin, E. Agerbo, and P.B. Mortensen, "Suicide Risk in Relation to Family History of Completed Suicide and Psychiatric Disorders: A Nested Case-Control Study Based on Longitudinal Registers," *Lancet* 360 (12 October 2002): 1126–30; A. Rot, "Family History of Suicide," *Archives of General Psychiatry* 40 (September 1983): 971–4.

42 J 46, 1019/1918, Lacey White.

43 J 46, 1324/1946, Timothy Enright.

44 J 46, 1464/1930, Joseph Ward.

45 JUS/N978/216, Jesse Dorrington.

46 JUS/N951/625, Andrew Carroll.

47 J 46, 950/1910, Alexander Krause.

48 J 46, 1132/1930, Henri Germane.

49 J 46, 318/1950, Charles Benton.

50 J 46, 837/1930, John Clark.

51 J 46, 86/1940, George Watson.

52 J 46, 564/1940, Gerald Matthews.

53 J 46, 62/1941, Robert Lockerbie.

54 J 46, 605/1930, Henare Maihi.

55 J 46, 753/1906, Peter Collins.

56 J 46, 154/1908, Alex Burgess.

57 David A. Jobes and Rachael E. Mann, "Reasons for Living versus Reasons for Dying: Examining the Internal Debate of Suicide," *Suicide and Life-Threatening Behavior* 29 (Summer 1999): 103.

58 JUS/N265/339, Charles Hickmott.

59 J 46, 218/1914, Richard Ward.

60 JUS/N320/137, John Gordon.

61 J 46, 107/1922, John Lepper.

62 J 46, 28/1927, William Aston.

63 JUS/N1057/6, Robert Hurst.

64 JUS/N408/505, Denis Downes.

65 The combination of Marxian thought and psychology that Richard Sennett attempted in several books many years ago has influenced some of the thinking that went into this chapter. See Richard Sennett and Jonathan Cobb, *The Hidden Injury of Class* (New York: Vintage Books, 1973), 53–118, 191–242.

66 J 46, 662/1904, James Mullins.

67 J 46, 283/1928, John Hewetson.

68 Janet Frame, *An Autobiography* (London: Women's Press, 1990; 1st ed., 1982), 212.

69 JUS/N791/23, Wallace Hudson.

70 J 46, 1364/1946, Andrew O'Brien.

71 Ibid.

72 J 46, 1366/1940, Katherine Smith.

73 William Lewis Robertson, "Final Statement: Part II" (unpublished ms.), 163, in Robert Ellis Papers, 88-077-2/02, Alexander Turnbull Library, National Library of New Zealand.

74 JUS/N564/523, Frank Beaumont.
75 J 46, 668/1938, Frederick Foster.
76 JUS/N245/360, Arthur Steele.
77 JUS/N709/417, Walter Ford.
78 JUS/N661/202,Roger Pendlebury.
79 J 46, 410/1914, Robert Gilchrist.
80 J 46, 1105/1940, Jean Hall.
81 J 46, 1312/1942, Constance Iris Elizabeth Smith.
82 JUS/N1504/1936, Isabella Symonds.
83 JUS/N742/45, Annie McGovern.
84 JUS/N678/700, Evelyn Drewe.
85 J 46, 206/1943, Emily Cundall.
86 JUS/N885/179, Doris Cooper.
87 J 46, 941/1938, Elsie Mary Dimond.
88 JUS/N262/182, John Grant.
89 J 46, 555/1924, Charles Tebutt.
90 JUS/N305/159, William John Gordon.
91 J 46, 1204/1930, John Miller.
92 JUS/N247/464, John Cahill.
93 JUS/N1042/188, Albert Harding.
94 JUS/N355/273, Gustav Klepsch.
95 JUS/N265/347, Alfred Atkins.
96 J 46, 1566/1936, Gew Yew.
97 J 46, 1539/1930, Leonard Bell.
98 JUS/N775/144, Patrick Kellett.
99 JUS/N609/244, John William Miller.
100 J 46, 549/1908, Albert Freeman.
101 JUS/N462/30, Max Mehner.
102 J 46, 253/1910, Thomas Christian.
103 J 46, 1101/1916, Charles Sheard.
104 JUS/N243/255, John Dandes.
105 J 46, 121/1914, Fletcher Hargreaves.
106 J 46, 413/1950, Leslie Buckingham.
107 J 46, 161/1938, Cornelius O'Leary; JUS/N1041/147, Oscar Willmott.
108 Len Bowers, *The Social Nature of Mental Illness* (London: Routledge, 2000),
     22.
109 J 46, 476/1900, Edward Frost.
110 J 46, 675/1900, William O'Connell.
111 J 46, 297/1906, William le Fleming senior.
112 J 46, 1083/1910, Daniel Kehely.

113 J 46, 399/1930, Alfred Derbridge.
114 J 46, 644/1920, Joseph Thompson.
115 J 46, 1079/1920, Edward Hay.
116 J 46, 897/1906, George Fryer.
117 JUS/N1010/288, Wilfred Burns.
118 Ibid.
119 J 46, 710/1926, Edward Scholz.
120 J 46, 384/1928, Minnie Knott.
121 J 46, 636/1914, George Lansdowne.
122 J 46 565/1950, John Smith.
123 J 46, 733/1918, Robert Smith.
124 J 46, 202/1902, William Cook.
125 J 46, 1336/1930, Frank McNeil.
126 J 46, 459/459/1904, John Northey.
127 Kenneth R. Connor, "A Call for Research on Planned vs. Unplanned Suicidal Behavior," *Suicide and Life-Threatening Behavior* 34 (Summer 2004): 89–95.
128 J 46, 20/1925, Frederick Frampton.
129 JUS/N 226/314, Joseph Hewitt.
130 J 46, 370/1902, Helen Deiderick.
131 J 46, 1313/1936, Helene Delabarca.
132 J 46, 64/1902, George Flanagan.
133 J 46, 770/1916, Ernest Timmins.
134 J 46, 236/1920, James Adam.
135 J 46, 1076/1910, Frederick Cullen.
136 J 46, 1296/1950, Lionel Barker.
137 JUS/N610/262, Frederick Box.
138 J 46, 161/1919, James O'Donoghue.
139 JUS/N606/182, Maria Millard.
140 J 46, 658/1902, Henry Weston.
141 J 46, 229/1920, Alfred Fitchett.
142 J 46, 1124/1930, Duncan McDonald.
143 J 46, 542/1930, William Thompson.
144 J 46, 117/1908, Joseph Breese.
145 J 46, 470/1908, Frederick Nekal.
146 J 46, 1002/1922, George Sanderson.
147 JUS/N501/387, Alfred Sylvester.
148 J 46,1365/1938, Frederick Thomas Bonham.
149 JUS/N289/438, Julia Hargreaves.
150 JUS/N918/819, David Flowitt.
151 J 46, 614/1910, Douglas Lawson.

152 JUS/N365/503, Hubert Durham.

153 JUS/N390/70, Hugh Fiddes.

154 J 46, 202/1919, Henry Saunders.

155 J 46, 520/1938, Alexander Aitken.

156 J 46, 1319/1926, George Bagria.

157 J 46, 1122/1920, Elizabeth Stevens.

158 J 46, 471/1951, Alice Burn.

159 JUS/N458/581, Elizabeth Maudsley.

160 JUS/N1015/539, Mary Legood.

161 J 46, 765/1936, Wiremu Matetata.

162 J 46, 159/1909, James Biggs.

163 JUS/N305/177, John Geddes.

164 J 46, 194/1926, Ivan Alexander Newdick.

165 J 46, 28/1927, William Henry Aston.

166 J 46, 121/1930, Reginald Robinson.

167 JUS/N978/244, Cyril Stuart Swift.

168 J 46, 355/1926, Robert Wilson.

169 JUS/N1049/512, Alfred Ward.

170 J 46, 1290/1926, Margaret Armstrong.

171 J 46, 222/1908, Rubina Livingstone.

172 JUS/N1010/269, John Kenneally.

173 J 46, 1141/1916, George McKeown.

174 J 46, 1061/1920, Charles Carter.

175 J 46, 195/1922, Ida Wells.

176 JUS/N288/381, Eliza Ruska.

177 J 46, 1571/1936, Alice Hill.

178 J 46, 1120/1928, Henry Wood.

179 J 46, 97/1928, Joseph Coombs.

180 J 46 1274/1924, Emei Larsen.

181 JUS/N306/245, George A. Fountain.

182 J 46, 1261/1924, Ivan Lulich.

183 On the religious beliefs of rural New Zealanders in the 1930s, see H.C.D. Somerset, *Littledene: Patterns of Change* (Wellington: New Zealand Council for Educational Research, 1974), 52.

184 JUS/N310/383, Charles Wentzel.

185 J 46, 1176/1930, Annie Trevor.

186 JUS/N491/151, Eliza Austin.

187 J 46, 862/1950, Margaret Dann.

188 J 46, 795/1924, Annie Law.

189 J 46, 1026/1930, Alfred Mulligan.

190 JUS/712/574, Mary Henley.
191 JUS/N505/495, Frank Tyler.
192 J 46, 1170/1926, Eric Wylie.
193 JUS/N206/490, William Hallinson.
194 JUS/N245/360, Arthur Edwin Steele.
195 JUS/N453/456, William Graham.
196 JUS/N550/177, George Coxen.
197 JUS/N914/650, James Shanks.
198 J 46, 1301/1940, William Richard Smith.
199 JUS/N748/778, Herbert Alfred.
200 J 46, 344/1924, Henry Savage.
201 J 46, 34/1927, Thomas Jackson.
202 JUS/N267/418, Francis Fay.
203 JUS/N556/312, James Kearnan.
204 J 46, 635/1908, Leslie Franklin.
205 J 46, 457/1926, William Anderson.
206 JUS/N1015/539, Mary Legood.
207 JUS/N947407, William Butt.
208 J 46, 875/1900, Henry Johnstone.
209 J 46, 248/1904, Charles McIntyre.
210 J 46, 1289/1916, Thomas Parkinson.
211 J 46, 536/1930, William Heare.
212 J 46, 633/1902, James Richardson.
213 J 46, 431/1922, John Bell.
214 J 46, 84/1910, Steven Burgess.
215 J 46, 1463/1920, James Graham.
216 JUS/N739/350, William Burton.
217 JUS/N320/04/115, Thomas Rea.
218 JUS/N492/165, Peter Cant.
219 JUS/N270/7, Sidney Grant.
220 JUS/N791/46, Peter Spaulding
221 J 46, 196/1906, James Lythgar.
222 J 46, 676/1900, Robert Jamieson.
223 JUS/N608/217, Charles Charman.
224 J 46, 580/1906, James Glover.
225 J 46, 535/1922, George Stevenson.
226 J 46, 1246/1930, Charles Edwards.
227 J 46, 1383/1942, Ethel Bird.
228 J 46, 704/1902, Thomas Heaney.

229 JUS/N709/411, Harry Webber
230 J 46, 479/1904, Isaac Cole.
231 J 46, 232/1908, Joshua Machlin.
232 J 46, 420/1940, Violet Grace.
233 J 46, 595/1940, Andrew Gray; J 46, 650/1940, Mary Jane Riley.
234 Bronwyn Dalley, "'Come Back with Honour': Prostitution and the New Zealand Soldier, at Home and Abroad," in *New Zealand's Great War: New Zealand, the Allies and the First World War,* ed. John Crawford and Ian McGibbon (Auckland: Exisle Publishing, 2007), 364–77.
235 Entry for 6 February 1936, Peter Cornford Lovell-Smith, Diary for 1935–36, MSX-5461, Alexander Turnbull Library, National Library of New Zealand.
236 JUS/N1011, Richard Harvey.
237 J 46, 319/1919, John Sherman.
238 J 46, 1019/1918, Lacey White.
239 J 46, 91/1912, Henry Smith.
240 J 46, 832/1906, Walter Bibbing.
241 J 46, 1297/1928, Peter Murphy.
242 J 46, 1186/1922, William Martin.
243 J 46, 1248/1938, William Frank Quick.
244 J 46, 1570/1938, George Smith.
245 JUS/N915/682 William Dale.
246 JUS/N710/494, Beatrice Brosnan.
247 J 46, 1273/1946, John Peter.
248 JUS/N456/537, John Miller.
249 J 46, 729/1922, Harry Edmonds.
250 J 46, 531/1902, George Mansell.
251 J 46, 800/1930, George Waugh.
252 JUS/N412/37, William Tracey.
253 J 46, 920/1900, James Thomas.
254 J 46, 448/1928, Walter Miller.
255 JUS/N454/479, Patrick McCarthy.
256 JUS/N710/453, William Campbell.
257 JUS/744/579, Richard Horrobin.
258 JUS/N750/882, Stefano Bongioni.
259 JUS/N921/20, Samuel Knight.
260 J 46, 455/1914, George Harrow.
261 J 46, 283/1900, Alfred Driver.
262 JUS/N441/164, Edwin Low.
263 JUS/N455/509, Richard Clunn.

264 J 46, 974/1938, Peter David Sandar; J 46, 1635/1938, Robert Thomas Flor-
     ence; J 46, 1996/ 1938, Alice Bertha Andrews.
265 Gregory R. Johnson et al., "Suicide among Adolescents and Young Adults: A
     Cross-National Comparison of 34 Countries," *Suicide and Life-Threatening
     Behavior* 30 (Spring 2000): 79.
266 J 46, 820/1924, Lawrence Wyatt.
267 J 46, 922/1928, Herbert Paterson.
268 A Brisbane newspaper in 1899 ran a feature article on botched suicides, pos-
     sibly to deter people. See "Hints to Young Suicides," *The Bulletin*, 19 August
     1899. I am indebted to Robert Thomson for this reference.
269 JUS/N607/206, Charles Ashcroft.
270 J 46, 647/1908, Alexander Beadie.
271 J 46, 426/1930, Eric Rodley.
272 J 46, 198/1927, Edward Huddleston.
273 J 46, 1444/1940, Hugh McDowell.
274 J 46, 600/1940, Hazel Osbourne.
275 J 46, 339/1928, Bertram Marshall.
276 J 46, 31/1928, Francis Dempsey.
277 "Six-Pennorth of Strychnine, Please!" *Brisbane Sunday Mail*, 27 September
     1936.
278 JUS/N363/467, John Dunlop.
279 J 46, 430/1930, Rudolph Ens.
280 J 46, 258/1922, Robert Cross.
281 JUS/N1086/863, Margaret O'Toole.
282 JUS/N267/428, Elizabeth Mattars.
283 JUS/N485/8, Elizabeth Bell.
284 On women and liquid poisons, see John L. McIntosh, "Changing Patterns in
     Methods of Suicide by Race and Sex," *Suicide and Life-Threatening Behavior*
     12 (Winter 1982): 231.
285 J 46, 621/1906, Cora Lancaster.
286 See, for example, JUS/Y13/334, Joan Robinson.
287 J 46, 417/1936, Emily Carr.
288 J 46, 1461/1940, Francis Doherty.
289 J 46, 760/1900, Arthur Gowing.
290 J 46, 865/1908, William Newman; J 46, 441/1909, Edgar Hill; J 46,
     936/1904, William Goodwin.
291 J 46, 936/1904, William Goodwin.
292 Shneidman, "The Commonalities of Suicide across the Life Span," 44–5
293 Ibid., 45.
294 Ibid., 51.

CHAPTER SEVEN

1 The quotation is from Sally Swartz, "The Great Asylum Laundry: Space, Classification, and Imperialism in Cape Town," in *The Confinement of the Insane: International Perspectives, 1800–1965*, ed. Roy Porter and David Wright (Cambridge: Cambridge University Press, 2003), 193. For examples of the literature on insanity in Australia and New Zealand, see Mark Finnane, "The Ruly and the Unruly: Isolation and Inclusion in the Management of the Insane," in *Isolation: Places and Practices of Exclusion*, ed. Carolyn Strange and Alison Bashford (London: Routledge, 2003), 89–101; Stephen Garton, "Bad or Mad? Developments in Incarceration in NSW, 1880–1920," in *What Rough Beast? The State and Social Order in Australian History*, ed. Sydney Labour History Group (Sydney: Australian Society for the Study of Labour History, 1982), 89–110. See, too, the collection of postgraduate student essays edited by Barbara Brookes and Jane Thompson: *"Unfortunate Folk": Essays on Mental Health Treatment, 1863–1992* (Dunedin; University of Otago Press, 2001). For the British Empire more widely considered, see Joseph Melling and Bill Forsythe, eds, *Insanity, Institutions, and Society, 1800–1914* (New York: Routledge, 1999); James E. Moran and David Wright, eds., *Mental Health and Canadian Society: Historical Perspectives* (Montreal: McGill-Queen's University Press, 2006); Jonathan Sadowsky, *Imperial Bedlam: Institutions of Madness in Colonial Southwest Nigeria* (Berkeley: University of California Press, 1999); James H. Mills, "Indians into Asylums: Community Use of the Brtish Colonial Medical Institution in India, 1857–1880," in *Health, Medicine, and Empire: Perspectives on Colonial India*, ed. Biswamoy Pati and Mark Harrison (Hyderabad, India : Orient Longman, 2001), 165–85; and Waltraud Ernst, *Mad Tales from the Raj: The European Insane in British India, 1800–1858* (London: Routledge, 1991). My thanks to Adam Montgomery for sharing his collection of this literature.

2 Catharine Coleborne, "Passage to the Asylum: The Role of the Police in Committals of the Insane in Victoria, Australia, 1848-1900," in Porter and Wright, eds, *The Confinement of the Insane*, 145–6; Stephen Garton, *Medicine and Madness : A Social History of Insanity in New South Wales, 1880–1940* (Kensington, Australia : New South Wales University Press, 1988), 147; Julie Parle, *States of Mind : Searching for Mental Health in Natal and Zululand, 1868–1918* (Scottsville, South Africa : University of KwaZulu-Natal Press, 2007), 115.

3 Janet Frame, *An Autobiography* (London: Women's Press, 1990), 190.

4 Ibid., 193.

5 On challenges to Michel Foucault's legacy, see Joseph Melling, "Accommodating Madness: New Research in the Social History of Insanity and Institutions," in Melling and Forsythe, eds, *Insanity, Institutions, and Society, 1800–1914*, 14–23.

6 Janet Frame wrote a fictionalized account of her experiences, which included electroconvulsive treatment. See Frame, *Faces in the Water* (New York: George Braziller, 1961), 22–6.

7 For Frame's statement, see Frame, *Autobiography*, 194–5. For a complex revisionist account, see Geoffrey Reaume, *Remembrance of Patients Past: Patient Life at the Toronto Hospital for the Insane, 1870–1940* (Toronto: Oxford University Press, 2000), 246.

8 Michael King, *Wrestling with the Angel: A Life of Janet Frame* (Washington, DC: Counterpoint, 2000), 69.

9 J 46, 1127/1918, David Clyde.

10 J 46, 1145/1912, George Mackinder.

11 JUS/N513/691, Mary Heenan.

12 J 46, 721/1922, William Wardell.

13 J 46, 1200/1916, Edward Alexander.

14 Tavistock Private Hospital and Hornby Mental Hospital were mentioned in several inquest files.

15 J 46, 298/1918, Ada Waters.

16 J 46, 1001/1906, Bart Dean.

17 J 46, 321/1916, Kathleen Mills.

18 J 46, 92/1922, William Todd.

19 J 46, 1392/1920, Margaret Ross.

20 J 46, 1561/1930, Walter Woodward.

21 J 46, 1116/1920, Margaret Hayes.

22 J 46, 1392/1920, Margaret Moss.

23 J 46, 727/1930, Lester Gardiner.

24 Heather Grant, *Great Queensland Women* (Brisbane: Queensland Government, Office of Women, 2005), 27–32. For Cooper's treatment of women with so-called nervous disorders, see JUS/N314/330, Mary Lawes.

25 John Bostock to Page Hanify, 11 May 1951, File on Department of Medical Psychology, box 7, John Bostock Papers, Fryer Library, University of Queensland (henceforth cited as Bostock Papers).

26 JUS/N1024/174, Edward Campbell.

27 Andrew Scull, "Rethinking the History of Asylumdom," in Melling and Forsythe, eds., *Insanity, Institutions, and Society, 1800–1914*, 303.

28 J 46, 1537/1930, Leonard Bell.

29 JUS/N1032/498, Michael Hayes.

30 JUS/N1023/104, James Evans.
31 JUS/N1023/130, Stewart Thompson.
32 J 46, 990/1920, Alex Dobbie.
33 J 46, 471/1908, George McIntyre.
34 J 46, 738/1908, Martha Milgrew.
35 J 46, 331/1918, Norman Kirkaldie.
36 JUS/N994/271, Josephine Fuller.
37 JUS/N1028/313, Ivey McInnes.
38 J 46, 83/1920, William Fawcett.
39 J 46, 1259/1920, Kate Feilder.
40 J 46, 1193/1912, Susan Smith.
41 J 46, 1254/1924, Agnes Benfield.
42 J 46, 1259/1920, Kate Feilder.
43 J 46, 776/1908, Janet Brown.
44 J 46, 360/1916, James Moir.
45 J 46, 343/1920, Walter Wilkes.
46 J 46, 1003/1910, Lillian Beaumont.
47 JUS/N1024/177, Reginald Houghton.
48 J 46, 547/1918, Paul Cressy.
49 JUS/N949/549, Gwendolyn Lihou; JUS/N1044/278, Robert Mitchell.
50 J 46, 689/1902, Randolph Miller; J 46, 259/1910, Percy Parish.
51 Memo on Mental Hygiene, Home Secretary's Office, Memorandum Book, 1938, A/26871, Queensland State Archives. Voluntary patients could consult with their medical advisers, and these doctors might consult with the superintendent of the mental hospital. The mental hospitals could provide private accommodation; the voluntary patients might have private nurses and private doctors. Private mental hospitals were brought under the terms of the act.
52 J 46, 822/1930, David Gillies.
53 J46, 910/1942, Claire Elinor Hammond.
54 The quotation appears in a letter from Dr J.D. Frankish to Edwin Arnold, 8 July 1904, Edwin Arnold Papers, MS-Papers-7237-11, Alexander Turnbull Library, National Library of New Zealand. Frankish was detained for years as criminally insane.
55 Stephen Garton, *Medicine and Madness: A Social History of Insanity in New South Wales, 1880–1940* (Kensington, Australia: New South Wales University Press, 1988), 32–40; Catharine Coleborne, "Making 'Mad' Populations in Settler Colonies: The Work of Law and Medicine in the Creation of the Colonial Asylum," in *Law, History, Colonialism: The Reach of Empire,* ed. Diane Kirkby and Catharine Coleborne (Manchester: University of Manchester Press, 2001), 106–19.

56 For a good example of a family-initiated process, see J 46, 951/1922, Nora Dunlop. For an employer-taken action, see J 46, 14/1902, Matthew Hooper.

57 J 46, 346/1922, Alfred Hanson.

58 J 46, 519/1904, Martha David.

59 J 46, 540/1930, James Broughton.

60 J 46, 728/1906, Robert Vincent.

61 J 46, 176/1902, William McNeill.

62 JUS/N247/464, John Cahill.

63 J 46, 624/1924, Evelyn Thomson.

64 JUS/N309/317, Thomas Cuddihy.

65 J 46, 155/1904, Ambrose Bearpark.

66 JUS/N558/356, John McDonald.

67 JUS/N238/25, Elizabeth Kenyon.

68 J 46, 1112/1920, Sidney Gibson.

69 On families and committal, see Nancy Tomes, *A Generous Confidence: Thomas Kirkbride and the Art of Asylum Keeping, 1840–1883* (New York: Cambridge University Press, 1984), 90–112.

70 Edward Shorter, *A History of Psychiatry: From the Era of the Asylum to the Age of Prozac* (New York: John Wiley and Sons, 1997), 61.

71 Bailey, *This Rash Act*, 54.

72 JUS/N396/216, Joseph McCarragher.

73 JUS/N1144/276, Alfio Sorbello. For a New Zealand example from the 1940s, see J 46, 1326/1942, Ethel Mary Dovey.

74 J 46, 933/1910, John Bulleid.

75 Shorter, *A History of Psychiatry*, 55.

76 In the 1940s in the United States, 15 per cent of male admissions were for dementia paralytica; for New South Wales from 1900 to 1940, 7.5 per cent of male admissions were for this organic disease of the nervous system. For Callan Park from 1910 to 1920, the figure was 12.9 per cent . See John Bostock, Lecture on Dementia Paralytica, box 13, Bostock Papers.

77 Barry Gustafson, *His Way: A Biography of Robert Muldoon* (Auckland: Auckland University Press, 2000), 20–1.

78 Mark Finnane, "The Ruly and the Unruly: Isolation and Inclusion in the Management of the Insane," in Strange and Bashford, eds., *Isolation*, 98.

79 JUS/N266/368, William Scott.

80 JUS/N263, William Webb.

81 JUS/N305/159, William Gordon.

82 JUS/N655, John Winkel.

83 JUS/N749/808, Theresa Loeffler.

84 JUS/N547/101, Sarah Martin.

85 JUS/N547/101, James Maloney.

86 Frame, *An Autobiography*, 193-4.

87 J 46, 270/1916, Isabella Hitchcock. Her brother mentioned the reports at the inquests.

88 Finnane, "The Ruly and the Unruly," 90.

89 JUS/N240/120, Catherine Gillick.

90 J 46, 765/1922, Isabella Ott.

91 J 46, 540/1930, James Broughton.

92 J 46, 283/1900, Alfred Driver; J 46, 476/1900, Edward Frost.

93 JUS/N352/176, Annie Fleming.

94 J 46, 270/1916, Isabella Hitchcock.

95 JUS/N609/239, Agnes O'Brien.

96 JUS/N657/11, Anna Potrezeba.

97 Frame, *An Autobiography*, 197.

98 Ibid., 214.

99 J 46, 154/1900, John Lawson.

100 J 46, 305/1904, Elizabeth Knox.

101 J 46, 1327/1916, George Barnes.

102 J 46, 390/1922, Joseph Henry.

103 J 46, 435/1930, Mary McWilliam.

104 J 46, 1092/1930, John O'Brien.

105 J 46, 910/1930, Mary Shanks.

106 J 46, 785/1914, Sarah Smyth.

107 J 46, 440/1920, William Sims.

108 J 46, 789/1902, Jessie Smith.

190 J 46, 138/1904, William Pinkerton.

110 J 46, 721/1902, William Driver; J 46, 452/1928, Margaret Ellen Marshall.

111 Martin Stone, "Shell Shock and the Psychologists," in *The Anatomy of Madness: Essays in the History of Psychiatry*, vol. 2, *Institutions and Society*, ed. W.F. Bynum, Roy Porter, and Michael Shepherd (London: Tavistock, 1985), 242–71.

112 For histories of shell shock as the precursor to PTSD, see, *inter alia*, Bill Rawling, "Providing the Gift of Life: Canadian Medical Practitioners and the Treatment of Shock on the Battlefield," *Canadian Military History* 10 (2001): 7–20; Harold Mersky, "Post-Traumatic Stress Disorder and Shell Shock – Clinical Section," in *A History of Clinical Psychiatry: The Origin and History of Psychiatric Disorders*, ed. German Berrios and Roy Porter (London: Athlone Press, 1995), 490–500; and Merskey, "After Shell Shock: Aspects of Hysteria since 1922," in *150 Years of British Psychiatry*, vol. 2, *The Aftermath*, ed. Hugh Freeman and German Berrios (London: Athlone Press, 1996),

89–118. For more critical examinations of the social construction of shell shock, see Edward Brown, "Post-Traumatic Stress Disorder and Shell Shock – Social Section," in Berrios and Porter, eds., *A History of Clinical Psychiatry*, 500–8.

113 Joanna Bourke, "Effeminacy, Ethnicity and the End of Trauma: the Sufferings of 'Shell-Shocked' Men in Great Britain and Ireland, 1914–39," *Journal of Contemporary History* 35 (2000): 57–69.

114 George Mosse, "Shell Shock as a Social Disease," *Journal of Contemporary History* 35 (2000): 101–8.

115 Bourke, "Effeminacy, Ethnicity and the End of Trauma." By contrast, Ben Shephard, in *A War of Nerves* (London: Jonathan Cape, 2000), has a less generous interpretation of the German response to shell shock.

116 Doris Kaufmann, "Science as Cultural Practice: Psychiatry in the First World War and Weimar Germany," *Journal of Contemporary History* 34 (1999): 125–44.

117 Peter Leese, "Problems Returning Home: The British Psychological Casualties of the Great War," *Historical Journal* 40 (1997): 1055–67.

118 Caroline Cox, "Invisible Wounds: The American Legion, Shell Shocked Veterans, and American Society, 1919–1924," in *Traumatic Pasts: History, Psychiatry, and Trauma in the Modern Age, 1870–1930*, ed. Mark Micale and Paul Lerner (Cambridge: Cambridge University Press, 2001), 280–306. For an analogous discussion of the role veterans' associations in the United States played in psychiatric classification, see Allan Young, *The Harmony of Illusions: Inventing Post-Traumatic Stress Disorder* (Princeton: Princeton University Press, 1995).

119 New Zealand, *New Zealand Expeditionary Force, Its Provision and Maintenance* (Wellington: Government Printer. 1919), 63.

120 This finding parallels that of Caroline Cox in her work on returning soldiers to the United States. She found activism on behalf of shell-shocked soldiers by the American Legion. In New Zealand the equivalent organizations originated in local patriotic associations, and the result was personalized lobbying. See Cox, "Invisible Wounds."

121 Archives New Zealand, Wellington, Army Department , Series I, AD 1, 49/301, Mental Patients, Memorandum, Federation of New Zealand Patriotic War Relief Societies to James Allen, Minister of Defence, 28 August 1917. (Henceforth the designation AD will be used for the Army Department, followed by the appropriate series number; 49 refers to a subseries and 301 to a subject file; the archives retained the army file numbering system.)

122 AD 1, 49/301, Mental Patients, Secretary, Rotoroa Returned Soldiers' Association, to Acting Director Medical Services (henceforth ADMS), Wellington, 2

December 1918; James Allen, Minister of Defence, to Miss Holland, Secretary, Victoria League of Auckland, 4 February 1919; F.S. Emmett to James Allen, 19 December 1919, 25 January 1920; AD 49/301/1, Mental Health Patients, NZEF (New Zealand Expeditionary Force), General File, William Power, Taranaki Provincial War Relief Association, to Minister of Defence, 16 June 1920.

123 AD 1, 49/301, Mental Patients, Secretary, Auckland Returned Soldiers' Association, to James Allen, Minister of Defence, 26 September 1919.

124 AD 78, 15/28, Mental Patients, Director of Base Records, to the Officer in Charge, New Zealand Record Office, London, 14 December 1917.

125 These two terms were related; they were used for supposedly light mental illness cases. The former largely meant somatic illnesses or those believed to be caused by brain lesions, while the latter was reserved for emotional trauma. At times, however, shell shock was the label applied to both concepts.

126 A.D. Carbery, *The New Zealand Medical Services in the Great War, 1914–1918* (Wellington: Whitcombe and Tombs, 1923), 225.

127 AD 1, 49/284/3, Neurasthenia Cases, Minute Sheet for Minister of Defence, 22 November 1918. The sheet mentioned studies and treatments.

128 AD 1, 49/921, Neurasthenia, M.M. Gardiner, Memorandum for Regimental Officers, 21 January 1921.

129 AD 1, 25/211, *Maheno* 3rd Voyage, Monthly Report for July 1916.

130 AD 1, 39/319, Hospitals – England, Report on Hospitals by [illegible signature] to General Officer Commanding, 14 August 1917.

131 National Archives of Australia, Army, 4364/48, Colonel [full name not cited] Downey, "Short Report on Shell Shock [1917]."

132 J.M.W. Binneveld, *From Shell Shock to Combat Stress: A Comparative History of Military Psychiatry*, trans. John O'Kane (Amsterdam : Amsterdam University Press, 1997), 86–7.

133 AD 78, 15/28, Mental Patients, F. Truby King to Col. Valintine and Dr Frank Hay, 3 June 1916.

134 Many reports for Hanmer survive from 23 October 1916 to 21 March 1920. These show average weekly admission rates of 4 (1916), 4 (1917), 9 (1918), and 6 (1919); multiplying these by the number of weeks (fifteen weekly reports were missing) gives an estimate of roughly 1,000. A separate report mentioned 481 admissions in 1920 and 368 in 1921, bringing the estimate to around 1,850 admissions from October 1916 to the end of 1921. These included a few patients receiving treatment for joint and chest problems. An inspection of Hanmer on 29–30 September 1917 showed that of 82 patients, 60 required massage treatment, so perhaps 20 per cent of patients were there for shell shock. In late March 1919 Hanmer became the designated army

centre for shell shock and neurasthenia. The anxiety of the DGMS over the mounting numbers of such cases in 1920 and 1921 suggests a rising proportion. If functional mental illness cases were around 20 per cent through 1916, 1917, and 1918, 50 per cent in 1919, and close to 100 per cent in 1920 and 1921, then perhaps 1,150 men had been treated for mental illness at Hanmer. A separate estimate can be made for soldiers in civilian mental hospitals. The minister of defence required sporadic reports to answer questions from critics. These documents provided cross-sectional glimpses. The following are the dates and number of soldier patients in all mental hospitals presented in scattered reports: 1914 (3), 1915 (23), 1916 (36), October 1920 (186), March 1921 (108), April 1921 (139), October 1921 (117), December 1921 (104), April 1922 (106). Seacliff held about a quarter to a third of the total number. A single report gave the total number of returned soldiers that Seacliff held from March 1915 to January 1920 as 94. Thus for that facility a total flow-through estimate of 130 to 150 soldier patients from March 1915 to January 1922 is reasonable. With about a quarter of all soldier patients in mental hospitals at Seacliff, it is possible that 400 men were in the hospitals during that period. From the start of the war until August 1919, returned soldiers at Avondale numbered 42, and a few more may have entered between August 1919 and January 1922. Several cross-sectional reports put the proportion of all soldier cases here at about one-sixth; an estimate based on Avondale would be roughly 300 soldiers in mental hospitals. Perhaps 1,500 men were institutionalized for assorted mental ailments, about 1150 at Hanmer and 300 to 400 in mental hospitals. See AD 1, 40/301, Mental Patients, Nominal Rolls of Military Patients at Mental Hospitals, 1921, McGavin to Secretary, National War Funds Council, 29 November, 1921; AD 1, 40/301, Mental Patients, Return of Soldiers Received into Seacliff Mental Hospital from March 1915 to January 1920, 17 January 1920; R. Heaton Rhodes to Secretary, Returned Soldiers' Association, Dunedin, 11 October 1920; DGMS to Dr W.E. Collins, 18 April 1921; AD 1, 64/30, Mental Cases in NZEF 1919, Ending 31 January 1918; AD 78, 15/28, List of Patients in Mental Hospitals [no date, but probably October 1920]; Return of Returned Soldiers, Mental Patients [no date, but probably March 1921].

135 See, for example, AD 1, 49/301, Mental Patients, NZEF, General File, Extract, Report on Marama, 29 May 1917; Extract, Report on Maheno, 14 January 1918; AD 1, 39/319, Hospitals – England, Report on Hospitals by [illegible signature] to General Officer Commanding, 14 August 1917.

136 AD 1, 49/301, Mental Patients, DGMS to Military Hospitals, Trentham, Featherston, Awapuni, 10 March 1916.

137 AD 1, 49/301, Mental Patients, Director of Military Hospitals to DGMS, 21 April 1916.

138 AD 1, 49/301, Mental Patients, Director of Military Hospitals to DGMS, 4 May 1916.

139 AD 1, 49/301, Mental Patients, W.E.A. Gibbs to [illegible], 1 February 1920. The letter's author was a relative of a man held at Seacliff, although the family had been led to believe he was at Karitane. The family objected to the illegality of his placement and to the place itself.

140 AD 1, 49/301, Mental Patients, Inspector General, Mental Hospitals, Department Memorandum, to Col. Valintine, 28 April 1916.

141 AD 1, 49/301, Mental Patients, DGMS to Truby King, [?] April 1916.

142 AD 1, 49/301, Mental Patients, Brigadier-General D.J. McGavin to Dr W.E. Collins, Chairman, New Zealand Executive, New Zealand Branch, British Red Cross and Order of St John, 18 April 1921; AD 78, 15/28, Mental Patients, Truby King to Inspector General, Mental Hospitals, 29 May 1916.

143 AD 78, 15/28, Mental Patients, Truby King to Inspector General, Mental Hospitals, 29 May 1916.

144 AD 78, 15/28 Mental Patients, Truby King to Col. Valintine and Dr Frank Hay, 3 June 1916.

145 Lloyd Chapman, *In a Strange Garden: The Life and Times of Truby King* (Auckland: Penguin Books, 2003), 49–101.

146 On the screening process, see J 46, 218/1919, George Martin, Deposition of William Baxter Gow, acting superintendent at Seacliff, 8 February 1919. For Truby King's observation about the need for some moral or emotional sense to work with, see AD 78, 15/28, Mental Patients, Truby King to Inspector General of Mental Hospitals, 29 May 1916.

147 AD 1, 49/301/1, Mental Patients, Superintendent, Mental Hospital, Seacliff, Memorandum for DGMS, 1 November 1920.

148 AD 1, 49/921, Neurasthenia, DGMS, Memorandum, Transfer of Patients, 30 October 1919.

149 AD 1, 49/301, Mental Patients, Secretary, Auckland Returned Soldiers' Association, to James Allen, Minister of Defence, 26 September 1919.

150 Archives New Zealand, Justice Department (JU), Series 9, Circular Memos, Item 16, Memo to Stipendiary Magistrates, 4 December 1918.

151 AD 1, 49/284/3, Neurasthenia Cases, Minute Sheet for Minister of Defence, 22 November 1918.

152 AD 1, 49/922, Training of Medical Officers in Psychotherapy.

153 AD 1, 49/922, Training of Medical Officers in Psychotherapy, minute on cable of 17 February 1919.

154 AD 1, 49/921, Neurasthenia, HQ (Medical), Canterbury Medical District, Memorandum for the DGMS, 27 March 1919.

155 AD 1, 49/921, Neurasthenia, Director, Division of Hospitals, to All Medical Practitioners, 10 February 1921.

156 Archives New Zealand, Health Department, Series 11, file 1/1, Queen Mary Hospital, Lieutenant Colonel P. Chisholm to D.S. Wylie, 12 October 1921.

157 There were Hanmer cases among the inquest files. See J 46, 1064/1926, Henry Taylor; J 46, 590/1938, George Hills.

158 AD 1, 49/261/1, Hanmer General File, Brigadier-General Donald Johnstone McGavin to Col. D.E. Kenwick, 23 December 1919.

159 AD 1, 20/68, Medical Conference at Headquarters, 18–21 March 1919, J.M. Christie, Consulting Surgeon to the Forces, Memorandum on Dunedin Hospital Outpatients, 10 March 1919.

160 AD 1, 49/921, Neurasthenia, A. Owen Johnson, Medical Superintendent, Grey River Hospital, Greymouth, 5 February 1921.

161 AD 1, 39/247, Health at Hanmer Hospital, Commandant to DGMS, 19 May 1919.

162 AD 1, 49/791, Alcoholism among Returned Soldiers, Report by the Special Committee Concerning a Visit to Roto-Roa, 8 July 1920.

163 AD 1, 49/921, Neurasthenia, Dr Marshall MacDonald to DGMS, 17 September 1920.

164 AD 1, 391/247, Health – Hanmer Hospital, DGMS, Memorandum for Officer Commanding Queen Mary Hospital, Hanmer, 23 December 1921.

165 JUS/N706/258, Wilfred Smith.

166 J 46, 1145/1930, Ena Gee.

167 National Archives of Australia, Department of Repatriation, Series A 2489/1, Item 1920/1447, "Shell-Shock Soldiers [Memorandum probably written by a Colonel Sinclair in the Department of Repatriation, 19-21 October 1919]." I am indebted to Jonathan Richards for this document.

168 John Bostock, "The Australian Association of Psychiatrists and Its Gestation" [unpublished address, 1952], File of the Royal Australian and New Zealand College of Psychiatrists, box 7, Bostock Papers.

169 Queensland established its first mental hospital (asylum), Wolston Park, in Goodna, on the Brisbane River, in 1865. It was known as Woogaroo and also Goodna. For an account of the changes in therapeutic practices there, see Mark Finnane, *Wolston Park Hospital, 1865–2001* (Brisbane, 2001). In 1948 the state had psychiatric clinics in Brisbane, Toowoomba, and Townsville. State mental hospitals were located at Brisbane, Toowoomba, and Ipswich. See Queensland State Government, Department of Health and Home Affairs, *A New Outlook on Mental Healing* (Brisbane: Government Printer, 1948), 3.

Also see John S.B. Lindsay, *Ward 10B: The Deadly Witch Hunt* (Main Beach: Wileman Publication, 1992), 63–4.

170 JUS/N794/178, Gertrude Ashley.

171 The board's minutes detail the rise of psychiatry as a recognized specialization. Without comparable records for New Zealand, the emergence of private psychiatric practices is more difficult to reconstruct, and for that reason the Queensland situation is now accented.

172 Queensland State Archives (QSA), A/38181, Queensland Medical Board, Minute Book, 17 February to 17 December 1925, Entry for 4 May 1925.

173 Ibid., Entries for 14 May and 16 April 1925.

174 QSA, A/38182, Queensland Medical Board, Minute Book, 14 January 1926 to 10 June 1937, Entry for 4 August 1927.

175 QSA, A/26872, Home Secretary's Office, Memorandum Book, 1939, Memorandum for Minister on Medical Bill, 23 August 1939.

176 QSA, A/38184, Medical Board of Queensland, Minute Book, 8 February 1940 to 16 December 1940, Entries for 10 July, 7 August, 11 September, 18 September 1941.

177 Finnane, "The Ruly and the Unruly," 12–13.

178 QSA, A/38182, Queensland Medical Board, Minute Book, 14 January 1926 to 10 June 1937, Entries for 12 February 1931, 11 February 1932, 12 May 1932, 9 June 1932; QSA, A/38187, Queensland Medical Board, Minute Book, 4 March 1943 to 8 February 1944, Entry for 9 September 1943.

179 John Bostock, Lecture on Opium and Morphine Addiction, box 13, Bostock Papers.

180 Entry on John Bostock in John Alexander, *Who's Who in Australia* (Melbourne: The Herald Press, 1941); Biography for Employment [1926], box 7, Bostock Papers.

181 C.A. Hogg, Inspector-General of Mental Hospitals, New South Wales, Memo, 6 July 1927, File on Letters of Recommendation, box 7, Bostock Papers.

182 Lindsay, *Ward 10B*, 63–4.

183 B.J. Phillip, "The Panegyric on John Bostock," 30 September 1987 [an address]; Obituary, *Australia and New Zealand Journal of Psychiatry*, March 1988, Biographical File, box 1, Bostock Papers.

184 B.E.H. Clifford, Captain, Military Secretary, Government House, 1 July 1920, File on Research Chair, box 1, Bostock Papers.

185 QSA, A/38216, File on Medical Board, Policy and Correspondence Files, Number of Specialists, 1941–1959.

186 QSA, A/38184, Medical Board of Queensland, Minute Book, 8 February 1940 to 16 December 1940, Entry for 11 April 1940.

187 Queensland State Government, *A New Outlook on Mental Healing*, 3; QSA, A/38188, Medical Board of Queensland, Minute Book, 8 February 1945 to 16 December 1949, Entry for 14 July 1949.

188 John Bostock, "Autobiographical Notes" [May 1965], Biographical File, box 1, Bostock Papers.

189 Ibid. Insulin shock treatment remained in use at least into the 1960s in New Zealand. See Dorothy Walker, "My Life," [unpublished memories of a schizophrenia patient], Dorothy Walker Papers, MS-Papers- 8001, Alexander Turnbull Library, National Library of New Zealand.

190 QSA, A/38347, File on Memos Concerning Nurses and Private Hospitals, Private Hospitals, Registrar to Under Secretary, Department of Health and Home Affairs, 18 December, 1953; List of Private Hospitals, 11 January 1939.

191 John Bostock, Lecture on Clinical Psychiatry: Admission of Patients to Mental Hospitals, box 13, Bostock Papers.

192 *Medical Journal of Australia Advertiser*, 5 March 1938, xv.

193 QSA, A/26871, Home Secretary's Office, Memorandum Book, 1938, Memo on Mental Hygiene. Voluntary patients could consult with their medical advisers, and these doctors could consult with the superintendent of the mental hospital. The mental hospitals could provide private accommodation; the voluntary could have private nurses and private doctors. Private mental hospitals were brought under the terms of the act.

194 John Bostock, Lecture on Anxiety States, box 13, Bostock Papers.

195 John Bostock, Lecture on Alcoholism, ibid.

196 JUS/N1055/816, Florence Reithmuller.

197 John Bostock, "On Therapeutic Judgment and Allied Problems," *Medical Journal of Australia*, 21 December 1940, 677.

198 Ibid.

199 John Bostock, "Nerves and Worry" [n.d.], File on Brisbane Clinic Brochures, box 1, Bostock Papers.

200 Royal Australian and New Zealand College of Psychiatry, File 11 on RANZCP, Memo on Fees [1958], box 7, Bostock Papers.

201 John Bostock, "How Civilization Manufactures Neuroses: A Survey of 200 Consecutive Cases," *Medical Journal of Australia*, 5 March 1938, 445–8.

202 Bostock may have used these selected cases for student examination purposes. See File of Case Notes [possibly from early 1950s], box 2, and Case Notes [possibly from 1940s], box 5, Bostock Papers.

203 John Bostock, Lectures on Cyclophrenia or Manic-Depressive Psychosis, box 13, Bostock Papers.

204 JUS/N 1090/742, Edna Watson.

205 John Bostock, "Mind Healing," *Medical Journal of Australia*, 4 February 1928, 146.

206 Bostock, "On Therapeutic Judgment and Allied Problems," 676.

207 John Bostock, "The Treatment of Nervous Diseases," *Medical Journal of Australia*, 21 September 1929, 4; John Bostock, *The Nursing of Nervous Patients* (Brisbane: Government Printer, 1942), 78 and 80.

208 John Bostock, "If You Have a Nervous Breakdown – What Then?" Radio Broadcast of 18 August 1948, box 2, Bostock Papers.

209 John Bostock, Lectures on Additions, box 13, Bostock Papers.

210 Bostock, "Mind Healing," 147; John Bostock, "The Treatment of Nervous Diseases," *Medical Journal of Australia*, 21 September 1929, 7; John Bostock and Evan Jones (examiner in psychiatry to the University of Sydney, medical superintendent at Broughton Hall Psychiatric Clinic, Sydney), *The Nervous Soldier: A Handbook for the Prevention, Detection, and Treatment of Nervous Invalidity in War* (Brisbane: University of Queensland, 1943, 77.

211 QSA, A/42311, Chief Secretary's Department, State Stores Board, 1943, Memo on Purchases, Inwards and General Correspondence.

212 John Bostock, "Borderline Cases and Their Treatment," File on General Lectures 1–14, box 2, Bostock Papers.

213 John Bostock, marginal note on Lecture on the Neurotic Personality, box 13, Bostock Papers.

214 Bostock, "Mind Healing," 150.

215 Ibid., 148.

216 JUS/N1032/489, Arthur Hayes.

217 John Bostock, Lectures on Clinical Psychiatry, box 13, Bostock Papers.

218 John Bostock, Lecture on Nervous and Mental Disorders, box 13, Bostock Papers.

219 Bostock, *The Nursing of Nervous Patients*, 77.

220 Bostock, Lectures on Clinical Psychiatry, box 13, Bostock Papers; Bostock, *The Nursing of Nervous Patients*, 59–68.

221 J 46, 331/1918, Norman Kirkaldie.

222 Bostock, *The Nursing of Nervous Patients*, 64.

223 King, *Wrestling with the Angel*, 96–7.

224 Frame, *An Autobiography*, 224.

225 John Bostock to the University Senate, 8 May 1945, File on the Department of Medical Psychology, box 7, Bostock Papers.

226 John Bostock and Bertram J. Phillips, "The Treatment of Psychoses and Psychoneuroses by Electroplexy (Electro Shock Therapy) in a General Hospital," *Medical Journal of Australia* [reprint], 3 January 1948, 5–8, File of Reprints, box 1, Bostock Papers.

227 QSA, HHA/D2, Health and Home Affairs, Memo by Basil Stafford, 28 May 1942.

228 QSA, JUS/Y 21 (Department of Justice, Police Investigations in Violent Deaths for Brisbane, Bundle 21), File 570.

229 Frame, *Faces in the Water*, 20–6.

230 Jill Trevelyan, *Rita Angus: An Artist's Life* (Wellington: Te Papa Press, 2008), 227–8.

231 John Bostock, "Borderline Cases and Their Management," File on Unpublished Manuscripts, box 2, Bostock Papers.

232 Louis Menand commenting on Eli Zaretsky's judgment in his cultural history of psychoanalysis in "Acid Redux: The Life and Times of Timothy Leary," *New Yorker*, 26 June 2006, 77.

233 John Bostock, *The Dawn of Australian Psychiatry* (Brisbane, 1951; mimeographed), 2.

234 Len Bowers, *The Social Nature of Mental Illness* (London: Routledge, 2000), 165.

235 Frame, *An Autobiography*, 197.

CONCLUSION

1 Susan K. Morrissey, *Suicide and the Body Politic in Imperial Russia* (Cambridge: Cambridge University Press, 2006), 158.

2 Thomas Szasz, *Fatal Freedom: The Ethics and Politics of Suicide* (Westport, Conn.: Praeger, 1999), 27.

3 Peter D. Kramer, *Against Depression* (New York: Penguin Books, 2005), 57–61.

4 Discussions with Chief Coroner Judge Neil MacLean and Wellington coroner Garry Evans, 30 July 2008.

5 Bijou Yang Lester, "Learning from Durkheim and Beyond: The Economy and Suicide," *Suicide and Life-Threatening Behavior* 31 (Spring 2001): 19–27

6 In the course of research for this project, I met with psychologists, psychiatrists, suicidologists, and suicide-prevention workers in Queensland and New Zealand. They all concurred that most of the individuals they interacted with had worked out a logic to self-destruction.

7 Victor Bailey, *This Rash Act: Suicide across the Life Cycle in the Victorian City* (Stanford: Stanford University Press, 1998), 31.

8 Ibid., 33.

9 Gary Greenberg, "Manufacturing Depression: A Journey into the Economy of Melancholy," *Harper's Magazine*, May 2007, 46. For a critical assessment of genetic research and of its hyped promises for improving health, see Grace

Budrys, *Unequal Health: How Inequality Contributes to Health or Illness* (Lantham, Md: Rowman & Littlefield, 2003), 125–42.

10 "Silencing of the Lambs," *Economist*, 10 May 2008, 90.

11 For a pertinent discussion of modernist-positivist, postmodern, and pragmatic psychoanalysis, see Elyn R. Saks, *Interpreting Interpretation: The Limits of Hermeneutic Psychoanalysis* (New Haven: Yale University Press, 1999), 34–79.

12 Dorothy Walker, notes in a diary, 2 February 1977, Dorothy Rose Walker Papers, MS-Papers-8001, Turnbull Library, National Library of New Zealand.

13 "Hope from a Pill," *Economist*, 11 March 2008, 84–5.

Index

An italic *f* following a page number denotes the presence of an illustration; an italic *g* denotes a graph; an italic *t* denotes a table.

marital problems, 169, 176,
180–2; and mental illness, 182,
234; and murder-suicide, 241,
242, 245–6, 251; in older men,
173–4; of physicians, 332; pubs
and publicans, 105–6f; reasons for
male alcoholism, 176; as self-
medication, 176, 350; and suicidal
resolve, 272–3; and suicide, 89,
98, 334, 350; suicide motives
related to, 89, 153, 156, 173–86,
175t, 177t, 184–5t; among
veterans, 187, 328, 329–30; of
women, 233–4, 350
alcohol psychosis, 179, 339
altruistic social forces and suicide,
49–51
Alzheimer, Alois, 88
American Association of Suicidology,
92
Anderson, Olive, 93
anger: impaired judgment with, 278,
283–4; role in murder-suicide,
245–6
Angus, Rita, 341
anomic social forces and suicide,
49–51, 65
antidepressant drugs, 90
anxiety neuroses or disorders, 138,
176, 339; melancholy anxiety (la
mélancholique anxieux), 65;
among women, 157, 334
Arnold, Edwin, 128
Ashburn Hall (New Zealand), 133,
308, 317
astrology, 287
attempted suicides, 81, 87, 96;
communication of intent, 295–7;
by women, 214–15. See also
parasuicide

attendants for suicidal individuals,
311–12
Austria, 140g

Baechler, Jean, 354
Bailey, Victor: on gender variation,
94; on home care vs mental
asylums, 315; on inquest testimony, 94, 149, 354; life-course
approach, 94, 348; on motives,
149, 153; on setting and social
meaning of suicide, 100; This Rash
Act, 97–8, 149, 348; on women,
94, 217, 228–9
Barnes, Jo, 241
Bassett, Michael, 125, 134–6
Bebel, August: Women in the Past,
Present and Future, 45
Belgium, 139g
binary thinking, 353–4
biological psychiatry, 80
bipolar disorder (Falret's syndrome),
22
Bostock, John: on alcoholism, 176,
234, 334; career, 332–3; on
psychiatry and psychiatric treatment, 331, 334–42
Bourdin, Étienne, 29t
brain biochemicals, 138
brain physiology, 88
Brierre de Boismont,
Alexandre-Jacques-François, 29t,
45, 48, 50, 54, 363n50, 370n38;
De suicide et de la folie suicide, 37
Britain: Bailey's study on Hull, 94,
228, 230, 315; monthly distribution of suicides in London, 139g,
142t; suicide studies in, 28t, 30,
59; view of shell shock in, 321–2
Broca, Paul Pierre, 88